The Pursuit of Excellence:

INTRODUCTORY
READINGS
IN EDUCATION

DONALD C. ORLICH   S. SAMUEL SHERMIS

Idaho State University

American Book Company   NEW YORK

1 3 5 7 9 EP 10 8 6 4 2

The authors gratefully acknowledge the permission of Holt, Rinehart and Winston, Inc. to reprint material from "Stopping by Woods on a Snowy Evening" from *Complete Poems of Robert Frost.* Copyright 1923 by Holt, Rinehart and Winston, Inc. Copyright 1951 by Robert Frost.

Preface

The answer to the question of what the student should study first is not easy for any discipline, even one—like mathematics and English— where mastery of certain "tools" is prerequisite to any real thinking in the discipline. It is especially difficult to answer this question for such subjects as education, where the mastery of special tools is more appropriate as one moves into special areas.

Certain "foundation" knowledges, however, apparently serve some of the same needs in the education curriculum that "tools" do in other curricula. It is *possible* to think about curriculum construction, for example, without knowing anything of the history of American education or the educational system as a social institution, but not to think *well* about it.

The cultural matrix—both historical and sociological—is one of these foundation areas. The theoretical or philosophical matrix is another, and we hope we have succeeded in unifying the information here available into a coherence not previously achieved.

Too often, we feel, these foundation knowledges are separated from their pragmatic implications. Our sections on financing the schools and influences on the curriculum are intended to anticipate this danger in the beginning student's orientation.

Finally, we feel that the prospective student should early get a sound general idea of the profession *as* a profession. Like the foundation knowledges, this knowledge can lend significance to all his later courses.

For their part in helping to make this book a realization, we extend our appreciation and gratitude to the many editors, publishers, and writers who gave us permission to use the materials quoted herein; to the many students who read and commented on the initial drafts; to Dr. Donald F. Kline, for his many constructive criticisms of the manuscript; and to Mrs. Arlene Bengal, who prepared the final copy. It was only with their assistance that we reached our goal.

DONALD C. ORLICH

S. SAMUEL SHERMIS

Pocatello, Idaho

Contents

I

History of American Education

The history of American education—like any other history—is both instructive and interesting. Unfortunately, we Americans are a peculiarly "unhistorical" people. Typically we neither study our own past nor learn from it.

This fact is demonstrated by recent events in education. Many critics of the educational system are advocating "solutions" to educational problems that have been tried already and found unacceptable. For example, there are critics who advocate "stiffening up" the curriculum so that those who do not succeed will simply be dropped. This was precisely the procedure in American education throughout the nineteenth century. What happened then was that the dropouts formed a large, semiliterate mass of young people who were incapable of doing much more than "dead-end work"—operating elevators, washing dishes, and digging ditches. Unfortunately, these three operations—and others like them—are now largely automated.

Even within the education profession, there is this same naïve and antihistorical attitude. Many educators are making claims for teaching machines and programmed learning like those made for workbooks forty years ago. Workbooks, as generally used, were (and are) deadly dull, irrelevant, mechanical devices. Once the novelty of gadgetry wears off, machines probably will become as deadening as workbooks.

Nevertheless, there are signs that we may well accept these old "solutions," which are as apt to fail now as in the past. Much fruitless "experimentation" could be avoided if American educators and the American people would develop the habit of looking into our historical past. It is for this reason—to initiate some historical perspective—that a section of essays and articles on American educational history is included.

"A Brief Survey of American Education," by S. Samuel Shermis, is an overview of American educational history. Beginning in the seventeenth century and tracing educational events to the present, this essay presents the bare outlines of curricular, methodological, philosophical, and other educational concerns.

Lloyd P. Jorgenson's "The Birth of a Tradition" discusses the origin of the public schools. You may be surprised to learn that public schools are a comparatively new institution in American history.

"McGuffey and His Readers," by Henry Steele Commager, is an enlightening discussion of the famous *McGuffey Readers*. These readers, used by almost three generations of Americans to learn their "letters," actually taught a good deal more than just reading and spelling. "Do Not Meddle," one of the many stories in the *McGuffey Readers*, illustrates the point.

"Country Schoolmaster of Long Ago," by the late Thomas Woody, gives not only facts but the "feel" of education in the nineteenth century. Woody's account follows "Do Not Meddle" to give us some idea of the complex life of the teacher using the readers. "Teaching McGuffey" was only a small part of the task.

"A Hundred Years of the Land-Grant Movement," by Oliver C. Carmichael, shows one method by which education became a truly public concern. It traces the history of college education from its aristocratic and church-affiliated origins to the development of state-supported institutions within reach of the working classes.

A Brief Survey of American Education

by S. SAMUEL SHERMIS

INTRODUCTION

What Is Education?   The word "education" is what is known as a weasel-word. That is, the term is ambiguous; it can and does mean a great many things to a great many people. To some, "education" is the same thing as "training"—when one is trained to do something, he is educated. But to the Greeks and Romans—and to many people today

—education is synonymous with development of the intellect, or freeing of mental powers. There are several other definitions, but the crucial point is that though "education" is a common, everyday term, its meaning is by no means clear.

Although this book is concerned with formal institutions of education, it is also important to study education from the standpoint of the social sciences, particularly anthropology.[1]

Anthropologists frequently define education as the transmission of the cultural heritage. But what is cultural heritage? A simple definition is that the cultural heritage is *all of man's learned behavior*. Whatever a group of people learns is its cultural heritage. The cultural heritage includes *tangible* items, such as clothing, tools, weapons, cooking utensils, buildings, and jewelry. It also includes *intangible* entities, or concepts, such as wishes, language, beliefs, religion, values, and desires. Although all peoples possess a cultural heritage, the extent and nature of this heritage vary greatly. All societies have governments, religions, languages, and food-gathering techniques, in one form or another. But one culture, such as our own, will have a very complex technology, whereas the technology of the Australian Bushman is limited to a bowl, a spear, and a spear-thrower. All cultures possess the institution of marriage, but some employ monogamy (one man marries one woman), while others employ plural marriage (one man may have several wives, or one wife several husbands). All cultures have some form of education—that is, they transmit their social institutions and other aspects of the cultural heritage to the young. They teach the young what they must know to become full-fledged, participating members of that society.

Education is a necessity for cultural survival. Unless children are carefully and systematically taught what they must know, they will not become accepted members of their society. However, education can proceed in many ways. In a preliterate society, one without an alphabet (and usually also without complex technology), education is informal. An older person, usually the parent or some other adult, teaches the young person what he should know—how to hunt, how to plant, the steps of important dances, the appropriate ways of showing respect for an elder, the words of a religious chant. A more technologically advanced society utilizes a more formal educational

---

[1] Anthropology, a fairly recently developed branch of the social sciences, is the study of man. Anthropologists study man in all his variety. They are concerned with man's physical characteristics and the way he behaves, with social institutions such as marriage and government, and with technology, food-raising, clothing, art, music, and religion.

structure—teachers, classrooms, textbooks, and schools. A culture that contains both a complex technology and a written alphabet and extensive literature must educate in a formal manner. Of course, informal education also takes place in such a society. Much of what you know you learned from your parents, your friends, the movies, television, and conversation—that is, informally, without your considering the process "education."

In addition to the distinction arising from the fact that a complex, technological culture educates formally and a preliterate culture educates informally, there is another important difference in education as it is found in the two types of cultures. In a simple, uniform culture, the transmission of the cultural heritage is a relatively uncomplicated affair. Most adult members of the culture know what is "right" and what is "wrong," what they should do and what they must not do, how to dress and what to eat, what religious rites are to be performed under what circumstances, and so on. Since these cultural patterns[2] are known by almost all adults, their transmission to the younger generation means the passing on of a well-known, respected tradition.

In a complex culture such as our own, the range of cultural patterns is likely to be extremely wide. Whereas the weapon-making techniques of the American Indian were quite limited, our own weaponry is unbelievably complex. The Indian generally used only one kind of flint and shaped that flint into an arrow in the one approved, traditional manner. In our own culture there are hundreds of different kinds of weapons and perhaps thousands of techniques used to make these weapons. Further, the techniques of weapon-making change rather rapidly.[3]

Other aspects of our culture change almost as fast as our technology. A particular value in a primitive society may endure unchanged generation after generation. But in the United States and other technologically complex nations, rapid and extreme shifts in the value structure can occur within one generation. For instance, at the turn of the century divorce was fairly uncommon, and a divorcée was apt to be stigmatized as a "fallen woman." Divorce is now fairly common, and, while regarded as unfortunate, is not usually condemned as immoral.

---

[2] A *cultural pattern* is some identifiable method, technique, or concept designed to indicate what is to be done. Examples of cultural patterns would be our habit of giving gifts on Christmas Day and the proper response to make when one is introduced to a stranger.

[3] Archaeologists indicate that a particular arrow-making technique often has lasted for many hundreds of years. In our own culture a weapon may be obsolete before it is off the drawing board. Jet fighters used in the Korean conflict during the early 1950's seem crude and "primitive" beside the very latest planes.

Our country has mixed as well as changed its cultural patterns. We have borrowed extensively from both European and non-European cultures. This borrowing, combined with rapid cultural change, has led to *cultural conflict*. That is, unlike a more simple and homogeneous culture, our own society suffers from internal disagreements; we lack substantial agreement about some very important values. Note the differences of conviction about whether there should be prayer in the public schools. One can assert neither that those who advocate some such religious observance are wrong nor that those who oppose it are deceived, immoral, or stupid: both groups offer rather convincing arguments. When it is difficult to see who or what is *ultimately* "right" or "correct," it is difficult to say that "We ought to do this" or "We ought to avoid that." This is the essential meaning of cultural conflict.

Cultural conflict raises some rather important problems for education. If education is the transmission of the cultural heritage, then the question is, "*Which* cultural heritage?" or "*What* cultural heritage?" In a society in which cultural patterns change rapidly and in which cultural conflict is the norm, it is by no means a simple matter to transmit *a* way of life. At no time is it clear *what* is to be transmitted, *how* this transmission is to take place, or to *whom* the culture is to be transmitted. We are not even sure of the *purpose* of this transmission—that is, we do not even agree as to *why* we are transmitting our cultural heritage.

Cultural conflict is evident in every aspect of our educational system. For some, the only legitimate curriculum—the only studies worthy of being taught—consists of those subjects that traditionally have been studied. (In our society these are usually mathematics, science, literature, languages, and history.) Others maintain that, in a technological society in which work is specialized and complex, the schools ought to teach vocational subjects, such as vocational agriculture, metal and carpentry techniques, and business skills.

Some people hold that the business of deciding what should be studied and when ought to be, as it generally is now, in the hands of adults. An experienced, mature, well-informed adult knows what is valuable. But this point—obvious as it is to some—has been contested by others, who maintain that this authoritarian approach to education is deficient—and even "undemocratic." To them, the young child ought to have an interest in what he studies, and to create this interest, children ought to be allowed *to help* choose their own curriculum.

There is a rather widely shared view that education should be designed to train an intellectual elite. Only those children who are verbally intelligent, it is argued, can truly profit from education. It is further argued that our society needs an elite, a group of intelligent persons with character, ability, and training, and that without such persons we shall surely perish.[4] Thus the schools exist to train an elite, those who will be the movers and designers of tomorrow. Many other people, however, believe that this is an archaic, reactionary, and undemocratic view. They hold that in a democracy schools exist for *all* young persons, regardless of their ability; education is not for an elite of any kind. Unless we wish to return to the Europe of five hundred years ago, we must provide the best kind of education for all children, regardless of their intelligence, background, abilities, and so on.

Given differences as to curricular values, teaching techniques, and goals—given conflict even over a question as basic as who is to be educated—we face extremely complex problems of education in our society. Before a prospective teacher can understand the educative process, he must learn something of what the basic problems are, how they developed, and what they mean. It is important to know how education "fits" in our culture.

THE EUROPEAN BACKGROUND

Americans tend to think that God created the world in 1620—that is, that nothing much of importance happened before the New England colonies were settled. This orientation—probably a result of our almost exclusive educational concentration on American history—tends to exclude an awareness of the very important contributions of Europe and Asia toward the shaping of American culture. The truth of the matter is, of course, that: (1) European colonists brought to the New World a rich cultural heritage, and (2) this cultural heritage was immediately modified by the conditions of the new land.

European educational systems were derived ultimately from the Greeks and Romans, the former dating to as early at 400 B.C. The Athenian Greeks thought of education as a process that developed both intellect and character. Education, the property of the ruling class, was to produce the kind of person who would naturally fit into that ruling class. For those who were not of the aristocracy, training in the manual arts would suffice. Roman education had a similar goal.

---

[4] See Samuel P. Huntington, "Conservatism as an Ideology," *The American Political Science Review*, 51 (June, 1957): 454-473. Other writers who have maintained this point of view include Russell Kirk and Clinton Rossiter. They also discuss the conservative position and educational theory.

The Hebrew concept, however, was considerably different. The ancient Hebrews contributed another educational goal that was at the same time a lasting ethical justification of education. By the first century B.C., they had created a rather well-developed educational system. Very young boys attended what roughly corresponded to our elementary schools. As they grew older, they began what was to be a lifelong study of the Sacred Scriptures.[5] The most promising went on to academies presided over by a rabbi, a learned scholar who was also often an important community leader. Apart from the structure of formal education there were numerous informal educational institutions, primarily adult discussion groups in which adults met to discuss informally some ethical or philosophical problem. Girls received little or no formal education, as was typical throughout the world until very recently. The significant contribution of Hebrew education—a contribution that has endured—was that education and the "Good Life" are inseparably linked.

The Hebrews believed that, for the good life to be lived and salvation attained, one had to be acquainted with religious truths. These truths, divinely inspired and transcribed in the sacred literature, were to be studied, understood, and memorized. Unless one possessed a deep understanding of the truths contained in the Scripture, neither the good life nor salvation was possible. Thus, by linking formal education to religion, the Hebrews began a tradition continued by the Christians, including the Puritans in America 1600 years later.

To summarize the contributions of the ancients, then, we find that: (1) A clear distinction between education and training was made by the Greeks and Romans. Education was the cultivation of both character and intellect, with a good man and a wise leader as the desired end result. Training, a kind of low-level habit formation whose end was vocational, was reserved for those members of the lower class who were to serve the elite. (2) The classical curriculum was seen as a proper blend of subjects, usually centering around a literary, philosophical, and mathematical core. (3) By wedding the educative process to their religion, the Hebrews made education sacred and indispensable.

All three of these contributions filtered into the Christian European world after the fall of Rome in 476.

The Medieval and Renaissance World   After the fall of Rome in the fifth century, Europe became a collection of isolated, separated,

---

[5] The Jewish Sacred Scriptures include the Torah, the first Five Books of Moses, also known as the Old Testament, and the Talmud, the later commentaries on the Torah.

competing states. Feudalism, the social system of medieval Europe, involved a complex tangle of duchies, kingdoms, monarchies, and margravates, ruled over theoretically by a Pope and an Emperor. The Pope, the head of the Catholic Church, represented the sacred world; the Holy Roman Emperor symbolized the secular life. Europe at that time was fundamentally a religiously homogeneous civilization.[6]

In view of the religiously uniform character of Europe, it is not surprising that for many years education was the exclusive possession of the Church. Education was by and for the Church. The young boy who showed intelligence and ability was educated by monks, who taught him Latin (the language of scholars), Church doctrine and theology, sacred music, and Biblical and perhaps other ancient history. Secondary schools slowly came into existence to provide advanced training for future religious or state leaders. Out of the medieval secondary schools there arose higher education, which at first was an amazingly simple affair: a master, usually a renowned scholar, and disciples who gathered around him. Eventually this master-disciple relationship became institutionalized, and in the thirteenth century there arose the European university. This was a state-approved institution in which there existed a kind of contractual arrangement between masters and students: the former agreed to teach and the latter agreed to learn.[7]

Gradually, however, European towns began to create both elementary and secondary schools, financed and controlled by the civil authorities. These schools, often referred to as "burgh" schools, were in part a response to the growing complexity of life and to the need for educating a class of merchants and tradesmen who were beginning to become more numerous and powerful.

In addition to the burgh and church schools, another type of educational institution, apprenticeship training, gradually arose, especially

---

[6] This despite the presence of Moslems and Jews in Spain until the end of the fifteenth century and the rise of the Greek Orthodox Church in the eleventh century. The influence of the latter was confined to the eastern portions of Europe.

[7] The medieval European university was not a stable, highly structured arrangement, as it is today. Laboratories, libraries, and other facilities were not of the essence. Indeed, frequently an entire university, professors and students, became irked with the townspeople and simply packed up and moved away to form a university in another town. In fact, the threat of a university's moving away was often enough to keep the townspeople in line. Then as now, relations between "town and gown" were not always cordial and pleasant. Students complained of poor food at inns and overcharging for rooms. The townspeople in turn often protested bitterly about the roistering, drunkenness, and fighting of students. There was little the townspeople could do about it, since the university had its own regulations and system of discipline; its students were not under the jurisdiction of the local civil authorities.

in England. When in the sixteenth century Henry VIII led England out of the Catholic Church and appropriated Church lands, a tremendous social upheaval resulted. Without the social-service institutions provided by the Church (including orphanages, old people's homes, Church-managed farms, and nunneries), population dislocations, unemployment, brigandage, and mass lawbreaking erupted throughout England. Further complications arose from the Enclosure Acts, which appropriated land for the purpose of raising sheep to supply wool for England's infant textile industry. The dispossessed farmers, driven off their land by sheep owners, tended to drift into the cities, aggravating the social dislocation. Thus England under Henry VIII and Elizabeth experienced severe social and economic problems. It was hoped that an adequate apprenticeship program would create trained workers and that this would lessen unemployment.

Various apprenticeship acts were passed making it mandatory for a master, the experienced craftsman, to board and train a beginner. In addition to giving technical training, the master was supposed to teach the apprentice the rudiments of reading and writing. While these acts were not always enforced and many masters merely exploited their young apprentices, a precedent was set. Eventually apprenticeship training was systematized, and a combination of simple elementary education and training in silversmithing, candlemaking, ironmongering, and other trades became an accepted part of European life. Thus Europe developed a somewhat rigidly divided educational system: a literary education for future leaders, and a training program for those who would work with their hands.

The Reformation An event of extreme importance in the history of education was the Reformation, also called the Protestant Revolution. Martin Luther, a Dominican monk, first attempted to bring about reforms in the Catholic Church of the sixteenth century. Eventually, however, he found himself leading a large part of the German population out of the Church. The theological, economic, political, and social aspects of the Protestant Revolution are too complicated and extensive to deal with here. Nevertheless, we should make brief mention of Luther's theology and consequent educational events.

As Luther's thinking developed, he began to feel that salvation could be achieved by faith and faith alone. Although the Catholic Church held (and still holds) that salvation could come about only by a combination of faith and good works, Luther—and other Protestant leaders—asserted that one was saved only by right belief. The source of this right belief was not the Church, but the Bible. The Bible was not only a moral authority but also the only reliable source of what would lead to salvation. Most of Europe's population were either illiterate or semiliterate. The people did not possess the skills to either read or interpret the Bible. Therefore Luther, assisted by the learned humanist and classical scholar Philipp Melanchthon, established a system of "public" education. They created new and expanded existing public elementary schools, gymnasiums (secondary schools), and universities. Luther translated the Bible into German and wrote a catechism, a manual of religious training, which became a basic reading text for hundreds of thousands of young children during the sixteenth century and later. The net result of this educational emphasis was to increase both the need for and the awareness of formal education.[8]

Another consequence of the Protestant Revolution was a reaffirmation of the educational assumption of the ancient Hebrews. By linking literacy with religion, the Protestants strengthened the ethical justification for education. Education, literacy, religion, and salvation became inseparably linked and culturally interacting elements. For the American colonists this religious sanction for education was of prime importance. The Puritans did not invent a new theological or educational theory; they built on and expanded their Protestant, European foundation. As the New England colonies acquired a measure of stability, educational institutions were established and regarded as an absolute necessity.

THE PERIOD OF TRANSPLANTATION

Those colonists who emigrated to this country brought with them the germ of the institutions they were to build. In particular, they began their American experiences with the following concepts:

1. Education as an inseparable part of religion.

2. An elite education for a ruling class and training for the masses.

3. Some embryonic ideas of specific educational institutions, including the idea of an elementary school, a secondary school, and some institution for higher education.

4. Educational goals concerning both the development of intellect and the improvement of character.

5. Two levels of curriculum: the first was an elementary curriculum to inculcate basic literacy skills, and the second the Seven Liberal Arts, or a curriculum for universities. Secondary education, as a separate and distinct institution, was not firmly established in Europe in the sixteenth century. It was not to become established in this country until the late-eighteenth and nineteenth centuries.

[8] This is a rather conventional picture of this time period. For a Catholic position, see Edward Power, *Education for American Democracy* (New York: McGraw-Hill, 1958), especially p. 135.

In addition to cultural patterns concerning education, sixteenth-century emigrants brought with them other cultural patterns they had learned in Europe. They carried to these shores a language and a well-developed literature. They possessed legal and political institutions, including forms of administration and the idea of representative government. A most important cultural concept was the English belief in stability, order, law, and property. Also included was the belief that it was important to conserve the past and that whatever change was needed could best come about slowly as the result of small parliamentary innovations and slight changes in attitude. This attitude toward law and order was later combined with the eighteenth-century French emphasis on liberty, equality, and brotherhood—the political freedoms. It is obvious that the English emphasis on law and property and the French emphasis on freedom and equality were not entirely consistent with each other. This inconsistency tended to create an American culture with some extremely sharp conflicts. The cultural conflicts have resulted in some rather serious strains and cleavages within our society. They also have contributed to the creative nature of our society.

The new arrivals to our country came slowly at first, then in larger numbers, and in the nineteenth century in a torrent. The early colonists arrived with a fairly extensive stock of ideas about education, government, philosophy, agriculture, finance, and trade. But almost immediately they discovered that many of their cultural patterns were completely inappropriate in the wilderness of North America.

The first winter of the Massachusetts Bay Colony in 1619-1620 was filled with starvation and wretchedness. But the forests were teeming with wild animals and the streams with fish. The principal problems were these: (1) the colonists did not know how to hunt and fish in the wilderness;[9] and (2) many refused to work, since manual work was obviously degrading and unsuited to a gentleman. Before the colonists changed their attitudes toward work and before they learned farming and hunting skills, they almost starved.[10]

[9] In England, as in most other European countries, the forests were owned by either a king or a noble. Poaching was a serious crime, punished by a fine, a severe whipping, or even imprisonment or death. Thus many American colonists did not possess hunting skills when they arrived on our shores early in the seventeenth century.

[10] The difficulty was compounded by many of the first colonists' rushing off into the hills to mine for gold. Contrary to most Americans' understanding of colonial America, not only the Spanish and Portugese searched for gold and precious stones. The English tried it too. Indeed, we can imagine the consternation of those colonists who shipped back to England a batch of yellow, shiny mineral only to find that it was iron pyrites—"fool's gold."

All successive streams of colonists discovered that they, too, would have to modify their European beliefs, customs, practices, and attitudes. Let us look at some of the cultural patterns brought over from Europe, where they had developed over centuries, but found to be inappropriate in the New World:

1. The notion of a centralized administrative authority, such as existed in England and France, seemed unworkable in a land as huge as North America. Kings could not send their deputies across the Atlantic Ocean to enforce decrees—as a succession of English kings discovered, much to their indignation. Thus, almost immediately, American colonists were forced to create their own administrative and judicial apparatus. This they did, and the results—which differed widely from area to area—formed a crazy quilt of often conflicting governmental and judicial procedures. English patterns of government required considerable alteration, and it is likely that central administration would never have been achieved in this country without the communications and transportation revolutions.

2. The mercantile economic system did not last long in the New World. The idea that guilds and governmental agencies could supervise production and distribution of goods, set prices, limit imports, and determine wages and conditions of labor did not work well in North America. In fact, much American colonial resentment toward England in the eighteenth century was due to the English attempts to control America's infant industries. The English did not succeed, and American financial and industrial enterprises grew in a breathtakingly rapid and uncontrolled fashion.

3. Religious unity did not last long in the New World. The belief that the state could and should regulate the religious beliefs of its subjects clearly could not long be sustained in a land to which religious dissidents flocked and in which new religious groups sprang up overnight. The result of religious pluralism was the "tolerance" that Americans have traditionally accorded different religions. It was felt that even though your neighbor with his strange beliefs was probably going to miss out on salvation, you might as well leave him alone; otherwise he might decide to interfere with your belief—the one True Religion.

4. The Continental class structure, with its strict divisions, duties, and obligations for all, and privileges mainly for a ruling class, did not become well established. With the exceptions of the Dutch patroon system in New York, the French seigneurial system in Canada, and the plantation society in the South, European feudalism did not flourish in the New World as it had in the old. It became obvious that a

man's ability, know-how, ambition, and hard work counted for more than the nobility of his ancestors. Thus—and the South is something of an exception to this—patterns of equality began to replace older European patterns of class and caste.

5. Related to the above and to education as well was the disappearance of a life style that was appropriate to a particular class. The European ruling class had developed a life style centering around leisure and material possessions, formalized entertainment, and a dabbling in art and literature. The new life in North America did not lend itself to a life style that featured a set of aesthetic and intellectual activities for a leisure, titled, wealthy class. Rather, many Americans developed a pronounced hostility to art, music, dancing, literature, and formal, scholarly education. This hostility was to have —and still has—considerable consequences for the development of education.

Many other European cultural patterns underwent considerable change. The very character of the wilderness required either the overhaul of older institutions or the formulation of relatively unique ways of doing things. To employ the historian Oscar Handlin's phrase, Americans were, in a real sense, "shaped by the wilderness."

COLONIAL EDUCATION

On the West Gateway at Harvard University there is a tablet that contains the following poignant phrase:

AFTER GOD HAD CARRIED <u>VS</u> SAFE TO NEW ENGLAND
AND WEE HAD BVILDED OVR HOVSES
PROVIDED NECESSARIES FOR OVR LIVELI HOOD
REARD CONVENIENT PLACES FOR GODS WORSHIP
AND SETLED THE CIVILL GOVERNMENT
ONE OF THE NEXT THINGS WE LONGED FOR
AND LOOKED AFTER WAS TO ADVANCE LEARNING
AND PERPETVATE IT TO POSTERITY
DREADING TO LEAVE AN ILLITERATE MINISTERY
TO THE CHVRCHES WHEN OVR PRESENT MINISTERS
SHALL LIE IN THE DVST.
NEW ENGLANDS FIRST FRVITS

When the infant colony was on fairly solid footing—with some towns established, agricultural techniques learned, and most towns prosperous—the New Englanders turned their attention and energy to creating an educational system. Oddly enough, the first educational institution to be established was a college—Harvard College, later to become Harvard University. A "worthy man," John Harvard, left a bequest for the college of about 260 volumes and £850, to which the Massachusetts legislature added, in 1636, another £400. Two years later Harvard, the first institution of higher learning in our country, was built. At first, as might be expected, Harvard (and later Yale, Columbia, and the other "Ivy League" colleges) specialized in producing ministers to supply the Christian faith with religious leaders.

In the decade of the 1640's, the New Englanders turned their attention to elementary education. The "Massachusetts Law of 1642" and the famous "Olde Deluder Satan Act" of 1647 were the first two pieces of legislation affecting education. Prefacing the Old Deluder Satan Act with the wish "that learning may not be buried in the grave of our fathers," the New England stewards created the beginnings of what was to become the American public-school system. The act required towns with a population of at least 50 families to establish a reading-and-writing, or elementary, school, and towns of at least 100 families to provide for grammar schools. Although the act was not always obeyed, as evidenced by the number of communities that had to be fined to require obedience, New England had a "public" school system. The early "public" schools, however, were essentially publicly supported parochial schools.

Although the very limited curriculum, the uncomfortable classrooms, and the frequently untrained schoolmasters were not impressive, this kind of educational apparatus did fulfill its major cultural imperative: it educated for godliness. New England colonists operated under the Calvinist assumption that man was inherently wicked: human nature was perverse, corrupt, and evil. This corruption, of course, was the result of the sin and casting out of Adam and Eve from the Garden of Eden. Because of Adam's primal sin, man was forever doomed to be a sin-ridden, perverted creature. And because of this, education was essential.

Education was an attempt to redirect man's wicked impulses. By being saturated with religion and godliness, by memorizing the cardinal rules of virtue (recall the ancient Hebrew child memorizing sections of the Torah), the young colonial child would at least have a chance to redirect his naturally wicked ways. Therefore the New England curriculum was basically religious, the discipline was religiously motivated, and the aim of education was religious.

The child, who may have attended a dame school, a nursery school conducted usually by an old widow, learned his ABC's. He then memorized a few hymns and learned some Biblical poetry and, of course, the basic postulates of Calvinism. Here, for example, are some rhymes by which children learned their alphabet:

A   In *Adam's* fall
     We Sinned all.
Z   Zaccheus he
     Did climb the tree
     His Lord to see.

Below is a portion of Westminster Catechism, taken from the *New England Primer*, one of the most frequently used textbooks in colonial New England:

Q. What is the chief End of Man?
A. Man's chief End is to glorify God and enjoy Him forever.
Q. What Rule hath God given to direct us how we may glorify and enjoy Him?
A. The word of God which is contained in the Scriptures of the Old and New Testament, Is the only rule to direct us how we may glorify and enjoy Him.

These phrases, prayers, hymns, and catechetical texts were memorized, were used as examples of writing, and were the subjects for innumerable sermons. The aim of this type of education, combined with strict laws, stern discipline, and harsh punishment for transgressors, was to redirect the child's naturally bad human nature, with salvation as the ultimate goal. It meant that education, as an inseparable part of religion, became an absolutely necessary part of the culture. Although the twentieth century has moved rather far from the Puritan seventeenth century, education is still conceived to be something all men need.

It was only in New England that "public" education achieved great significance. By and large, education in the Middle Colonies was essentially parochial. Education was generally controlled by the dominant religion in the area, and since there were so many different religions in the Middle Colonies, there were many different patterns of education.

In the South the situation was somewhat different. Instead of either public education (and in the seventeenth and eighteenth centuries "public" meant education provided by and for the local township) or parochial education, the South provided either private education or pauper education. Of course, there was some public education and some parochial education, but neither was characteristic of the South as a whole. Those Southern families who could afford it tended to employ private tutors to teach their children the "Three R's" and those subjects appropriate for an elite class—art, dancing, music, and the like. There was pauper education provided by such organizations as the Society for the Propagation of the Gospel in Foreign Parts. A missionary would teach children of the poor their letters and some hymns and prayers. The schoolhouse was often an abandoned building on a worn-out piece of land; hence, you may find the pauper education of this era referred to as "old field schools."

There was almost no education provided for Negroes. Indeed, in the South it eventually became a serious crime to teach Negroes to read. In South Carolina in the eighteenth century a fine of 100 pounds could be levied against a person for teaching a Negro to read. In Massachusetts at the same time an entire city would be fined 5 pounds for not establishing a school!

After the founding of Harvard in 1636 by the Puritans, other religious sects soon founded their own colleges. Today the Ivy League (Harvard, Yale, University of Pennsylvania, Princeton, Columbia, Dartmouth, Brown, and Cornell) is composed mainly of these early American institutions. These are still in operation today and are still among the leaders in the field of higher education.

In the eighteenth and nineteenth centuries all American colleges were, in some sense, church-oriented—that is, church-affiliated or church-directed. Whether the colleges were founded solely for the purpose of perpetuating the faith or whether they had a wider aim, their orientation was toward a particular denomination. In a recent study of American colleges and universities, Frederick Rudolph points out that, although the direction of colonial American colleges was religious, there was still a good deal of diversity in the structure and curricula of higher education. The denominational rivalry encouraged "toleration," but this rivalry was detrimental to the higher-education movement in colonial America.[11]

The curriculum of the colonial American college was both religious and classical. It attempted first of all to inculcate the dogmas and religious beliefs of a particular denomination. Otherwise, the curriculum generally was restricted to a study of the Greek and Latin classics. As in its European counterpart of a few centuries earlier, much of the learning was verbal, centering around debate, rhetoric, and disputation.

Colonial colleges, unlike present-day colleges and universities, were aristocratic by tradition, and they were designed to serve the aristo-

[11] *The American College and University* (New York: Knopf, 1962), p. 18.

cratic elements of colonial society. However, this aristocracy was continuously being subjected to "American" conditions, which tended to modify it.[12]

The classical curriculum and the emphasis on verbal acquisition contributed to a sterility of the colonial and the eighteenth- and nineteenth-century college so marked that it has led both Messerli and Rudolph to attribute any effectiveness of the college to either extracurricular or noncollege factors.[13]

Therefore, if we wish to understand the chief significance of colonial education as a force in shaping the destiny of this country, we must concentrate on the embryonic public schools of New England.

THE PERIOD OF INNOVATION AND CONSOLIDATION

One cannot date precisely the period of American educational innovation. In a sense, the period began when colonists landed on our shores. As noted in the previous section, early American education was extremely restricted, guided by religious ideals, and not genuinely "democratic"; much change was necessary before American education could be characterized as "democratic."

The changes that came about during the nineteenth century were the result of a number of forces:

1. The increasingly democratic nature of other American political and social institutions, particularly those associated with Jacksonian democracy in the midnineteenth century.

2. The arrival of a torrent of European immigrants who needed to be rapidly enculturated.

3. The increase in industrialism, which demanded a much higher level of literacy skills.

4. Related to the above, an increased urban population. City life is inherently more complex than rural and requires more skills to provide for the interdependence growing out of the need for sanitary facilities, judicial institutions, specialized occupations, and greater social interaction.

---

[12] *Ibid.*, p. 19.

[13] In an account of the college life of Horace Mann, often called the "father of American public education," Jonathan C. Messerli says, "If one is to judge from Horace Mann's own account, the period of 1816 to 1819 which he spent at Brown University had little significance as preparation for his future educational work." See Jonathan C. Messerli, "Horace Mann at Brown," *Harvard Educational Review*, 33 (Summer, 1963): 285. Rudolph says, "In the extracurriculum the college student stated his case for the human mind, the human personality, and the human body, for all aspects of man that the colleges tended to ignore in their single-minded interest in the salvation of souls." See Rudolph, *American College*, p. 155.

5. The growing sensitivity of the Americans. Eventually, education was viewed as something that went beyond individual or state concern. Education was considered a necessity that society should guarantee to everyone.

6. The importation of rather unique educational theories. The views of Jean Jacques Rousseau, an eighteenth-century French writer and philosopher, generated a great number of later educational philosophies, including those of Johann Heinrich Pestalozzi and Friedrich Froebel. The practical effect of their writings was to make education in general considerably more pleasant and effective.

Let us discuss each of these factors in some detail:

1. *The increasingly democratic nature of American political and social institutions.* "Democracy" means, in part, self-government. That is, the people as a collective body make those decisions that affect them. In a monarchy or an aristocracy an individual (the monarch) or a group of individuals (the aristocracy) makes the important decisions. In a democracy individuals rule themselves, either directly or through elected representatives. Much of colonial America of the seventeenth century was a kind of theocracy[14] ruled by Puritans or patricians.

As democratic beliefs and institutions spread, the notion that the people were capable of ruling themselves also spread, as did awareness of the need for education. Decision-making on the part of the people meant that they would need the facts and information to make decisions; it also meant that the people would need to know how to obtain information. Thus a need for information created a simultaneous need for literacy, and the people realized that increased literacy was a prerequisite for democracy. Little by little the "common" school arose— that is, a school for the children of the common man. By the middle of the nineteenth century, most Americans believed that elementary-school education was a necessity.

2. *The arrival of immigrants.* The characteristics of the mass immigration from Europe changed considerably in the nineteenth century. Instead of drawing almost exclusively from England and Germany, America began to draw immigrants from southern and eastern Europe. Famines, repressive governments, the desire for religious freedom and, most important, a hunger for land vastly increased immigration to this country during the nineteenth and early part of the twentieth century. Italians, Russians, Lithuanians, Yugoslavs, Irish, Chinese, and people of many other nationalities arrived by the hundreds of thousands and, between the Civil War and 1920, by the millions!

---

[14] A "theocracy" is a government in which an elect few, who claim to represent the divine will, rule in the name of God.

As we already noted, it is essential for the young, immature person to develop and become a part of the society in which he lives. For the immigrant a similar process—acculturation—must take place. To become acculturated means to learn the ways of a culture that is not your native culture. The torrent of immigrants had to learn a new language, a new monetary system, a new set of attitudes toward government—in general, they had to remake their lives.

It was the task of our educational system to turn the newly arrived immigrants into Americans. Schools, principally in large cities, received the immigrant children,[15] although many immigrants settled in farm areas—as the Germans did in the Dakotas. By and large, the schools succeeded in their task of acculturation. They succeeded in providing the immigrant child with literacy skills, promoted certain democratic attitudes, inculcated the American ideal of upward social mobility and, in many cases, taught immigrants occupational skills. The last point is most important, for many European immigrants came to this country with skills that were either inappropriate or unwanted in the United States. Manual-arts schools and polytechnical institutions, particularly in the East, imparted occupational skills that were more useful in a society becoming industrialized.

3. *Increase in industrialism.* By the third or fourth decade of the nineteenth century New England had become industrialized, while the South relied on cotton as its economic mainstay. The Civil War provided a tremendous impetus to industry both in New England and in the Middle States. By the end of the nineteenth century and the beginning of the twentieth century, the United States had charted its course as an industrial nation. Our country experienced a need for trained financial experts, as well as for manufacturing experts. Banking, investments, merchandising, and import-export businesses also thrived in the industrial age.

An increased need for trained workers and highly educated professionals developed. Little by little the semiliterate factory worker and the uneducated ranch hand began to pass from the scene. Individuals needed to possess computational and literacy skills far in advance of what had been needed in, say, 1800. Therefore, both secondary schools and institutions of higher education were given the job of seeing to it that a growing, technological culture would have sufficient numbers

15 And adults, too. Adult education played an extremely important part in the acculturation of the new immigrants. For a humorous and sympathetic portrayal of an immigrant striving to become Americanized, see Leonard Q. Ross (pseudonym for Leo C. Rosten), *The Education of H*Y*M*A*N K*A*P*L*A*N* (New York: Harcourt, Brace, 1937).

of adequately trained workers. The character of both secondary schools and colleges changed drastically during the late nineteenth century. The academy and the liberal-arts college of the early nineteenth century, designed to develop a genteel, elite class, began to decline in relative importance, although there are still many such schools, especially in the East and South. The comprehensive high school, originating in 1821 in New England, became more important than the private academy. After 1863, land-grant colleges and universities sprang up by the dozen.[16] Their objective, in addition to the perpetuation of the liberal arts, was to create trained professionals—physicians, attorneys, and scientists. They also had to create scientific agriculturists, journalists, teachers, businessmen, and a host of needed professional specialists. Hence expanding American industrialism created a pressing need for a highly skilled and literate populace.

4. *Increase in urban life.* The nineteenth century saw the beginning of the flow toward the cities. Better jobs, a more comfortable way of life, and (less strongly) a higher level of culture (art, music, drama, and lectures) were some of the many attractions that lured people away from the farms and into the cities and suburbs. It has been estimated that during the Revolutionary War in 1776 about 90 percent of the population lived on farms. Present-day statistics indicate that about 70 percent of the American people live in either cities, towns, or suburbs. We are no longer basically an agrarian nation.

To accommodate itself to an inherently more complex way of life, education underwent both quantitative and qualitative changes. In place of only the "Three R's," schools began to offer a much wider curriculum. In place of insisting on education for a rather limited number of children, Americans began to take it for granted that any normal child should receive schooling. And in the twentieth century even subnormal children are expected to receive some kind of education or training. For a person to be able to work, vote intelligently, buy insurance, choose a home or a car, talk about national or international events, deal with questions of fire and police protection, understand something of the art, literature, and music that surround him—in other words, for all of the complex skills involved in city life—a more sophisticated and a wider level of education was needed. The twentieth century has seen constant debate as to just what *kind* of education this is to be, but most persons take it for granted that their children will

[16] See Oliver C. Carmichael, "A Hundred Years of the Land-Grant Movement," *Saturday Review*, 45 (April 21, 1962): 58-59, 71-72 (which is reprinted in this section), for an interesting account of land-grant colleges and their impact on American higher education.

be educated. The debate is now over means—how it is to be accomplished.

The impact of what is known as "mass media" has been huge. In the nineteenth century, books, magazines, journals, and newspapers created a considerable cultural need for increased literacy. The twentieth century has added radio, movies, and television. Communications media in both centuries have interacted with our culture: they have required increased literacy skills to be understood, and they have increased the desire for literacy.

5. *The growing sensitivity of the American people.* The nineteenth century saw a uniquely American phenomenon: the growth of a tremendous faith in education. No matter how he defines education, almost everyone agrees that education is desirable. Education makes "something" out of a person that he would not be without it. What that "something" is has not been completely clear. But as Americans have viewed their goals, education has been seen as that which fulfills a person and that which helps an individual develop his potentialities. Aside from the fact that a formal education opens up occupational vistas, many, if not most, Americans seem to feel that the more formal education a person has, the better he is.[17] Americans have had a good deal of faith in education. The more widespread this faith became, the more it created a demand for elementary, secondary, and higher education.

6. *Importation of European educational theories of the eighteenth and nineteenth centuries.* In the eighteenth century, Rousseau devised a revolutionary educational theory. In brief, Rousseau believed that education ought to be pleasant and "natural." He assailed those schoolmasters who drove their lessons in with the cane, ruler, and switch. Disparaging memorization of unrelated and obscure concepts, Rousseau believed that the young child ought to be given an education that followed both his "real" human nature and natural laws. Rousseau's writ-

---

[17] Though this belief is widely held, the opposite belief is also entertained by many: education is often seen as a kind of frill that one does not need. Many people can be heard to say something like, "No, I didn't have much formal education, and perhaps I would have gone further with more. But I have not done badly as it is. I learned in the school of hard knocks; I learned by experience. In fact, I would say that the kinds of experiences I have had have done more for me than college has for many of the college-educated kids I hire." This position may well be the minority viewpoint, but it clearly exists as an alternative. It appears to reflect an older belief that if an individual is good, if he has the capacity, he will develop without an education. The extreme position is that formal education may well be a handicap to one's development. Remember that many preachers are "called" to preach the word of God—without formal seminary training. And it is often held erroneously that a good teacher is "born," not "made," and really does not need formal training.

ings, especially his book *Émile*, had considerable influence on Europeans during his lifetime, but their real impact came after his death in 1778. A somewhat eccentric Swiss schoolteacher named Heinrich Pestalozzi attempted to put Rousseau's theories into action. He opened several orphanage schools and attempted to teach young waifs to read and write, to learn a useful occupation, and to appreciate the wonders of nature. Of course, he had to modify Rousseau's ideas considerably, for Rousseau was not a schoolteacher; he was a theorist whose writings were imaginative and insightful but whose views were quite impossible to implement. Pestalozzi's theories came to this country in various ways.[18] They became known as "objective teaching," and soon enthusiastic disciples of Pestalozzi's methods were teaching his principles at normal schools and teacher-training institutions throughout the country.

Other European educational theorists included Joseph Lancaster and his so-called Lancasterian system, a monitorial method in which the brighter and more advanced child taught platoons of other children; Friedrich Froebel, a disciple of Rousseau and Pestalozzi who developed many theories and methods of childhood education; and Johann Friedrich Herbart, another German, who attempted to make a science of education.

By the end of the nineteenth century disciples of Pestalozzi, Rousseau, Frobel, Herbart, and other European educational theorists had brought their theories and methods to this country. The effect was to revolutionize American education. Teacher-training institutions began to teach educational sociology, psychology, and philosophy. Courses in methods, curriculum, and administration were added. In the twentieth century education courses have been combined with a liberal-arts curriculum. In essence, in America—and, of course, in Europe—there began to develop the idea that education is a complex undertaking that requires specially educated and intelligent practitioners. The American people have very, very slowly realized that truly good education also requires libraries, laboratories, teaching materials, and adequate classrooms.

The higher the level of educational aspiration, the more essential education became. The more education was viewed as essential, the more widespread educational institutions became.

---

[18] For a recent excellent discussion of Pestalozzi, see Charles Brauner, *American Educational Theory* (Englewood Cliffs: Prentice-Hall, 1964), especially Ch. 3, "Feeling as a Basis for Thought: Object Teaching."

THE MOLD IS FORMED—THE DEVELOPMENT
AND GROWTH OF INSTITUTIONS

By the beginning of the twentieth century, American educational institutions were established and formed. With two exceptions—the junior high school and the junior college—the major American educational institutions with which we are all familiar developed in the seventeenth, eighteenth, and nineteenth centuries. Let us review the kinds of educational institutions that have developed in the United States.

In the first place, common schools were created for all of the children of all the people.[19] In part through the efforts of Horace Mann and Frederick Barnard, public schools became part of what is loosely but with great conviction called "the American way of life." In the first half of the nineteenth century, education passed from either private or parochial hands and became a more public institution. By the time of the Civil War, most Americans expected a "common school"—that is, an elementary-school—education for their children.

Secondary schools developed from the academies of the eighteenth century. Benjamin Franklin's educational dream of a secondary school that would meet the practical needs of the American people resulted in the academy, whose heyday was from 1750 to 1820. The academy was an improvement over the Latin grammar school in at least two respects: it expanded the curriculum to include modern languages, science, and commercial and vocational subjects; and it considered girls as being educable. (The last point is most significant, for Western civilization has not, by and large, considered girls to be the equal of boys.)

In 1821 a high school was opened in Boston, and during the next fifty years the high school grew rather slowly.[20] In 1872 an important legal decision arising out of the famous Kalamazoo case made it possible for cities to levy taxes to support public secondary schools. After this decision by the Supreme Court in Michigan, the number of high schools began to increase rapidly. The comprehensive high school, which offers three types of curricula—college preparatory, terminal, and vocational—is considered by some to be the crowning glory of

[19] This is the claim, and it is generally true. But we must not lose sight of the fact that the formal education of Negroes and girls is a fairly recent phenomenon.

[20] Why the name "high school" was chosen is not clear. There is a German word, *Hochschule*, which does not mean high school; it has the designation of "higher education." An ambitious graduate student might find a doctoral dissertation in research on the origin of the name "high school."

America. By the end of the nineteenth century, the high school was an important institution.

America has had colleges since 1636. These institutions were exclusively undergraduate, liberal-arts institutions. The midnineteenth century saw the creation of the university, a grouping of colleges and professional schools. A typical university has an undergraduate college of liberal arts, a graduate school, and various professional schools, including law, education, medicine, engineering, nursing, and religion. Some institutions of higher education are noted for their concentration on some particular subject. For example, in California, Fresno State College and the University of California at Davis offer intensive specialized training in agriculture; Eastman Conservatory at Rochester, New York, provides advanced training in music.

In 1875 Daniel Coit Gilman established what was to be the first true graduate school in the United States. His institution, Johns Hopkins, provided for education beyond the B.A. degree. Previously, Americans who wished an M.A. or Ph.D. degree had to attend a European university, frequently German. By the end of the nineteenth century, American graduate schools were attracting graduate students who otherwise would have gone to Europe for their advanced degrees.[21]

Specialized institutions of higher education and specialized secondary schools also arose in the nineteenth century. Secondary schools for future machinists, dressmakers, electricians, and so on developed in large Eastern cities. Colleges of agriculture, engineering, and forestry also arose at this time. The status of these schools remains somewhat ambiguous. While they fill a real need, many would question their classification as truly educational institutions. Be that as it may, they are a part of the entire system of American education and are likely to continue as such for a long time to come.

Night schools—college-extension and adult schools—as previously indicated, increased greatly during the nineteenth century. Night schools and adult schools had a variety of purposes, ranging from basic literacy and citizenship training to training in hobbies, continuation school, vocational training, and even college course work. In the nineteenth century, colleges and universities began offering courses to people who could not go to the colleges. Instructors went to the villages and towns of rural America to teach the latest and most efficient methods of canning, planting, sewing, insect control, and the like. The

[21] For a good short summary of graduate schools, see the chapter entitled "Long-Range Forces That Have Shaped Doctoral Work," in Ernest V. Hollis, *Toward Improving Ph.D. Programs* (Washington, D.C.: American Council on Education, 1945).

twentieth century has seen a continuation and expansion of these activities. Many teachers drive long distances in an evening to teach extension classes in communities far from the home institution.

Negro education developed only after the Civil War. Although it was still a crime in several Southern states to educate a Negro, the ending of the Civil War saw a tremendous rush on the part of Negroes to learn to read and write. Many missionary-type educators from the North went to the South to open schools for Negro children and adults. Soon formal educational institutions for Negroes arose, such as the vocational institutes established by Booker T. Washington. By and large, Negro education centered around providing basic literacy and training in skilled occupations.[22] In part because of segregation and discrimination, few colleges and professional or graduate schools for Negroes arose in the nineteenth century. However, a few Negro colleges and universities, such as Howard, Tuft, and Dillard, did offer an opportunity for Negroes to obtain a higher education. In the 1950's and 1960's there has been a vigorous attempt on the part of Negroes to obtain integrated education, and elementary schools, high schools, and universities have very slowly opened their back gates to Negro students.

Education for women was another ideal promulgated during the nineteenth century in this country. As we noted, in Western civilization girls and women were long considered incapable of benefiting from formal education; their education was usually of the homemaking-vocational type. But institutions called "female academies" first opened their doors in the nineteenth century. In addition to the usual academic work, these academies attempted to provide upper-class polish for girls, who were instructed in foreign language, some art, music, fancy crocheting, and the other "polite arts."

Beginning with Oberlin College in Ohio in 1838, American colleges began to offer higher education to women. In both the nineteenth and twentieth centuries, colleges established exclusively for women provided an excellent education for the "bright, rich, and beautiful" girls of upper-middle- and upper-class American families. Some of the more famous women's colleges are Mt. Holyoke, Smith, Vassar, Radcliffe, Sarah Lawrence, and Bennington.

[22] For an interesting treatment of Negro education, see the *History of Education Journal*, 7 (Summer, 1957). There are two articles of considerable importance: "Forty Acres and a Mule and a Speller," by Edgar B. Wesley, discusses Negro education in general after the Civil War. "The Washington-DuBois Controversy and Its Effect on the Negro Problem," by C. Spencer Poxpey, deals with the long controversy between two Negro leaders, Booker T. Washington and W. E. DuBois.

Eventually most colleges and universities and many professional schools opened their doors to young women, and soon the "co-ed" became accepted in higher education. However, a new set of problems has been created, centering around the question of what should be done by the college-educated women who rears a family and makes no *use* of her formal training. One investigator has found a high incidence of emotional disorders among college-educated women and has suggested that the whole problem reflects a general cultural dilemma: How we can utilize the hard-won skills of the college-educated woman in a culture in which the dream-desire of woman is to be wives and mothers.[23]

To summarize: By 1900 the United States had developed most of the educational institutions we have today. Established and consolidated between 1870 and 1900 were elementary schools open to all, secondary schools, institutions of higher education, schools for Negroes and for women, specialized vocational educational facilities, graduate schools, teacher-education institutions, and a wide variety of adult-education facilities.

A PRELUDE AND TWO REVOLUTIONS

That tremendous educational progress took place in the nineteenth century is undeniable. That most or even many Americans were completely satisfied with the quantity and quality of schooling their children received, however, does not necessarily follow. As the nineteenth century closed, both the amount and the bitterness of criticism leveled at educational institutions increased.

Why were Americans critical of their schools? What did they find wrong? What kind of education did they want? In a recent book Lawrence Cremin discusses both the reasons for American dissatisfaction and the revolution that took place in the opening decades of the twentieth century.[24] The reader must remember that the decade of the 1890's and the first ten or fifteen years of the twentieth century were also periods of dissatisfaction with many other American institutions. The "muckrakers" wrote and lectured on every conceivable kind of evil, from the savage tactics used by the "robber barons" to build empires in the industrial and business world to impurities in food and

---

[23] For a sympathetic discussion of this problem, see Betty Friedan, *The Feminine Mystique* (New York: Norton, 1963).

[24] *The Transformation of the American School* (New York: Knopf, 1962).

drugs, from crime and poverty in the cities to the inadequacies of the medical profession.[25] The period between the Civil War and the early twentieth century saw the rise of almost unrestricted capitalism. The cities were growing much faster than facilities could be devised to take care of the many immigrants and native Americans who wished to live there. One could go on at great length describing both the social problems and the critics and reformers of this era. Suffice it to say that in every aspect of our social life pressing social problems arose to demand attention, and there was no lack of editors, writers, lecturers, novelists, social workers, and other critics to expose these problems to the American people and to suggest solutions.

One of the first educational critics to attract considerable attention was a physician, Joseph Rice. Becoming interested in what went on in classrooms, Rice traveled and observed many schools. What he saw horrified him. Classes were tremendously overcrowded. Desks were bolted down in rows and students sat in them, woodenly repeating what they had memorized. Corrupt political influence sent the incompetent niece of the local politician to teach school. Administrators who ruled like autocratic tyrants over their cowed teachers were common. The teachers themselves were disorganized, poorly trained, and ineffective. The school buildings were frequently unsanitary and dilapidated. The curriculum, teaching methods, textbooks, and facilities were outdated and ineffective. A continuing problem was the constant use of corporal punishment. Students of both sexes were beaten, flogged, whipped, and switched. Some were made to stand in uncomfortable positions for hours. It seemed to Dr. Rice that sadism and cruelty were dominant elements in American schools.[26]

In both the country and the city these conditions resulted in a high mortality rate. Many students, finding nothing of value in their classes, simply dropped out of school and went to work. (The con-

---

[25] See Ida Tarbell's *History of Standard Oil Company*, Upton Sinclair's *The Jungle*, Lincoln Steffens' *The Shame of Our Cities*, Gustavus Myers' *History of Great American Fortunes*, Jacob Riis's *How the Other Half Lives*, John Spargo's *The Bitter Cry of the Children*, Frank Norris's *The Pit*, and George Kibbe Turner's *Daughters of the Poor*. For a discussion of the "muckrakers" and other reform movements, see Samuel Eliot Morison and Henry Steele Commager, *The Growth of the American Republic* (5th ed.; New York: Oxford U. Press, 1962), II, Ch. 16, "The Progressive Movement, 1890-1917," pp. 440-475.

[26] See James P. Jewett, "The Fight Against Corporal Punishment in American Schools," *History of Education Journal*, 5 (Autumn, 1958): 1-10; and Paul Nash, "Corporal Punishment in an Age of Violence," *Educational Theory*, 13 (October, 1963): 295.

cern about "dropouts" is by no means of recent origin. American schools have always had a dropout problem. The recent publicity probably means that we are becoming more aware of it!) Most frequently it was the children of the poor, the immigrant, the racial minority who cut their education short. This made it painfully obvious to Rice and others that our schools were far from democratic and were actually being operated by and for a rather limited segment of our population. The charge (and documentation) that schools operate under this bias has been made so often since the 1890's that it is no longer capable of arousing shock. However, when Rice, Kilpatrick, Dewey, Lynd, and other educational critics brought this to the attention of the American people four, five, and six decades ago, it did arouse shock and resentment. How could schools, it was asked, which were supposed to be dedicated to the democratization of all the people, be so fundamentally undemocratic?

The undemocratic character of schools revealed itself in both the curriculum and the teaching methods. After "mastering" the basics, the "Three R's," students would presumably go on to more advanced learning. This learning, though it sometimes included geography, science, art, and music, most often tended to center around the classics, ancient history, mathematics, foreign languages, and literature. These subjects, hallowed by the years, were defended as excellent means of disciplining one's mind.[27] That subject matter could be intrinsically interesting or that it could have application in any practical sense was not widely believed. Without knowing basically what the classics meant, both teachers and those laymen who approved of the classics tended to see them as necessary.

The necessity of a secondary-school curriculum based on the classics seemed, to many, to be but a poor rationalization for an educational system designed exclusively for an elite, ruling class (held in disrepute in this nation). Historically such a curriculum had indeed been designed for a ruling class in Europe, and to many it was outmoded. Defenders of the classics replied that the very fact that a classical curriculum was ancient was sufficient reason to retain it: it must have had some value, or it would not have been kept for so many centuries.

Whatever the "ultimate" truth of either argument, the fact remained that the classical curriculum did indeed have little appeal to the sons and daughters of bricklayers, factory workers, farmers, and other members of the working class. Why, they asked frequently and with bitterness, could schools not teach something that was useful, helpful,

[27] See the essay "Influences on the Curriculum: Theories of Mind" in this text.

and practical?[28] Thus little by little there arose an increased demand for vocational subjects and a curriculum that would, somehow, be useful to students.

In brief, American education (then as now) was under heavy attack for offering outdated curricula, employing obsolescent and often unreadable textbooks, being influenced by corrupt politicians, utilizing incompetent and poorly trained teachers, and making almost sadistic use of corporal punishment. The entire school, from the classical curriculum to the tyrannical administrator, seemed an island of antidemocratic practices in a land supposedly democratic. Finally, learning often was entirely a matter of rote memorization, with things repeated and completely misunderstood by or having little meaning for most students. These were the accusations; how accurate they were is difficult to say. That they were partially valid is undoubtedly true. That they represented a completely accurate picture of the schools might be doubted: those who are trying to reform a situation invariably both exaggerate the evil of the status quo and tend to overlook any virtues that exist.

No institution in this country, particularly one so close to the people as the schools, can long remain indifferent to widespread criticism. Almost immediately, reform elements began to attempt solutions.[29] The reform movement followed a variety of paths. Parents of school-age youngsters grouped together to find out just what was happening to their children's classrooms. States passed laws to establish at least minimal standards for teachers. Commissions of inquiry sought to discover more about education at all levels. But perhaps the most important reform was made by educators themselves—the creation of a kind of educative method known as "Progressive Education."

[28] The entire argument is difficult to assess, even a half century later. First, the same argument—should schools offer "practical" curricula or should studies be designed to "train the mind" for a later time—is by no means dead. Second, with few exceptions, no one had even the foggiest notion just what subjects could be considered "practical"; in fact, the term "practical" is extremely difficult to define. Third, the entire argument involves the traditional American distaste for theoretical, abstract, or intellectual subjects, and different people use the same argument with very different underlying assumptions or reasons.

[29] In other areas as well as education. Laws to control abuses in our factories were passed—often to be struck down by the Supreme Court. Attempts were made to redress the grievances of farmers. In 1905 Congress passed a pure food and drug act. Citizens began to band together to fight political corruption in cities. The entire wave of criticism and reform culminated in Woodrow Wilson's first term in office. The reader is referred to Ch. XVIII, "The New Freedom, 1913-1917," in Morison and Commager, *The Growth of the American Republic*, II, 522-545, for a brief but excellent discussion of this era.

Though the battle over whether our schools should adopt the program proposed by those known as Progressive Educators has passed, the phrase "Progressive Education" is still a fighting word to many. To some, Progressive Education was a profoundly humanitarian experiment designed to democratize education by making it more "natural" and humane. To other extremely vocal groups, Progressive Education was the most damaging and the most unfortunate disaster that ever afflicted American education.

Progressive Education was neither a single idea nor the result of the contributions of a single person. As one might expect in our culture, it represented the pooled beliefs and philosophies of a variety of persons. The spiritual father of the Progressive movement in education was undoubtedly Jean Jacques Rousseau, the apostle of naturalism in education. Rousseau's theories, modified and put into practice by Heinrich Pestalozzi in Switzerland, formed a set of assumptions that were to guide Progressivism a century later. In the nineteenth century the pioneer in childhood education, Friedrich Froebel, a German philosopher and educational theorist, further developed the Rousseauean and Pestalozzian philosophy. John Dewey, in the late-nineteenth and early-twentieth century, provided some important ideas for this movement.[30] Finally, William Heard Kilpatrick, the much-beloved professor of education at Columbia Teachers College, probably did more to shape Progressivism than any other single person. Other significant Progressive Education advocates were H. Gordon Hullfish, Carleton Washburne, Harold Rugg, George Counts, Jesse Newlon, and Bruce Raup. The Progressives wrote voluminously—books, journal articles, speeches, tracts, pamphlets, and essays. Those theorists referred to above are but a tiny fraction of the active Progressive Educational theorists. These persons, and many more, were heavily influenced by naturalism, romanticism, the scientific method, democracy, and humanism.

The second aspect of the revolution was created by a rather different group of theorists who, while they joined with the Progressives, nevertheless held views quite different from theirs. We are referring to the Science of Education group.

If the Progressives were interested in naturalism and democracy in education, the Science of Education movement, as its name implies,

---

[30] Although John Dewey is often blamed as the evil genius of Progressivism, he in fact had comparatively little to do with it. He was not a particularly active participant in the Progressive Education Association and as early as the late 1920's criticized Progressivism severely for its shortcomings. The reader is cautioned to take all impassioned attacks on Dewey and Progressivism with a grain of salt.

was heavily influenced by "science." The methods of science had spread from the physics and chemistry laboratories and were applied, in the late-nineteenth century, to the study of human behavior. Psychologists, sociologists, and certain professors of education felt that the methods of science could be applied both to human behavior and to education. One could formulate hypotheses, gather data, and treat them statistically and through the experimental method decide what should be taught and how it should be taught. To this end, the Science of Education advocates turned their attention to virtually every aspect of education. They measured the neatness of handwriting and the accuracy of spelling. They evaluated the reading speed and comprehension of students. They devised tests designed to measure aptitudes, achievement, and (much less successfully) personality characteristics. They attempted to find out precisely how much money was spent by schools and how this money could be spent more wisely. They investigated the rate at which children learn to divide by a two-digit number and the speed with which they forget what they learned. They measured children's manual dexterity and their ability to handle abstract concepts. A Stanford University professor, Lewis Terman, improved on the French intelligence tests and came up with one of his own, the Stanford-Binet Test (called frequently but incorrectly the "I.Q. Test").

Science of Education enthusiasts investigated the curriculum and decided that it could be made truly useful by carefully analyzing what people actually did in their daily lives. For instance, in the eighteenth and nineteenth centuries students learned to use such fractions as 19/37, 5/19, and 11/23. The Science of Education curriculum devisers discovered that people in the business and industrial world rarely used these fractions; they more often used halves, thirds, fourths, and fifths. Therefore, the Science of Education people replaced the complex, rarely used fractions with those most typically employed by persons in their daily lives.

The most important name associated with the Science of Education movement was Edward Lee Thorndike. For almost forty years, during which time he was a professor at Columbia University, Thorndike was the acknowledged leader in educational research. Not only did he formulate the theory of stimulus-response psychology, but he conducted research in teaching methods, testing, curriculum construction, learning theory, and virtually anything else that touched on education. Thorndike's findings and theories had an enormous impact on education, probably every bit as great as that of Progressive Education.

The two movements that comprised the educational revolution, the Science of Education and Progressive Education, were radically different in orientation, approach, and consequences. Unfortunately, the differences between the two schools were not appreciated. Both schools were lumped into one movement, with neither the general public nor many professional educators discriminating between the two. In the textbook *Foundations of Method* William Heard Kilpatrick, who studied under both Dewey and Thorndike, attempted to combine the theories of both educational theorists without realizing that these theories were not harmonious.

Progressive Educators, such as Kilpatrick, assumed that people learn as they grow and develop—that is, there is a kind of built-in urge that enables persons to develop from stage to stage. The Science of Education advocates, such as Thorndike, believed that most learning is the result of outside influences. This is not simply a theoretical difference: these two theories result in two radically different conceptions of teaching!

If a child grows and develops in a predetermined fashion, much as a plant grows from seed to bud to full-grown plant, then education is a matter of teachers (1) finding out just how students grow and (2) allowing students to learn just what is in line with their natural development. Therefore, Kilpatrick and other Progressives believed that students ought to determine the major portion of what they are to learn and of how they are to learn. Students should study what *they* feel is important, and then *they* should plan their courses of study. Students ought to be responsible for executing these plans and, finally, they should play a major part in evaluating what they have studied. Progressive Education, therefore, placed heavy emphasis on student interests. Instead of the teacher giving assignments, hearing students recite, and testing them, the teacher should act as a guide. He should assist students in the learning process but should not dominate it.

The Science of Education movement had quite different notions of what education should be. The teacher must first of all know what is to be taught. He must then present the material to students. Then he must test them to determine how much they learned. In practice, this meant that teachers introduced small units of work and drilled students in the work until they made the correct responses. Correct responses were evidence that the student truly had learned.

Progressive Education led to spontaneity, an interest in the arts, and emphasis on self-expression. It led to a curriculum in which student interests dominated and to teaching methods in which the teacher accepted the secondary role of a guide. The Science of Education led to the teacher-dominated classroom, in which teachers initiated, planned, presented, and judged. One can perhaps get an insight into both approaches by looking at a typical unit of work.

In a Progressive classroom the students might decide that they wanted to learn about animals, and therefore that a field trip to the zoo was in order. Before they went on the field trip, all students would probably read about the animals they would see. Some might give reports on certain animals, others might construct clay models of giraffes and elephants, and others might paint a mural of a zoo. All the students would then go to the zoo, with the teacher acting as guide. When they returned, there would likely be a class discussion of what they had seen. The class would cooperatively decide what testing procedures would enable the students to show what they had learned. That is, they would decide on the best method of evaluating the "experience"—a key term in Progressive Education—that they had "undergone." Perhaps the zoo unit would lead into the next unit, as students would build plans for future learning on present knowledge. Throughout the unit many skills would be utilized—reading, arithmetic, discussion, writing, research, oral reports, and the like.

In a classroom conducted by a disciple of the Science of Education the teacher would decide, for example, that it was important for students to learn about the exports of the United States, so that as adults they could make intelligent economic decisions in the light of their knowledge about geography, agriculture, industry, and the like. In all likelihood, the teacher would give students a pretest to see what they knew. Students would read a geography book, concentrating on the chapter entitled "The Exports of the United States." The teacher would then ask questions designed to elicit correct responses—that is, to indicate whether or not there was an accurate understanding of the subject matter. After the recitation students would take an objective test, with their answers being compared with those on the pretest.

Both the Progressive movement and the Science of Education influenced educational theory and practice. Not many people today are "pure" Science of Education or Progressive advocates. But it is this eclecticism, the indiscriminate mixing and joining of two different theories, that has provided some rather serious problems for teachers since the 1920's.

Teaching on the early elementary level tends to follow Progressive patterns. The children are given a good deal of freedom to initiate and perform. Their interests are frequently taken as the starting place for most activities. Art, music, and enjoyable subjects play an important part in the curriculum. As children reach the third or fourth grade, however, the picture changes: in place of freedom, interest, guided activities, and field trips, the emphasis switches to subject-matter-to-be-covered. Workbooks, "units" of study, drill, mastery of information, and other curricular concepts associated with the Science of Education dominate. Not many persons have asked, "How desirable is it for children to experience this abrupt change in the educative process?" Nor is it frequently asked whether one or the other of the learning theories *is better*. It is assumed, without awareness, that younger children have different education goals, learn differently, and require different teaching than intermediate-aged children.

Today the curricular and methodological contributions of both movements are so ingrained in American education that they appear to be natural. This is a typically American pattern: the combination of theoretically inconsistent beliefs without concern for the inconsistencies in either theory or practice—as long as it "works." But it is crucial to ask, "What does it mean for something to 'work'?"

THE AMERICAN DEPRESSION OF THE 1930'S

In October of 1929, as most people know very well, the stock market fell apart. Financial chaos precipitated by the stock-market crash deepened into a depression in which the reduction of consumer demand led to the laying off of workers. Unemployment led to still further reduction in demand, and the vicious cycle continued, until in the early 1930's between 7 and 13 million workers—perhaps 6 percent to 11 percent of the population of this country—were out of work. This, however, is only an estimate, because no one is certain as to the precise number of unemployed. Savings were soon depleted; jobs became impossible to find; men and boys by the hundreds of thousands roamed the country, often riding the rails in a desperate and usually unsuccessful search for work—any kind of work.[31] Marriages were postponed, and couples deliberately reduced the number of children they would have. Breadlines and free soup canteens appeared in major cities. Agricultural regions also experienced crises, for the reduced demand affected the raising of crops. Indeed, so low were the prices for agricultural products that it became "good economic sense" to pour milk into sewers, to plow oranges into the ground, and to slaughter immature animals so that agricultural products would not glut the market and reduce prices even further.

[31] One estimate in a 1934 newspaper was that 1,000,000 men and boys were "bumming the rails."

It became obvious to most Americans that something was basically wrong. There was no good reason that a nation of 123 million previously rich, proud, and comfortable people should suffer a catastrophic depression. Yet, unless one wished to believe that the depression was a punishment from heaven, it appeared obvious that it must have been man-made. For ten or more years, writers, economists, educators, and philosophers search for an answer, or the answers that would help explain the depression. The answers that were given all involved the belief that our basic social philosophy was wrong and that education had failed to create desirable social attitudes in the young.

Many influential educational critics in this country, from John Dewey on down, offered analyses that went something like this: The economic and social philosophy of the eighteenth and nineteenth centuries is inadequate for today. The capitalistic philosophy of Adam Smith[32] emphasized that unrestricted economic activities of individuals would somehow create a desirable economic situation for all. That is, the fewer the controls and restrictions on individual entrepreneurs, the more prosperous any country would become. The trouble with this philosophy, said its critics, is that it tended to make the selfish desires of individuals the basis of all morality. In place of the cooperative member of society, this nineteenth-century capitalism set up the aggressive, profit-seeking, power-hungry businessman as the moral model for all Americans. It was further concluded by the critics that unrestricted competition and uninhibited profit-seeking as the supreme values were at the root of our troubles. The schools simply cooperated in passing on this selfish, antisocial morality.[33]

The answer: *Let the schools lead the nation in devising and passing on a new social philosophy!* Those who advocated this point of view were called Social Reconstructionists, for they wished to reconstruct our society and fervently believed that teachers should lead the American people to a better tomorrow. Educational theorists such as George Counts, author of *Dare the Schools Build a New Social Order?* formed a new curricular movement. They published a journal, *The Social Frontier*, which reflected their beliefs. Soon other professors of edu-

---

[32] Adam Smith, a Scottish economist and philosopher, wrote his *Wealth of Nations* in 1776. This book, which became the bible of nineteenth-century capitalism, expounded the basic beliefs and assumptions of capitalism, including the importance of private property, unrestricted economic activity, and profit.

[33] If this sounds like a left-wing argument, it is not surprising. Many American critics of the 1930's who were not themselves Marxists or Communists were heavily influenced by a Marxist position. To a historian of the depression, it may seem almost as if the Communists had a monopoly on social criticism, although they did not.

cation, speakers, and textbook writers adopted the viewpoint that the schools should lead society.

Instead of schools simply transmitting the cultural heritage, schools would *change* the cultural heritage. Teachers would see to it that students learned how to criticize social institutions and, in the act of criticism, would come to prefer a more rational, a more just, a more democratic, and a more equitable way of life. In place of the nineteenth-century capitalistic philosophy and the egocentric Protestant ethic,[34] the schools were to transmit a new cooperative ethic, one based on the scientific method of knowing, on democracy as a way of life, on equality, and on progressive amelioration of the socioeconomic scene.

The Social Reconstructionists did not go unchallenged. Boyd Bode, an associate of John Dewey who interpreted Dewey's pragmatism to teachers and professors, raised one major objection. He accused the Social Reconstructionists of attempting to indoctrinate children in liberal, left-wing philosophy. To Bode, indoctrination in education was to be avoided, whether it was left-wing or conservative indoctrination.

Bewildered as Americans were by the depression of the 1930's, they were not quite ready to turn schools over to what appeared to them to be left-wing Utopian dreamers.[35] The movement lost steam and slowly died out. On December 7, 1941, the entire question became academic, for Americans faced another challenge that completely eclipsed the problems and questions that arose during the depression years.

Despite the death of Social Reconstructionism as a meaningful movement in American education, the controversy surrounding it raised numerous issues that are still relevant. First, the controversy established the fact that, far from being morally neutral, schools are indeed in the business of passing on some kind of philosophy. Second, it highlighted the enormous importance of education. More and more people began to see the schools as a battleground on which was being

[34] The origin and meaning of the phrase "Protestant ethic" cannot be discussed here. However, the student is invited to do some research to understand the significance of an ethical principle that blended capitalism and seventeenth- and eighteenth-century ethical beliefs. See, for example, Vernon Parrington, *Main Currents in American Thought* (New York: Harcourt, Brace, 1927), I and II; and Crane Brinton, *The Shaping of the Modern Mind* (New York: Mentor, 1953).

[35] Most of the original Social Reconstructionists, such as Newlon and Rugg, have passed on. Counts is retired and is pursuing other interests. The only remaining forceful advocate of this position is Theodore Brameld. See his *Philosophies of Education in Cultural Perspective* (New York: Holt, 1955).

fought a crucial war—or rather, a series of crucial wars. And more and more organized pressure groups began to want to take a part in this struggle for children's minds.

As far as making any real change in the social-studies curriculum went, the Social Reconstructionist movement was a failure. The course called "social studies," despite numerous formal changes (called "integration," "correlation," "fusion," and the "Core"), has remained essentially the same as it always was—a collection of frequently unrelated facts, taken from history, economics, and geography, which is concerned with the formal structure and function of our society and very little else.[36]

FROM 1945 TO THE PRESENT

The end of the Second War in 1945 saw the beginning of a new set of questions for American education. In place of "What is wrong with American society and how can we improve?" the question became, "How under the existing democracy can we: (1) continue to lead the world as an industrialized, democratic society and (2) develop the talents of *all* our children?" One assumption behind these questions was that our democracy and economic system were quite adequate. All existing inequalities and weaknesses, it was widely believed, would soon be ironed out as appropriate legislation was passed to remedy the situations.

The other assumption was that America faced a new enemy. In place of the defeated fascist and nazi regimes of Germany, Italy, and Japan, a new movement—international communism—presented us with a new challenge. Communism, which combines some extremely appealing and humanitarian goals with oppressive measures to reach those goals, appeared to be a formidable opponent. It became obvious to most Americans in the days following World War II that America was destined to lead the Western world against an aggressive international communistic movement.

The conflict between America and other Western democracies and the Soviet Union and its allies became known as the Cold War. The Cold War has had an enormous impact on American education in a variety of ways. First, it can be claimed that much of the national wealth that might have been channeled into education has been spent

---

[36] For a sharp criticism of the social studies, see Martin Mayer, *Where, When and Why* (New York: Harper and Row, 1963). For a more scholarly and balanced approach to the social studies, see Maurice Hunt and Lawrence Metcalf, *Teaching High School Social Studies* (New York: Harper, 1955).

and is being spent on building and maintaining a huge defense apparatus of men and machines. Second, much of our educational energy is spent on Cold War-related activities, such as the recent legislation (known as the National Defense Educational Act, or the NDEA, which was passed by the Congress in 1958) to create more trained personnel in science, foreign languages, and mathematics. This emphasis has created curricular distortions, for it has meant that the humanities—philosophy, art, literature, music—have had to take a back seat to science and mathematics. Third, the Cold War has meant that the social studies are given over, to a rather large degree, to prodemocratic and anticommunist indoctrination. That is, in place of objective study, students are often exposed to a one-sided dose of propaganda in which "we" are the "good guys" and "they" are all bad.

In addition to the Cold War, other movements and events have had considerable consequences for the programs of American schools. Let us describe the educational scene briefly:

1. *Population expansion.* In 1930 our country had about 123 million people; in 1940 that figure was 132 million; in 1950 we had attained a population of 151 million. And in the 1960's our population will grow to 200 million. What this means is that schools are "bursting at the seams." At the elementary, secondary, and university levels, more and more students are in school. These huge numbers of students are taxing the facilities of schools—crowding lecture rooms, laboratories, and classrooms, exhausting the often meager stock of books in libraries, and requiring a wide variety of ingenious inventions, such as teaching machines, which we shall discuss in a moment. Education is not only big business, it may well be second in size only to national defense.

2. *Technology.* Technological advances have had a wide variety of effects on schools. The increasingly complex level of technology in our country has made education more and more important. In our recent past there was always some kind of job for the illiterate or semiliterate workers; they could pick cotton, run elevators, or dig ditches. Now we have cotton-picking machines, automatic elevators, and high-speed ditchdiggers. The term used to describe this increasingly complex technology in which ingeniously sophisticated machines do the work formerly done by human beings is "automation."

Though automation has displaced hundreds of thousands of workers, it has given work to many others. People have to design, produce, sell, and service these wonder machines, and these people must be rather well educated. Thus there is an enormous need for programmers, electronic technicians, repairmen, and the like. Our educational system, it must be noted, is responding rather slowly to the new needs of our society, for most high-school vocational classes are teaching skills that are either inappropriate (to the need) or are and have been obsolete for years. A startling evidence of educational lag is the fact that, despite the *decreasing* need for farmers, many states still offer vocational agriculture as the primary vocational course.

Another effect of automation on education has been an increase in the number of gadgets in classrooms. Educational television, programmed learning, including teaching machines, and a wide variety of other audio-visual materials are increasing at a rapid rate. Many universities and high schools are experimenting with language laboratories, and several states in the Midwest have experimented with an airborne educational television station that beams a televised lecture to many thousands of students.

The actual value of all of this experimentation is most debatable. That educational television and teaching machines save teacher time and are efficient is granted; that they actually result in the desired and desirable kinds of learning is not so certain. After all, as has been pointed out, one cannot talk back to a machine, and "talking back" may well be an indispensable element of education.

3. *Experimentation.* The tried and true arrangements in education are being questioned by almost everyone. The notion (found, incidentally, in the Old Testament) that the ideal classroom consists of one teacher and twenty-five students is now being challenged by proponents of variable-sized classrooms. It has been found that the size of a class can—and perhaps should—vary from small seminars to huge lecture audiences, with from a few students to several hundred.

Similarly, the *modes* of teaching are being debated. There is a rather ancient idea that a teaching situation is one in which a teacher, an expert in some branch of subject matter, transmits information to students, whose main job is to "get" that information. This idea has been challenged by a number of theoreticians. First, some say that teaching which follows exclusively the ancient pattern of transmitting information is simply poor teaching. It usually results in a low retention rate and in poor motivation. Second, most areas of knowledge have expanded so rapidly that it is quite impossible to know all there is to know in one field. Therefore, some educators talk about learning how to inquire—that is, learning how to formulate important questions and how to discover their solutions. Educators also discuss the structure of a field of knowledge and what it means to learn this structure.[37]

---

[37] One of the major exponents of this point of view is Jerome Bruner, *The Process of Education* (Cambridge: Harvard U. Press, 1961).

Experimentation to improve the teaching of mathematics and the natural sciences is now in full swing. New and rather radical curricula are proving effective. The BSCS (Biological Science Curriculum Study), a modern approach to high-school biology, has attempted to get away from the old practice of memorizing vast amounts of conceptually unrelated information—names of animals, species, parts of the body, and so on. The new approach emphasizes the process of scientific inquiry—the nature of a hypothesis and of data. It makes extensive use of laboratory-type situations, which replace the almost exclusive use of a textbook. Similarly, the SMSG, School Mathematics Study Group (to name one of the organizations interested in improving the teaching of mathematics), has attempted to introduce new teaching concepts. This approach emphasizes the nature of the deductive process in mathematics, stressing the logical progression of propositions. Those of us who suffered through a geometry course in which we "proved" that something or other is congruent with angle X without understanding what we were about are especially happy to hear of this new approach.[38]

One could describe a good many other rather exciting experiments in education today. Suffice it to say that every aspect of education is undergoing scrutiny and that rather ancient, long-accepted practices are in process of being drastically overhauled. This is true from the elementary-school level to postgraduate education. It is affecting every subject-matter specialty and every method of teaching. Just where it is all leading is difficult to say now, for those in the midst of a revolution scarcely know its direction.

4. *Expanding humanitarianism.* The idea that our country ought to educate each person to the full limits of his capabilities is becoming stronger and more persuasive with each passing year. While there are many barriers in the way of this extremely humane goal, there is evidence that we are moving toward it successfully. For instance, the present concern with our rather high dropout rate means that we no longer feel quite so unconcerned about the waste inherent in a half-finished education. Thus many experiments are being attempted today to see what can be done to salvage dropouts, from before potential dropouts begin kindergarten to after they have officially quit school. Efforts ranging from nursery-school training for slum children to work-study programs for dropouts seem to hold promise for rehabili-

[38] See Allen F. Strehler, "What's New About the New Math?" *Saturday Review,* 47 (March 21, 1964): 68-69, 84.

tating children who would otherwise become half-literate castoffs, unfit for anything but poorly paying, dead-end jobs.[39] Another manifestation of growing American social sensitivity is our concern with special education. "Special education" refers to the teaching of children who deviate rather widely from some accepted norm. This group includes the blind, the deaf and dumb, the mentally retarded, the cerebral-palsied, the emotionally disturbed child, and the child with speech defects, on the one hand, and the extremely bright child, on the other. Special teachers are being trained to work with these children and, assisted by psychological, medical, neurological, and genetic research, they are accomplishing a great deal. It is becoming increasingly apparent that those children formerly considered too stupid or too deviant to be helped really can be helped.

The significance of our efforts to help the culturally deprived, the handicapped, and the brilliant child is this: The idea that education exists in part to develop the potentialities of *all* children to their limit has been extended to include those children who have many and apparently insurmountable barriers to an adequate development of their potentialities and those who, because of superior intelligence, cannot benefit from the "standard" curriculum. What has historically been available to a comparative few is now being made available to the many.

5. *Changes in the profession.* As we shall point out in the essay on professionalism, teaching has been accorded somewhat too little respect. The notion of a teacher as a semieducated, not especially talented person—either man or woman—is slowly giving way to the idea of a teacher as thoroughly educated, intelligent, and effective. This ideal has by no means been attained, but there are signs that both the profession and its practitioners are improving.

For example, both the National Education Association and the American Federation of Teachers are attempting to improve salaries and conditions of work. This improvement is attracting more capable people to teaching. Those persons who have heretofore looked to the more settled professions for a career are beginning to be drawn to teaching as it carries with it higher salaries, desirable fringe benefits, a chance to improve one's skills constantly, and an opportunity for upward social mobility.

This improvement will not come about, however, without considerable friction, debate, and hard feeling. For teachers all over the coun-

---

[39] For an interesting and rather poignant treatment of these attempts, see "School for Poverty's Children," *Life*, 56 (April 3, 1964): 71-89.

try to make rather substantial improvements in their way of life, power necessarily will slowly drift from the local level to the professional association of teachers. That is, as teachers become more militant and better organized, they will make more and more decisions previously left to the superintendent and the board. What this amounts to is a weakening of representative democracy at the local level. It would appear, however, that either teachers will gain in power and improve their profession by establishing strong state and national organizations or most educational decisions will continue to be made at the local level. And what this latter alternative has meant historically is that the board and the superintendent, single-mindedly devoted to lowering educational costs, hire young, inexperienced teachers for low wages and provide them with inadequate facilities.

6. *Changes in teacher preparation.* Numerous improvements are reported in the area of teacher education. For years there has been debate and wrangling, often savage and acrimonious, over the question of the kind and extent of teacher education. Apparently there is a definite move on the part of college professors to talk to each other about just what kind of course preparation is essential for teachers.[40]

The result of this dialogue has been agreement on some basic issues: teachers need to know what to teach—that is, the subject matter—and they need to know something about teaching—that is, children's growth and learning patterns, teaching techniques, philosophy of education, and the organization and function of schools. It is also generally (although not by any means completely) agreed that the previous practice of allowing people with two or three years of college education to teach is no longer desirable—if it ever was. Most teacher-education institutions and many state departments of education are now thinking of certifying only those teachers who have a four-year degree. Some states are even talking about the necessity of either a five-year college program or a Master's degree.

7. *Higher education.* Higher education, too, has undergone a variety of important changes. In addition to the most obvious change —more and more students taking a greater variety of specialized course work—there are other important modifications.

Junior or community colleges have arisen by the hundreds during

[40] The history of this problem is ably reported in G. K. Hodenfield and T. M. Stinnett, *The Education of Teachers* (Englewood Cliffs: Prentice-Hall, 1961). See also James B. Conant, *The Education of American Teachers* (New York: McGraw-Hill, 1963). Conant's ideas have drawn the wrath and scorn of a number of professors of education.

this century. Junior colleges have at least four functions: (1) continuing the high-school curriculum; (2) providing the first two years of college at a minimal cost; (3) providing terminal training; and (4) supplying adult or continuing education. The junior college may well be the solution to the vexing problem of how to provide further education for those who may not have the interest or intellectual ability to profit from a regular college experience.[41]

Graduate schools have increased in number and offer a greater quantity of course work. More and more people in a variety of fields are discovering that they need advanced study. Graduate schools in every field from physics to packaging are offering advanced study. Graduate study is quite unlike undergraduate work. The emphasis in graduate study is on individual study, research, small classes, and intense concentration on some limited aspect of a field.

Research is far more important to colleges and universities than it was a few years ago. Those in higher education, which both creates and disseminates knowledge, have discovered that the production of new information requires staff members and facilities that the institution usually does not have. Therefore wealthy foundations, private industry, and government have increasingly come to subsidize research in many fields.[42] The salaries of professors are augmented, buildings are constructed and expensive equipment acquired, and graduate students and secretarial help are secured; the result is a flood of articles, pamphlets, books, and monographs on every topic, from the sex life of the blue whale to the reasons for delinquents and delinquency.

The rapid increase in graduate research, however, has not been uncriticized. First, since there is more money and prestige in research than in teaching, many professors tend to emphasize research and publication at the expense of their students. Second, research can actually distort the program of an entire university. If a great deal of money and professors' energies are channeled toward research, fewer resources are expended on undergraduate teaching. In addition, questions have been raised about the ultimate value of this research. It is difficult to tell, at any given time, whether a particular bit of research is really useful and significant or mere academic boondoggling. Finally, the research itself is apparently one-sided; there is a heavy concentration

41 See Clyde E. Blocker, "Comprehensive Community College," *NEA Journal*, 51 (September, 1962): 20-21.

42 For a most interesting treatment of both higher education and graduate research, the reader is referred to Christian K. Arnold's "Higher Education: Fourth Branch of Government?" *Saturday Review*, 47 (January 18, 1964): 60-61, 75-77.

on the physical sciences and much less on the humanities and the behavioral sciences.[43]

8. *Vocational education.* Since our culture, with its increasingly complex technology, requires special training for certain vocations, the problem of vocational education is increasingly becoming one for the public schools. Although we have had vocational education since the turn of the century, when the Smith-Hughes and Smith-Lever Acts subsidized vocational training in agriculture and home economics, vocational education has been something of a stepchild. Frequently the vocational school has been a dumping-ground for students who could not do well in an academic program, and frequently it has trained students in obsolescent skills on obsolescent machines.

However, it appears that there is a considerable awakening to the need for a modern, useful vocational education program in our secondary schools. Although only about 2 percent of federally reimbursed programs in six states sampled currently offered training in trade or industrial occupations,[44] there is reason to believe that this picture will change. We are beginning to realize that we can no longer turn masses of teen-agers loose in the employment market with either no skills or obsolescent work skills. Therefore, there are studies presently in progress that are attempts to determine the types and curricula of vocational education. The next step is to design the kind of vocational education program that will keep abreast of the rapidly changing employment picture.

IN CONCLUSION

This rather brief summary of the history of American education is only a bare outline. Many events and a great many significant figures who have affected education have not even been mentioned. However, the student should be cognizant of the following important ideas:

Education began as a rather humble, local, religious-oriented project. It has turned into a complex, nationwide enterprise that—in one way or another—affects everyone in this country.

Education began as a privilege for a fairly small elite. It is now regarded as the birthright of all Americans.

[43] Insofar as overemphasis on published research is concerned, in a case reported in *Time Magazine*, 83 (April 24, 1964): 86-87, a professor was fired for lack of research, even though he had written a rather famous book—out of his field. This subtle administrative "coercion" is known in the field as "publish or perish." For a scholarly discussion of this general issue, see Theodore Caplow and Reece J. McGee, *The Academic Marketplace* (New York: Basic Books, 1958).

[44] J. Chester Swanson, "Whither Vocational Education?" *NEA Journal,* 52 (October, 1963): 59-60.

Certain persistent problems have troubled this culture since the seventeenth century. Precisely who is to be educated? What are the students to learn? For what purpose are they to learn? The extent and intensity of educational controversies indicate that we are not very close to finding solutions.

Because of the pluralistic nature of our society, education will continue to be rather responsive to the wishes of different groups. This is both a value and a problem. It makes education a servant of our needs, but at the same time it makes it difficult for professional educators to know what to teach.

If the above conclusions are correct, there is a rather disturbing implication: every social problem is eventually an educational problem.

The Birth of a Tradition*

by LLOYD P. JORGENSON

Lloyd P. Jorgenson is professor of education at the University of Missouri, Columbia. He is widely known in the field of history of education and has contributed to the leading journals in this field, in addition to having written THE FOUNDING OF PUBLIC EDUCATION IN WISCONSIN.

The distinction between "public" and "denominational" schools, so important to later generations, was quite unknown throughout most of the Colonial period of our history. To be sure, wherever one denominational group enjoyed a dominant position the schools were, in a sense, under "public" sponsorship, but this was only because in such cases church and state were one. Schooling was, first and foremost, a function of the church, and all denominational groups accepted this responsibility, whether or not they were in a position to enlist the aid of the state.[1] The same blending of state and denominational

* Lloyd P. Jorgenson, "The Birth of a Tradition," *Phi Delta Kappan* 44 (June, 1963): 407-414. By permission of the editor.

[1] Bernard Bailyn effectively points out the fallacy of trying to make a distinction between the denominational and public aspects of colonial education in his *Education in the Forming of American Society*, Chapel Hill: University of North Carolina Press, 1960, pp. 10-11. Essentially the same point had been made earlier by Charles A. and Mary R. Beard in *The Rise of American Civilization*, Vol. I, New York: Macmillan, 1927, p. 52.

resources was present in the founding and support of the colonial colleges. They were creatures of the state as well as of the denominations they were designed to serve, and "whether they should be thought of as state colleges or as church colleges is a problem in semantics that is perhaps best resolved by calling them state-church colleges."[2]

Public education as we know it was not a product of the seventeenth century, either in Europe or in the United States. The origins of the idea are to be found in the revolutionary period, although the early assertions of the right of the state in education brought meager results. The grandiose schemes of the French *philosophes* came to naught; the contribution of the French Revolution to education, said Guizot, was *"un déluge des mots."* And the much-quoted phrase of the Ordinance of 1787—that schools and the means of education should forever be encouraged—remained for almost half a century little more than a pious wish.

But the role of the state was to become in the nineteenth century increasingly important in every sphere of life, and nowhere was this more true than in education. That a struggle should ensue as the state reached out for the control which historically had been exercised by the church was inevitable. Although the solutions devised were everywhere different, the problem was in each case the cause of prolonged and sometimes bitter struggle. In France, the revolutionary aspirations for a purely secular system of education were modified by Napoleon's Concordat with the Pope, and even more so by the return of the Bourbons. Guizot, as minister of education during the time of the founding of the French elementary school system, wished to return to a secular system. But this view was abandoned in the conservative reaction after 1848, and for a generation France again had publicly-supported denominational schools. The Third Republic swung back to the other extreme, instituted the principle of the *école laïque,* and almost succeeded in excluding the church entirely from the field of education.

In England, a basically different approach was adopted. The first steps of the state in education were designed to support and subsidize the denominational efforts already in existence. This decision was not a deliberate choice; it was made because the churches were adamant in their opposition to any public encroachment upon their work. It may well be that the conflict between the Anglicans and the Non-

---

[2] Frederick Rudolph, *The American College and University, a History.* New York: Knopf, 1962, p. 13.

conformists delayed for fifty years the creation of a national system of education in England.[3]

In the United States, also, the assumption of a more positive role by the state was the occasion for a serious struggle. It is of course true that the Common School Movement was, first and foremost, political in nature. Its leaders regarded education as the necessary safeguard of republican institutions, or indeed as the basic method of democratic social control.[4] But if education was a matter of political importance, it was also more than this. For education, even under civil control, had a religious dimension, and the tradition of church-state cooperation in education therefore persisted well into the national period. So far from prohibiting public support for private and denominational schools, the early state constitutions and statutes actively encouraged this policy. Grants of both money and land were made extensively to schools of all levels. Indeed, public aid to denominational schools increased considerably until about 1820, and persisted, in diminishing but still significant amounts, until well after the Civil War.[5]

In the realm of higher education the distinction between public and private institutions was even later to appear. During the first half of the nineteenth century, denominational colleges vigorously opposed the claims of the new state institutions for a share of the public funds which they had come to consider as rightfully their own. Even after the Civil War, the tradition of public support for denominational colleges was still strong enough to permit six states to assign the revenues from the first Morrill Act lands to church-affiliated institutions.[6]

But the tide had begun to turn earlier, in the Thirties, as the Common School Movement gained momentum. The development of the

[3] A. D. C. Peterson, *A Hundred Years of Education*. London: Duckworth, 1952, pp. 25-40. It must be remembered that England's "national system" is a union of civil and denominational sponsorship of schools.

[4] Rush Welter, *Popular Education and Democratic Thought in America*. New York: Columbia University Press, 1962, Chaps. 3-7; Lawrence A. Cremin, *The American Common School: An Historic Conception*. New York: Bureau of Publications, Teachers College, Columbia, 1951; R. Freeman Butts, *The American Tradition in Religion and Education*. Boston: Beacon Press, 1950.

[5] Richard Gabel, Jr., *Public Funds for Church and Private Schools*. Washington, D.C.: Catholic University of America Press, 1937, pp. 147-262.

[6] U. S. Office of Education Bulletin No. 9, 1930, pp. 17-18. The institutions aided were Yale and Dartmouth, Congregationalist; Brown, Baptist; Rutgers, Reformed; Clarflin and Corvallis, Methodist. Brown and Yale sued when the states later tried to transfer the funds to new public institutions, and both collected damages.

public school idea in Massachusetts under the leadership of Horace Mann has been accorded much attention by historians, and justly so. Mann fully accepted the proposition, almost universally held in his day, that religious instruction was an indispensable part of the work of the school. However, he argued, the inclusion of the doctrines unique to any one sect would alienate all other sects. The public schools would therefore have to be non-sectarian schools. As he and others of like mind often expressed it, the great "common truths" of Christianity should be taught—but anything more than this would be sectarianism and hence inadmissible.

But the task of providing religious instruction in the schools and at the same time avoiding sectarianism proved to be extremely difficult. The evangelical wing of Protestantism, for reasons which will be discussed later, strongly supported Mann's position, although even from this quarter there were at first some bitter attacks. Much more serious, however, was the reaction in the older denominations, which had a long tradition of support for parochial schools.

For the Lutherans, the answer was already clear. Although everywhere a minority group during the Colonial period, they had established during that time more than 400 schools, of which at least 342 remained at the end of the period. This tradition was carried over into the national period. In Pennsylvania, where they were numerous, the Lutherans created the largest denominational school system in the country before the era of public education, with about 240 schools in operation by 1820.[7] The advent of the public school movement created much apprehension among the Lutherans here, and they were the principal supporters of a massive petition calling for repeal of the free school law of 1834.[8]

The dominant Lutheran elementary school system early became that of the Missouri Synod, which steadfastly emphasized the importance of parochial schools, from the time that the first German immigrants established themselves in the Middle West in 1838 and 1839. The first constitution of the synod contained detailed and explicit

[7] Walter H. Beck, *Lutheran Elementary Schools in the United States*. St. Louis: Concordia Publishing House, 1939, pp. 47 and 73.

[8] J. P. Wickersham, *History of Education in Pennsylvania*. Lancaster: J. B. Lippincott Co., 1896, pp. 320-331. A committee of the state legislature regarded this petition as proof of the indifference of German Lutherans to education, and pointed out that most of the 32,000 signatures were not in "English script." The signatures were, of course, in German script, and less than one-fifth of one per cent signed by making a cross, indicating an illiteracy rate approaching zero, whereas among native-born Americans at the time illiteracy was all too common.

instructions for the establishment of parochial schools, the content and nature of textbooks, the training of teachers, and other matters.[9]

In the Episcopal Church the circumstances were different. The parent Church of England had a long tradition of interest in elementary education, but this concern seemed to wane as the American church drew away from its English moorings. As the Common School Movement dawned, it had very few schools left.[10] The initial success of the Common School Movement, however, aroused concern among many Episcopal leaders. In the General Convention of 1838 a strong sentiment for the establishment of church schools appeared. The leading denominational journalists were all critical of the public schools. During the 1840's and 50's several committees urged the General Convention to endorse officially the principle of church-sponsored schools. Although it did not take official action, the convention displayed a sympathetic attitude toward such proposals, and by 1862, Episcopal parochial schools had been established in at least eleven states.[11]

The Presbyterian denomination mounted an even more ambitious program for parochial schools. As early as 1799 the General Assembly of the church had deplored the "vain and pernicious philosophy" of the public schools, and in 1811 a committee of the assembly submitted a report declaring that education is "the legitimate business of the church, rather than of the state."[12] As in the case of the Episcopal Church, the initial successes of the Common School Movement served as a catalyst to revive the church's interest in parochial schools. In 1845 the Synod of New Jersey adopted a resolution strongly affirming the principle of public support for denominational schools. The following year the national assembly of the major wing of the denomination (the "old school") launched a program to establish parochial schools. Dr. Charles Hodge, the most influential leader in the movement, charged that the common schools were "positively anti-Christian," and declared that parochial schools offered the only hope of providing an adequate education. These schools were entitled to receive public

[9] Beck, op. cit., p. 106.

[10] Clifton H. Brewer, *History of Religious Education in the Episcopal Church to 1835*. New Haven: Yale University Press, 1924, pp. 103ff.

[11] Francis X. Curran, *The Churches and the Schools: American Protestantism and Popular Elementary Education*. Chicago: Loyola University Press, 1954, pp. 26, 29.

[12] Lewis J. Sherrill, *Presbyterian Parochial Schools, 1841-1870*. New Haven: Yale University Press, 1932, p. 2.

funds; to deny them such funds, he asserted, was "unjust and tyrannical."[13]

Obviously, the movement to make education a function of the state had aroused serious misgivings in some segments of American Protestantism. What the outcome would have been had America remained almost solidly Protestant is impossible to say. As it was, the immigration of Catholics in large numbers served to cast the question in an entirely different light. For there can be no doubt that Catholic opposition to certain practices in the public schools served to unite Protestants in their support of these schools and to hasten the success of the movement.

Perhaps the most serious weakness in standard accounts of the Common School Movement is their neglect of the fact that the movement took place at a time when the country was in the throes of the most bitter and violent wave of anti-Catholicism it has ever seen. Not only were these two developments contemporaneous; they were inextricably bound up with each other.

BEGINNINGS OF THE NATIVIST MOVEMENT

To be sure, hostility to Catholicism had been a part of American thought from the very beginning. But the arrival of large numbers of immigrants in the 1830's and 40's, many of them Catholic, seemed to many to be a menace to the national security, and resulted in a strong nativist movement. Concurrent with this nativist movement, and closely related to it, was the growth of a revivalistic spirit in Protestantism, and the founding of a number of religious societies and publications. The first of these to take a stand openly against Catholicism was the American Bible Society, founded in 1816. By 1827, forty Protestant religious newspapers had been founded, all of them distinctly anti-Catholic, and the stage had been set for the nativistic drama.[14]

When Horace Mann entered upon his educational work in 1837, the nativist movement had already reached alarming proportions. Three years earlier a nativist mob, inflamed by the anti-Catholic sermons of Boston clergymen, chief among them the Reverend Lyman Beecher, had put to flames the Ursuline Convent school on the out-

---

[13] *Ibid.*, pp. 15, 24-36.

[14] Ray A. Billington, *The Protestant Crusade, 1800-1860: A Study of the Origins of American Nativism.* New York: Macmillan, 1938, pp. 41-47. Although this account concentrates on the anti-Catholic component of pre-Civil War nativism, and overlooks the social and economic causes of the movement, it is still the standard work on the subject.

skirts of the town. In 1836 the greatest of all the nativistic propaganda works had appeared, Maria Monk's *Awful Disclosures of the Hotel Dieu Nunnery of Montreal,* a lurid account of alleged immorality in Catholic convents. The account was soon disclosed to be a monstrous fabrication. Maria Monk's venture was, in fact, sponsored by a number of Protestant ministers, one of whom wrote her book, aided by an equally unscrupulous Catholic priest. Maria Monk died in prison in 1849, but the continued popularity of her book revealed the strength of anti-Catholic sentiment in the United States. Three hundred thousand copies of this *"Uncle Tom's Cabin* of Know Nothingism" were sold prior to the Civil War, and numerous editions appeared thereafter.[15]

Although the thinly veiled pornography of the "exposure" literature held credulous Protestants by the thousands under its spell, there were more basic issues at stake. The educational reformers and the nativist leaders (and in at least some instances they were the same persons) were in full agreement on two propositions: 1) that the Bible should be read in the public schools and 2) that public funds should not be used for parochial schools.

Minor skirmishes on these issues had occurred in many places, but in New York City in 1840 the contending forces faced each other in a dramatic struggle which attracted national attention. The city did not as yet have a system of public schools. Instead, most of its schools were under the control of the Public School Society, a philanthropic association. The Common Council of the city turned over to this society the bulk of the school funds received from the state.

Although nominally non-sectarian, the schools of the Public School Society were strongly Protestant in flavor. The prayers, songs, and religious instruction were of a Protestant nature, and the King James version of the Bible was read daily in all schools. Even more offensive, from the Catholic point of view, was the Protestant bias of many of the textbooks, with their allusions to "deceitful Catholics," and to the Pope as the "man of sin, mystery of iniquity, son of perdition."[16]

Governor William H. Seward, himself a Protestant, estimated that 20,000 foreign-born children in the city were being kept out of the society's schools because of the sectarian nature of the instruction provided. Probably encouraged by this attitude, a number of Catholics requested that a portion of the school funds be allocated to their parochial schools.

[15] *Ibid.,* pp. 98-108.

[16] *Ibid.,* pp. 142-145. A more extended account of the controversy is provided in Edward M. Connors, *Church-State Relationships in Education in the State of New York.* Washington, D.C.: Catholic University of America Press, 1951, Chap. 2.

The petition aroused furious protests. The Protestant press represented it as further proof that Catholics were opposed to the Bible,
and indeed opposed to all education, preferring to hold their subjects
in illiterate bondage. Intemperate criticisms of the society's schools by
Catholic leaders added to the flames. In a public hearing on the petition, Catholics were denounced as worshipers of idols, intent on the
murder of Protestants and the subversion of democratic ideas. It would
be easy merely to dismiss this as bigotry—which indeed it was. But
it was also a revelation of the deep fear of Catholicism harbored by
Protestant leaders—a fear nurtured through many centuries, and now
intensified by the sustained and vicious anti-Catholic propaganda campaign which had been raging for twenty years.

The petition was overwhelmingly defeated in the Common Council (15-1) and Bishop Hughes, spokesman for the Catholic cause, then
launched a movement, supported by some liberal Protestants, to extend
to New York City the system of school administration which existed
throughout the state, a public system, administered by elected board
members. The result of such a change would be, Hughes thought, a
completely secular system of education which, though far from ideal,
would be preferable to the sectarianism in the Public School Society's
schools. The 1841 fall elections in the city were fought largely on this
issue, and public opinion divided along clearly religious lines. It was
a novel spectacle: Catholics appeared as the champions of a publicly
controlled school system and Protestants as its opponents. The Demo-
crats in the legislature, courting Catholic support, favored the proposal and the bill was enacted into law. That night the streets of the
city were filled with mobs which pursued Irish immigrants and stoned
the windows of Bishop Hughes' home. Governor Seward bore his
share of the abuse, and it was his stand on the school question which
eventually cost him his office.[17]

A BIBLE READING CONTROVERSY IN 1844

But the worst was yet to come. In Philadelphia, in 1844, a controversy over Bible reading in the public schools led to violence and
bloodshed. The immediate cause of the controversy was a school board
ruling to the effect that Bible reading in the schools could be, in the
case of Catholic children, from the Douay version. Incensed by this
action, a Protestant clergymen's association launched a campaign of
inflammatory anti-Catholic propaganda. Tension mounted in the weeks

[17] *Ibid.*, pp. 148-157.

that followed, and finally erupted into open warfare. Before order was finally restored, at least twenty persons had been killed, and three times that number wounded. Entire blocks of homes belonging to Irish immigrants had been put to flames, in addition to three Catholic churches and a seminary. It was no doubt American Protestantism's darkest hour. But a city investigating committee laid the blame for the riots entirely on the Irish, and a grand jury investigation reported that the trouble had arisen as a result of "the efforts of a portion of the community to exclude the Bible from our Public Schools."[18]

If there had ever been any possibility of a rational consideration of the points at issue, this possibility had now been lost. In two almost savage encounters, the Catholic initiative had been repulsed with scant thought of compromise. The Catholic position now came to be the lodestar about which Protestant educational thought revolved.

Perhaps there had never been any possibility for an accommodation. The theory of the religious but non-sectarian school, even in its most limited form as espoused by Mann, was a purely Protestant concept. Its central feature was the reading of the Bible, without comment, a direct application of the basic Protestant doctrine of individual inter-pretation of the Scriptures, and an idea quite unacceptable to Catholics. A Catholic spokesman had stated the question succinctly during the New York controversy:

> The Catholic Church tells her children that they must be taught by *authority*. The sects say, read the Bible, judge for yourselves. The Bible is read in the public schools, the children are allowed to judge for them-selves. The Protestant principle is therefore acted upon, silently incul-cated, and the schools are sectarian.[19]

But the point was lost on most Protestants. To them, anyone who could object to a practice so wholesome as Bible reading must of neces-sity be perverse—or, more likely, under the spell of sinister forces.

In practice, religious instruction in the common schools meant much more than Bible reading. Of the textbooks in common use, perhaps the least sectarian were the beloved McGuffey readers, but even these were suffused with the ideals of a rural, Protestant America.[20] Many other authors were not so circumspect, however. The widely used

[18] *Ibid.*, pp. 221-231.

[19] William O. Bourne, *History of the Public School Society of the City of New York*. New York: Wm. Wood & Co., 1870, p. 329.

[20] Lewis Atherton, *Main Street on the Middle Border*. Bloomington, Ind.: Uni-versity of Indiana Press, 1954, Chap. 3.

books of S. G. Goodrich (Peter Parley) were flagrantly anti-Catholic in tone. Of "Rome Under the Popes," Goodrich declared:

> They called themselves the successors of St. Peter, and said that the keys of heaven and hell were given into their custody. No other tyranny had ever been like theirs, for they tyrannized over the souls of men.[21]

Not infrequently publications which spoke for the state itself, directly or indirectly, contained similar statements. The *Wisconsin Journal of Education*, official organ of the Department of Public Instruction and the State Teachers Association, was presumably committed to the non-sectarian policy laid down by the constitution of that state. Yet the editor, a Protestant minister, saw no impropriety in publishing an article declaring that in pre-Reformation days priests "ignorant of the spirit of Christ, sought to procure power for themselves by . . . practicing all kinds of frauds. . . ." And the *New York Teacher* published a long poem which contained the charge that

> The Romish Church God's holy word
> Forbade the right to search,
> Except to priests, who taught a blind
> Obedience to the church.[22]

It is impossible to understand the nature of the Common School Movement without taking into account yet another factor: Its leadership was provided, in large part, by Protestant clergymen. In Kentucky, the first seven state superintendents (1838 to 1859) were Protestant clergymen. Of them, the greatest was Robert J. Breckinridge, who with good reason has been considered the father of the public school system of that state.[23] Earlier, as a Presbyterian minister in Maryland, he had been a prominent leader in nativist activities and

---

[21] S. G. Goodrich, *Peter Parley's Common School History*, 1838, pp. 187-88. Abbeys and monasteries, Goodrich explained, were "seats of voluptuousness" where monks and friars and nuns, "while they pretended to be engaged in religious duties, screened from the eyes of the world, often gave themselves up to luxurious pleasures." For a complete account of the Protestant bias in textbooks, see Marie Leonore Fell, *The Foundations of Nativism in American Textbooks*, 1783-1860. Washington, D.C.: Catholic University of America Press, 1941.

[22] *Wisconsin Journal of Education*, 6:182-183, December, 1860; *New York Teacher*, 1:330, August, 1853.

[23] Barksdale Hamlett, *History of Education in Kentucky*, Bulletin of the Kentucky State Department of Education No. 4, Frankfort, 1914, pp. 15-78. In fact, eleven of the fourteen men who held this office between 1838 and 1899 were clergymen.

had helped to lay the foundations for the period of turmoil which in the late Fifties gained for Baltimore the title of "mob-city."[24]

This may have been an extreme case, but the prominence of ministers during the formative period of American education was everywhere evident. Calvin Stowe of Ohio, Caleb Mills of Indiana, John D. Pierce of Michigan—all of them Protestant ministers—were the acknowledged leaders of the public school movement in their respective states. Indeed, one might reasonably ask how the movement could have been carried on without the leadership of Protestant clergymen. They served as superintendents at all levels, as officers in teachers' associations, as school principals, and leaders of teachers' "institutes."[25] Even after the Civil War, the role of ministers was not to be disregarded; about one-third of the contributors to Barnard's *American Journal of Education* were ministers.[26]

The Common School Movement was, therefore, in its inception and development, a distinctly Protestant phenomenon. As noted earlier, many of the older denominations at first had serious misgivings about the movement. But the main body of Protestantism accepted it from the outset. This was particularly true of the most rapidly growing groups, the Methodists and Baptists. Congregationalists, although a few demurred at first, soon joined in. And as the Catholic position on the school question came into prominence, the leaders of these groups surged forward to defend the public school.

In so doing, they made explicit what they had always assumed— that the public schools were Protestant institutions. The public schools were a legacy from their "Puritan ancestors," declared a committee report to the Massachusetts General Association of Congregationalist churches in 1848. And the leading journals of the denomination repeatedly explained that the public school was essentially a Protestant institution.[27] Methodist and Baptist spokesmen also identified the public schools with Protestantism.[28]

[24] Mary St. Patrick McConville, *Political Nativism in the State of Maryland,* 1830-1860, Washington, D.C.: Catholic University of America Press, 1928, pp. 88-90, 121.

[25] Lloyd P. Jorgenson, *The Founding of Public Education in Wisconsin.* Madison: University of Wisconsin Press, 1956, pp. 122-124.

[26] Richard Thursfield, *Henry Barnard's American Journal of Education.* Baltimore: Johns Hopkins Press, 1945, p. 87.

[27] Curran, op. cit., pp. 40, 47, 49.

[28] *Ibid.,* pp. 87-88, 101-105.

PUBLIC SCHOOLS A DEFENSE AGAINST CATHOLICISM

Not only was the public school regarded as a Protestant institution; it was also the first line of defense against the growth of Catholicism. A Methodist journal, the *Christian Advocate*, during the heat of the New York controversy, published a series of articles entitled, "The Common Schools, the Antidote of Jesuitism."[29] The *Watchman*, a Baptist weekly, was even more outspoken:

> If the children of Papists are really in danger of being corrupted in the Protestant schools of enlightened, free and happy America, it may be well for their conscientious parents and still more conscientious priests, to return them to the privileges of their ancestral homes, among the half-tamed boors of Germany. . . .[30]

Protestant journals consistently portrayed the Catholic church as the enemy of the public schools. "The Pope hates our free schools," said the Baptist *Examiner*, and it denounced the plot of the "Man of Sin" to keep the masses in ignorance. Congregationalist and Methodist journals voiced whole-hearted agreement.[31]

The defense of the public schools against alleged Catholic attacks thus became the *leitmotif* of educational discussions in these denominations, and they embraced the public school movement with militant enthusiasm. The historical claims of the church in the field of education seemed to be forgotten, as their spokesmen ardently championed the rights of the state. And it was not long before they reached the only logical conclusions which could ensue from this type of reasoning: that elementary education should be a monopoly of the state, that only public schools were truly "American," that all children should be compelled to attend the state schools, and that denominational schools should not be allowed to exist. This position was actually stated by many spokesmen in all these denominations as early as the 1840's. The Baptist *Examiner* expressed it in strong words in 1870:

> When a father proposes to put his boy into the hands of masters whose alphabet of truth is that the ecclesiastical law or the church canons rule the civil law of the country, a State might be justified in interfering, and taking the boy away from father and master, placing him in a system less inimical to its own safety.[32]

[29] *Ibid.*, p. 85.

[30] *Watchman*, June 25, 1841, cited in Curran, p. 101. The vehemence of the language used in denouncing Catholicism was sometimes startling. In 1874 the *Watchman* announced its discovery of a plot by the Catholic heirarchy to overcome the United States "by the porcine virtue of fertility." Curran, p. 110.

[31] Curran, op. cit., pp. 39, 87-88, 102, 105.

[32] *Examiner*, Feb. 3, 1870, cited in Curran, p. 106.

Methodist journals also insisted that all children should attend public schools—and that the Catholic hierarchy should be permitted no voice in the management of these schools.[33]

Although these denominations maintained virtually no elementary schools, they had long sponsored secondary and higher education. And, although they all strongly affirmed the rights of the state in elementary education, they just as strongly denied the rights of the state in secondary and higher education. The Congregationalist *New Englander* denied the right of the state to tax for secondary education.[34] Baptist spokesmen also on many occasions explicitly denied the right of the state to enter these fields. But the weakness of this position was sharply revealed by two editorials which appeared in the same issue of the *Watchman* in 1873. One asserted the right of the Baptist church to maintain its schools; the other denied the same right to Catholics. To maintain a position so equivocal as this proved to be impossible, and by the end of the century Protestant leaders had given up any claim for church priority in secondary and higher education as well.[35]

The older denominations also felt the effects of the nativistic and Know-Nothing movements. The Missouri Synod was not deflected from its course, but the Episcopal and Presbyterian parochial school movements foundered, and within a few years collapsed. When the Episcopal *Churchman* in 1851 editorially approved of Bishop Hughes' request for public support for parochial schools, a Methodist journal shrilly denounced this coalition of "Romanist and High-Church influence."[36] A Congregationalist clergyman admonished his erring brethren in other folds that parochial schools, whether Catholic, Episcopal, or Presbyterian, were "sectarian, divisive, narrow, clannish, anti-republican." And *The Independent*, an influential Congregationalist journal, expressed regret that Episcopalians and Presbyterians were following the bad example of Catholics in establishing separate schools. A Presbyterian editor, stung by the remark, resented this "shameless" effort to place Presbyterians "by the side of Roman Catholics."[37] Rebukes from official sources no doubt also dampened the enthusiasm of Protestant parochial school advocates. When Presbyterians pressed their demands for a share of the public school monies in the state of New York in 1850, the state superintendent replied by asking them whether

---

[33] Curran, op. cit., pp. 87-88.
[34] *Ibid.*, pp. 53-55.
[35] *Ibid.*, pp. 105, 110-117.
[36] *Ibid.*, p. 87.
[37] *Ibid.*, p. 46.

Roman Catholics should also receive their share of the tax funds for their schools.[38]

As the Know-Nothing excitement of the 1850's mounted, the enthusiasm of Presbyterians and Episcopalians for parochial schools waned. The change was sharply illustrated in the policy of the Episcopal *Church Review*. In 1855 this journal had sharply criticized the public schools; only a year later it reported a plot "on the part of the Romish priesthood, either to banish the Bible from our Public Schools, so as to make them absolutely atheistic in character, or else to break down the whole Common School System altogether." It was therefore incumbent upon all Christians to support the public schools, because they alone could create "true American nationality of character."[39] By 1870 the support for parochial schools was all but gone. In that year the Episcopal Convention approved of parochial schools "where they are practicable," but noted that they could never take the place of public schools, which should have the support of the church not only for patriotic reasons but "for the sake of Christianity itself."[40]

From this point, it was not far to go to open opposition to the parochial school, and the *Churchman* reached this position in 1875:

> Let the Roman Catholic have his own school, if he will, and withal be exempted from taxation for the schools sanctioned by the State; but let the inevitable result be, loss of all qualifications as a voter.[41]

The Presbyterian parochial school movement also entered upon a decline, starting in the Fifties. It had been a difficult task from the beginning, and it was rendered more difficult by the fact that the venture, although officially endorsed, did not have the full support of the denomination. Indeed, some were strongly opposed to the venture, among them the Reverend Robert J. Breckinridge, a fiery anti-Catholic, state superintendent of common schools in Kentucky. Although the number of schools reached about 250 at one time, the movement could not be sustained. The Presbyterian board and assembly finally came to the realization that the venture had failed, and it was officially discontinued in 1870.[42]

---

[38] Samuel S. Randall, *History of the Common School System of the State of New York,* Troy, N.Y.: Johnson and Davis, 1871, p. 286.

[39] *Church Review,* 8:23, 1855-56, cited in Curran, p. 28.

[40] Curran, op. cit., p. 32.

[41] *Churchman,* Oct. 16, 1875; cited in Curran, p. 33.

[42] Sherrill, op. cit., pp. 51-68.

PROTESTANTS NOW UNITED FOR PUBLIC SCHOOLS

With the exception of the Lutherans, therefore, American Protestantism now was united in its support of the public elementary school. (Actually, several of the Lutheran synods had embraced the public school by the latter part of the century; the Missouri Synod came to be the only major Protestant body committed to the parochial school idea.) The defection of the Lutherans was a major one, but it was tempered in American minds by the fact that this group, largely of German origin, had remained somewhat aloof, insisting upon the preservation of its own customs and language—an attitude which before long was to bring it under sharp attack by native Americans.

By the time of the Civil War, the issues which had been debated so heatedly for two decades were rapidly moving toward their solution. The solution had been foreshadowed by the position taken by the more militant Protestants in the 1840's. The basic factors in the settlement were that public funds were not to be used for sectarian schools, and that Bible reading in the public schools was to be encouraged and, if possible, required.

Nowhere was the relationship between the nativist movement and the school question more vividly illustrated than in Massachusetts. Here in 1854 the Know-Nothing Party won a sweeping victory, and promptly enacted into law a series of discriminatory measures. One restricted the suffrage to those with twenty-one years of residence and another the right to hold office to native-born citizens. A Nunnery Investigating Committee found no evidence of sin in Catholic institutions, but the conduct of its own members was so shameless that even their fellow legislators were taken aback. The enactment of a law denying public funds to sectarian schools was a foregone conclusion— although care was taken to use the term "schools," a term specifically not intended to include colleges and academies, most of them sponsored by Protestant denominations—and the courts upheld this interpretation. Also adopted was a bill to require the daily reading in the public schools of some portion of the Bible in the "common English version." This was explicit enough, although the Senate had attempted to specify the King James version by name.[43]

In other states also the nativist excitement was at least a contributing factor to such legislation. Prior to 1835 only three states had legisla-

---

[43] Sherman A. Smith, *The Relation of the State to Religious Education in Massachusetts.* Syracuse: Syracuse University Bookstore, 1926.

tion prohibiting the use of public funds for parochial schools, and in these states the legislation was openly disregarded.[44] Michigan enacted such legislation in 1835; three more states enacted such legislation (constitutional or statutory) in the 1840's, nine in the Fifties, and nine more in the Sixties.[45]

With Bible reading in the public schools, the development was similar. Prior to the time of the large Catholic immigrations, no legal authority for Bible reading in the schools existed because none was necessary; the right was simply taken for granted. Horace Mann declared in his 1848 Report that he did not know of a single school in the state in which the Bible was not used. As the practice of Bible reading increasingly came under attack, a number of states saw fit to provide legal sanction for the continuance of the practice. Seventeen states enacted such legislation by the end of the century.[46]

Although the "school question," as Catholics had come to call it, was to enter an even more crucial stage later, the basic outlines of the settlement were now clear. Public funds were to be used only for public schools, nominally non-sectarian but actually Protestant-oriented. The reading of the Bible had been preserved and specifically legalized—a principle upheld in the large majority of state court decisions to this date. On occasion, the terms of the settlement were imposed by force. In Oswego, New York, a Catholic child was whipped by a teacher for refusing to read from the King James version and in Boston and New York City in 1858 and 1859 students were expelled from school for the same offense.[47] In Maine the struggle over Bible reading led to a momentous judicial decision in 1854. A Catholic girl was expelled from school for refusing to read from the King James version of the Bible, as ordered by her teacher. The father appealed and the case reached the state supreme court, which held that the school board regulation requiring reading from the King James version was constitutional, and that it was binding on all students in the school, even though they might be of different religious faiths.[48]

---

[44] Burton Confrey, *Secularism in American Education: Its History*. Washington, D.C.: Catholic University of America Press, 1937, p. 123; Gabel, *passim*.

[45] *Ibid.*, p. 123.

[46] *Ibid.*, pp. 123 ff.

[47] Billington, op. cit., pp. 290-294.

[48] *Donahoe* v. *Richards*, 38 Me. 379.

A VICTORY THAT TURNED AGAINST THE VICTORS

The policy of public support for public schools only was later to become, in the minds of its proponents, a matter of abstract justice, founded on the Constitution, and, indeed, it did come to have this status. But originally, it was a policy forged by a society still predominantly Protestant, a policy frankly advocated as a means of curtailing the growth of a minority group. It was a decisive victory for the Protestants, but their doctrine of non-sectarianism was in time turned back against them. It was destined finally to destroy what they had originally sought to preserve—religious instruction in the public schools.

McGuffey and His Readers*

by HENRY STEELE COMMAGER

Henry Steele Commager, a prominent American historian, is Winthrop H. Smith Professor of American History and American Studies at Amherst College, Massachusetts. Among the many books that he has written, edited, or collaborated on are DOCU-MENTS OF AMERICAN HISTORY; THE AMERICAN MIND; FREEDOM, LOYALTY AND DISSENT; THEODORE PARKER, YANKEE CRUSADER; and THE GROWTH OF THE AMERICAN REPUBLIC.

When in 1891 William Venable wrote his classic "Beginnings of Literary Culture in The Ohio Valley," he found room for William Holmes McGuffey and his schoolbooks in a footnote. Within a generation such distinguished public figures as Hamlin Garland, Herbert Quick, and Mark Sullivan were to hail the McGuffey Readers as major influences not only in American education but in American morals and culture as well. Still another generation and the McGuffey Readers became the darlings of conservatives who found in them the very symbols and citadels of traditionalism, and used them to counter and repel all that they thought pernicious in "progressive" education.

* Henry Steele Commager, "McGuffey and His Readers," *Saturday Review*, 45 (June 16, 1962): 50-51, 69-70. By permission of the author and the editor.

In a perverse way the conservatives were right: the Readers were conservative, even pedagogically. William McGuffey—their chief producer—showed no awareness in his Readers, or in his college and university teaching, of those progressive educational ideas which had their origins in Germany, penetrated into France and England, and had spread to New England, where Bronson Alcott's Temple School anticipated by more than half a century the benign teachings of Jane Addams and John Dewey. Nor was there even an awareness of those new but entirely respectable ideas that Horace Mann was expounding in that wonderful series of annual reports to the legislature of Massachusetts. The McGuffey Readers were improvements on the Webster Readers and Spellers and on Lindley Murray's widely popular series of Readers, but they differed from these in degree rather than in kind.

One thing the McGuffey Readers shared with schoolbooks everywhere, and indeed with most literature and art of their day, was the notion that education itself was primarily moral, and only secondarily intellectual. It had long been taken for granted in England, even in the grammar schools and the universities (it was in this perhaps that English education differed most strikingly from the Continental), that the primary business of schools was to train character. The Puritans, far more interested in education than most of their contemporaries, added to all this a special emphasis on religious training. If Puritan schools were not designed to produce Christian gentlemen, they were certainly designed to produce Christians. The attitude explicit in the school laws of the Bay Colony was that "one chief project of ye old deluder Satan [is] to keep men from the knowledge of the Scriptures. . . ." This was the preliminary justification for the famous Act of 1647 requiring every town to provide elementary education for its children. The generation of the Founding Fathers looked to education to train character. Schools, Benjamin Rush thought, should be "engines for Republicanism." So, too, the Northwest Ordinance stated that as "religion, morality, and knowledge" were "necessary to good government and the happiness of mankind, schools and the means of education shall forever be encouraged." McGuffey's generation took this principle for granted and carried it into the Ohio country and beyond. Even the great educational reformers of the Thirties and Forties did not reject or seriously modify this concept. Horace Mann himself thought education primarily moral, and insisted that intellectual training must always take second place after moral instruction; to this principle his great co-worker Henry Barnard readily subscribed.

Certainly what is most impressive in the McGuffey Readers is the morality. From the First Reader on through the Sixth, that morality is pervasive and insistent. There is rarely a page but addresses itself to some moral problem, points some moral lesson. This morality has sometimes been associated with the character and needs of the West, as if the Readers were themselves, somehow, a product of the Ohio frontier. Actually, the morality of the Readers was that of the Victorian age everywhere in the Western world. It can be read in almost all the children's books of that time—in the pious stories of Maria Edgeworth or Charlotte Yonge, of Mrs. Ewing and Mrs. Molesworth in England; in the scores of volumes written by our own Peter Parley (he was Samuel Goodrich) and by Jacob Abbott of "Rollo" fame, or in the Sunday School papers that the young were expected to read, or in the pages of the *Youth's Companion*. Thus the prospectus of that famous magazine asserted (1827) that "this is the day of peculiar care for Youth. Let their minds be formed, their hearts prepared, and their characters moulded for the scenes and duties of a brighter day." And when Franklin Edmunds launched a little series of books for boys he reassured anxious parents that "all stories of an exaggerated style and false sentiment will be avoided and nothing presented but what will be calculated to inculcate some moral lesson."

What was the nature of the morality that permeated the Readers?

It was deeply religious, and in those mid-century years in America, religion meant Protestant Christianity. More, it was a Christianity closer to Puritanism than to that Unitarianism which was even then making its way out of New England and into the Ohio country. God was omnipresent. He had His eye on every child every moment of the day and night, watched its every action, knew its every thought. He was a just God, but a stern one, and would not hesitate to punish even the smallest children who broke His commandments. The world of the McGuffeys was a world where no one questioned the truths of the Bible, or their relevance to everyday conduct, and where the notion that the separation of church and state required the exclusion of religion from the school-room or from school-books seemed preposterous. The Readers, therefore, are filled with stories from the Bible, and tributes to its truth and beauty.

Yet for all its preoccupation with religion, the morality of the Readers was materialistic and worldly. It taught a simple system of rewards and punishments. Virtue was rarely its own reward: the kind old lady found out that the vagabond she had befriended was really a rich nephew returned from the gold fields; the honest farmer was given five hundred dollars by his rich neighbor as a reward for his honesty; the poor boy who helped the old man across the street was promptly provided with a job, the little chimney sweep who resisted the temptation to steal a gold watch was adopted by its enraptured owner. Wickedness, too, was invariably detected and punished, and once again the punishments were material and physical. The disobedient boy drowned; the greedy boy found himself in want; the rude boy, the meddlesome boy, the inquisitive boy, failed to get the job, or forfeited the rewards that went to his more exemplary companions. Nothing was left to the imagination, nothing to chance, and nothing, one is tempted to say, to conscience. It is an intriguing—but unanswerable—question whether this kind of moral arithmetic eventually did more harm than good. Those who are today infatuated with the morality of the Readers might reflect that the generation most elaborately and persistently exposed to it—the generation roughly from the 1840's to the 1880's—was probably the most materialistic generation in our history.

It was a middle-class, conventional, and equalitarian morality, one that derived from Benjamin Franklin and his careful Rules of Good Conduct, rather than from the Puritan austerity of a John Adams, or the Enlightenment of a Jefferson. Industry, sobriety, thrift, propriety, modesty, punctuality, conformity—these were the essential virtues, and those who practiced them were sure of success. Success, too, for all the patina of morality that was brushed over it, was clearly material. It was a job, a farm, money in hand or in the bank. Failure was, just as clearly, the consequence of laziness or self-indulgence, and deserved, therefore, little sympathy:

> There is a class of people (asserted the Fourth Reader) who are the pest of every community, workmen who do not know their trade, businessmen ignorant of the first principles of business. They can never be relied upon to do well anything they undertake. They are always making blunders which other people have to suffer for, and which react upon themselves. They are always getting out of employment, and failing in business. To make up for what they lack in knowledge and thoroughness, they often resort to trick and fraud, and become not merely contemptible but criminal.

In all this the Readers performed for a rural America pretty much the function that the Alger books were to perform for an urban America.

The McGuffey morality had many similarities to that of Dr. Pangloss: no matter how distressing things might seem, all was for the best. The workings of Providence, the arrangements of society, the vicissitudes of the economy—all would come right in the end. Does the widow starve? It is not her fault, to be sure, but neither is it the fault of society, and if she bears up, charity will take care of her. Are orphans bereft? Society has no responsibility for them, but there is always some great-hearted man who will come to their rescue or some kind woman who will adopt them. Does the laborer lose an arm or a leg in the factory? The kind employer will reward him. Is the upright man out of work? That is one of the hardships of fate but, if he is willing to turn his hand to anything, someone will surely recognize his virtues and give him work. Life is full of hardships, but be of good cheer. God watches over His own, most men are kindly and generous, and in the end virtue will be rewarded.

All this was in the spirit of self-reliance and of individualism, and reflected, too, that distrust of the State which was implicit both in much of Puritanism and in Jeffersonianism. Yet the heirs of the Puritans in New England—even the author of "Self-Reliance"—did not carry that virtue so far, or forgive the State from any responsibility for the operation of the economic order. McGuffey, and his collaborators and successors, lived in the midst of the greatest reform era in our history—an era when all the institutions of society were being called before the bar of Reason and asked for their credentials, and when the State was required to take on some responsibility for the welfare of the "dangerous and perishing classes." But the Readers show no awareness of this ferment of ideas, confess no temptation to challenge existing institutions, and reveal no inclination to enlarge the concept of social or political responsibility.

In nothing are the Readers more Victorian than in their pervasive sentimentality. As in so much Victorian literature—on the European continent as in England and America—sentimentality washed over children, dogs, and horses, found expression in flowers and trees, adored the primitive (especially in Nature) and romanticized the farmer. Even its piety was romantic. Curiously enough it was fascinated with death, and even children were expected to ponder the moral implications of death. One is sometimes reminded of Poe's definition of the perfect subject of a poem as the death of a beautiful maiden. Surprisingly, Poe himself is represented in the Readers only by "The Raven."

What of the contribution of the Readers to education? Here they performed a signal service, but it was not the service most commonly attributed to them by their admirers, and perhaps not even the service designed by those who wrote and edited them. For it was intellectual rather than moral, and cosmopolitan rather than nationalistic.

We have only to turn to most of the textbooks and readers current in mid-century America to see how great an improvement the McGuffeys inaugurated. That improvement was not merely pedagogical—the Rhetorical Guide, for example, the elaborate exercises, the careful vocabularies, the rich body of illustrations. More important was the marked improvement in the content itself. The best examples of this are the Fifth and Sixth Readers—the first to include a really substantial selection from literature.

What is striking about the Readers—it was probably not so much a product of policy as of habit—was that they made so few conscious concessions to immaturity. There was no nonsense about limiting the vocabulary to familiar words, for example. There was no effort always to be entertaining, and no policy of easy familiarity between young and old. There was no drawing back from many of the harsher experiences of the grown-up world. If the McGuffeys did not ransack literature quite as thoroughly as Hamlin Garland and Herbert Quick seemed to remember (the Readers are notable for the classics that they leave out as well as for those they put in), they did draw generously on modern English classics, and on such American books as might be supposed to be classics, and they took for granted that the young would understand them, or that teachers would explain them —something publishers never appear to think of today!

A second major educational contribution of the Readers was their cosmopolitanism. It is customary to emphasize the ardent Americanism of the Readers, and Richard Mosier, in his "Making the American Mind," has devoted a persuasive chapter to this theme. Certainly an emphasis on nationalism would not have been surprising, for this was the period of national self-consciousness everywhere, of Manifest Destiny, of the apotheosis of the Founding Fathers and the rediscovery of the Pilgrim Fathers, and of the struggle for Union. The temptation to use the Readers to inculcate patriotism and nationalism must have been well-nigh irresistible. In so far as the Readers drew on the classics of American literature and politics they did doubtless contribute something to cultural nationalism. But what is astonishing is how little of this there really is. Though the original volumes of the Readers appeared when men could still remember the Revolutionary War and the War of 1812—McGuffey himself lived through that war, and on the Ohio frontier, too—there is no ardent hostility to Britain, no execration of George III, no atrocity stories about the Indians. And though new Readers, and revisions of old Readers, poured from the presses all through the era of the Mexican War, of Manifest Destiny, and of Young America, the Readers reflect none of this. Even the Oregon Trail and the gold rush to California were not allowed to ruffle the serenity of their pages. Even more startling is the fact that

those who later revised the Readers—the 1879 edition of the Fifth
Reader is a good example—managed to avoid the Civil War! Aside
from Francis Finch's "The Blue and the Gray"—a masterpiece of
impartiality—the war might never have happened as far as the Readers
are concerned. The editors even brought themselves to omit the whole
body of Civil War songs—"Battle Hymn of the Republic," "Tenting
Tonight," "Maryland My Maryland," the "Conquered Banner," and
all—though these were already the common property of the people,
cherished then as now.

In the substantial attention the McGuffeys gave to American literature, in the celebration—or at least the affectionate recollection—of
Washington and Franklin, Patrick Henry and Daniel Webster, they
contributed no doubt to foster a sense of patriotism in the young.
But there was no deliberate attempt to do this. The McGuffeys perhaps realized—what so many of our professional patriots do not realize
—that in a sound and fortunate society patriotism can be trusted to
take care of itself.

A more important contribution to nationalism was equally uncalcu-
lated, though by no means fortuitous. It lay in providing the school
children of the mid-nineteenth century with a common body of
allusion and a common frame of reference. Justice Holmes said of
John Marshall that part of his greatness was in being *there*. So, too,
we can say that part of the greatness of the McGuffey Readers was
that they were *there* at the right time. They were *there* to be read by
millions of children from all parts of the country, from all classes, of
all faiths. They gave to the American child of the nineteenth century
what he so conspicuously lacks today—a common body of allusions, a
sense of common experience and of common possession. That, no
doubt, was what made the Readers so cherished in retrospect. They
were always there to be remembered and quoted, and you could be
reasonably sure that your audience would share your recollection and
recognize your quotation.

Here they are—to be taken seriously, to be taken humorously—
but always to be taken and to be remembered: the boy who stood on
the burning deck whence all but he had fled; the captain's daughter
strapped to the mast in the "Wreck of the Hesperus"; the old oaken
bucket; the story of Mr. Idle and Mr. Toil which had the simplicity
of an Andersen fairy tale; Whittier's "Fish I Didn't Catch" which was
so useful as an aphorism; Abou Ben Adhem, whose name led all the
rest; the easy rhymes of "The Melancholy Days" are come the saddest

of the year; the declamations of a Patrick Henry; the wild courage of
Arnold of Winkelried ("Make way for Liberty he cried, Made way
for Liberty, and died"); the simple morality of the "Psalm of Life";
the touching story of Maud Muller and the proud Judge: "Of all sad
words of tongue or pen, the saddest are these, it might have been"; and
even a bit of Shakespeare, just enough to whet the appetite.

It is here that the Readers made, perhaps, their greatest contributions, and it is here that they have something to teach us. For one of
the things that has disappeared from much of current study of literature and history on the elementary level is this common body of allusion and of reference. That our children, today, are better taught
than were their luckless predecessors is generally conceded, though
we are sometimes puzzled that we have not produced a generation
of statesmen as distinguished as the Founding Fathers—products of
rural academies and embryo colleges—or a generation of men of
letters as distinguished as that of the Golden Day—products, again
of frontier schools, village academies and struggling colleges. But
even those most confident of the virtues of our current educational
practices, and most proud of our textbooks—so handsomely printed,
so lavishly illustrated, so elaborately provided with pedagogical apparatus that they leave nothing to either the child or the teacher—may
wonder what has happened to that body of common knowledge that
was in fact common in an earlier generation.

All of this was a benevolent, not a chauvinistic, expression of
nationalism—pride in the virtues or the beauties of the nation, not in
its prowess, or its superiority to other nations. Indeed the effect of the
Readers was cosmopolitan rather than parochial—something those
infatuated extremists who seek to exploit them for chauvinistic purposes might ponder. Children exposed to them—particularly to the
Fifth and the Sixth—could not fail to have a lively sense of the past,
and of the rich cultural tradition of other nations. The Greeks were
here, and the Romans, William Tell and Arnold Winkelried, Hamlet
and Shylock, and the Highland clansmen. Irving described the
Alhambra, and Southey celebrated the Battle of Blenheim, and Thomas
Campbell provided a sample of the Scots dialect (not surprisingly,
the Scots were favorites of the McGuffey brothers) and Charles Wolfe
lamented the death of General John Moore fighting Napoleon in
Spain: "We carved not a line, we raised not a stone but we left him
alone with his glory." Above all, the Readers provided an introduction, and more than an introduction, to the literature of England, and
that literature, with its far-flung imperial interests, has always been

cosmopolitan. Where McGuffey's great predecessor Noah Webster, set himself to eradicate Anglicisms from the Amercian language, and to foster a sense of American cultural independence ("America must be independent in literature, as she is in politics") the McGuffeys refused to be distracted by cultural chauvinism. They saw no reason why political independence should cut young Americans off from their cultural heritage, and they deliberately gave to generations of boys and girls growing up on the prairies of the West a sense of membership in a larger community of history and literature.

The McGuffey Readers, then, are far more than an historical curiosity. They played an important role in American education, and in American culture, and helped shape that elusive thing we call the American character. If they did not themselves provide the stuff of culture and morality, they were one of the chief instruments for weaving this stuff into the fabric of American life. Their contribution was, on the whole, beneficent.

*Do Not Meddle**

1. About twenty years ago there lived a singular gentleman in the Old Hall among the elm trees. He was about three-score years of age, very rich, and somewhat odd in many of his habits, but for generosity and benevolence he had no equal.

2. No poor cottager stood in need of comforts, which he was not ready to supply; no sick man or woman languished for want of his assistance; and not even a beggar, unless a known impostor, went empty-handed from the Hall. Like the village pastor described in Goldsmith's poem of "The Deserted Village,"

> "His house was known to all the vagrant train;
> He chid their wand'rings, but relieved their pain;
> The long-remembered beggar was his guest,
> Whose beard descending swept his aged breast."

3. Now it happened that the old gentleman wanted a boy to wait upon him at table, and to attend him in different ways, for he was

* From *McGuffey's Fifth Eclectic Reader* (rev. ed.; New York: American Book, 1921), pp. 54-58.

very fond of young people. But much as he liked the society of the young, he had a great aversion to that curiosity in which many young people are apt to indulge. He used to say, "The boy who will peep into a drawer will be tempted to take something out of it; and he who will steal a penny in his youth will steal a pound in his manhood."

4. No sooner was it known that the old gentleman was in want of a boy than twenty applications were made for the situation; but he determined not to engage anyone until he had in some way ascertained that he did not possess a curious, prying disposition.

5. On Monday morning seven lads, dressed in their Sunday clothes, with bright and happy faces, made their appearance at the Hall, each of them desiring to obtain the situation. Now the old gentleman, being of a singular disposition, had prepared a room in such a way that he might easily know if any of the young people who applied were given to meddle unnecessarily with things around them, or to peep into cupboards and drawers. He took care that the lads who were then at Elm Tree Hall should be shown into this room one after another.

6. And first, Charles Brown was sent into the room, and told that he would have to wait a little. So Charles sat down on the chair near the door. For some time he was very quiet, and looked about him; but there seemed to be so many curious things in the room that at last he got up to peep at them.

7. On the table was placed a dish cover, and Charles wanted sadly to know what was under it, but he felt afraid of lifting it up. Bad habits are strong things; and, as Charles was of a curious disposition, he could not withstand the temptation of taking one peep. So he lifted up the cover.

8. This turned out to be a sad affair; for under the dish cover was a heap of very light feathers; part of the feathers, drawn up by a current of air, flew about the room, and Charles, in his fright, putting the cover down hastily, puffed the rest of them off the table.

9. What was to be done? Charles began to pick up the feathers one by one; but the old gentleman, who was in an adjoining room, hearing a scuffle, and guessing the cause of it, entered the room, to the consternation of Charles Brown, who was very soon dismissed as a boy who had not principle enough to resist even a slight temptation.

10. When the room was once more arranged, Henry Wilkins was placed there until such time as he should be sent for. No sooner was he left to himself than his attention was attracted by a plate of fine, ripe cherries. Now Henry was uncommonly fond of cherries, and he

thought it would be impossible to miss one cherry among so many. He looked and longed, and longed and looked, for some time, and just as he had got off his seat to take one, he heard, as he thought, a foot coming to the door; but no, it was a false alarm.

11. Taking fresh courage, he went cautiously and took a very fine cherry, for he was determined to take but one, and put it into his mouth. It was excellent; and then he persuaded himself that he ran no risk of taking another; this he did, and hastily popped it into his mouth.

12. Now, the old gentleman had placed a few artificial cherries at the top of the others, filled with Cayenne pepper; one of these Henry had unfortunately taken, and it made his mouth smart and burn most intolerably. The old gentleman heard him coughing, and knew very well what was the matter. The boy that would take what did not belong to him, if no more than a cherry, was not the boy for him. Henry Wilkins was sent about his business without delay, with his mouth almost as hot as if he had put a burning coal into it.

13. Rufus Wilson was next introduced into the room and left to himself; but he had not been there ten minutes before he began to move from one place to another. He was of a bold, resolute temper, but not overburdened with principle; for if he could have opened every cupboard, closet, and drawer in the house, without being found out, he would have done it directly.

14. Having looked around the room, he noticed a drawer to the table, and made up his mind to peep therein. But no sooner did he lay hold of the drawer knob than he set a large bell ringing, which was concealed under the table. The old gentleman immediately answered the summons, and entered the room.

15. Rufus was so startled by the sudden ringing of the bell, that all his impudence could not support him. He looked as though anyone might knock him down with a feather. The old gentleman asked him if he had rung the bell because he wanted anything. Rufus was much confused, and stammered, and tried to excuse himself, but all to no purpose, for it did not prevent him from being ordered off the premises.

16. George Jones was then shown into the room by an old Steward; and being of a cautious disposition, he touched nothing, but only looked at the things about him. At last he saw that a closet door was a little open, and, thinking it would be impossible for anyone to know that he had opened it a little more, he very cautiously opened it an

inch farther, looking down at the bottom of the door, that it might not catch against anything and make a noise.

17. Now had he looked at the top, instead of the bottom, it might have been better for him; for to the top of the door was fastened a plug, which filled up the hole of a small barrel of shot. He ventured to open the door another inch, and then another, till, the plug being pulled out of the barrel, the leaden shot began to pour out at a strange rate. At the bottom of the closet was placed a tin pan, and the shot falling upon this pan made such a clatter that George was frightened half out of his senses.

18. The old gentleman soon came into the room to inquire what was the matter, and there he found George nearly as pale as a sheet. George was soon dismissed.

19. It now came the turn of Albert Jenkins to be put into the room. The other boys had been sent to their homes by different ways, and no one knew what the experience of the other had been in the room of trial.

20. On the table stood a small round box, with a screw top to it, and Albert, thinking it contained something curious, could not be easy without unscrewing the top; but no sooner did he do this than out bounded an artificial snake, full a yard long, and fell upon his arm. He started back, and uttered a scream which brought the old gentleman to his elbow. There stood Albert, with the bottom of the box in one hand, the top in the other, and the snake on the floor.

21. "Come, come," said the old gentleman, "one snake is quite enough to have in the house at a time; therefore, the sooner you are gone the better." With that he dismissed him, without waiting a moment for his reply.

22. William Smith next entered the room, and being left alone soon began to amuse himself in looking at the curiosities around him. William was not only curious and prying, but dishonest, too, and observing that the key was left in the drawer of a bookcase, he stepped on tiptoe in that direction. The key had a wire fastened to it, which communicated with an electrical machine, and William received such a shock as he was not likely to forget. No sooner did he sufficiently recover himself to walk, than he was told to leave the house, and let other people lock and unlock their own drawers.

23. The other boy was Harry Gordon, and though he was left in the room full twenty minutes, he never during that time stirred from his chair. Harry had eyes in his head as well as the others, but he had more integrity in his heart; neither the dish cover, the cherries, the drawer knob, the closet door, the round box, nor the key tempted him

to rise from his seat; and the consequence was that, in half an hour after, he was engaged in the service of the old gentleman at Elm Tree Hall. He followed his good old master to his grave, and received a large legacy for his upright conduct in his service.

Country Schoolmaster of Long Ago*

by THOMAS WOODY

Thomas Woody, late professor of education at the University of Pennsylvania, wrote or edited the following books on early American education: EARLY QUAKER EDUCATION IN PENNSYLVANIA; EDUCATIONAL VIEWS OF BENJAMIN FRANKLIN; *and* A HISTORY OF WOMEN'S EDUCATION IN THE UNITED STATES.

Every generation has those who cry against its decadence. In one sense, and to a degree, they are always right: in life there is death; social growth entails destruction; but this is not the view of those who lament. Growth and destruction, especially at times of marked acceleration, occasion emotional reactions—apprehension for the future, nostalgia for the past. This nostalgia is a common affliction of parents, newspaper editors, clerics, teachers—and occasionally students. Others experience attacks now and then, but they are less articulate.

Schools and teachers throughout the ages have been blamed for the evils of the new day, as though they created societies. In this respect, 1954 is not unlike fifth century Athens before the Christian era, and the last century of the Roman Republic. Names have changed, certainly: then it was philosophers and orators; today, it is scientists, and pedagogues who study their profession, who are blamed—for philosophers have retired from active duty, and orators are seldom heard.

Reflecting thus upon the nostalgic temper of modern prophets of pedagogical and social doom that awaits us, unless we return speedily to the good old days, the image of an old master and his school came to mind. The image is particular, the master real. The writer tells the story as he heard it. The general may dwell in the particular, but no effort is intended to draw it forth. If it should occur to any who

* Thomas Woody, "Country Schoolmaster of Long Ago," *History of Education Journal,* 5 (No. 2, Winter, 1954): 41-53. By permission of the editor.

come upon this fragment, however, that on balance they prefer the new school—learning without larruping; reading without tears—such occurrence may be put down to personal idiosyncrasy; and if others, at this glimpse of the old school, find their longing for the past enhanced, let them be nostalgic still.

D. S. Domer, who attended a far away class, should have published his own story, which he was persuaded to tell the writer. Since he did not find the opportunity, it is hoped that, though belatedly and much shortened, his desire may be partially realized; and, at the same time, remembrance may be kept of a master of the old school.

It is now [1929] fifty-five years ago that I first entered the public schools of Pennsylvania, in the little village of Springville, now Florin. The experiences related of going to school in the early seventies and eighties, the trials of teaching, the methods, discipline, buildings, mode of recitation, the teachers who taught me, and other matters, are vivid memories and can be verified.[1]

The village was mainly Pennsylvania Dutch, of whom I am a descendant. At the age of six I was scarcely able to speak a word of English. We lived about a block from the school. The building was an old moss-covered structure, built long before my entry. It was of brick and had three windows on each side and a door at one end. There were no cloak rooms, but a row of hooks to the right and left of the door, where hats and coats were hung, often three deep. If one kept his own wearing apparel for the whole term, he was lucky.

The seats were plain pine board benches; the desks, of the same material, had plain tops, with backs raised about two inches above the top. Legs were two by four uprights, fastened to the floor. Two sat at each desk; a partition inside it was designed to keep books and materials of pupils separate. The floor was oak boards, split and rough hewn. Walls were partly wainscoting. The "blackboard" was painted on the walls; slate, just coming into use, was opposed as a too expensive luxury. The rest of the walls and the ceiling were plastered with a mixture of lime, sand and clay, and whitewashed about twice a year, at the beginning of the term in autumn and again at holidays. There were no blinds; but outside shutters, partly closed, kept out sun-glare; when entirely closed, to keep out cold and wind, the room was so dark, it was almost impossible to see to work, unless the oil lamps hanging on the wall were lit.

The school had forty or fifty pupils. The boys sat on one side of a wide aisle, the girls on the other. A platform ran across the front of the room. Long benches stood against the wall, where the class reciting was

[1] Mr. Domer showed me documents which he had preserved, to vouch for some of them.

seated. The teacher usually turned his back to the recitation he was hearing; it was not safe to turn his back to the rest of the school, for some culprit would try "heathen tricks" on him; and if he went to the other end of the room, the reciting class would make trouble. Teaching by moral influence had not yet superseded the hickory rod.

Little pedagogy and less psychology were used. A recitation—geography, for example, covering the United States, its location, extent, and development—was conducted as follows: the lesson was assigned; questions, numbering often twenty or thirty, came at the end of the chapter. If the class had ten pupils, it was easy for us to learn the lesson. The pupil at the head of the class learned No. 1, the next one No. 2, and so on to the tenth; the first then studies No. 11, and so on through the entire list. Each had his question and answer well studied, and a perfect recitation could be recorded. It seems not to have occurred to the teacher to vary the order of the recitation. Routine dominated method; it went over big, it was easiest for teacher and pupil alike; it was followed in all subjects having questions and answers. That was the day of formal teaching, variations were avoided, originality was frowned upon. Promiscuous asking of questions was taboo; the child had no right to think; he was to do just what the teacher said.

In a school where 31 classes were heard in about 300 minutes—an average of about 10 minutes to a class—little more could be expected than a rapid question and answer method. The same routine obtained in all classes. In arithmetic the pupil solved his problem, read it from the board, was excused, another was called on, and so on to the end; a new lesson was assigned, and the class was dismissed, either by taps on a bell or counting one, two, three—stand, pass, sit. Seldom did the teacher explain the lesson; his object was to get through the day and cover all the ground. This continued throughout the year; at the end of six months we had often "gone through" the book twice. In one term we even "went through" the same book three times.

Until I was fifteen, while I was at this type of school, I had "gone through" my grammar, arithmetic, geography, speller, and the rest, a dozen times or more. There were no "grades" or "promotions" then. You were placed by the book you were reading. In my first three years I had completed my Third Reader; at twelve or thirteen I reached the Fifth and Sixth. We used Sander's, McGuffey's and Swinton's readers; Appleton's were more difficult, and I read the Fifth Reader several years. Tests or examinations were never held. If we did what was in the book, it was a mark of perfect scholarship, and that was all that was required.

When eight years old, I was afflicted with a malady which crippled me badly, so I could not play games, or move rapidly. It grew worse; I had to use crutches; for seven years there seemed no prospect of recovery, and I was threatened with spinal paralysis. Finally, after much deliberation and opposition, an operation at Jefferson Hospital saved me from the blighting effects of deformity, and enabled me to carry on my profession, though always incapacitated for physical labor.

Due to poverty, I was compelled to learn some trade; and my illness dictated that it should be something I could do with my hands while my body remained quiet. My cousin, A. B. Kreider, was both teacher and cigar-maker—which was not contrary to the ethics of that time. After long consultation with my mother, it was decided I should become his ward, attend his school, and learn cigar-making at the same time. I began the trade in the Spring of 1884, and entered his school that Fall. I worked morning, noon, and night, attending school from 9 to 12 and 1 to 4. After supper I applied myself to my books by the kitchen stove, with the aid of a kerosene lamp, often till one and two o'clock next morning. Summers, I spent the day in the shop, and read at night, chiefly history, for my benefactor had a good library for that time. Thus I was occupied from 1884 to 1888.

It was at Salunga Public School, under the solicitous teaching of my cousin, that I prepared, during the winter of 1887-1888, to become a teacher. I remained in his school till I was twenty. For three months I went to night school. In day school I studied the common branches; at night school, I read and recited pedagogy and several advanced studies. After school closed in March, I was tutored for my first county teachers examination, which came in June, 1888.[2]

On my way to the examination I met the County Superintendent, M. J. Brecht. We walked a half mile together from the train, and I have no doubt I won his sympathy, which may have stood me in good stead. There were then no uniform State examinations. The County Superintendent, chosen by the trustees of the school districts, was the sole authority. At nine o'clock, the mill began to grind—operated by one-man power, the Superintendent. The first subject was arithmetic. The Superintendent read a set of questions, prepared in advance in his office or propounded extemporaneously. About 40 minutes were allowed to solve them. There were problems in mental arithmetic, to be solved on the spot, and on one's feet. Sometimes only the method of solution was called for. When each candidate finished one examination, his papers were taken up, read, and graded then and there by the official. All the nine common branches were treated the same way during the day.

At last the end approached. At four o'clock we would know our fate. If one passed, his name was called, and a certificate was handed him. If he failed, his name was not called, which saved some embarrassment. The subjects were rated 1, very good; 2, good; 3, middling.[3] If the sum total were more than 24, no certificate could be issued. Per cent grades

[2] Mr. Domer's memory slipped here; his first certificate shows May.

[3] Mr. Domer's memory varied from the documents later shown me, which are followed here.

were not then popularized in Lancaster County. Later, when I followed Greeley's advice and went West, my Ohio certificate, issued in 1891, used per cents. My total the first time was 23¾. If I had added a quarter to my total, my hopes would have received a rude shock; but I lowered my integers and raised my standard enough so that I was on the road I longed to travel. I still treasure my first three certificates.

Thus armed, I was ready, whether "qualified" or not, to enter upon the noblest work of man. The preparation I then had at the age of twenty might now be matched by a pupil in Junior High School. My first school was a man's job—64 pupils, ranging from 6 to 20, more than half being under 10 years of age—but I set to work with serious intent to apply my little store of pedagogy and psychology.

Getting my first school proved to be an experience never to be forgotten. After receiving a certificate, one looked for a school—unless it had been promised earlier on condition of passing. I had no such promise, but the County Superintendent suggested several places to look up. I selected one and notified the Board I would present myself.

A word on the administration of common schools may be useful. Lancaster County had township organization. The township I first taught in had forty districts, all under the direction of six school trustees, chosen annually. Each trustee had an area, or number of schools under his oversight, and he reported to the Board each month. At such meetings the trustees also examined teachers' reports and paid their salaries. The Board could be quite autocratic, might disregard even the suggestions of the County Superintendent, for he himself held office at their pleasure.

The Board I approached wanted a "man" teacher. They met on a Saturday in August (1888), 20 days before the beginning of school, to hire the teacher. These six representatives of the community were indeed an august body—but their names are all forgotten now, save those of the president and one other. It was with some trepidation that I came before this body, for they met in the back end of a barroom in the village of Schoeneck. As I entered the room, I met the gaze, the inspection, and then the quiz of these patriarchs of education.

I had applied in writing for a school a short way from the village, and the application was filed here with others. When I was seated at one end of the long table around which the Board sat, I was asked by the chairman whether I believed in the "three R's"; but he, to relieve me of any fear, at once assured me they stood for "Radcliffe's Ready Relief." Of course, they had already read the applications and had really decided by a previous vote to let me have the school at the munificent salary of $28.00[4] a month for a term of six months. I was

[4] The County Superintendent rated teachers "1 plus, 1, 1—, 2 plus, 2, and 2—." From "2—" up each grade meant a $5.00 raise. I was raised to $33.00 the second year, and received $40.00 the third.

to be my own janitor, sweep out, and keep fires going. But before I was to sign the contract, a surprise awaited me.

"Mr. Domer," the President began, "we have decided to give you the M——— School, and we think you are all right. Now since one good turn deserves another, we think you ought to set up the drinks to us for the favor; so if you want to sign the contract, go and bring a bottle of whiskey and six glasses for us, and we will then close the deal." The Almighty was witness to such an act, no doubt. With disgust and dejection I acted on the suggestion of the venerable President of the Board. That a body of men could be so enslaved to drinking on all occasions, and to bind a contract by treating a set of men in the deal, was indeed dumbfounding to me, an incident in my young life that I can never erase. For I had been under the tutelage of a radical prohibitionist, and had signed the temperance pledge on the sixth of May, 1886, which I have kept all these years.

Nevertheless, I turned on my heel and went to the barroom; there, across the bar were handed me a bottle and six small glasses. Returning to the room with the loaded tray, I placed it on the table in front of the President of the Board. He acted as host to the rest of them, poured six glasses full, passed one to each of the members, and all drank to my success as a teacher, swallowing all at one gulp, without even a twitch of the mouth, so habituated to liquor were these men. When they had all drunk, I took the tray-load back to the bartender, who took my word for it that only six glasses full were used. I paid him 60 cents for the drinks, the price of my contract. When I returned, they told me I was a good sport, and could now sign the contract, as they had already done. Seating myself next to the clerk of the Board, I attached my signature. Many reflections have come and gone since I traded six glasses of whiskey for a teacher's contract. Nothing like it has happened to me from that day to this. Whether it happened so to other young men who sought positions, I do not know. The moral effect on me was profound. Raised in a home which was opposed to strong drink of any kind, and tutored by a man who was a leader in the anti-whiskey forces, I felt I had done wrong; but as I was not a professing Christian at the time, and I was anxious to get a school, I soon cleared my conscience and started on the first Monday in September to teach school.

I chose a place to room and board a few days in advance of opening school. It was about ¾ of a mile away, and I covered the distance, walking, or catching a ride when possible. In sloppy weather I wore high top rubber boots, changed to shoes at school, and wore the boots home in the evening. Board, room, and washing cost $10.00 a month.[5] It was an old-fashioned farm home, and one lived with the family. There was

<hr>

[5] The salary of $28.00 was really far more than it seems now, for prices were low; a suit cost $8.00 to $10.00; hat $1.00 to $1.50; shoes, made to order, $4.50 to $5.00.

plenty to eat, a good bed (a wooden bedstead, rope springs, straw mat-
tress, feather ticks, and blankets), and woven carpets on the floor. Wood
and an old-fashioned cookstove furnished heat for kitchen, dining room,
and all the rest of the house, upstairs and down. Hot water was provided by a tea kettle and a reservoir in the stove itself.

I went to the schoolhouse alone the Saturday before school began.
The building, located on an acre for a playground, was not significantly
different from the one where I first went to school. It was of brick, dirt
cheap, burned in a nearby kiln for the purpose. Aesthetics had not yet
taken root among patrons, trustees, or teachers. The inside was as dull
as a leaden sky in December, save as it was sometimes brightened by
leaves in autumn, or some pictures could be borrowed from the pupils'
homes. The desks were a little better than I had first used at school, but
single seats had not yet appeared. The double-seated desks were a source
of trouble: they induced whispering, idle mischief, neglect and dis-
honesty in studies; books got mixed up, articles were stolen, and property destroyed. I counted the seats, made up a tentative programme,
set the clock, put shoe mats in place, had two water buckets (one for
waste, for there was no drain) and two tin cups ready for thirsty
children. Sanitary rules were then unknown in country districts, and
often in small towns, too. Water was brought from the nearest farmer's
well. With 60 children, a bucket full would not last long. Sometimes
trustees paid a monthly tax to the farmer for the water used at school.
Toilets were outdoors, and exposed to public view. A partition separated boys and girls. Obscenity was bound to result from such conditions. More than one problem arose from this source to confront me in
my early teaching.

Monday, the first day of school, came. It was with no little emotion
that I faced a small army of motley-dressed boys and girls. They had
arranged themselves in two rows of about equal length along the pathway, and I had to run the gauntlet of inspection. No sooner was the
door opened than a rush for seats was made; for it was customary there,
that the first arrivals should have the choice of seats. One can imagine
the tumult: about 60 pupils, six to twenty, dashing through the door
before I could say "Stop!" Such a scramble meant that half the seats
were unsuitable to those who first claimed them, so teacher's job, and
a lot of trouble it was, too, loomed before him. But with a show of being
master, after an hour's work the "seating" of the school was completed,
the small ones up front, the rest, according to size, reaching back to
the rear.

Classifying pupils was the next task that taxed my ingenuity. I had
them write their names, if they could, and the Reader they were "in"
at the previous school term. This showed me at once who were the
writers. Some who could not write, printed their names. The beginners
were interviewed personally, to get their names. These would be the

A B C class. Placing the others was more difficult. Some brought an advanced Reader, but could not read it at all, when put to the test. The promotions and demotions made some parents glad and others mad; mothers came and wanted their children changed. I made enemies the first day. I was obdurate; I was running the school, and I would not change pupils unless I was convinced they could do the work that was assigned them. I handled some cases by calling the pupils to read in the presence of their parents, who could then see and hear the child could not read, or do the other work of the class they had wanted to enter. The oldest pupils, whose records I could learn from the register left by my predecessor, I simply directed to the programme placed earlier on the blackboard.

The programme went like this: I opened with Bible reading, repeating the Lord's prayer, and singing a familiar song. Then came, first, the beginners; then arithmetic; reading classes; grammar, elementary and advanced; geography; history; physiology; and finally three or four spelling classes. The beginners recited three or four times a day; altogether thirty-three classes were heard in about 310 minutes, an average of less than 10 minutes to each.

Rules, all of which I thought very necessary at the time, were posted in a conspicuous place for the observation of all. Among them were: no whispering, sharpening pencils, throwing stones, name-calling. They were to raise their hands when anything was wanted; they were to stand, pass, and be seated, as I counted one, two, three, or tapped a small bell. All seemed sensible then, but they appear nonsensical now. The most ridiculous rule I made was that no German should be spoken on the playground at recess; and no swearing, either in German or English, would be permitted. My intentions were good, I tried to enforce the rules I made; but my pedagogy was bad, I went at teaching character the wrong way. I soon saw my entire code was out of place, and I learned to put children on their honor more and more, charging them with only two things: Do right; and make life worth while. These I tried to exemplify before them. But the public moral atmosphere was very much lower then than it is today. Children's conduct was not so well looked after as it is now; and pupils were not so independent and self-reliant as they are today.

The school classified, programme and rules posted, I was ready to teach. One of my first difficult problems was due to the community, which was Pennsylvania Dutch. More than half the children were unable to speak a word of English, and did not understand them even when they read English words. How could it be otherwise? They spoke Dutch or German at home; and all the religion they knew was in German. Doubtless many a Pennsylvania German felt as did the old man who insisted, *Der Herr Gott war ja Deitsch*—The Lord God was indeed German. To the beginners, then, I was the interpreter of a foreign tongue, not just a teacher of written forms for a language already known by daily use. I devised my own method. As I happened to be a good artist, I would draw pictures on the "board"— a hat, a fly, a moth, a ball, a knife, etc., write the Pennsylvania Dutch names shouted by the pupils (they seemed to like the pictures) and then the English terms. Thus I helped each one to the English for various objects, increasing their vocabulary.[6]

As for other teaching, I followed a method my mother had used forty years earlier, the same by which I had myself been taught. We memorized the alphabet and the abs—combining all the vowels with the twenty-two consonants, thus: ab, eb, ib, ob, ub; ac, ec, ic, oc, uc; ad, ed, id, od, ud; and so on through the alphabet. However nonsensical it may seem now, it was then considered a splendid method, and was exhibited on the pages of many a textbook. This was formal discipline with a vengeance; if a child could remember this, he could very well remember a lesson in spelling, reading, history, or any other fundamental subject. As a good method, it had the stamp of approval of the County Superintendent and other pedagogical leaders of the day, though it seems "devilish" to critics now.

When ab, eb, ec, and so on had been learned, pupils went to the First Reader, and learned to use words in sentences. The name of the letter was essential then. When "A" was put on the "board" it meant "A," and not another sound. O, Y, T meant O, Y and T. If a child saw T O Y on the board, he spelled it out, naming the letters, and then pronounced the word. Phonics were unknown; if we had tried to introduce such "tomfoolery," it would have brought the wrath of parents on our heads. In every word he built, the pupil must know the letters; no one was allowed to read unless he knew his letters forward, backward, and crosswise. Reading was not dramatized, one read to increase vocabulary, and to see who could read farthest without a mistake, noticing all the *marks*.

In geography the question and answer method was thought the best. Map study was an art. Every town, city, river, mountain peak, bay, gulf, lake, island, strait, isthmus, peninsula, and sea were hunted up. It was a contest in acquiring information. "Trapping" was a game in every class; the one who could stand at the head of the class longest was the best scholar. History was a matter of chronology, as many old textbooks show. Arithmetic was extremely formal; the one who got the answers to the most problems was the best mathematician. I myself committed almost all the problems of a Mental Arithmetic to memory, together

---

[6] Mr. Domer seems not to have known Sander's *Bilder Fibel*. This book (1846) showed pictures, gave German and English in parallel columns and pages, and thus facilitated transition from the tongue of family and community to the idiom of the school room. It was to be an introduction to Sander's First Reader.

with the answers for each. It was a feat to be proud of! It was a day of memorizing; not much reasoning was sought or developed.

Grammar was chiefly the committing of the parts of speech, conjugations, and paradigms to memory. We went through the modes and tenses of every regular and irregular verb. Parsing and diagramming were a mental acrobatic stunt. It was pure memory drill. Writing compositions was a Friday afternoon exercise, not a regular curriculum subject. It was chiefly to increase vocabulary, not for literary value. No one thought of having children read good books, tell stories, write narratives, or descriptions, or dramatize a scene from life. Such things, if tried, would have been criticised violently and reported to the School Board as proof of a lack of sense and the qualifications of a good teacher. Children went to school to "learn," not to be entertained.

Penmanship was simply drill in following a copy. Each pupil had a Spencerian copybook, or the teacher wrote a "Copy" to follow—often a very fine model, expressing good moral precepts to be followed in later life. The Palmer system came into use later, then the vertical system—and a ruinous system it was. Finally there came scales to mesaure the quality of writing.

Thus my first three years were spent practicing what I thought was common sense in teaching, committing the rules of grammar, the rules of arithmetic and of spelling, and the location of every mountain and molehill in the United States to memory. I knew little or nothing of principles of pedagogy or laws of psychology, except the little gained from reading a few books. While pedagogy classes were offered in Normal School, I had not attended such an institution before beginning to teach. Hence my knowledge was extremely limited. I passed from the rural school to the small town school, where "grades," "method," and "psychological teaching" were unknown. It was just a question of the smartest pupil going on to higher classes as fast as he could make them.

Discipline was a large part of the old school. No other phase of teaching has undergone such a thorough change. Discipline, when I began teaching, depended more on physical strength, the ability and the will to give punishment, than any other thing. One of the first questions I was asked upon applying for the school, was whether I believed in "licking," and whether I was afraid of the boys in school. A negative answer to the first question, or an affirmative answer to the second, would have ended my career then and there.

The kind of school one had was a reflection of the government and discipline he employed. In my own school days it was not uncommon to see a large bundle of "hickories" behind the teacher's desk, ready for use. I can not even estimate the number of punishments I received with the "rod"; but I can well remember some of them, administered by a strong arm, justly or unjustly. It was not uncommon forty or fifty years ago for a master to wear out a heavy "hickory" on an obstreperous boy, or even a girl, as I have seen. I vividly recall one occasion, a real fight between a teacher and a pupil, resulting from the teacher's attempting to thrash a large boy. Teacher and pupil both "went to the mat," and fought from the desk to the door, while smaller children crouched in fright under seats, or ran to the older ones for protection. The teacher came out second best, with bruised face, torn clothes, while the bully walked out of the room with an oath on his lips. Nothing was done to either pupil or teacher; it was purely a matter of discipline; if the teacher could not "handle" the boys, he must resign; and if a boy did not like the teacher's rule he could take a licking or leave school. But sometimes he did neither. This particular young ruffian never came back to school.

As for my own school, much of my time was spent showing boys, and girls too, how strong I was, and what feats of strength I could perform. It was a day of weight-lifting. I became adept at lifting with my arms and gripping with teeth and hands. It was no small trick to place a twenty-five pound bag of shot on my left shoulder, and then reach my right hand over my head and lift the weight single handed to the right shoulder. I moved the big stove around the school room, held pupils in or out of the room by bracing myself against them in the doorway; let the pupils hang on my arm, extended against the wall; had pupils strike my chest; lifted heavy objects on the school grounds, and did feats of strength at neighborhood gatherings, such as lifting bags of wheat with my teeth, and wheeling heavy loads in a wheelbarrow. These I did when "living round" with patrons of a district.

By such demonstrations I showed I would be physically able to punish boys as old and big as I was, and the girls too, for they were sometimes hard to keep obedient to the rules laid down. It was sometimes necessary to demonstrate competence. I did not hold to the notion that it was always necessary to thrash pupils to make them mind, but it was sometimes necessary, seemed a fairly effective remedy, and, in fact, was mandatory from headquarters. Several teachers had been run out before I came. Laws governing conduct of pupils in the late eighties, save by such means as have been named, were not thought of, and the teacher had to be a law unto himself when emergencies demanded quick action.

The last school I taught in Pennsylvania was chiefly of boys, and they were hard to handle. Coming, as they did, from a community that had little culture, and composed mostly of pioneers and sons of first and second generations, it was necessary for me to do more fighting and to use more physical punishments in this school than I had in the two years before. Some boys came from homes of veriest ruffians. Belligerent and rebellious towards school discipline, I could not have dared to show the white feather. They would not hesitate to "double team" the teacher, as they had the year before. But I was on guard. With vigilant eye, I was constantly on watch for any concerted action of these fellows.

One day, towards the middle of the term, I saw a move was on foot to play horse with me in a spelling class. Every word that came to a group of boys was misspelled; after the second round, I pronounced the same word to the same boys, and they all misspelled it again. I then told them that if they missed another word during that recitation, I would thrash every one of them individually. I meant what I said, I placed a large "gad" where I could reach it, and I put the stove-poker next to it, to let them know that I would be boss, even if I had to kill some of them.[7] Things moved along very quietly after that, and I finished the term "to the satisfaction of the trustees."

But I could not reconcile myself to such teaching, where one had to declare war on incorrigibles. Patrons offered to make up five dollars extra pay, over the regular salary of forty dollars; but I had "Western fever," and turned down all inducements. I exercised such discipline for three years in the public schools of Pennsylvania, never lacking the courage to put it into execution when needed. But times have now changed; no more does a teacher have to be a branch of the War Department to teach successfully.

A Hundred Years
of the Land-Grant Movement*

by OLIVER C. CARMICHAEL

Oliver C. Carmichael is former president of the Carnegie Foundation for the Advancement of Teaching and is currently a consultant to the Ford Foundation. He has written several books pertaining to higher education, among them THE CHANGING ROLE OF HIGHER EDUCATION; GRADUATE EDUCATION: A CRITIQUE AND A PROGRAM; *and* UNIVERSITIES: COMMONWEALTH AND AMERICAN.

The most revolutionary single development in the history of American higher education is the "land-grant college movement,"

[7] Mr. Domer's vigorous discipline recalls another redoutable teacher who brought learning to the Pennsylvania Germans. He was an Irishman; and oh, how he clobbered the Dutch! *(Er war en Eirischer; ach, wie hott er die Deitsche verkloppt.)*

* Oliver C. Carmichael, "A Hundred Years of the Land-Grant Movement," *Saturday Review,* 45 (April 21, 1962): 58-59, 71-72. By permission of the editor and the author.

initiated just a century ago by the Morrill Act of 1862. It is difficult to conceive what the United States would be like today if the land-grant college act had failed to pass or if President Lincoln had refused to sign it. Educationally, economically, and politically, it would be a different land and would occupy a different place in the international community. With all its shortcomings and the vagaries of its early history, not all of which have yet been eliminated, the net effect of the land-grant college movement, after a century, is a stronger, more imaginative, more enterprising, and more democratic America.

It would be a mistake to ascribe to this movement all the contributions of the land-grant colleges and universities because a number of universities have incorporated the land-grant program as only one of their divisions of instruction and research. Cornell University, for example, is a privately supported institution which operates its "land-grant college" under a contract with the state of New York. The University of Missouri had been in operation for twenty years, and the University of Minnesota for eleven years, before the Morrill Act was passed. Rutgers was founded in 1766 but added engineering and agriculture to its curricula in 1864. Several states added their own funds for state universities to the federal funds provided by the Morrill Act.

The essential provisions of the act introduced by a Vermont Congressman can be stated in a single sentence: "The Morrill Act of 1862 provided land grants to each state for the endowment, support, and maintenance of at least one college where the leading object shall be, without excluding other scientific and classical studies, and including military tactics, to teach such branches of learning as are related to agriculture and the mechanic arts, in such manner as the legislatures of the states may respectively prescribe in order to promote the liberal and practical education of the industrial classes in the several pursuits and professions in life." This plan was revolutionary in three aspects. It provided for instruction in subjects not previously considered worthy of university study; it was designed to reach a segment of society not hitherto served by higher education, and, finally, it involved a new conception of the role of higher education in our society.

It is not only contrary to the tradition of American higher education which was, in 1862, well into its third century; it was an even more startling departure from Anglo-Saxon theory and practice in university education which dated back to the founding of Oxford some 700 years earlier.

There were a few departments of engineering in the United States before 1862 but they were not of college grade. Rensselaer Polytechnic Institute and the Military Academy at West Point inaugurated civil engineering early in the nineteenth century but these programs were modeled after the French polytechnic institutes, not after their universities. Technical training was already being provided in Britain, by the middle of the century, but this was offered in the technical colleges primarily. The University of London had three engineering departments but these were of little or no influence on university education at that time. The polytechnic institutes in Europe were not affiliated with universities and did not offer university grade programs.

The land-grant colleges introduced a new set of courses quite different in character from those found in traditional universities and, by their example, encouraged other institutions to follow suit. The lofty conception of the ideal university as expressed so eloquently by Cardinal Newman was lacking; a pragmatic, practical type of education was emphasized. These colleges were designed to serve, not the few who wished to enter the learned professions, but the many who desired to enter "the several pursuits and professions in life." The purpose and the vision of a working man's college was their novel element, and they prepared students for a wide variety of vocations.

This fact has been responsible for much of the trivia found in college and university programs in the vocational and professional areas. The land-grant colleges cannot be held accountable for all the vagaries of American higher education but the fact remains that a trend which has led institutions astray was initiated by the program launched in 1862. Courses proliferated unduly and many did not represent genuine university work. This does not mean, however, that the "land-grant" development has not justified its existence. Indeed, among the three seminal movements in higher education in the nineteenth century, the program arising out of the Morrill Act has been perhaps the most significant in its effect on American life. The other two, the elective system and the conception of the modern university, have both been affected by the land-grant college development and have, in turn, contributed tremendously to it. For example, if the stranglehold of the classical curriculum had not been broken the new courses would never have been admitted. Similarly, if the modern university with its emphasis on research had not developed, the agricultural experiment station would probably never have been established.

The elective system provided the demand for new courses. The "modern university" emphasis upon research influenced the methods employed in higher learning. But the land-grant college plan introduced new subject matter and thus affected substantively the direction of university development perhaps more than any other reform during the past one hundred years. In breaking away from the philosophical moorings of the past the land-grant movement, in 1862, set sail on an unknown sea without chart or compass and has been exploring new areas of educational service for a century. All the while it has been exerting a significant influence on colleges and universities both public and private not only in the U.S. but throughout the world.

Undoubtedly, the scientific, technological, and technical development of the past 100 years has been largely due to the emphasis on science and technology in American higher education, which in turn stemmed largely from the land-grant college movement. The success of America economically and industrially has inspired other nations to follow its lead in their educational programs in the scientific and technological fields. Thus the influence of the Morrill Act has been widespread both at home and abroad.

Certain questions arise when we consider these facts. Why did the proponents of agricultural and engineering education succeed in the 1860's when they had failed in the 1850's? What were the forces that gave rise to the land-grant idea? How did the act happen to get through Congress at a time when the country was in the midst of bitter civil strife and its resources already severely strained?

The interest of the federal government and the substantial land-grants were doubtless responsible for the success of the program in "agriculture and the mechanic arts." These subjects would probably not have been accepted by the faculties of higher education if there had not been the stimulus of federal aid. The fact that many of the programs originally established were set up as divisions of state universities also helped. Even with these great assets the land-grant college programs were not readily accepted and recognized as bona fide university subjects. It was well into the twentieth century before the new programs gained general acceptance. Indeed, it may be said that the full flowering of the land-grant colleges did not occur until after World War II. University emphasis upon science and technology in the past two decades has eclipsed all previous records, not only in the United States, but in universities throughout the world.

When Congressman Morrill introduced his bill, the public apparently was ready for it. The Industrial Revolution was well under way but college curricula had not yet adapted themselves to it. The Civil War had revealed the need for technological training and, for at least a decade, there had been demands for additions to the curriculum and for the student's right to select his own subjects. All these facts pre-disposed Congress, as well as the general public, to favor an educational program designed to produce agricultural and industrial leadership.

The evolution of the land-grant college programs is an interesting story in itself, but too long to detail here. All the land-grant institutions had difficulty finding teachers and suffered from low standards, even lower than those prevailing in other colleges and universities. But as they grew in numbers and in support, standards were gradually raised until they are generally on a par with other state-supported institutions.

In addition to the land-grants to establish these institutions under the Morrill Act of 1862, there was a second Morrill Act passed in 1890 that made possible regular federal appropriation for the support of these institutions. The Hatch Act of 1887 provided for agricultural experiment stations and the Smith-Lever Act of 1914 for farm and home demonstration agents.

The magnitude of the service rendered under the Smith-Lever Act is illustrated by the fact that more than 10,000,000 homes were served by the home demonstration agents in 1961. The farm demonstration agents were equally widespread. These agents have access to the latest research findings of the home economics faculties and of the agricultural experiment stations, as well as the agricultural faculties of the sixty-nine land-grant colleges and universities serving the continental United States, Hawaii, Alaska, and Puerto Rico. The effect of these services on the standards of living of millions of Americans is beyond the reach of one's imagination. In assessing the factors that contribute to the high living standards of Americans, this factor is usually underrated or ignored.

The struggle to establish and maintain standards characterized the first three or four decades of the land-grant college movement. In the beginning there were few people qualified to give instruction in either agriculture or engineering. The faculties had to be developed on the job. The result was that in the early years the quality of work, particularly in the independent institutions, was poor. This added to the difficulty of building prestige for the new program. In many instances the vocational and technical curricula were substandard and the non-professional courses little, if any, better. In some sections of the country it was a half-century before the program measured up to the low standards of other institutions of that period. However, in a few instances the independent land-grant institution outstripped the state university in number of students attracted, in range of curriculum, and in quality of work.

With the improvement in standards, growth in prestige, and increase in enrollments, the independent colleges began early to aspire to university status. Indeed, the Ohio Agricultural and Mechanical College, which was established by statute in 1870 and gave its first instruction in 1873, changed its name to Ohio State University only five years later (1878). This trend has continued until now some forty of the sixty-nine land-grant colleges in operation are universities. The original Morrill Act which provided specifically for "scientific and classical studies" laid the foundation for a broad university program and thus encouraged this trend. In the past decade Pennsylvania, Michigan, and Alabama have substituted *university* for *college* or *institute* in the title of their land-grant institutions.

The federal fund grants now constitute a very small fraction of the support of the land-grant colleges and universities. For example, in 1954 the total of federal grants under the Morrill, Hatch, and Smith-Lever Acts amounted to $50,487,737, while the aggregate budgets of these institutions, not including buildings, amounted to $840,482,000.

In those states which have a land-grant institution separate from the state university there is frequently a struggle over the amount of state support each shall receive. Often the land-grant college has more grass-roots support than the university, partly because the former has more contact with citizens of the state through the farm and home demonstration agents, and partly because its program makes a wider appeal to the citizens generally than that of the state university. This gives the land-grant college or university great political strength, which is no mean asset in dealing with legislative budget committees. The appeal of the land-grant program is also effective in the recruitment of students.

Any account of land-grant colleges would be incomplete without a brief look at the contributions which they have made to scholarship, to American higher education, to economic progress, and to American democracy.

Their chief contribution to scholarship has been in the field of applied science. Some basic contributions to the life sciences may perhaps be ascribed to them but land-grant programs have been mainly concerned with the applications of scientific knowledge. This has proved a highly significant contribution. It has meant greater realism in scholarship. Metaphysical speculation, which dominated the universities of the Middle Ages and later, had still not lost its hold upon scholarship in the early nineteenth century. The emphasis upon the application of scientific theory to practical affairs did much to bring the scholar out of his ivory tower and into the market place. While basic scholarship may have suffered somewhat from the diversion of the scholars' energies from pure science to its applications, that was probably more than offset by the gains that were derived from it. It affected the outlook of the general public as well as the scholar and in the long run may have strengthened basic science. The test of the usefulness of knowledge has doubtless had some adverse effects upon scholarly pursuits. It may have contributed to the weakness of fundamental scholarship and of pure science, but it is more than likely that it has helped rather than hindered basic investigation.

While no one can say with certainty what the effect of emphasis on technology has been on the progress of science, this much is certain: It has had a profound effect upon the economy of the country and upon the standard of living of the American people. With the advance of automation the effects of technology will appear still more evident. For the first time in history a nation is able to produce more than it needs. The economic and industrial power of the United States is without a peer in our modern world and without a precedent in history. This is due to the advances of science and technology which were, to a marked degree, stimulated by the land-grant college movement.

The effect of the land-grant movement upon the educational system has been no less profound. It was designed to democratize higher education. In reforming the university curriculum, by adding a vast number of new subjects, it made higher education attractive to a large segment of the country's population who previously had no interest in it. This accounts largely for the growth of college and university enrollments, which increased twentyfold between 1850 and 1900, when the census showed only a threefold expansion, and tenfold between 1900 and 1950, when the total population only doubled.

The emphasis upon practical education initiated and stimulated the growth of vocational education and training. Our far-flung vocational educational program appears to have been largely inspired by the new type of college that had its origin in 1862. This development has had its drawbacks. It has been responsible for a kind of chaos in the public mind, which has, in many ways, retarded educational progress. The American public has often confused *education* with *training* and frequently has wanted the latter when it needed the former. This is one of the reasons for the sad plight of liberal education today. Parents who insisted that four years in college have been wasted, if they have not prepared Johnny or Mary for a vocation, are victims of the widespread confusion which prevails.

Thus, while the land-grant college movement did much to democratize education at all levels, it introduced, at the same time, some serious problems. There is confusion not only in high schools and colleges but at the graduate level as well. This is illustrated by the trend toward granting more and more Ph.D.s for work in applied science fields, whereas a few short years ago the highest degree was granted only by basic science departments or in collaboration with them.

The land-grant program not only contributed to the democratization of American education; it was essential to the democratization of America. So long as higher education was beyond the reach of the "industrial classes," because it had nothing to offer them, there could be no genuine democracy. In other words, so long as the classical curriculum dominated the university program true democracy was not attainable; this the legislator from Vermont seemed to understand.

As they enter upon their second century, the land-grant institutions are riding the crest of the wave of popularity, as indicated by the place of science and technology in the modern university curriculum. Their future will depend upon the kind of leadership they command. If it is imaginative, realistic, and dedicated, aware of certain obvious weaknesses, alert to the changing needs of society, and determined to build upon the sound elements in the foundations already laid, their prospects are bright.

A central problem of higher education in the decades ahead will be that of reconciling its aim with the traditional purpose of the higher learning, whether its subject matter and methods are traditional or novel. That purpose, "the pursuit of truth," is still the goal of true university education that should be sought not only by the land-grant institutions but by all other universities.

SUGGESTED ACTIVITIES

1. Visit a public or college library and select three *National Geographic* magazines—a recent one, one from the year 1930, and one from the year 1915. Read several advertisements and note the kinds, varieties, and functions of appliances for the housewife. Note how many more appliances are advertised in a recent issue, and notice, too, how much these appliances can do. Then ask yourself this question: "Have the increased and more efficient appliances changed the role of the housewife?" If so, how? How does this question relate to the first

section on technological change and cultural patterns, including educational techniques?

2. Look through two high-school yearbooks, one containing a picture of the senior class in the year 1930 and the other portraits of last year's seniors. Note that most of the graduating class of 1930 appear to be older than those in the more recent one. *Are* they older? If so, what does this fact mean?

3. In most preliterate cultures there is much less bickering among brothers and sisters and between children and parents than there is in our culture. In the light of the author's discussion of cultural patterns, why do you think this is so?

4. Consider for a moment those students who graduated from your high school and went on to college. Some of the graduates went to "prestige" colleges. Others went either to a junior college in the community or to a state university or college. Compare the economic circumstances of the two groups. From your results, what tentative conclusions can you draw about the meaning of the word *democracy* as it applies to higher education?

5. In many European countries the street cleaner or dishwasher sings the lyrics to Italian or German operas. In this country only a tiny minority seem to appreciate and enjoy opera. What could account for this difference?

6. Ask your grandparents whether they approve of corporal punishment for youngsters. Ask this same question of your mother and father. Now ask yourself this same question. To what do you attribute differences in the responses?

7. In "A Brief Survey of American Education," p. 15, the author notes that the South was tardy in establishing a true public-school system. Some years ago Prince Edward County, Virginia chose to close its public schools rather than integrate. Is there any connection between these two phenomena? Discuss.

8. Visit the registrar's office or library and examine a few of the hundreds of college bulletins collected there. How many different kinds of institutions of higher learning can you classify?

9. Professor Rudolph, in *The American College and University*, praises the extracurriculum of nineteenth-century American colleges

as providing elements of **true education** not found in the formal curriculum. Poll three students, one a fraternity member, the second an
active club member, and the third a participant in student government.
Ask them the following question: "What values do you feel that you
are obtaining from your extracurricular activities?" As you reflect on
the answers, ask yourself the following question: "Would it be possible for these values to be obtained in the formal college classroom?"

SUGGESTED READINGS

BALDWIN, LELAND AND KELLEY, ROBERT. *The Stream of American History.*
3rd ed.; New York; American Book, 1965.   A standard text which takes
full account of sociological, economic, and cultural forces as well as political
and military events in the development of American civilization.

BARTKY, JOHN A. *Social Issues in Public Education.* Boston: Houghton
Mifflin, 1963.   A good introduction to the social foundations of education; requires an understanding of basic sociological concepts.

BRAUNER, CHARLES J. *American Educational Theory.* Englewood Cliffs:
Prentice-Hall, 1964.   A work, designed for the advanced student of educational history and philosophy, which gives a detailed description of
theory and practice. Brauner's iconoclastic approach to the commonly held
assumptions about education makes the book interesting and informative.

BROOKOVER, WILBUR B. AND GOTTLIEB, DAVID. *The Sociology of Education.*
2nd ed.; New York: American Book, 1963.   A standard text in the social
order of the school, including school-community relations.

BUTTS, R. FREEMAN. *A Cultural History of Western Education.* 2nd ed.;
New York: McGraw-Hill, 1955.   A standard textbook in educational
history.

EBY, FREDERICK. *The Development of Modern Education.* Englewood
Cliffs: Prentice-Hall, 1959.   The companion work to the Eby and Arrowood book listed below.

EBY, FREDERICK AND ARROWOOD, CHARLES F. *The History and Philosophy of
Education Ancient and Medieval.* Englewood Cliffs: Prentice-Hall, 1960.
A standard reference in the field. Contains a wealth of detail.

EGGLESTON, EDWARD. *The Hoosier Schoolmaster.* New York: Macmillan,
1928.   An accurate and colorful description of teaching in "the good
old days."

FRENCH, WILLIAM M. *America's Educational Tradition, An Interpretive History*. Boston: Heath, 1964.   An objective, colorful, curriculum-oriented description of American educational institutions.

FRIEDAN, BETTY. *The Feminine Mystique*. New York: Norton, 1963. Discusses the plight of the educated housewife who is torn between utilizing her intellectual skills and obeying the cultural norms that tend to force women into the roles of wife and mother.

GABRIEL, RALPH HENRY. *The Course of American Democratic Thought* New York: Ronald, 1956.   A summary and interpretation of the significant social and philosophical movements affecting democracy in the United States. Primarily for the more advanced student.

GOOD, HARRY G. *A History of Western Education*. New York: Macmillan, 1962.   A standard reference in educational history.

GROSS, CARL H. AND CHANDLER, CHARLES C. *This History of American Education Through Readings*. Boston: Heath, 1964.   Note especially the selections by Cotton Mather, Samuel E. Morison, Edward Eggleston, and Washington Irving.

GROSS, CARL H., HANSON, JOHN, AND WRONSKI, STANLEY F. *School and Society*. Boston: Heath, 1962.   A collection of essays in the social-foundations area. Part I, "The Role of Education in Society," is most relevant to the first part of our essay, "A Brief Survey of American Educational History."

HOFSTADTER, RICHARD. *Anti-intellectualism in American Life*. New York: Knopf, 1963.   Treats the American tendency to reject intellectualism in and by business, labor, agriculture, religion, and education.

HOLLIS, ERNEST V. *Toward Improving Ph.D. Programs*. Washington, D.C.: American Council on Education, 1945.   The chapter entitled "Long Range Forces That Have Shaped Doctoral Work" is an excellent summary of the history of higher education in this country.

KALLENBACH, W. WARREN AND HODGES, HAROLD M., JR. *Education and Society*. Columbus: Merrill, 1963.   A collection of readings in the fields of anthropology, psychology, and sociology, selected for undergraduate students.

KNELLER, GEORGE F. *Foundations of Education*. New York: Wiley, 1963 Essays on the relationship between education and society. The essay by Ruth Landes, "Culture and Education," is of special interest.

KNIGHT, EDGAR AND HALL, CLIFTON L. *Readings in American Educational History*. New York: Appleton-Century-Crofts, 1951.   Documents per taining to American education from its beginnings to the middle of the nineteenth century.

MORRIS, VAN CLEVE, *et al. Becoming an Educator*. New York: Houghton Mifflin, 1963.   The second section contains two relevant chapters, "The History of Education" and "The Sociology of Education."

POWER, EDWARD J. *Education for American Democracy*. New York: McGraw-Hill, 1958.   A competent treatment of American education from a Catholic viewpoint. Chapters on educational history are found throughout the book.

———. *Main Currents in the History of Education*. New York: McGraw-Hill, 1962.   A comprehensive treatment of educational history from primitive times to the present. Designed for the advanced student, the volume contains a wealth of detail.

ROSTEN, LEO C. *The Education of H*Y*M*A*N K*A*P*L*A*N*. New York: Harcourt, Brace, 1937.   A poignant, humorous, and delightful description of the difficulties of an American teacher in introducing newly arrived immigrants to American language and customs.

RUDOLPH, FREDERICK. *The American College and University*. New York: Knopf, 1962.   A well-written account of the history of American higher education.

SPINDLER, GEORGE D. *Education and Culture*. New York: Holt, Rinehart and Winston, 1963.   Reflects the recent interest in applying the insights of anthropology to education. A collection of interesting though difficult essays.

THAYER, V. T. *The Role of the School in American Society*. New York: Dodd, Mead, 1961.   A thorough discussion of the relationship between educational institutions and social and philosophical currents.

THUT, I. N. *The Story of Education*. New York: McGraw-Hill, 1957. A concise but extremely useful interpretation of educational history.

ULICH, ROBERT. *The History of Educational Thought*. New York: American Book, 1950.   A penetrating treatment of the chief contributions of both academic and nonacademic people to thinking about education.

WILDS, ELMER H. AND LOTTICH, KENNETH V. *The Foundations of Modern Education*. New York: Holt, Rinehart and Winston, 1961.   One of the best histories of educational theory and practice. Primarily an attempt to relate intellectual, social, cultural, and philosophical movements to education.

II

Educational Goals

Most societies—and most individuals—are unaware of their own values, beliefs, attitudes, and goals. Both societies and individuals do, in fact, *have* beliefs and goals; but the mere possession is different from a conscious, clear knowledge of the nature and meaning of these beliefs and goals.

Education is a field heavily laden with subjective values—that is, everyone has his own educational philosophy. One is tempted to say that there are too many aims and values regarding the educative process. We say "is tempted" because in a pluralistic society the growth of many different values and aims is inevitable. However, it is also true that most Americans are not aware that, as a nation, we entertain widely varying goals for education. Most people naïvely believe that their particular aim or goal of education is the "right" one and that goals which differ from theirs are, to some extent, wrong or inappropriate. Students, teachers, parents, and other members of a community are often surprised, indeed, to discover that there *are* other positions—a good many other positions—regarding the goals of education.

As a matter of fact—and whether Mr. Jones and Mrs. Smith are aware of it or not—one of the outstanding characteristics of American education is the fact that the cultural plurality of our society has led to a plurality of educational goals, values, beliefs, and attitudes that come into considerable conflict. There are several aspects of the multiplicity of goals in American education that will be illustrated in the reading selections.

S. Samuel Shermis' article "Conflicting Goals of Education" examines the character of our many conflicting educational goals. The essay explores the philosophical background and implications of some theories of education that have been important in our society since 1620.

"Whose Values Should Be Taught?" by Max Birnbaum, develops further the idea that American pluralism has created some almost insoluble problems for public schools.

In "A Crisis of Purpose," Arthur E. Bestor speaks out for the one goal of intellectual training. Bestor is one of many who believe that "social, psychological, and vocational purposes" should not be included as curricular goals.

Harold G. Shane, in "We Can Be Proud of the Facts," writes what may be considered a rebuttal to some of the recent derogatory statements made by critics of American education. Can you imagine what Bestor might say in reply to Shane's arguments? How would he handle the concrete facts which Shane presents?

"Stop Pampering Gifted Children," by Bruno Bettelheim, would appear at first glance to be a rather strange addition to a collection of general essays on education. Actually, the significance of this article lies in the educational assumptions of the author rather than in his statements about how the gifted should or should not be taught.

The final reading has been carefully selected to leave a shade of reasonable doubt with the reader. William H. Boyer's "Have Our Schools Kept Us Free?" focuses our attention on a possible failure to attain the most important objective of all.

Conflicting Goals of Education

by S. SAMUEL SHERMIS

American education three centuries ago had one goal: to train people to live in a way that would secure eternal salvation for them. But as time went on, education became a matter of national concern; a hundred problems clamored for immediate solution.

OUR PLURALISTIC SOCIETY

Our country has often been referred to as a melting pot. Actually, it resembles a stew more than a melting pot. In a melting pot elements are mixed so that they lose their original identities. A stew, on the other hand, is a mixture in which the original elements, although each has been affected by the others, retain their identity and can be distinguished one from the other.

Our society is composed of many, many different elements, and while the characteristics of these elements have altered a good deal over the years—like the beef and carrots in a stew—the elements are still recognizable. We retain a good many of our Puritan characteristics, and the original thinking and customs of the Southern planters of the eighteenth century have by no means completely vanished. Both Puritan beliefs and Virginia's aristocratic attitudes, although considerably modified and changed during the last two or three centuries, are actual, living, and vital forces in our way of life. Since our older attitudes and practices continue to exist side by side with one another and with our newer ways—*and since this is not recognized*—these older characteristics cause a good deal of trouble. The problem of conflict between older and newer ways of thinking combines with yet another fact of American life to intensify conflict further. This fact of our life is known as "pluralism"—a term describing a mixture of many nationalities, races, classes, religions, occupational groupings, philosophies, value systems, and economic theories.

First, we are a nation of different nationalities. Our heritage is predominantly English, but alongside the English-speaking people we have Slavs, Chinese, Japanese, Hungarians, Scandinavians, Italians, Latin Americans, Irish, French, and people of many other nationalities from Europe, Africa, Asia, and South America. People of these various nationalities, as the historian Oscar Handlin has pointed out, attempted to become Americanized as soon as possible.[1] They gave up their language, their cooking, their dancing, and many of their other customs—but not entirely. For example, the English, throughout their history, have tended to emphasize and seek stability, law, order, legal procedures, and gradual reform. This is an important part of our heritage. But the French have contributed quite a different heritage: an emphasis on revolution and freedom and the belief that people should be as free as possible from external restrictions. Our country has incorporated both these sets of quite different and frequently unharmonious attitudes and values.

Second, we are a nation of different races. Predominantly, we are Caucasian. But there are in the United States twenty million Negroes and nearly one-half million persons of Oriental descent. The mere fact of different races living together does not automatically mean that a

---

[1] *Race and Nationality in American Life* (New York: Doubleday, 1957).

problem will be created. But in our society, it certainly has meant that. Third, we are a nation of different classes. Sociologists generally accept the existence of a three-class system: upper, middle, and lower.[2] While most Americans are middle-class, know this, and are proud of it, a very large number are lower class. The middle-class teacher may be confronted with a student who is driven to school each day by a chauffeur; but more likely the middle-class instructor has to face children who do not value education, are indifferent to cleanliness, believe in fighting as a means of settling quarrels, and live by relatively loose sexual codes. These values, which are those of the lower class, create monumental problems for the middle-class teacher, who is often both bewildered and angered by them. Since the schools are middle-class oriented, from teacher to curriculum to textbooks,[3] the lower-class youth does not easily fit in. The rural Mexican boy or the Puerto Rican slum dweller or the child of the migrant fruit picker has little stake and little interest in what goes on in the typical classroom.

Fourth, we are, in addition, a nation composed of people of different religions and those who oppose religion. Though the United States is predominantly Protestant, there are now about forty-five million Catholics and perhaps five and a half million Jews. Protestants range from Episcopalians, with one set of dogmas, beliefs, and practices, to Southern Baptists, with quite another. The Mormons and Christian Scientists broaden even further the Protestant spectrum. The presence of these different religions has raised quite a number of issues in or involving the nation's schools: federal aid to parochial schools, Bible reading and prayers in public schools, treatment of religious topics in the classroom—even the celebration of Christmas. Further, these various religious groups entertain very different beliefs with regard to everything from sexual morality to certain civic functions.

Fifth, sectionalism is by no means a dead issue in America. If one happens to have been brought up in Idaho, one's views are apt to be different than they would be if one were brought up in Mississippi. Idaho certainly does not have the racial problems of Mississippi. But there are few states as large or geographically isolated as Idaho, and a resident of Idaho will have problems different from those of an inhabitant, say, of New England. It is obvious that whether a given area

---

[2] W. Lloyd Warner and Paul S. Lunt, *The Social Life of a Modern Community* (New York: Yale U. Press, 1949). Other books on this subject include those by Richard Centers, Robert Lynd, and Allison Davis.

[3] For more information on this point, see William O. Stanley, *et al.*, *Social Foundations of Education* (New York: Holt, 1956), Sec. 7, "The Impact of Class, Ethnic Groups, and Welfare Levels on the School."

is densely populated or sparsely settled, heavily agricultural or strongly industrial, consisting of old-stock Americans or recent second-generation immigrants will help determine the views and values of its inhabitants.

Sixth, occupational patterns help determine people's views. In a town in which most persons are engaged in the same occupation, one tends to find a rather uniform outlook on issues. But, in a town with a wide variety of occupational and professional groups, there follows disparity in attitudes and values. Teachers tend to look at certain issues in a similar way, just as do steelworkers, potato farmers, and small businessmen. The existence of so many occupations and professions adds to the already existing complexity of attitudes, outlooks, and values.

And last, people in the United States entertain a variety of social, political, and economic philosophies. In a group of ten men chosen at random, we might expect to find at least one who violently opposed any further "meddling" of the government in local affairs and one who welcomed government "support and assistance" in that same area. We might find a person who took the position that we should establish much higher tariff barriers on, say, figs, because he was being hurt by the importation of Turkish figs. Another might argue that, since we belong to a world community, we must cooperate economically; he would therefore advocate the immediate and complete abolition of all tariffs and other trade barriers. One person might assert that some races are just naturally inferior, that the Lord made them so, and that they should be segregated from the others. Another would be quite certain that democracy means that everyone is completely equal and that there are no differences among groups and races. There is no one American socioeconomic philosophy.

Interpersonal Relations We in the United States have many religions, nationalities, races, classes, occupations, philosophies, attitudes, outlooks, and values. This pluralism has created at least two kinds of major problems: *interpersonal* and *intrapersonal*.

Our nation is composed of competing, opposing factions. This point was first made by Alexander Hamilton in *The Federalist Papers,* and it is even truer now than it was over 170 years ago. What is desired by one group may be violently opposed by another. The property owner naturally wishes to see lower taxes on his property. The parent of the school-age child wants higher taxes to be used for education. The nature lover wishes to keep the wilderness primitive and undeveloped so that all may enjoy the beauties of nature. This same area is viewed by a lumber merchant as something to be developed for profit.

One group is opposed to gambling on moral grounds. Another group welcomes gambling for its effect on tourism and the increase in state income therefrom.

In many important social areas there is little unanimity. We cannot "get together" simply and quickly and agree about what should or should not be done. Even when we can agree on *what* ought to be done, we often don't agree on *why* or *how* it should be done.

Now what has actually happened is that our country has somehow, in a way not at all clear to any thinker, managed to "get by." Some writers see our country functioning as a series of alliances in which combinations of power groups "get together" briefly and temporarily to bring about this or that.[4] These power alliances last just as long as the individual group needs to cooperate. Then the alliance is disbanded, and the groups may, and usually do, return to fighting each other. For example, the Women's Christian Temperance Union in the last century cooperated with other groups, including trade unions, to help bring about the establishment of sanitary conditions in factories, abolition of heavy labor by women in factories, and industrial reform. However, on the issue of prohibition of alcoholic beverages, the WCTU worked for action that many union members opposed. Thus, on national as well as local issues, combinations of groups who make themselves heard determine what gets done. They pressure the legislatures, both state and national, propagandize on radio, television, in the newspapers, and on the speaking platforms, and work on a person-to-person basis.

Thus we are a society consisting of many little groups, factions, and interests that express a welter of views and beliefs. Each group— or combination of groups—operates to realize the values it holds dear. Ordinarily there is some conflict between these values, so that our society is a collection of competing groups. What determines the most important value or, to put it another way, what determines what gets done and who gets what, is simply the totality of power that can be mustered in support of any program.

Intrapersonal Relations   With such a widely varied and often self-contradictory social heritage, a single individual often incorporates very different and unharmonious beliefs and values. The same individual who talks loudly about—and probably sincerely believes in—

[4] The first well-known treatment of pressure groups in the United States is in *The Federalist*, a collection of 85 essays by Alexander Hamilton, John Jay, and James Madison. See especially essays 9 and 10. An inexpensive edition of *The Federalist* is the Modern Library edition. A contemporary author who deals with the same topic is John Kenneth Galbraith, *American Capitalism: The Concept of Countervailing Power* (Cambridge: Riverside, 1956).

the fact that God created all men equal may refuse to sell his house to a Negro. The person who believes that all youth, including his own children, ought to be encouraged to be independent will refuse his teen-age son the right to make many decisions for himself. In these two cases one individual holds two contradictory beliefs.

For the most part, these individuals are not aware that they disagree within themselves; they believe that they are being quite consistent. If you were to ask the father of the teen-age boy how he can believe in the importance of independence for young people and at the same time withhold independence from his own children, he would doubtless give a reply that was completely satisfying—to himself.

Intrapersonal and interpersonal conflict can create energy, and out of this creative energy may come something of real significance. Conflict between groups or individuals may cause opposing ideas to be brought out into the open, where lines of action are plotted and alternative points of view are examined. For example, out of the clash between two political candidates who really disagree on important issues may come public enlightenment.

However, there is another side to this coin. Interpersonal conflict in our society may often produce useless friction, the result of which is antagonism, hatred, ill will, and acrimony. This weakens the common ties that bind people together. And intrapersonal conflict, the conflict within a person, often carries even more severe consequences. The conflict within a person can tear him apart. For example, many teen-agers have grown up in an environment that holds that premarital sexual intercourse is wrong. When these teen-agers find themselves away from the restrictions of parents, church, and school, when they are told that "everyone does it," and when they have also been exposed to another, very different belief—that sex is a good, healthy thing and that the sexual urge needs to be satisfied for "happiness" to be achieved—they often experience emotional agony, no matter what they do.

Intrapersonal conflict has other effects. The individual who strongly believes in two opposing values does not know which one is really "right." Sometimes the result of this ambivalence is indecision involving an important choice, and the ultimate result of the delay is tragedy. Another consequence of intrapersonal value conflict is inconsistency. An individual may behave in line with one value at one time and in line with another, quite different, value at another time. A mother, believing that her children should be allowed to express themselves freely, will give them free rein at one time. At another time, she may recall the value of firm parental discipline and severely punish her children for behavior she allowed earlier.

There is yet another consequence of intrapersonal conflict. The individual goes ahead and does something because it seems "good" and "right" to him, and then, after he does it, is visited by anxiety and guilt. Two teen-agers in a parked car may afford an example of just this effect of intrapersonal conflict.

The important fact about intrapersonal conflict is that it is largely unconscious. The individual who experiences doubt and confusion often does not know *why* he feels as he does. The conflicting values were learned without the individual actually being aware that he was learning them. Thus, an individual who, for instance, resents his teachers probably does not know *why* he feels the way he does.

Summary   Our society, consisting of a wide variety of groups and beliefs, entertains values that are often contradictory. These contradictory beliefs are transmitted, usually without their being conscious of the transmission, to the young people in our society. Young people internalize these contradictory values, which in time come into conflict with each other, and the result is intrapersonal conflict. Intrapersonal conflict involves an individual at war with himself for reasons that usually are not very clear to him. Interpersonal conflict refers to value conflict between one individual and another, between one group and another, or between a group and an individual. These kinds of conflicts generate remarkable energy, even though they also create a good deal of disharmony and hatred.

In the following section, we will attempt to describe the effects of pluralism on education, especially on the goals, or aims, of education. We are using the words "goal" and "aim" to mean an overriding principle, a major value that acts to give direction to a particular undertaking. In any given task the goal or aim helps determine the means by which a task is to be accomplished.

PLURAL AIMS OF EDUCATION

In a society as pluralistic and diverse as ours, one would expect to find a good many aims and goals. One would expect also to find that these goals are often at cross-purposes with one another. This is exactly what we do find. Let us now examine some of the many contradictory goals that have given direction to American schools for three hundred years.

Religious Goals   The educational goal of the Puritans was the eternal salvation of souls. And while some customs and beliefs change considerably through the centuries, others tend to persist with a good deal of vigor. The goal of the Puritan colonists has persisted. Although public education became more secular, religious motives and values have not died out in our society. The three major religions are very much alive and actively attempt to breathe religious values into their followers. Catholics, Protestants, and Jews still learn about the nature of man and God, about the goals of their religion, about desirable behavior. Therefore, while our schools are technically secular, many teachers still hold clearly religious values which, often quite unconsciously, they attempt to impress on their students.[5] Many teachers still believe that the purpose of this life is to gain entry into the higher, more perfect world of heaven. We would expect teachers in a parochial school to hold this goal, but many teachers in secular, public schools also have this, often without being aware of it, as their overriding aim.

A teacher who holds this goal believes that God has revealed how man shall enter the kingdom of heaven. The Old and New Testaments contain a series of injunctions, rules, laws, and commandments, which all men must follow. Thus, the teacher constantly attempts to see to it that students both believe and behave in certain ways. She tells Johnny, whom she has caught cheating, that God has forbidden man to lie or cheat. Lying and cheating violate a God-given rule, and that is why Johnny is not to cheat. She attempts to see to it that Johnny learns and believes in a particular religious dogma or ritual.[6]

Vocational Goals Religious goals are not the only ones in our society, of course. A prospective teacher, asked what his educational aim would be, replied simply, "To provide every child with an effective occupation." This, of course, is quite different from the religious aim, and it is a goal sought by many Americans who believe that schools should be essentially vocational in nature. That is, many hold that the function of the school is to see to it that each student is fit for some occupation, whether a profession or a skilled trade. These people would select a curriculum with either an immediate or a long-range vocational purpose. English would be taught because communication is necessary for employment. Social studies would be taught because every effective worker needs to know about social, political, and economic matters. Such a curriculum, naturally, would make great use of "shop," home economics, journalism, and similar courses, as opposed to, say, Latin and literature.

[5] Robert Brackenbury, *Getting Down to Cases* (New York: Putnam, 1959). See pp. 97-117.

[6] *Ibid.*, pp. 97-117.

Intellectual Goals Vigorously opposed to this particular aim are those thinkers called "classical realists." Classical realists believe that there exists a body of knowledge which *everyone* must possess, that without this body of knowledge the individual cannot deal satisfactorily with the world. They believe that this body of knowledge really does not change; it is always essentially the same, with only minor modifications over the years.

What kind of curriculum would the classical realist stress? Classical realists insist that everyone must be acquainted with his cultural heritage, for, they ask, how can an individual survive in a culture about which he knows nothing? Therefore, the classical realist's curriculum consists of the transmission of Western culture built up over the centuries. Literature, language, history, government, and mathematics are heavily stressed. Classical realists also insist on the complete mastery of basic skill subjects—reading, writing, and arithmetic—in the elementary schools.[7] Classical realists, although they are not numerous, are extremely effective in publicizing their views. As is their right in a pluralistic democracy, they have persuaded many of the correctness of their position.

Improvement of Society In this century another group of thinkers, called "pragmatists," became quite active in formulating goals of American education. Led by the American philosopher John Dewey, pragmatists saw the goal of American education as twofold: to transmit our way of life to school children and, at the same time, to improve this way of life.[8] Actually, of course, all education is designed to pass on a particular way of life; Dewey and the pragmatists did not come up with anything new in this respect. But the second part of Dewey's goal was somewhat novel. The belief that schools exist to improve our society gripped the imagination of many teachers and educators.

Such a philosophical goal is rather difficult to understand and to implement. Exactly how do teachers go about deciding what needs to be improved? Obviously, in a pluralistic society, there will be a good deal of disagreement as to what should be retained, what should be refined, modified, and improved. In our society some people would love to see a return of our nineteenth-century economic system; some are quite happy with economic policies the way they are now; and

---

[7] The most widely read advocate of this point of view is the former chancellor of the University of Chicago, Robert M. Hutchins. Most of his books deal with his educational proposals. See, for example, *The Higher Learning in America* (New Haven: Yale U. Press, 1937).

[8] John Dewey, *Democracy and Education* (New York: Macmillan, 1916).

others wish to change many types of economic arrangements. This, of course, raises the following question: Since there is very little agreement as to the goodness or badness of our economic system, which aspects of our economic way of life should be retained and which should be changed or eliminated? Needless to say, this question has not been solved to the satisfaction of many people, in or out of education.

Development of Critical Thinking   Another group of thinkers, also influenced by John Dewey, has a somewhat different educational goal. Briefly, this goal is to develop the thinking abilities of all students. Advocates of this goal wish to see students taught to become proficient thinkers. The problem here, of course, is deciding exactly what is meant by "thinking" and "good thinking" and who is to decide.[9] The proponents of this goal answer that by "thinking" they are referring to a process called either "decision-making" or "problem-solving." And they wish to see each student become an individual who can take responsibility for making his own choices. They deplore unthinking, blind conformity to custom. By setting up a curriculum that would give students experience in choice-making, or thinking, they believe they can improve both the individual and society.

Development of the Individual   There is another goal of education that probably commands the allegiance of almost all American public-school teachers. This goal, simply stated, is to allow each student to develop to the maximum limits of his ability. This particular goal has its roots in our own history and is probably a peculiarly American ideal. What it means is that each and every student, no matter what his race, religion, or nationality, is to have those experiences in schools that will make him the best, most completely fulfilled person he is capable of becoming.

That such a goal is lofty and ambitious is obvious. That it has commanded the allegiance of many people—teachers and laymen—for many years is also obvious. What is not obvious is just how this goal is to be realized. What does it mean to "develop" a child? Can we identify the traits or talents that ought *not* be developed? How, in a class of thirty children, is one teacher supposed to develop each individual? What are the techniques of "developing"?

These questions cannot be answered definitively because most educational aims have a major weakness: They are usually worded so vaguely that it is impossible to know what they mean. That is, the

---

[9] One author who attempts to deal with this question is Ernest E. Bayles, *Democratic Educational Theory* (New York: Harper, 1960).

average teacher does not know how a given aim is to be understood or implemented in the day-by-day work of the classroom.

Character Building   There is still another aim of education, one that is quite attractive to many. Although this goal is quite difficult to describe, it has to do with the creation or formation of a very desirable kind of person. The advocates of this aim are often called "idealists." ("Idealism" as used here is a technical educational term and is not to be confused with the ordinary use of the word "idealist" to mean someone with high ideals.) There is not complete agreement among idealists as to exactly what this very desirable person would be like. However, most idealists agree that the person would have such traits as generosity, concern for others, unselfishness, cooperativeness, ability to carry through with a hard job, good work habits, and honesty. In addition, the idealist is much concerned that education should teach all children to appreciate beauty in their lives. The curriculum of the idealists, as might be expected, is heavy with languages and literature, art, and music. In addition, students are constantly impressed with the need to develop character traits such as those mentioned above. The idealist teacher wishes to mold his students to become truly good persons.

Eclectic Goals   Eclecticism is usually defined as the mixing of components of different theories. The author believes that there is no one overriding goal of American education; rather our educational system has incorporated all of the above goals—and more, too! If each teacher in our country were committed to but one educational goal, and if all teachers had the same goal, there would be no major social problem involving educational aims. But this is just not so: the people of the United States are extremely eclectic in their educational aims.

Eclecticism needs to be seen in light of intra- and interpersonal conflict. Most teachers in parochial schools believe in the goal that emphasizes the creation of persons holy enough to reach union with God. It is very likely that many—perhaps most—teachers (and professors) of science hold to a view like classical realism; they wish to acquaint their students with a body of knowledge that they consider absolutely essential. Many teachers of literature and the arts are somewhat inclined to accept an idealistic educational aim; they seem to think that students who study the lives of great and noble men will develop desirable character traits.[10] Many instructors of social science (or, as it is called in public schools, social studies) hope that their students

---

[10] See Sherwin S. Shermis, "Education and the Absolute Temper," *The Educational Forum*, 26 (May, 1962): 481-485.

will learn enough about the operations of society so that they will be able to improve it. And in all likelihood, most teachers would acknowledge the importance of developing clear thinking habits.

But eclecticism leads to a fundamental problem on an *intra*personal level. A given teacher may wish to further two, three, or all of the educational goals described above. Like the person with a noneducational intrapersonal conflict, such a teacher may believe in one goal at one time and another goal at another time. Or he may hold two or more goals simultaneously.

The questions then arise: Why can't a teacher be eclectic about his educational goals? What's wrong with holding two, three, four, or all these goals? These are very difficult questions to answer. Much depends on one's philosophical assumptions. It is obvious that it would be silly, in a society as pluralistic and eclectic as ours, to label eclecticism a terrible folly. However, we should like to point out the actual operational difficulties with conflicting goals of education.[11]

For instance, a teacher who has decided that producing a good person is a valid educational goal and who has also decided what a good person ought to be like quite naturally will do everything he can to make his students "good." He will reward "good" behavior and punish "bad" behavior. If he values loyalty, for example, he will attempt, by word and deed, to make his students intensely loyal; any behavior that seems disloyal will be dealt with as bad behavior. The student will be admonished to change his ways.

But the goal of developing independent thinking is often in direct conflict with the desire to make students into "good" people. What the teacher who advocates independent thinking wishes to accomplish is to get his students to understand the issues—on their own. He will guide thought, of course, but he will carefully refrain from forcing his own convictions on his students. What he wants is students who can think their way clearly to their own sets of personal convictions; students who understand, students who, independently of their teacher, can judge a situation and carefully and deliberately make a choice.

What happens to the teacher who unconsciously adopts both of these frequently conflicting goals? How is it possible for him to persuade students at 9:00 A.M. of the essential goodness and truth of his position and at 10:00 A.M. guide his students to reach (perhaps quite different) decisions independently? Implementation of the first goal

---

[11] An educational theorist who dealt with this topic at considerable length was the late Boyd Henry Bode, an associate of John Dewey's. See, for instance, Bode's *Conflicting Psychologies of Learning* (Boston: Heath, 1929).

necessitates the teacher's persuading and convincing his students. Implementation of the second goal involves permitting students to arrive at decisions of their own. Since the furthering of each of these educational goals leads in different directions, the teacher who incorporates both of them is like the man who mounts a horse and rides off in all directions. Teaching that "rides off in all directions" is at best ineffective and at worst extremely confusing.

We have by no means described all of the goals of education. Some of these aims stand in sharp conflict with each other. Most teachers do not appear to realize that there are many, different, and conflicting educational values. Consequently most teachers tend to be eclectic, now holding to one aim of education as being the most important, now emphasizing another, quite different end. The consequences of this eclecticism are ineffectiveness and confusion. The teacher who holds conflicting goals is apt to confuse his students, for inconsistent beliefs —to repeat the point—lead to inconsistent practices.

*Whose Values Should Be Taught?**

by MAX BIRNBAUM

Max Birnbaum is Education Consultant of the American Jewish Committee and a staff member of the Boston University Laboratory of Human Relations. Mr. Birnbaum has written widely about adult education in professional journals and was a contributing author to the HANDBOOK OF ADULT EDUCATION, 1960.

In a society in which there is general agreement on what constitutes the good, the true, and the beautiful, the task of teaching values is a simple one. The consensus is clear and, even if minority views exist, they do not challenge the majority judgment effectively. But in a pluralist society, in which no general agreement has been reached, the problem becomes infinitely more difficult.

* Max Birnbaum, "Whose Values Should Be Taught?" *Saturday Review*, 47 (June 20, 1964): 60-62, 67. By permission of the editor and the author.

Teaching values in American classrooms today, therefore, is an awesome assignment. For, as a nation, we are caught between the myths of a rural past that has all but disappeared, and the new urban present that has not yet achieved its final form. While our backs were turned, profound changes took place not only in our values, but in the very sources from which they come. While our sights were focused on older, simpler patterns of thought and conduct, far more complex problems and issues were beginning to challenge our society. No longer, for instance, can we teach the principle of equality for all without recognizing its unique meaning for the American Negro; nor can we discuss traditional concepts of religious liberty without taking into account the recent Supreme Court decisions on Bible reading and prayer in the classroom, and the role played by the new assertiveness of Catholics and Jews in many areas of our national life.

(Some teachers who live and work in areas of the country where religious, racial, and ethnic differences are not acute will insist that such problems are alien to the American Way. But many others have experienced the problems of emerging difference at first hand and are aware of the vast changes that have taken place.)

Yet the dramatic changes that have marked the development of contemporary attitudes did not come without warning. If we take even a brief backward look at our nation's history, we can see that they evolved over a period of several decades.

The American colonies were settled originally by Protestant, English-speaking people of Anglo-Saxon origin. Almost from the beginning this group was joined by those who were non-Protestant, non-Anglo-Saxon, and even non-English-speaking. But the names of the signers of the Declaration of Independence and the membership of the Constitutional Convention, almost 150 years after the earliest settlements, still reflected the continued dominance of the first group. This persistence of control is most remarkable in view of fairly sound historical evidence that almost 40 per cent of the inhabitants of the United States in 1790 were of non-English-speaking origin.

American culture, its values, institutions, and mores are primarily, although not exclusively, the creation of that remarkable group of men whose origins, immediate and remote, were the British Isles. To be sure, the group absorbed innumerable sons and daughters from other religions and cultures, but its Protestant Anglo-Saxon imprint continued to be highly visible.

The Civil War and the rise of industrial America contributed directly to changes in the religious and ethnic composition of the nation.

Most new immigrants in the years immediately after the Civil War were German and Irish. These were followed by people from Southern and Eastern Europe, of Slavic and Italian origin and Jews from the Austro-Hungarian empire, Poland, and Russia. Part of the native American's horror-stricken reaction to the city of the late nineteenth century came from the fact that it was crowded by people with strange tongues and stranger behavior. By the turn of the century, when immigrants of English origin were fast becoming a minority, voices were saying that unless something were done to stem the tide, the character of our civilization would change drastically.

Just as the Civil War was in many ways the "Second American Revolution" in its impact on our society, so 1914 marked the end not only of our isolation from world involvement, but also of our unitary society. The values and mores derived from our historically dominant religious and ethnic groups were being challenged. As a result, in the years following 1914, we witnessed the imposition of immigration quotas based upon a philosophy of Nordic Supremacy, the Great Depression and the fundamental changes it brought in the relations of the state to our citizenry, and the successive challenges to the old order by Catholic, Jew, and now the Negro. In the light of these swift and truly revolutionary changes, it is not remarkable that our schools have had difficulty in promulgating a common set of values. What is amazing is that they have done as well as they have.

Of the half century since 1914, perhaps the most significant years were the 1920's. For they marked a climactic period during which those conflicts that had raged sporadically just beneath the surface of public awareness were revealed publicly. The fears of those who felt that this country was theirs by right of birth and ancestral domain were intensified by the 1910 steel strike and rumors of Bolshevik infiltration. The American Legion had been organized in Paris in response to similar fears, when all of Europe appeared to be going communist. The United States, with its polyglot population, seemed a natural target for such subversion. But the most significant impact on America came from the immigration debates that raged for almost a decade in Congress and throughout the nation, in which terms such as the "alien flood," the "barbarian hordes," and the "forign tide" were freely used.

The debates when stripped to their essentials reveal that: (1) the dominant voices in our society used basically racist arguments to stigmatize those who had immigrated from Southern and Eastern Europe; (2) descent from English-speaking ancestors from the British Isles was deemed sufficient guarantee of superior capacity to assume the responsibilities and privileges of American citizenship; (3) American labor, despite its origins, was willing to be swayed by economic need to shut the doors of the nation even against its own kin; (4) the new American patriotic coalition, which emerged at this time, spearheaded the drive for restriction of immigration as an expression of nationalism and a fear of socialism and communism.

Although minority peoples formed protective organizations in response to a variety of special needs, the defensive character of these groups was intensified by the use of ethnic group classifications in the National Origins Act that determined all future quotas for immigration into the United States. From that point on, the right to enter America and become a citizen was defined not in individual but in group terms. The Irish had already learned the uses of ethnic group politics; other immigrant groups were now to follow in their footsteps, and group pressures soon became common in all areas of national life, including the schools.

The end of unrestricted immigration created a condition quite different from that which had been intended by the architects of the restrictive immigration policy. In two generations, all citizens of Eastern European descent had become native, rather than foreign-born Americans. But for many the group consciousness stimulated by the National Origins Act helped to strengthen rather than lessen their adherence to the values of the groups from which they sprang. Aided by awareness of service on behalf of country in two World Wars, the minority religious and ethnic groups began increasingly to assert their rights. Subsequently, the American Negro returned from the Allies' victory over German Nazism, determined to destroy racism here as well.

The decade of the Thirties witnessed two events of overwhelming importance to all Americans that had special poignancy for Catholics and Jews—and that also demonstrate the complexity of group loyalties in American society. The first was the Spanish Civil War. The nation, with the exception of the Catholics, was largely sympathetic to the Republican cause. The fact that Germany and Italy were aiding Franco, and Soviet Russia was aiding the Loyalists, created disastrous divisions among religious, ethnic, and political groupings. The issue was in large measure, for the Catholics and Jews, a matter of opposing the ally who was most threatening to them at the time. For the Jews it was obviously Hitler; for the Catholics it was Stalin; Protestants, and the unchurched generally, except for those who feared and hated the Soviet more than anything else, were either neutral or pro-Republican.

Then came the war against the Axis powers. A significant number of Americans, reflecting predominantly Catholic and Protestant groups, some of whom were of German ancestry, felt that we were fighting the wrong enemy. When Stalin and the Soviet Union became our major antagonists in the period after the Second World War, those group that had opposed our fighting as an ally of Russia came into their own. Their passionate opposition to American foreign policy had been long pent-up and the beginning of the Cold War provided them with final justification for their feelings.

Senator McCarthy was in many respects a charismatic champion of this submerged cause. A Midwestern Irish Catholic, elected from a state with a very large German ethnic population, he provided precisely the kind of ruthless hostility toward Communism that would satisfy the loose coalition of those who had always felt that Russia was the true threat to America. A Gallup Poll during the period of McCarthy's greatest influence showed Jews overwhelmingly opposed to him, the Catholics strongly in his favor, and Protestants divided. The strongly Protestant hinterlands of the Middle West and Southwest supported him, and the urban, Northwestern, and Far Western Protestants strongly opposed him. The endurance of attitudes based on religious and ethnic considerations has rarely been more clearly demonstrated than during this conflict. And, as we shall see, recent problems and patriotism are still intertwined with this legacy of the past.

At this point it should be revealing to analyze three basic issues that have presented serious problems for teachers, in terms of the group forces operating in our contemporary society. Obviously, the most significant value-laden issues for public schools have been the place of religion and religious values in the curriculum, the teaching of patriotism, and the closely related issue of teaching about communism. The impact of race on our schools is also of prime importance, but this will be treated separately because of the unusual character of the group forces reflected in the racial crisis.

Before applying a group relations theory to explain these complicated issues, however, certain qualifications should be stated. No one theory can explain complex group behavior. Few observers after the election of 1960 would deny the persistence of religious, ethnic, and racial loyalties. The significant shift of Democratic Protestants to Nixon and a similar shift of Republican Catholics to Kennedy is evidence enough. What is not explained by any simple cause and effect analysis is why so many Protestants, for example, voted for

Kennedy, and why so many Catholics voted for Nixon. Economic factors, ethnic backgrounds, regional biases, personal preferences largely free of group loyalties or pressures, would have to be investigated. Jews and Negroes, on the other hand, voted in overwhelming numbers for Kennedy. The Democratic Party, especially in the Northern cities, still retains the loyalty of these and other minority religious and racial groups. The appointment of two Jews to Kennedy's Cabinet, and the subsequent appointment to that powerful and symbolic body of an Italo-American and a Polish-American, with a tacit commitment to include a Negro eventually as well, makes very plain indeed that the old Protestant, Anglo-Saxon order has changed.

With this *caveat* stated, let us consider the two major problem areas that have both openly and subtly affected the teaching of values and value-laden subjects during the past two decades—religion and patriotism. Both problems differ markedly from region to region and stubbornly refuse to respond to simple analysis. But after saying this, we are also reasonably certain that on both issues Catholics and Jews have been overwhelmingly on opposite sides, and that Protestants, once again, have split down the middle, in a pattern very similar to that which prevailed during the 1930's and through the McCarthy period.

The growing agreement between the politically and theologically liberal Protestants and the Jews with similar views has been an important factor in Protestant sensitivity to Jewish hostility toward religious influences in the public schools. Prayer, Bible reading, and excessively Christological observances of Christmas and Easter are cases in point. And most of the leaders of the larger Protestant denominations, together with a few Catholics, have gone along with the recent Supreme Court decisions on prayer and Bible reading. (To be sure, the awareness of Protestant leaders that the more important issue is public support of parochial education undoubtedly influenced many to make what is a comparatively small sacrifice in order to build additional legal bulwarks against the potential diversion of public funds.) Common commitment to public education, similar attitudes on censorship, birth control, and a host of other religiously value-laden issues make for easy communication and accommodation between these Protestants and most Jewish groups.

Most Catholic spokesmen, on the other hand, originally opposed the Supreme Court decisions in terms that were surprisingly similar in tone to the declarations of the Protestant South and Middle West. Increased secularization of the public schools is seen as a direct threat to conservative Protestants, and as an attack on religion in public life by Catholics.

Beyond this point, however, the two groups differ. And unless the essentially unstable character of this coalition is comprehended, it is virtually impossible to understand the unpredictable strengths and weaknesses of its pressures on the schools. The largest segment of Protestants opposed to the elimination of prayer and other religious observances in the classroom also opposes with the greatest vigor any grant of public funds to Catholic parochial schools or any move that would increase Catholic influence. Fundamentally, the purely religious loyalties of the two parties to the coalition are directly opposed to each other. For instance, consider the Catholic opposition to public school baccalaureate services throughout the Middle West and the opposition of Protestants to an ambassador to the Vatican.

When the topics of divorce, family relationships, and the nature of authority arise, members of each of the two coalitions again find themselves in agreement. The question of school discipline is a revealing touchstone, for here, too, with some exceptions, the Jews and liberal Protestants tend to be more child-centered and less concerned with traditional forms of authority and discipline. The fundamentalist Protestants and most Catholics tend in the opposite direction. Attitudes toward the subject of mental health divide similarly. What we have in essence is a serious culture conflict, with powerful groups arrayed against each other along fairly distinct religious lines.

The issue of patriotism and the related problem of communism are directly associated with this culture conflict. Reliance on familiar religious forms, hostility to anti-religious forces, zealous support for traditional forms of authority, a highly developed sense of individual property rights, plus a strong nationalist bias would immediately predispose the conservative coalition to react to the serious threat of the cold war with traditional solutions. Their support for a program of indoctrination in the schools, the feeling that there should be no compromise with evil, and a strong sense of what is right and what is wrong, the insistence that there is good only on our side and nothing but evil "out there" are but a public restatement in pedagogical terms of the manner in which members of the coalition were reared—or believe they were reared.

The opposite approach is also easy to comprehend if we interpret the religious, ethnic, and regional influences on those who support it. The coalition of liberal Protestants and Jews reflects basically a yearning for peace, an effort to achieve possible accommodation with the cold war enemy, and a recognition that authoritarian solutions are difficult if not impossible to achieve. (To be sure, the liberal coalition has at times seemed to be so unaware of the harsher realities of peace and power politics as to cause their opponents to question both their patriotism and their competence to administer affairs of state.) This group also displays a considerably smaller degree of nationalism, and their support of the U.N. is, therefore, firm. In direct contrast, the conservative religious coalition reflects strong suspicion and outright hostility to the U.N. and its affiliated agencies, especially UNESCO. And finally, the liberal coalition's memory of Hitler predisposes its members to be especially vigilant in opposing any excessive anti-communism that tends to bracket communism with liberalism.

What impact the recent shift in emphasis and viewpoint within the Roman Catholic Church will have on issues that concern the public schools is a matter for speculation. Very likely, leading Catholic spokesmen will join with the liberal coalition on selected issues at first, but ultimately, the full import of the Catholic Church's ecumenical effort to reorient itself for participation in a religiously and racially pluralist society will make itself felt—and with profound effects on the American public school scene. This realignment will not only have profound influence on the atmosphere in which values are taught— possibly making the job easier—but it may also lead to further experiments in closer cooperation between public and parochial schools such as shared-time programs.

The racial problem has been reserved for separate treatment for several reasons. Race in our culture has been an infinitely more difficult barrier to surmount than religious or ethnic background, and the Negro has been compelled to condense into a few short years what for other groups has been decades of organization and effort. The violence of the Negro thrust can only be understood when we remember what happens when a coiled spring, compressed to its utmost, is suddenly released. The election of 1960 was won with the strong surge of Negro votes in the major Northern city strongholds of the Democratic Party. What has happened since has been the presentation of a bill for payment for services rendered. This process is as old as the political realities of American elections.

The Negroes, who are primarily Protestant, although there is a sizable Catholic minority, have hardly engaged in "religious politics"; their overriding concern has been the question of race. So basic is the issue of color that increasingly the Negroes have become a separate entity, considered as a third force in addition to the two religious coalitions. This condition will undoubtedly continue for some time to come. Ironically, in the last few years the cause of equality for the Negro has become the first occasion for a remarkable degree of cooperation and collaboration among the three major religious faiths. Short of war, this has not happened before. (There are other signs that cooperation on behalf of the cause of the Negro may be the first of a series of collaborations on crucial issues, such as U.N. support and world peace.)

The Negro, with the help of his white allies, has turned to the schools with a host of demands that have upset public education as seldom before. This is true not only in the South, where the issue has been a matter of constitutional right, but also in the North, where the school has become the major instrumentality for the symbolic—if not actual—end of racial segregation. Balked at ending residential segregation immediately, and unable to secure the kinds of jobs that satisfy their rising expectations, the Negroes have turned on the schools with a series of demands. Almost overnight the problems of the education of deprived children and the school drop-out have become predominantly the problems of Negro children. They have also become the two most discussed educational problems since the post-Sputnik overhaul of science and mathematics teaching. The reverberation of this onslaught will affect the teaching of history and social problems, textbook revision, the nature of teaching, the organization of schools, and practically every other facet of education. But what is perhaps most meaningful for the teaching of social values is that the militancy of the civil rights movement has heightened our awareness of the fact that so many of our values reflect a white culture with unconscious as well as conscious biases. These will be repeatedly challenged from now on. Excessive sensitivity that has led to attacks on *Huckleberry Finn* and other classics will undoubtedly abate in the future, but the period immediately ahead promises to be a very stormy one for schools and teachers.

The gradual dissolution of a homogeneous, Anglo-Saxon, Protestant society, the appearance of the conservative and liberal religious coalitions, and the emergence of the racial crisis will necessarily lead either to a truly pluralist society or to chaos. The problem for the public schools, of course, is especially acute. Caught for the past two decades in a religio-ethnic crossfire, they are suddenly also beset by racial conflicts. Their only salvation is to begin immediately to bring to bear all our present knowledge and experience to develop ground rules for teaching and learning in a diverse society that will conserve our basic values and still accommodate the emerging social order. Fortunately,

such a pluralist solution is in harmony with the spirit of our democratic ideal and the reality of our constitutional tradition. But the task
will be a difficult one—far more difficult and complex than most of us
have yet admitted.

A Crisis of Purpose*

by ARTHUR E. BESTOR

*Arthur E. Bestor is professor of history at the University of
Washington, Seattle. He is famous as a critic of American education, being the former president of the Council for Basic Education and having written two scorching criticisms of American
schools—*THE RESTORATION OF LEARNING *and* EDUCATIONAL
WASTELANDS. *Mr. Bestor has also written or collaborated on a
number of books in the field of history.*

The present crisis in the American public-school system is, at bottom, a crisis of purpose. Low achievement is the consequence of low
aims. Confusion about the purposes of the high school has produced
the shortcomings so appallingly evident today. In an article published
in 1952 I spoke of the problem as "Aimlessness in Education." May I
repeat what I said then, five years before Sputnik: "If we really believe
that education is vital to our safety, then we need to know exactly
what kind of schooling constitutes genuine education, and what kind is
merely a gaudy show."[1]

For twenty-five years, at least, the purposes of our high schools
have been determined by a narrow group of educational theorists who
like to describe themselves as "professional" educators—thereby imply-
ing that a college professor in the liberal arts or sciences (who may
devote a lifetime to teaching) is somehow an amateur in education.
Contemptuously rejecting the views of the scholarly and scientific
world, these professional educationalists have redefined the purpose of
both elementary and secondary schools in terms that are almost com-

* Arthur E. Bestor, "A Crisis of Purpose," *Vital Speeches of the Day*, 24 (September 15, 1958): 723-728. By permission of the publisher and the author.

[1] *Scientific Monthly*, vol. 75, pp. 109-116 (August 1952).

pletely non-intellectual, and that are often belligerently anti-intellectual. Year by year, the high-school curriculum has come to have less and less connection with the real world of mature intellectual activity. As a consequence, the American high school now prepares its students for a grotesque dream world, where science and mathematics do not count (though in the real world they underlie our whole technology), where foreign languages are unnecessary (though in the real world our responsibilities as a world power make them indispensable), where history can be overlooked (though the real world is a changing world, which history alone can interpret).

The educational theory that dominates our public-school system today is an attempt to escape from reality, not an effort to grapple with the actual intellectual problems of the contemporary world. To conceal this fact, professional educationists insist that the school should not be judged in terms of the intellectual achievement of its students. The school is to be looked upon as a welfare agency performing a variety of social services, of which intellectual training is merely one and a relatively minor one. Let us examine this argument in its own terms.

The public schools enroll virtually all the young people of the nation. These young people are facing all sorts of personal problems. They must all eventually make a living, hence the question of a well-paid future job is much on their minds. They are all growing up—a disconcerting, even painful, experience—and they can well be "mixed up" without being "crazy." A substantial number of these young people have a most unsatisfactory home life. Poverty, the divorce of their parents, discriminations practised against them as members of a minority group create in them deep-seated emotional and psychological disturbances. Problems like these are much more real to vast numbers of the young people than are the problems presented by *Macbeth*, by algebra, by grammar, by the American constitution, or by the reaction of hydrochloric acid with zinc.

Taking these facts as their starting point, professional educationists insist that the public school must try to solve all the resulting problems. "It is the job of the school," according to a pronouncement of one of the most influential bodies of American professional educators, "to meet the common and the specific individual needs of youth."[2] Because a young man's need for a job is so evident, the school should make every effort to help him "develop salable skills." For a young

[2] National Association of Secondary-School Principals, *Planning for American Youth* (Washington, 1944), p. 10.

woman, cooking and sewing and homemaking should be a central feature of the program. If a child comes from a broken home, then the
school must devote its main effort to giving him a sense of security.
When young people reach adolescence, and begin to feel excited and
disturbed about the opposite sex, the school must move in on the problem with courses in sex education. If accidents are increasing, the
school must teach youngsters to drive. Since personal appearance
counts for so much, the school ought to show girls how to dress attrac-
tively and how to use make-up, and boys how to be well-groomed.

Educationists who look upon the school's responsibility in this way
believe that every school activity must be placed on a par with every
other. If a pupil is getting some kind of practical training that he
needs, then he is being "educated," regardless of any intellectual content in what he is doing. To say that one activity is any more "educational" than another—to treat one kind of study as intrinsically more
worthwhile and important than another—would be undemocratic. The
Educational Policies Commission (set up by the National Education
Association and one of its departments) undertook a few years ago to
describe an ideal school program in an imaginary community, which
it called Farmville. The Commission stated the principle thus: "There
is no aristocracy of 'subjects' in the Farmville curriculum. Mathematics
and mechanics, art and agriculture, history and homemaking are all
peers."[3]

Intellectual training gets short shrift in such a conception of education. Educationists who view the school program in this way are apt
to think of intellectual training as simply a special form of vocational
training, rather than as an exciting venture in ideas, important in its
own right and vital to intelligent citizenship. Science and mathematics,
these educationists assume, are appropriate only for the few who are
going to be scientists or engineers or doctors. History and English,
they believe, are for the minority who plan to be writers or historians
or lawyers. Pupils destined for other jobs, the educationists insist, can
get along without these forms of knowledge, or with minimum dos-
ages.

Another aspect of this philosophy must be noted. Many of the social
and psychological problems of young people can be handled more
effectively through extra-curricular activities—editing the school paper,
planning class parties, running student government, managing athletic
teams, and the like—than in a formal classroom. Because the handling

[3] Educational Policies Commission, *Education for All American Youth* (Washington, 1944), p. 142.

of these personal problems is so important, educationists wish to erase the traditional line between the curriculum (the course of study) and the other activities connected with the school, thus permitting youngsters to devote all or most of their time to activities rather than studies.

The shift of emphasis from intellectual to non-intellectual activities in the school leads to some extremely odd statements about the things with which the school should concern itself. One such document from Illinois is worth citing. Under the auspices of the state, a certain professor of education undertook to list the "real-life problems" of young people, which the school should attempt to deal with by a "reorientation" of its curriculum. Among the fifty-five items on the list there was no mention whatever of any branch of science or mathematics, though "camping" and "doing parlor stunts" rated specific attention. Here are some of the problems, put forward in all seriousness as proper concerns of the school: "The problem of developing one or more 'making things,' 'making it go,' or 'tinkering' hobbies," "The problem of improving one's personal appearance," "the problem of developing and maintaining wholesome boy-girl relationships," and "the problem of selecting a 'family dentist' and acquiring the habit of visiting him systematically."[4]

I have no doubt that some thoughtless adolescents consider these "problems" significant enough for them to spend precious school time— *their* time, paid for by their parents and by the rest of us—in learning the answers. Did the American people, however, create a nationwide public-school system to deal with problems like these? They did not. Neither parents nor citizens at large originated these proposals. They were devised by doctrinaire educational theorists. Whatever public acceptance they have won is the result of irresponsible, high-pressure salesmanship on the part of professional educationists.

The argument, briefly put, is that because a social need exists the school must therefore attempt to satisfy it. This is a complete *non sequitur*. The school is only one of the agencies that eixst to satisfy the needs of society. Each agency has its own area of responsibility, because each possesses a particular sort of competence. The particular competence of a school is in providing intellectual training. It was created for this purpose and its facilities and techniques—classrooms, laboratories, libraries; assignments, recitations, lectures, examinations— are adapted to this particular end. To subordinate this end to something else (no matter how worthy) is to deprive society of a vital service that no other agency can provide.

[4] Harold C. Hand, "Problems of High School Youth," in Illinois Secondary School Curriculum Program, Bulletin No. 11, pp. 30-32 (August 1950).

When a school takes over a function that it is less competent to perform than some existing social agency, the net effect is to impair the welfare of society, not to improve it. Family life is said to have deteriorated in the United States. The public schools have made a great fuss over courses in "home and family living." Nothing in the present situation suggests that such courses have succeeded in reducing the divorce rate or accomplishing any of the other results so glowingly promised. On the other hand, there is good reason to believe that the influence of the home upon young people has been seriously undermined by the very effort of the school to take over functions properly belonging to the family. The promise that the school will effectively perform these functions is a promise that cannot possibly be kept. Nevertheless the irresponsible utterances of educationists about taking over responsibilities that the home has neglected contribute to the very breakdown they are talking about. Their words are an encouragement to weak-minded parents to dump their problems on the school instead of dealing with them as they should.

There is, of course, one kind of school that can and does assume responsibility for the entire life of the young person in its charge. This is the full-time residential or boarding school. Such a school stands *in loco parentis*, exercising the authority and assuming the responsibility of the home. It provides medical services. It enforces discipline twenty-four hours a day. It furnishes recreation. It usually sponsors religious services, making itself the channel through which the church performs its functions. Under these circumstances the influence of every social agency except the school is suspended, and the school not only can but must take over their duties.

A strong argument can be made (as, indeed, Admiral Rickover has done) for creating in the United States a large number of full-time residential schools, in which public funds would provide both subsistence and tuition for the students enrolled. Such schools would be capable of assuming the responsibilities that American educationists are talking about. But educationists are not urging the creation of such schools. They are asking that the public schools, as they now exist, assume these wide-ranging responsibilities. They close their eyes to the basic fact that the American public school is a *day school*, which has charge of the student for no more than half (and usually much less than half) of each waking day, for only five days out of each week's seven. During the greater part of his conscious life, a student is under the influence of—within the sphere of control of—other institutions of society, upon which responsibility also rests. There must be a distribution of function among the various agencies of society, the school included, because there is a distribution of time among them. The school has responsibility for part, but only part, of his time. *Which* part of the child's upbringing, given this distribution of function, is the peculiar and inescapable responsibility of the school?

The experience, practice, and policy of a residential school is peculiarly relevant in this connection. Though such a school must assume responsibility for the entire life of its students, it never permits a blurring of the line that separates the curriculum from the rest of its activities. Formal classroom periods are devoted to basic intellectual disciplines and uninterrupted study periods are set aside. All other functions are performed outside the curriculum. Now, the time available to the day school is roughly the equivalent of the time devoted in a residential school to the curriculum proper. A student can expect to receive an education of equal depth and value in a public day school only if the same number of classroom periods are devoted to serious intellectual training as would be the case in a residential school, and only if the public school insists upon homework equal in amount to the work done in the study periods that a residential school sets aside in the evenings and on weekends and holidays. If a public day school purports to offer a genuine education—rather than a watered-down imitation—then it must prevent any and every encroachment upon the time that students devote to study of the fundamental intellectual disciplines. School administrators must draw a sharp line between the curriculum and extra-curricular activities. In the time available to the school for the latter—for activities over and above the basic curriculum —it can accomplish many desirable vocational and social ends. Athletics, shop-work, cooking, and driver-training are perfectly legitimate *extra curricular* activities, recognized as valuable in the most traditional schools. "The battle of Waterloo," Wellington is supposed to have said, "was won in the playing fields of Eton."[5] Every good school accomplishes much besides intellectual training. Only by distinguishing clearly between the classroom and the playing field, however, can serious and honest results be achieved by either.

The school must plan its program in terms of the time that has been made available to it. Most of the time made available in America to the public school is *curricular* time, within which the school is under solemn obligation to plan a continuous, cumulative, uninterrupted program of intellectual training. A small balance of time is also available for extra-curricular activities under supervision of the school. The school, if honest and responsible, must promise, in the way of voca-

[5] *Oxford Dictionary of Quotations* (2nd ed., London, 1953), p. 564.

tional training and social conditioning, no more than it can perform within the limits of this *extra-curricular* segment of time. Before embarking on vast programs purporting to advance social, psychological, and vocational purposes, the school must demand and receive from society whatever additional allotments of student time (as well as whatever additional allotments of money) may be necessary to carry out such programs. If, for example, the school is really to take over the responsibilities of the home, it must take time away from the home life of the student and must be vested with the disciplinary authority of the home. Barring such a grant of time, authority, and money (a grant most unlikely to be forthcoming), the school has no business promising—or even consenting—to assume responsibility for tasks that are outside its province. Indeed, until the school has proved itself willing to carry out honestly, thoroughly, and unremittingly its assigned task of intellectual training, there is no reason in the world for society to say to it, "Well done, thou good and faithful servant: thou hast been faithful over a few things, I will make thee ruler over many things."

The contention that American public schools can carry on the miscellany of activities that professional educationists advocate, can introduce these activities into the curriculum itself, and can at the same time provide basic intellectual training of undiminished quality is a preposterous contention on its very face. The hard, unyielding statistics, moreover, show that American public schools, taken as a whole, have failed—calamitously failed—to provide the mass of our young people with intellectual training of the quality and thoroughness required in the modern world. The frantic efforts of professional educationists to manipulate and, as a last resort, to suppress the figures have not succeeded and will not succeed in concealing the facts of the present situation from a deeply alarmed citizenry.

Suppression is a harsh word, but what other term is applicable to the letter sent out on 25 March 1958 by the National Association of Secondary-School Principals (a department of the National Education Association) over the signature of its executive secretary, Dr. Paul E. Elicker? In a series of articles entitled "Crisis in Education," the magazine *Life* had expressed views which the directorate of this Association disliked. Promptly Dr. Elicker wrote officially to the 19,000 school administrators—public officials, mind you—enrolled in his organizations, using the following words:

> The only way to be effective in combatting a continuance of this type of irresponsible reporting is to write a letter to protest NOW to Mr. Roy Larsen, President, LIFE. . . . We know from experience with

another magazine a few years ago that your most effective weapon wi be to question the continuation of subscriptions to the LIFE and TIM publications in your school as long as they have an attitude and polic inimical to education.

Also, we suggest that you urge teachers, parents, and citizens to writ similar letters to Mr. Larsen. Of course, the force of your letter will b discounted if you indicate that you have been advised to write such letter.

I agree with the editorial in the Detroit (Michigan) *Free Pres* which commented that this clandestine effort to suppress free discus sion "exhibits motives no less base than those of a frightened but ruth less dictator." With a stroke of his pen, Dr. Elicker has done mor damage to public confidence in our schools than any man in our his tory. The secondary-school principals of the country—whose integrit and whose belief in democracy Dr. Elicker has gravely compromise in hundreds if not thousands of communities—should demand hi resignation.

Certain aspects of this sorry story have not received the attention they ought. Dr. Elicker based his undercover boycott on an allegation that certain statistical statements presented by *Life* were "mistakes an misinterpretations," and he circulated a memorandum by Professo Harold C. Hand to support the accusation. Many newspapers an individuals who condemned the boycott, nevertheless assumed tha *Life* had probably misrepresented the statistics, as charged. In fact, the magazine had done no such thing. Those who attacked *Life* were the ones who manipulated the figures. Let us look briefly at Professo Hand's memorandum. He first takes issue with the following statemen in *Life*: ". . . only 25% [of high school students in the United States are studying physics." This is the figure given by the United State Office of Education in its study of *Offerings and Enrollments in Sci ence and Mathematics in Public High Schools, 1956*. The enrollmen in physics was 24.3 percent of the total enrollment in the twelfth grad in that year.[6]

What does Professor Hand do to this straightforward, official sta tistic? Here are his words:

> We shall begin with the datum for physics. This figure of 25% is th
> approximate fraction of the students in grade twelve, the school level a

[6] Pamphlet No. 120, compiled by Kenneth E. Brown (Washington, 1957), p. 12 Actually, if *Life*'s statement were taken literally the figure it should have given would have been 4.4 percent not 24.3 percent, because the smaller precentage is the enroll ment in physics expressed as a percentage of *all* high-school students. Life took the base *most favorable* to the public-school record.

which this subject is usually taught, who are enrolled in physics. By the time they complete high school, then, this fraction of today's high-school student body has taken physics. This is about three-fourths of those in the upper third of the intelligence distribution, hence about three-fourths of those who presumably could do well in physics if they were to enroll in it.

What does this rigamarole come to? Professor Hand takes the unquestioned percentage and deliberately alters it, justifying his manipulation by the completely undocumented assertion that only the top third of the population is capable of studying physics. By this sleight-of-Hand, 25 percent miraculously becomes 75 percent. But even granting the right of Professor Hand to manipulate the statistics in this way, the final figure he gives is false. There are 2,300,000 seventeen-year-olds in the population.[7] The upper third would come to 767,000. Only 310,000 seventeen-year-olds are enrolled in physics.[8] This is not 75 percent of the upper third of the relevant population. *It is only 40.4 percent.* Professor Hand, moreover, conveniently forgets to mention that in the Soviet Union today, *100 percent* of those in the "upper third of the intelligence distribution" are studying physics, not for *one* year (as with us) but for *five.* Moreover, 100 percent *of the entire population* are studying it for two years—in the seven-year school, attendance at which is compulsory for all.[9]

Of all the statistics that are now available on Soviet education, the ones that reveal most strikingly the failure of our own school system are those that pertain to the curriculum of the first seven years. During these years, schooling has become universal in Russia as here. Our system has attained universality for a longer span of time, it is true—ten years instead of seven. But with three more years, we have failed to bring our students in mass up to the level, so far as fundamental fields are concerned, that is attained for the whole mass of Soviet students and attained at an earlier age.

Let me summarize the record, reminding you that I am comparing not a selected student body with an unselected one, but the student bodies of the two countries *for the period during which schooling is compulsory and universal for both.*

In the Soviet Union every young person reaches maturity with some knowledge of algebra and geometry, because two years of this

[7] Ibid., p. 44.

[8] Ibid.

[9] Alexander G. Korol, *Soviet Education for Science and Technology* (New York, 1957), pp. 3, 17, 26, 55, 57. These agree with the findings of the U.S. Office of Education, *Education in the USSR* (Bulletin, 1957, No. 14).

are required in the grades where universal schooling is in effect. In the United States only 60 percent of our young people reach maturity with some knowledge of algebra and geometry.

In the Soviet Union every young person reaches maturity with some systematically taught knowledge of biology, chemistry, and physics, derived from one to four years of course work in these specific fields in the first seven years of the Soviet schools. In the United States only three out of five of our young people reach maturity having had a course in biology, less than one quarter having had a course in chemistry, and little more than one-eighth having had a course in physics.

In the Soviet Union every child has studied a foreign language for at least three years before drop-outs begin. In the United States, fewer than one young person in twenty reach the age of eighteen having had three years of a foreign language.[10]

If we go on to the last years of the secondary school (the ten-year school in the U.S.S.R. and the high school in the U.S.), the comparisons are even more devastating. In what follows, be it observed, I am not offering unfair comparisons between selected and unselected Student Bodies. I am comparing *the proportion of total population* which reaches a give level of intellectual attainment in the Soviet Union, with the proportion of the total population which reaches the same level "or a lower one" in the United States.

In the Soviet Union the top third of all young people reach maturity with a knowledge of mathematics at least through trigonometry, normally the highest branch taught in secondary schools. In the United States only the top one-twelfth of all young people are reaching maturity with a command of mathematics at this level.

In the Soviet Union the top third of all young people reach maturity having studied physics for *five* years. In the United States only the top one-eighth reach maturity having studied physics for *one* year. Not a single American, in all probability, has studied the subject systematically for five years in an American high school.

In the Soviet Union the top third of all young people reach maturity having studied a foreign language for six years. In the United States, less than one percent of the population get as far as the fourth year of a foreign language in high school.

Let me remind you of the point of these comparisons. No one in

---

[10] Figures based on the studies previously cited. They are analyzed in greater detail in the author's article "The Choice Before Us in American Education," National University Extension Association, *Thirty-Second Discussion and Debate Manual,* 1958-59 ed. by *American Education:* Bower Aly, Vol. 1, pp. 65-86.

his senses would suggest that the United States should take over the Soviet educational system. There are far sounder and far better balanced school programs in the democratic countries of Western Europe. The question in any case is not whether we should have an American educational system or a European one. The question is whether the American educational system should be a good one or a poor one. The most important thing we can learn from European experience is to raise, immediately and by a substantial amount, our judgments about the intellectual ability of young people. Our expectations must go up, and our standards with them. We must repudiate the view that only a minority of American young people can be taught the basic subjects. Noting that Soviet educators harbor no such contemptuous opinion of the intellectual capacity of their own young people, we must deliver a stinging rebuke to those professional educationists who have persistently slandered the children of the American people as uneducable, and have used this malicious judgment as an excuse for selling them down the river.

With the restoration of faith in our young people will come a restoration to the school system of a clear sense of purpose. To replace the educational aimlessness of recent years, we need only return to the principles and aims that inspired the American public-school system at its creation. A simple definition of education, and a simple democratic corollary thereof, will suffice:

It is the job of a school to teach young men and women to think. It is the job of a *democratic* school to teach *all* young men and women to think.

If this is, in fact, the central purpose of education, the school must recognize, at the very outset, that certain studies are vastly more effective than others in developing the capacity to think clearly, seriously, and sustainedly. The school must, accordingly, select its subjects of instruction with infinite care. Typewriting, for example, is a very useful practical skill. It is a training of the fingers, however, rather than of the mind. History, by contrast, is a most unpromising pathway to lucrative employment. (I am an historian, and I speak from experience.) But history is a study that involves the careful weighing of evidence and the continuous exercise of critical judgment. Properly taught, it develops the kind of intellectual power that a democratic nation requires of all its responsible citizens. No matter how skillfully taught, typewriting cannot possibly lay claim to equal educational significance.

A school can do only a few things well, consequently the things it does must be the things of very greatest worth. Moreover, the school must organize its work carefully in order to do these things in the most effective way possible. How can one determine the things that it is most important for the school to do, and the ways of doing them that will be most effective? The answers to both questions can be found in the accumulated experience of three thousand years of intellectual and educational history.

Let us begin by examining the second question—the question of the most effective way of organizing school instruction. Many persons imagine that there is something arbitrary about the various fields of learning as they exist today. The phenomena of nature are all interrelated, they point out. Why isolate one aspect from another and make separate fields out of chemistry, physics, geology, botany, and zoology? Why not deal with the whole at once? The same argument is applied to society. Why study its various aspects separately under the labels of history, economics, political science, and jurisprudence? Again, why not tackle at once the living whole?

The best answer is that the experience of thousands of years has shown that the human mind is best able to grapple with complicated problems by breaking them down into their component parts. Once experience has been *analyzed*, it becomes possible to develop specialized intellectual skills for dealing with the different aspects of experience. These skills can be organized systematically, can be taught, and can be applied with enormous effectiveness to new problems. These organized skills constitute the various scientific and scholarly disciplines. (The latter is the scholar's word; the popular term "subjects" much used by educationists, is inaccurate and misleading, because it suggests that the disciplines are mere collections of facts, rather than methods of investigation and of thought.) Mathematics, history, economics, geology, chemistry, and psychology are examples of such disciplines. The reason for planning an educational curriculum in terms of them is that mankind has discovered that effective, creative, critical thinking can best be done by employing these systematic, organized tools of thought.

The scientific and scholarly disciplines, well-defined and efficiently organized, constitute the foundations of mature intellectual effort. These foundations must be laid in the elementary and high schools. Such, in brief, is the educational theory of scientists and scholars. Which disciplines, then, are basic to the *high-school curriculum?* The question is not really as difficult to answer as some people suppose.

In every age and every country, a person deemed educated must be able to use his own language correctly and fluently, and must be widely read in its literature. Accordingly, English is basic in an American school curriculum. This is obviously a scientific age, hence mathematics, physics, chemistry, and biology are obviously basic. We live in a rapidly changing world, hence history (whose subject is change) belongs among the basic secondary-school disciplines. International contacts are rapidly multiplying, hence foreign languages must be considered essential. Emphasis on the disciplines I have mentioned is simply a matter of common sense, dictated by the obvious facts about the intellectual life in the contemporary world.

Contrary to popular belief, scientists and scholars, both here and abroad, agree pretty well on the desirable basic curriculum of the secondary school. I know no reputable scholar who is anxious merely to advance his own subject. Scientists are as convinced of the importance of English and foreign languages as I (an historian) am convinced of the importance of science and mathematics. With very few dissenting voices, the scholarly world agrees that the high school should focus the efforts of all students upon five principal fields: the student's native language and its literature; at least one foreign language; mathematics; the natural sciences (specifically biology, chemistry, and physics), and history. The fine arts and music should have a recognized place, though perhaps on the basis of individual instruction. The various social sciences (economics, political science, sociology) might be introduced alongside, but not in replacement of, history, because their full elaboration usually takes place at the college level.

What we are after, of course, is not a mere list of "subjects," but a training in the basic disciplines of thought. The desirable curriculum can be described in terms of the intellectual skills that the high school should impart. It must, first of all, furnish its students with a store of knowledge, so that they will not be obliged to make bricks without straw. Secondly, it must require them to practice unceasingly the use of the recognized tools of language and thought: reading, mathematics, grammar, logic, and the rest. Beyond this, the school must give its students, at first hand through laboratory work, a grasp of the method of scientific investigation. It must teach them to weigh evidence as an historian does, and to construct therefrom a framework of chronology and historical explanation adequate to organize their accumulating knowledge about the development of their own country and the world. It must make them acquainted with the great ideas embodied in literature, and with the varied forms (poetry, fiction, drama, philosophic discourse) in which great ideas are expressed.

The school, moreover, must go at these tasks systematically. To think means to apply the mind continuously, often over long periods of time, to the problem at hand. The student must use his mind in this way in school. If he is expected to pick up "snippets" of information from one "project" after another—if his program skips about from topic to unrelated topic—then he will not go forth with a disciplined mind. He will have been trained as a mere intellectual grasshopper. Certain contrived "experiences" may be needed to arouse the first interest of young children, but once serious work has begun, the directing force of further study should be intellectual curiosity, and its organization should represent the logical unfolding of the subject itself. Once a serious subject is taken up there must be continuity, usually over a period of years. Four years of a foreign language, for example, are not twice as valuable as two, but ten or twenty times as valuable, thanks to the cumulative character of learning.

Progression, as well as continuity, is essential. The school must push its students steadily forward from simple intellectual tasks to increasingly complex and abstract ones. Mere "enrichment"—the multiplying of tasks at the same level of abstraction—does not mean intellectual growth; it may mean intellectual stagnation. Above all, the school must require its students to write, write, write—themes, examinations, original productions in prose and verse; each one to be corrected and criticized, for form as well as content—until young men and women are able, almost instinctively, to set down their own ideas, whatever the subject may be, with clarity, accuracy, cogency, and fluency.

An education of this kind is not one among several equally valuable kinds of education. It is the one kind that deliberately sets out to produce men and women capable of serious and sustained thinking. If we really believe in democracy, this is the kind of education we ought to bestow upon every single one of our future citizens. If we offer a portion of our children an education different in kind and hence inferior—narrow job-training or shoddy "life-adjustment"—then we are treating them as second-class citizens. We are not providing equality of educational opportunity, we are withholding it.

A high-school curriculum based squarely upon the basic intellectual disciplines is neither designed nor intended to produce an aloof, self-conscious intellectual *elite*. Quite the reverse. It is designed to give *every* citizen in a democracy a share in the intellectual life of the Republic, by providing him with the kind of education that was once reserved for a small aristocratic class.

The central problem of education in a democracy is to make intellectual training available to all. This is a difficult task, like all the other tasks of making democracy work. It presents a problem to be solved, however, not one to be avoided. Vocational training and "life adjustment" education are not solutions, they are attempts to dodge the problem, to run away from it yet to conceal the retreat behind high-sounding words. Programs for the slow learner are required, but programs in *the basic intellectual disciplines*. Both the student himself and the nation are betrayed by school programs that substitute something else for intellectual training. Only when we possess the kind of public-school system in which able students can push ahead as fast and as far as their minds can carry them, and in which every other student can tread the same path, at the best pace which he is capable of maintaining, will we have a truly sound and democratic educational structure, worthy of the American Republic.

We Can Be Proud of the Facts*

by HAROLD G. SHANE

Harold G. Shane is dean of the school of education at Indiana State University, Bloomington. He has written extensively in educational journals and has written or collaborated on several textbooks, including EVALUATION AND THE ELEMENTARY CURRICULUM; THE AMERICAN ELEMENTARY SCHOOL; *and* IMPROVING LANGUAGE ARTS INSTRUCTION IN THE ELEMENTARY SCHOOL.

During the last six or eight years, criticisms of education have become familiar to most school people and to seasoned members of boards of education. Also, since 1950, numerous professional and popular magazines have published a variety of "replies," "corrections," "denials" and rebuttals of all kinds whenever a critic has lambasted the schools.

In the heat of discussion, however, there rarely has been time for us to take a long, careful look at the last fifty years in order to locate the facts that contradict the vague claim that schools in the United States are cheating children out of a first-rate education. Here are some of the blunt questions raised about schools in America and some forthright factual answers. They suggest that public education is something of which to be proud rather than apologetic.

* Harold G. Shane, "We Can Be Proud of the Facts," *The Nation's Schools*, 60 (September, 1957): 44-47. With permission of *The Nation's Schools* and the author. Copyright 1957, The Modern Hospital Publishing Co., Inc., Chicago. All rights reserved.

Are elementary schools "too easy" on children? First let's look at the field of elementary education. Is our average 6 to 12 year old youngster doing much more than merely earning an "A" for digging in sandpiles, a pat on the back for neat paper cutting, or a gold star for being a "good relaxer" during rest period?

Despite widespread opinion to the contrary, elementary school age children are learning the fundamentals, the 3 R's, more thoroughly than in 1900. Studies of test scores extending back to 1844 show that each successive generation is learning more subject matter than did past generations.[1] For instance, a top official in one of the largest companies publishing our public school reading and arithmetic tests recently reviewed the test scores made by 230,000 pupils. Even in so brief a period as the past decade there was indisputable evidence of the increased intellectual attainments of children. The average child's reading, mathematics and language usage scores *on the same tests* improved by 12 per cent over a 10 year period.[2] And this despite the fact that a study just completed in New York proved that the average child in a given grade today is *one full year younger* than was the average child of 35 years ago![3]

One research worker in a midwestern city gave third and fifth grade children the same tests used in 1934 and compared their arithmetic and spelling achievement with that of the past generation. What happened? Today's children made significantly higher scores than did mother or dad.[4] At least 16 similar investigations tell the same story about every one of the 3 R's.

Modern education, often given the vague label "progressive" education, has long been accused of debasing our schools academically. Actually, modern educational practices have been maligned by writers who have given any shoddy educational practice the name "progressive."

As schools interpret the term today, so-called "progressive" or modern educational methods are designed to help children learn more than they once did and to make learning have more meaning. For example, certain arithmetical processes today are commonly introduced about

[1] Rock, B. R.: *Children's Achievement: Today and Yesterday.* Austin: The Texas Elementary Principals and Supervisors Association, 1952.

[2] *Bulletin of the California Test Bureau: A Comparison of Pupil Achievement Before and After 1945.* Los Angeles. P. 8.

[3] Wrightstone, J. Wayne: *Class Organization for Instruction.* Washington, D.C.: Department of Classroom Teachers and American Educational Research Association of N.E.A. 1957, p. 4.

[4] Lanton, Wendell C.: "The Proof of the Pudding," *The Phi Delta Kappan, 36:* 136, December 1954.

a year later than they were in the elementary school of the 1920's. This change was not made to soften the curriculum. Rather it was made in order to help children master content in a few weeks rather than wasting months trying to learn abstract number concepts before they were intellectually mature enough to grasp them.

Clearly, schools today are *not* trying to produce "—at great expense and with the most incongruous self-congratulation—a nation of Henry Aldriches."[5] After 25 years in the field of education I have yet to meet either a teacher or professor of education who believed that "it really isn't important what children learn, just so long as they're happy." (The cartoon about the second grade child who asked the teacher, "Do we *have* to do what we want to do today, Miss Jones?" was amusing but sadly misleading when it appeared in a popular magazine.) The improving levels of national standardized test scores clearly suggest that the fundamentals, far from being neglected, are now taught more thoroughly than ever. The scores also contradict the statement that "all children are promoted" regardless of whether they have learned the "essentials." Today's high standards of academic achievement patently were not reached by de-emphasizing the importance of study.

What has happened to history and geography? Nor does the evidence support the vague claim that social studies in the elementary school (and "life adjustment" courses in the secondary school) are reducing the teaching of history and geography to a heap of rubble. In the majority of schools the social studies period is one in which geography and history are taught as one subject in order to make clear to young children the way in which the two fields are related.

Are we "brain wasting" gifted children? Do elementary schools, or high schools for that matter, merit the charge that they are "brain wasting" by neglecting gifted children? A gifted child is one with an intelligence quotient or I.Q. of 140 or above. In an exhaustive study of such brilliant youngsters one of the country's top psychologists found that even some years ago nine-tenths of our gifted children were being identified by their teachers. Far from being neglected, the typical gifted children who were tested were achieving 44 per cent higher test scores than were their less able classmates. That is, gifted fourth grade children had learned approximately as much in four years as the average child learned in eight years of school.[6] All large

[5] Bell, Bernard Iddings: "Know How vs. Know Why," *Life* 29:89-98, Oct. 16, 1950.

[6] Terman, Lewis M., et al.: *Genetic Studies of Genius.* Stanford University Press, p. 306.

school systems, and many small ones, have for years made special provision for the intellectually promising boy and girl. There is relatively little brain wasting here considering how limited school funds are.

Further evidence of the fact that mass education has *not* harmed quality education is afforded by a 20 year study of 1,470 young men and women of top intellectual promise. Nine out of 10 of this genius-level group went on to college, and two-thirds of the men and one-third of the women completed at least one postgraduate university degree.[7]

But at the same time we cannot afford to be complacent about the educational opportunities of our top-flight students! Rear Admiral H. G. Rickover, the gifted engineer-scientist who created the atomic submarine *Nautilus,* was completely correct when he stated earlier this year that ". . . our schools are not equipped to do justice to the special needs of such pupils."[8] *Truly, the accomplishments of our schools often have been made in spite of limited funds with which to nurture the truly gifted!* If we are not to waste "our most precious natural asset," as Admiral Rickover called the brain power of our genius, the schools must be given additional means to increase their underfinanced programs for the gifted. In view of what the schools have already done on shoestring budgets they will accomplish wonders when stimulated by an awakened public interest in and support for education which challenges our gifted youngsters. We have the wealth to do the job, but often have lacked the vision to invest sufficient capital in the "cold war of the classrooms" in an era when our national survival depends on the outcome.

Are Europe's elementary schools better than ours? Both prevalent and inaccurate is the view that the instructional programs in American elementary schools are markedly inferior to the European variety. The results of tests administered *in Europe by Europeans* indicate that the reverse may be true. One report published recently by the University of London Press revealed that children in the United Kingdom were below a comparable group of our children in reading ability.[9] This was despite the fact that the children overseas often began their reading instruction earlier than those in the United States. "Worriers" who are alarmed lest American reading is handled too lightheartedly

[7] Terman, Lewis M., and Oden, M. H.: *Genetic Studies of Genius: The Gifted Child Grows Up* (Vol. IV). Stanford University Press, 1947.

[8] Rickover, H. G.: "Let's Stop Wasting Our Greatest Resource," *The Saturday Evening Post, 229*:108, March 2, 1957.

[9] Taylor, C. D.: "The Effect of Training on Reading Readiness," *Studies in Reading.* University of London Press, 1950. Vol. II, pp. 63-80.

in the primary grades will be pleased to know that a study (made by a Scot in the ruggedly academic schools of Scotland) showed that only about half as much time was spent on reading in these schools as in American ones at equivalent age levels.[10]

Speaking of European schools, the "childhood disease" of leisure time comic book reading proved to be roughly twice as widespread among 11 to 15 year olds in England as in the U.S. Two recent British polls of comic book reading habits published in a European psychological journal pointed to this conclusion.[11,12]

Despite the reassuring evidence, we cannot be smugly satisfied. While our schools do at least a comparable and perhaps a better job of educating a large number of students than Europe's schools, we do our least effective work with our most able pupils.

Have our high school programs deteriorated? Since factual information supports a proud 50 year record in elementary education, what about the record of the American high school? It was stated recently that "the schools have retreated from modern life" because of the way they have de-emphasized science and mathematics. The speaker, an articulate and ardent proponent of a return to "basic education," contended that the percentage of high school students taking science and mathematics had declined from approximately 85 per cent to about 55 per cent since 1900.[13] These figures are a beautiful illustration of how information, taken out of context, can be used to support a faulty argument.

As I write, I have before me recent official records from the U.S. Department of Health, Education and Welfare.[14] These reports show, in round numbers, that 400,000 children were taking science and mathematics courses at the turn of the century out of a total population of 75,603,000. Fifty years later, while our population increased by some 100 per cent, the number of high school students enrolled in science had increased by 600 per cent and mathematics class enrollments have grown by 900 per cent.

[10] Inglis, W. W.: "The Early Stages of Reading." *A Review of Recent Investigations, Studies in Reading.* University of London Press, 1948. Vol. I, pp. 1-92.

[11] Stewart, Mary: "The Leisure Activities of Grammar School Pupils," *British Journal of Educational Psychology, 20:*11-34, February 1950.

[12] Williams, A. R.: "The Magazine Reading of Secondary School Children," *British Journal of Educational Psychology, 21:*186-98, November 1951.

[13] Bestor, Arthur: "We Are Less Educated Than 50 Years Ago," *U.S. News and World Report, 41:*68-82, Nov. 30, 1956.

[14] U.S. Department of Health, Education, and Welfare: *Offerings and Enrollments in Science and Mathematics in Public High Schools,* Washington, D.C.; U.S. Govt. Printing Office, 1956. Pp. 24. Supplementary population figures cited are from the *Biennial Survey of Education (1950-52)* also issued by the Govt. Printing Office.

Bear in mind that this tremendous gain was registered during a period in which nearly all our children had an opportunity to go into high school, not merely the children of the socially or economically privileged. The schools certainly have not "retreated" when today from six to nine times as many of our intellectually competent boys and girls are taking science and mathematics courses as were taking these courses at the century's turn.

Are languages being ignored? The status of foreign language teaching also has been viewed with alarm by the proponents of "fundamental" education. Here, again, the story is an interesting one. According to the careful records of the Modern Language Association, there was a 400 per cent increase at the elementary level in the teaching of a second language in Grade 6 and below in a recent three-year (1951-54) period.[15] By 1957 the total number of young children engaged in foreign language study hovered near the 400,000 mark. At the high school level the number of pupils studying one of the four major languages most commonly offered (Spanish, Latin, French and German) has increased threefold while the U. S. population has merely doubled.[16] The number of children taking high school Spanish, for instance, was too small to be recorded by the Office of Education in 1900; about a half million students are now enrolled.

Latin class enrollments have proportionately kept pace with the national population increase, and 10 children take French today for every one who studied it in 1900.[17] Only German language teaching has shown a net decline, and this is traceable in part to an antipathy to all things Germanic during two World Wars. During these periods some schools dropped the language in response to public demand.

How competent are our teachers? In view of the academic record made by children and youth it seems self-evident that the vast majority of teachers know their subjects as well as their teaching methods. Nevertheless, it is reassuring once again to examine the evidence. In the first major survey of teacher status, made in 1911 by a gentleman who later became president of the University of Minnesota, the findings were sad indeed. The average teacher was young, poorly paid, and had begun teaching *without completing even one year of college*

[15] Mildenberger, K. W.: *The Status of Foreign Language Teaching in American Elementary Schools.* Washington, D.C., U.S. Dept. of Health, Education, and Welfare, 1955.

[16] U.S. Office of Education: *Biennial Survey of Education (1948-50).*

[17] *Ibid.*

study.[18] Today it is the rule rather than the exception to find elementary schools hiring teachers with a B.A. degree, while secondary schools often require the M.A. degree. Also, particularly at the high school level, state requirements have been stiffened tremendously with respect to the subject matter courses teachers must complete in order to qualify for a license to teach.

Does job tenure protect teachers, as critics of the schools have claimed, if such instructors are inefficient in the classroom? This charge is only a half-truth at most, since states with tenure laws generally require that teachers prove their skill over a two or three year period before they go on tenure. Also, state laws permit teachers to be fired for incompetence.

Job protection legislation pertaining to teachers was enacted to protect them from peremptory dismissal but also allows school boards to shield children from those who might harm them intellectually or physically. It is true, however, that teachers are sometimes removed from the classroom only with much difficulty and red tape. Trouble is especially likely to arise when a dismissal becomes a *cause célèbre* and is fought by organized teachers' groups. Also, in all fairness, it must be recognized that, with the present shortage of teachers, people of marginal ability are sometimes retained because no better qualified persons can be hired. The same generalization holds true, of course, for engineers, stenographers or ribbon clerks!

Does public education cost too much? One of the proudest achievements of our public schools is the way they have given the public its increasingly high level of pupil achievement *at increasingly lower cost!* A typical misrepresentation of the cost of education appeared in a recent article, circulated among businessmen. The writer pointed out that ". . . we are now spending three times as large a part of our national income, *after war costs,* on education than [sic] we did in 1900."[19] The catch is in the phrase "after war costs."

Actually, the proportion of our national income spent on education has averaged approximately 3 per cent for many years and has shown little significant variation for decades. Yet the proportionate number of students has greatly increased. In 1900, there were 699,403 students in our high schools. In 1956 there were 8,472,478! We now educate 12 or 13 children at the high school level for every one

18 Coffman, L. D.: *The Social Composition of the Teaching Profession.* New York: Bureau of Publications, Teachers College, Columbia University, 1911.

19 Freeman, Roger A.: "Dollars and Sense in Education," *The Civic Federation,* Bulletin 498, November 1956, p. 3.

enrolled in 1900, yet the percentage of income invested in their education remains identical.

What do report cards report? The charge has often been made by critics that schools have disregarded parental opinion by dropping the ABC type of marking system on report cards. This point is cited as an example to prove that the public isn't getting what it wants from the schools. Let's explode this myth!

In the first place, most high schools and virtually all universities and colleges continue to use grades of the ABC type, a fact many critics ignore. Even at the elementary school level traditional report cards are the rule. A student in one of my classes polled the 15 largest cities in his midwestern state and found that all but one of these school systems still used ABC grades, even at the elementary level. As a further check I polled 35 suburban school systems noted for their distinguished educational programs. In Grade 6 and below a substantial majority of my replies stated that ABC grades (which are sometimes coupled with parent conferences) were currently in use!

In the second place, there is reason seriously to doubt that parents really want ABC type grades. Recently I asked 700 Chicago area parents what they most wanted to know about their child in elementary school. Most of them wanted to be assured that he is an effective human being and that he is getting along well with other children. Only about one parent in three was primarily interested in grades. In short, the hubbub raised about marks in school not only conceals the fact that most schools still have ABC grading systems, but ignores the fact that many parents probably want to know more about their children than a grade of "C" or "A" reveals.

Does education lack purpose? It seems fitting to close this review of the reassuring achievements of our public schools with a passing glance at the fuzziest of the criticisms they have received. "The schools have lost their purpose," it has been alleged, because "unessential activities are squeezing out the basic subjects."

Enrollment trends and test scores, previously mentioned, clearly show that relatively more children are taking basic subjects today than in the past, and that the individual child (despite the one year decrease in his age in a given grade) is learning more subject matter than ever before. Obviously, the schools have not defaulted on their academic goals. But are the schools doing more than merely passing along the best in our cultural heritage? Are they preserving and extending moral values? The answer is a resounding Yes, and the evidence is abundant.

The products of our educational system are, with each passing decade, demonstrating our growing maturity as a nation. They are making real the American dream that human beings can live together with dignity and self-respect.

In 50 years the integrity of our country has stood firm through many harsh tests. In depression and war the graduates of our schools and colleges have proved that, while a few of us may be petty or mean, the average American is someone to be proud of. He has shown vision that lifts him above himself. He is friendy and basically respectful to others, but he has proved he can and will fight in every quarter of the globe for the things in which he believes. The typical product of our educational system may occasionally be misdirected or misinformed, but in the long run he stands for what proves to be right.

These qualities are no happy accident. They have been fostered and strengthened by the objectives of our schools which, like home and church, are the repository of the ideals that make up the American dream of a better world. Truly, we have more often succeeded than failed as a people, and a substantial measure of credit for this success is due to the effectiveness of public education.

Stop Pampering Gifted Children*

by BRUNO BETTELHEIM

Bruno Bettelheim is professor of educational psychology at the University of Chicago and is the principal of the Sonia Shankman Orthogenic School. Among the many books he has written are THE INFORMED HEART: AUTONOMY IN A MASS AGE; DYNAMICS OF PREJUDICE; LOVE IS NOT ENOUGH: THE TREATMENT OF EMOTIONALLY DISTURBED CHILDREN; TRUANTS FROM LIFE: THE REHABILITATION OF EMOTIONALLY DISTURBED CHILDREN; and SYMBOLIC WOUNDS.

For several years it has been fashionable to maintain that our schools fail to develop our gifted children. Ordinary classwork, so the argument runs, doesn't challenge bright youngsters to excel, and the result is a "tragic waste" of that "precious national resource"

* Bruno Bettelheim, "Stop Pampering Gifted Children," *The Saturday Evening Post* (Speaking Out), 237 (April 11, 1964): 8-9. By permission of the author.

called "brainpower." To meet this criticism the schools have devised complicated new systems of education which segregate the more able students and provide them with intensive instruction.

As a psychologist with a special interest in education, I believe this is a mistake. Taking the gifted child out of the regular classroom and pushing him ahead as fast as he can move creates very serious problems for the child and for all society. Segregating the gifted, I am convinced, harms both the advanced student and the not-so-advanced.

The demand for special schooling blossomed spectacularly in that memorable autumn of 1957 when the first Russian *Sputnik* soared into the sky. All across the country millions of people were appalled by Russian scientific progress and felt that the American educational system had failed. They wanted immediate reforms. The nation had to have more and better scientists; its schools had to produce them, and right away.

Thus we came to think of our children not as human beings but as commodities—as "resources," as assets of society which could and should be exploited for the social good. This attitude is wrong. Certainly our children need to be as well-educated as we can make them. But they need that for themselves and not for society, not to win the Cold War, not to prove democracy superior to Communism. In any case, education benefits children to the degree that the children want it and not to the degree that parents want them to want it.

Parents and others who insist on special classes for the gifted claim the gifted are held back—possibly thwarted—by learning at a pace designed for the average child. They argue that the gifted child becomes bored in regular classrooms, loses interest in learning. Although I have spoken with many gifted children, I find they rarely make this complaint about school—unless they are parroting what they have heard their parents say. It cannot be denied that some children at the top of their class may be bored in school. But it is usually the poor learner who daydreams in class, who doodles, who gets into mischief.

Advocates of special education argue that the school experience of most gifted children involves "overlearning," that the gifted child must often repeat tasks he has already mastered. He repeats these tasks, they say, not for his own benefit but to accommodate the slower learner; therefore his time is wasted. This argument neglects an important point: It is quite possible that the gifted continue to outdo their classmates just because of this "overlearning." I believe the repetition helps to produce a greater recall and an emotional ease in meeting intellectual tasks.

If the assigned task does not hold the student's attention because he masters it quickly, the result is not necessarily boredom. If he is really gifted, then other intellectual interests fill the vacant time. Not having to pay rapt attention to get the point the teacher is making, the gifted student may have time to wonder if the point is worth making at all.

I have observed what happened to a number of gifted children who were taken out of a highly accelerated, highly competitive private school and placed in a public high school of fair academic standing. There, by comparison, the work was so easy as to be "boring," or at least so their parents claimed.

The students themselves, however, belied the claim. In the special school for the gifted, they had shown little ability to use their own critical judgment; instead, they had relied heavily on their teachers' direction. But in the slower-paced school, no longer busy with keeping up, they began to reflect spontaneously on many problems, some of which were not in the school program. On their own, they acquired a much deeper appreciation of life, of the arts, and above all of the human beings around them.

The gifted child in the ordinary classroom reaps another benefit. Because he learns easily, he becomes confident. This prolonged, rarely threatened intellectual security may be the very best preparation for courageously besieging the uncharted outposts of knowledge. On the other hand, if the gifted child is put into a special class where learning is not easy for him, where he is only average among a group of extremely gifted youngsters, he may feel his abilities are only average and later lack the courage to take on difficult problems.

By putting a gifted child in a special class and by demanding high achievement from him, we may also push him beyond what is good for him. We may encourage him to strain his abilities so that the end of his school career finds him intellectually exhausted by the too-rapid pace. Or he may suffer still more serious damage: He may settle for intellectual success as his only satisfaction in life, independent of its meaning or purpose.

It is very difficult to cheat a gifted child out of making good use of his intellectual abilities, but it is very easy to cheat him out of his childhood. While it is doubtful that learning a lot of math and science will necessarily produce a future scientist, there is no question that enjoying childhood experiences to the full is the best preparation for becoming a mature adult. Some very brilliant people, who as children were prematurely pushed toward achievements beyond their age, remain immature as adults.

There can be little doubt that special classes for gifted children can help them to graduate earlier and take their place in life sooner. But there is also little doubt that special schooling teaches them at an early age to look down on the rest of the population as inferior. And this is my greatest fear, that by separating the gifted from the rest we may well end up with something like what George Orwell predicted in his novel *1984:* a world of big brothers who hold little brothers at their mercy because the little brothers can't speak their language or even hold the same view of this world.

Some who concede this danger nevertheless argue that to mix gifted and average children is undesirable because it makes the slower learners anxious. Perhaps it does. But how do anxieties become manageable? Through a friendly working relationship with those who we feel are superior—in this case, the faster learners in the classroom. If you were inexperienced at mountain climbing, you would obviously welcome proficient climbers in your party. In mountain climbing the experts usually distribute themselves among the beginners, who are placed in the center of the group. If the beginner has an expert before him and an expert behind him, the likelihood is great that he will learn quickly and well. However, if we put all the good climbers in one party and all the poor ones in another and expect all of them to make the perilous ascent to adult maturity, we virtually insure that our second group will stumble badly or perish altogether. If teamwork is there, we can afford to put the awkward among the skillful, and as likely as not, all will succeed. What worries me about classes for the gifted is that the good mountain climbers will stop feeling any ties or obligation to those they have left far below.

Do we even know who the gifted are? The younger the child, the more his school achievement and his attitude toward learning reflect parental attitudes. In the early grades the child is strictly the product of his home, for the school has barely begun to exert its full influence. Not until high school is the young adult usually free enough from his home background for his native talents fully to unfold. If children are grouped before they reach high school, their schooling, far from equalizing their differences in background, only widens the gap by adding intellectual differences.

Thus, early grouping discriminates against children who do not come from "nice" homes. In order to do well in school, lower-class whites and Negroes need to be challenged and motivated by example. Grouping deprives these children of this stimulation. Denied inspiring companionship in school and given little support at home, they find themselves in a predicament they are poorly prepared to overcome. Dimly realizing the powerful odds against them, they often succumb to hopelessness. And if any children in the nongifted group show unusual ability, they are drawn away to join their intellectual peers in the gifted group, leaving the nongifted group more impoverished than ever.

Behind the conscious concern for the gifted there seems to lie an unconscious desire to create a segregation based on intellect. Many of the intelligentsia can advocate desegregation of the public schools today because their own children, the "gifted" children, white and Negro, are already segregated from the rest of the integrated schools. These children are attending special classes for gifted children in public schools. Or they are attending private schools. Or they attend schools in the suburbs. They are already enjoying the benefits of their particular brand of segregation.

These parents, whether they know it consciously or not, wish to establish an up-to-date elite—a white-collar elite of the intellect, of scientists—an elite they hope will replace the old aristocracy of money or family. Such an intellectual elite will consist of highly educated people of all colors. Their education, language, manners and outlook on life—rather than racial barriers—will set them apart.

In past centuries the dominent problem of society was to make life secure by mastering nature. For this, society required scientists and technicians. But today fewer people are needed and employed in production for survival, in making the goods we need to be housed, clothed and fed. The greatest need of man is no longer to learn more about the world but to learn about himself and his relations to others.

Again and again, college and graduate students ask me why they were never told in high school what life in our cities is really like. Why, they ask, weren't they told about poverty, about mental disease? These questions they ask openly. Only in secret do they ask the more devastating questions: Why am I so lonely? Why am I afraid of my own feelings, my desires, my fantasies? Why do we have to suppress our sensitivities?

I think what our children need most to learn is not physics or math but the answers to these perturbing questions. They must learn about the inequities that still exist in the world and their causes, and why we do not apply the remedies already at hand. Most of all, they need to learn all we know about the true nature of man—his outer face and his inner turmoil, the prevalence and the power of both his social and asocial tendencies, and how the one can domesticate the other without destroying his freedom. I hope it is clear by now that I am talking about the acquisition not so much of knowledge as of values.

Children can secure their full identity only after they have become deeply committed to values. Yet values do not exist in a void: They flow out of the life process.

How can we educate for value? I do not know the full answer. I can only propose a first step—I suggest we have high-school boys and girls, perhaps in their junior and senior years, learn about human behavior by working in day nurseries for three- and four-year-olds, particularly from underprivileged homes.

At present, we collect all children at the ripe age of five or six and drop them into one and the same school situation. We carefully follow this routine even though their preparation varies. We hope that by high school the socially handicapped children will catch up with the others. But why couldn't we change this practice? Why couldn't we take steps to help the children who come from homes that do not prepare the child to make the best use of classroom learning?

If we devoted a year or two to this job, we might speed up the slow learners before they fall behind. We might win over the children who come to school doubting that the classroom is a good place for them. We could teach these youngsters the manners, the attitudes, the skills—as simple as the knack of sitting still and concentrating— that are necessary to make the best use of teacher and school. We could, in short, help most of those who would otherwise be slow learners turn into at least average, if not fast, learners before they enter first grade.

LEARNING FROM CHILDREN

At the same time the adolescents assigned to the nurseries would be introduced to what will be the major task of their generation— social service. And they would learn how to be good parents to their children.

Working with small children would teach the teen-ager to understand himself better, to recognize those areas where he is still an infant emotionally and those areas where he is already becoming a mature adult. Most of all, it would teach him that one enriches oneself by enriching the lives of others.

When the children now entering school will be grown up, the scientific revolution will be largely behind them. Ahead will lie a psychological revolution. What is sorely lacking in our education—and will have to stand at the heart of our efforts in the future—is the education of the emotions, an education which will permit people to live at peace with themselves and others.

In this kind of education, giftedness is totally irrelevant, because if the issue is to know oneself, it matters little how fast one learns to read or count. While the talent to push ahead of others develops early, and while schooling can be pushed, it takes a child a great deal of time to develop insight into himself. Learning how to help others to live a good life comes only slowly.

Have Our Schools Kept Us Free?*

by WILLIAM H. BOYER

William H. Boyer is an associate professor of education at the University of Hawaii, Honolulu. He has written widely in the field of educational philosophy and is concerned about academic freedom.

The most difficult goals for people to pursue are often those they claim to prize most highly. In American culture, the word *freedom* has a halo of esteem, yet the goals that Americans actually pursue are often inconsistent with the freedom they supposedly revere. Educators, themselves sensitive to cultural ideals, often praise the record of education by asserting, "Our schools have kept us free."

The statement is difficult to verify or to refute. But the assertion has such important implications that it is worth examining relevant information to see whether the evidence suggests the schools have, in fact, kept us free.

The first problem is to define the term *freedom*. Given certain definitions, one might examine any of a variety of educational outcomes and show that in some fashion each contributes to freedom as defined. If the outcomes are also desirable in a totalitarian society, they are not central in a discussion of freedom, for they do not distinguish a free society from a totalitarian society.

Freedom can be defined to include many of the elements of both a democratic (free) and an autocratic (totalitarian) education. In the Soviet Union, a modern autocratic political state, skills like reading,

* Reprinted from "Have Our Schools Kept Us Free?" *The School Review*, 71 (No. 2, Summer, 1963): 222-228 by William H. Boyer by permission of the author and The University of Chicago Press. Copyright 1963 by the University of Chicago.

writing, and computation are intentionally developed without being inconsistent with the totalitarian ideology. Scientific information and a wide variety of technical skills are also taught. Education is free in the sense that there is no tuition, and it is universal so that all may receive it. Since these objectives are also important in a modern "free" democratic state, they are not distinguishing features of either system. What should be learned in a democratic society to free its citizens in a way that cannot be permitted in an autocratic society?

Since an autocratic society must retain an essentially closed system of ideas, thoroughly open criticism of goals and procedures is threatening to the system. Conversely, a democratic society builds its goals and procedures on the results of unrestricted critical examination. Democracy, therefore, depends on maximum criticism while autocracy considers maximum criticism intolerable. Since social criticism and the institutionalization of this process are essential features of a democratic society, though destructive to an autocratic society, criticism may be considered the most distinguishing characteristic of a free society. An explicit statement of these principles of freedom can provide an evaluative criterion for examining the contribution that schools make to freedom. The criteria may be stated as follows: first, individuals should understand their society and be intelligently critical of it; second, individuals should defend the institutions that are necessary to the maintenance of unrestricted social criticism.

These may not be the only criteria of education for freedom. There are others which are necessary, some of which aim at the development of individual abilities and, therefore, free the individual from what would be otherwise personal limitations. These criteria are submitted as two that are essential to education in a free society and inconsistent with education in an autocratic society. If these two criteria are among those that distinguish an education for freedom, it then becomes possible to examine the record of American education to see whether the schools have contributed significantly to these objectives. If they have not, the assertion "Our schools have kept us free" is not adequately supported.

It is not the purpose of this paper to introduce new evidence but to refer to studies that have already been conducted to see whether present evidence supports the two criteria.

The theocentric education of early America obviously made no contribution to the two criteria. The period when education might have contributed to freedom is from the mid-nineteenth century to the present, when the curriculum became secular and education became universal. However, since only a minority of the total population received a college education, the record below the college level is the most relevant.

Before the twentieth century, when the majority of students did not attend school beyond eighth grade, it is questionable that education at the elementary-school level could have made a significant contribution toward the two criteria under consideration, even if it had tried. It is evident that the elementary schools did not try, for the studies at that level were either formal or vocational, and all were noncontroversial.

During the twentieth century the high school has been the institution that has been able to affect the lives of nearly all Americans at a time in their development when principles of freedom could become meaningful. The American high school is therefore the institution of primary interest in this study.

Some of the most useful information on the history of freedom in the schools came from Howard Beale's studies in the 1930's, sponsored by the American Historical Society. Beale conducted the most comprehensive study of freedom in American schools that has been undertaken. The findings were published in 1941 in two volumes. One volume, called *A History of Freedom of Teaching in American Schools* (1), covered the entire period of American education. The other volume, *Are American Teachers Free?* (2), concentrated on the period after World War I. The following statements are from Beale's conclusions:

> Teachers in each century and locality have been allowed to discuss subjects that did not seem to matter and denied freedom on issues about which men did seriously care [1:xiii].
>
> It is questionable whether the teacher of 1939 is freer to criticize the capitalist system than the teacher of 1859 was to oppose slavery [1:247].
>
> Whether teachers are actually more free in matters that vitally interest the public than they have been in other days is doubtful. There seems to have been many more open violations of freedom in the past ten years than in all the rest of our history together [1:263-64].
>
> The majority of teachers . . . are usually not aware of their own extreme conventionality. Furthermore, they have never done enough thinking or reading to know a "controversial subject" when they see one, for in their mind there can be no "controversy" or possibility of difference of opinion on any of them [1:247].
>
> The average administrator opposes real freedom for teachers [2:744].

The study showed that there was little concern in the schools for social criticism or for the institutions that supported such criticism. Merle Curti, who conducted a historical study of the social ideas of American educators during the same period, stated: "It would seem that science, religion, and philosophy were less important in determining the social thinking of educators than the pressure, however unconscious it may have been, of the dominant economic forces of the day" (3:589).

If such conclusions are thought to be influenced by the reformist period in which Beale and Curti were writing, studies of other leading historians of education writing more recently can be cited. In 1947, John Brubacher wrote:

> The rise of the public school system put a premium on keeping controversial issues out of the classroom. The success of the shift from private to public support of education depended in large part on keeping a united public opinion behind the public school [4:634].
>
> In the classroom below the college grade the problem of academic freedom was not even raised in nineteenth century America. There was no reason why it should be. The common school curriculum was so devoted to the three R's and the academy and high school curricula were so absorbed in either classics or the practical studies necessary to getting ahead in a rapidly growing country that no one even thought of making room for a study of current social issues of a controversial nature [4:633-34].

Even more recently Freeman Butts has stated:

> Social pressures upon teachers have been great. The public has been very eager to make its teachers toe the mark of respectability and conform to the dominant mores of the community [5:544].
>
> In the 1940's and 1950's the hottest issues centered upon "subversive" ideas and actions of teachers. . . . Several kinds of steps were taken to ensure the orthodoxy of teachers and to weed out those thought to be dangerous and disloyal. . . . More serious than all other aspects of these campaigns for orthodoxy was the atmosphere of fear, suspicion, timidity, and anxiety that developed in schools and colleges throughout the land. Self-appointed censors and accusers kept after teachers so energetically that few dared to discuss even the basic issues of public policy that filled the press, radio, and television [5:545-46].

These historians indicate that the schools were not making significant contributions to the kind of freedoms under discussion. Other studies have provided relevant information about the recent practices of schools and the behavior of high-school students.

Late in 1955 a survey of high-school teachers was conducted throughout Arizona to determine the restrictions teachers believed existed in their teaching and in their role as citizens of the community. The findings indicated fewer restrictions than in the 1930's on the more innocuous personal activities such as drinking, smoking, and dancing. But in the freedom to teach controversial issues no improvement over the 1930's was indicated. Nearly all issues connected with sex, politics, or religion were assumed to be "dangerous." Society's more important problems were considered the least acceptable for study. The lack of freedom was attributable in part to external pressures but was based more significantly on the voluntary submission of teachers themselves. Teachers used the term "teachers' ethics" only in reference to their reason for capitulating to arbitrary social power. "Teachers' ethics" were never associated with an obligation to take action against pressures that restricted academic freedom (6).

In 1957, Remmers' *The American Teenager* summarized a fifteen-year study by social scientists at Purdue University (7). One of the findings was that the majority of teen-age students did not believe in civil liberties. Sixty per cent believed that censorship of books, newspapers, and magazines is warranted. "A third of them believed American free speech should be denied certain people if it seems convenient. Another 13 per cent would restrict by law religious belief and worship" (7:16-17).

A recent statement by Jules Henry bears on the criteria being examined. Henry, an anthropologist, has developed an outline of education based on many different cultures, including American education. Henry wrote, "Nowadays, in America, there is much talk about teaching children how to think. In five years of observation in American schools, however, we have found very little that tends in this direction" (8:274).

These statements are not evidence in themselves, yet they summarize findings that do constitute evidence. Possibly there is other equally creditable evidence that affirms the contribution the schools have made to American freedom. The evidence that has been cited, which seems to be representative, does not support the assertion that the schools have made significant contributions to either of the two criteria of freedom—intelligent social criticism or defense of institutions maintaining social criticism. If there is agreement on the way freedom has been defined, and if these findings are representative, it must be conceded that the assertion "Our schools have kept us free" does not correspond with available evidence. Below the college level the curriculum, teaching methods, administrative practices, and the attitudes, beliefs, and knowledge of students have provided no basis for concluding that there has been any significant concern for freedom as it has been defined here.

There may be little consolation in assuming that colleges have a substantially better record than high schools. The Jacob study suggests that the great majority of students are no more intelligently critical of their society when they graduate from colleges and universities than when they enroll; however, they do show a gain in the ability to adjust socially and to earn a living (9).

Possibly Americans have always exaggerated their freedoms, because they have interpreted freedom largely as the absence of the tyranny of government. There are other forms of tyranny that are not always labeled as such. According to Beale, "The tendency to coerce conformity and to resort to mob violence against the dissenter from popular opinion has been much greater in American history than men have realized or like to admit" (2:19). In recent times, as William Whyte has shown, the corporation has often sought total control over men's lives, for their behavior even in activities outside of their salaried services has been judged to reflect on the image of the corporation (10). It appears that the statement "Our schools have kept us free" indicates only an overly generous assumption about the state of American society.

American education has surely served as a useful success ladder even if its contribution to the kind of freedom under discussion has been questionable. Merle Curti once said that our schools teach "subordination to existing institutions . . . inculcating the ideals of efficiency and success" (3:586). In our quest for national purpose we need to face the question as to whether efficiency and success are presently our central goals, and if they are to decide whether such goals are likely to develop the kinds of individuals and the kind of society we really wish to have.

If we actually believe in human freedom, there is no reason why our schools could not, in fact, help develop a free people. However, to make significant progress in the future will require far more energy and clarity of purpose directed toward achieving greater freedom and far less time spent proclaiming ourselves free than has been true in the past.

REFERENCES

1. HOWARD K. BEALE. *A History of Freedom in American Schools.* New York: Charles Scribner's Sons, 1941.

2. HOWARD K. BEALE. *Are American Teachers Free?* New York: Charles Scribner's Sons, 1936.

3. MERLE CURTI. *The Social Ideas of American Educators.* New York: Charles Scribner's Sons, 1935.

4. JOHN BRUBACHER. *A History of the Problems of Education.* New York: McGraw-Hill Book Company, 1947.

5. FREEMAN BUTTS. *A Cultural History of Western Education.* New York: McGraw-Hill Book Company, 1955.

6. WILLIAM H. BOYER. *Conformity Implication of Certain Current Secondary Educational Theories,* pp. 180-232. Unpublished dissertation, Arizona State University, 1956.

7. H. H. REMMERS and D. H. RADLER. *The American Teenager,* pp. 16-17. New York: Bobbs-Merrill Company, 1957.

8. JULES HENRY. "A Cross-Cultural Outline of Education," *Current Anthropology,* I (July, 1960), 274.

9. PHILIP E. JACOB. *Changing Values in College.* New York: Harper and Brothers, 1957.

10. WILLIAM WHYTE. *The Organization Man.* New York: Simon and Schuster, 1956.

' SUGGESTED ACTIVITIES

1. Make an informal survey to determine the following differences among the students in one of your classes: nationalities, religions and various forms of Protestantism, apparent social class differences, and different sections of the country from which they come. Make an educated guess at how these factors affect the attitudes expressed by these students toward their reasons for being in higher education.

2. Assume that the authors are correct in their analyses of intra- and interpersonal conflict. Explain the following situations:

a. A man wishes his wife to lose weight but insists that she keep a plentiful supply of pastries in the house.

b. A father lectures his eight-year-old son on the virtues of honesty and then asks the boy to keep sharp watch out of the back window of the car while he double parks.

c. Any expression of sexuality on the part of adolescents is almost universally frowned on by Americans. At the same time, sexual themes are becoming more and more dominant in the movies and in literature.

d. Many Americans express the feeling that it is most important for young married couples to stay out of debt. Yet economists regard installment indebtedness as one sign of a "healthy" economy.

e. Teachers are frequently harsh with children who "act up" in class. Nevertheless, they agree that self-expression is a most desirable trait.

f. Teen-agers possess good reflexes and coordination and fast reaction time. But teen-age boys have more than their share of automobile accidents. (See if you can go beyond the assertion that they lack "common sense." Seek a better analysis than that.)

3. Consult educational publications which report research, such as the yearbooks of the National Society for the Study of Education, *Phi Delta Kappan*, or the *Journal of Educational Research*, for evidence that recitation of a prayer or the reading of the Bible in the classroom improves students' morals. Report your findings.

4. Which of the educational goals discussed in this section would seem to be most important to the following commentators on education: Arthur E. Bestor, James B. Conant, Bruno Bettelheim, and Harold G. Shane?

5. Assume that Shane and Bestor had unlimited funds to establish a public-school system from kindergarten through grade twelve. In what ways would their school systems differ?

6. Consult three art teachers and three science teachers. Ask each of them the following question and record their answers as precisely as you can: "If you had to choose three values that can be brought about by study of your subject, what would they be?"

Are there differences in their answers? If so, how would these differences affect (1) the students, (2) the public, (3) the fields of art and science?

7. Ask your history or foreign-language professor the following question: "What kinds of youngsters are entitled to a college education?" Ask the same question of a member of the college of education. Do the answers agree? If not, how do they differ? What do you consider the reasons for the difference?

8. If you are an active member of a religious faith, ask your rabbi, priest, or minister the following question: "Which function do you consider the most important: that of teacher, preacher, or administrator?" As they answer, see whether you can determine the relationship between the teaching function and the other functions. Summarize your conclusions.

9. Americans often verbalize a great deal of faith in education. Ask a member of your community who has not gone beyond high school what values he thinks are provided by higher education. Ask the same question of your physician, a lawyer, an engineer, and a high-school principal. Compare their answers, and attempt to account for agreements or disagreements.

10. The Russian people are *not* having a major debate as to the purpose of their educational system. We *are* having such a debate. In each case, why?

SUGGESTED READINGS

BAYLES, ERNEST E. *Democratic Educational Theory*. New York: Harper, 1960.   A collection of essays many of which bear directly on educational goals. Though the writing is clear and sharp, the concepts are difficult and will require attention.

BERKSON, I. B. *The Ideal and the Community*. New York: Harper, 1958. Written by a philosophical idealist, this book is an attempt to criticize the pragmatic position and to provide an alternative.

BIGGE, MORRIS L. AND HUNT, MAURICE P. *Psychological Foundations of Education*. New York: Harper and Row, 1962.   Chapter 14, "What Is the Cognitive-Field Theory of Learning?" and Chapter 15, "How Is Learning Related to Teaching?" Discuss the goals of reflective thinking and its relationship to teaching.

BLOOM, BENJAMIN (ED.). *Taxonomy of Educational Objectives: The Classification of Educational Goals*. New York: McKay, 1956.   An attempt by a committee of educators to classify and interpret various educational aims with respect to their ability to produce behavioral changes within an individual.

BRACKENBURY, ROBERT L. *Getting Down to Cases*. New York: Putnam's, 1959.   A "problems approach" introduction to philosophy for the non-specialist. It presents the varying goals and philosophies of education in an interesting, conversational manner.

BRAMELD, THEODORE. *Toward a Reconstructed Philosophy of Education*. New York: Dryden, 1956.   Brameld's position, one first developed in the 1930's, is that schools should attempt to reconstruct our society.

BROUDY, HARRY S. *Building a Philosophy of Education.* 2nd ed.; Engle-wood Cliffs: Prentice-Hall, 1961.   A textbook on the philosophy of edu-cation by a classical realist. See Chapter 2, "The Good Life as the Aim of Education."

BRUNER, JEROME. *The Process of Education.* Cambridge: Harvard U. Press, 1961.   A brief but important book in educational theory. The author discusses the results of a conference that led to important revisions in educational theorizing.

The Central Purpose of American Education. Washington, D.C.: National Education Association, 1961. (The Educational Policies Commission.) Sets forth the goals of American education as seen by a commission of the NEA.

Goals for Americans. Englewood Cliffs: Prentice-Hall, 1960. (The Report of the President's Commission on National Goals.)   Could serve as an excellent guide for discussion of our national purpose. The report presents the thinking of eleven American leaders from various walks of life.

HENRY, NELSON B. (ED.)   *The Forty-First Yearbook of the National Society for the Study of Education.* Chicago: U. of Chicago Press, 1942. (Part I, *Philosophies of Education.*)   A classic in the field. Eminent philosophers attempt to explain and develop their points of view.

———. *The Fifty-Fourth Yearbook of the National Society for the Study of Education.* Chicago: U. of Chicago Press, 1955. (Part I, *Modern Philos-ophies and Education.*)   The follow-up volume to the one above. It revises and updates the philosophies of education.

HULLFISH, H. GORDON and SMITH, PHILIP G. *Reflective Thinking: The Method of Education.* New York: Dodd, Mead, 1961.   The second section of this book is an exhaustive examination of the process of problem solving. Attempts to shed some light on the pragmatic educational goal, which has stressed the reflective, or scientific, method of thought.

HUNT, MAURICE and METCALF, LAWRENCE. *Teaching High School Social Studies.* New York: Harper, 1955.   The first section discusses the reflec-tive method of thought. The authors propose an entirely new curriculum for the social studies, one based on the "closed areas," those topics fre-quently barred from discussion and inquiry. The authors suggest that stu-dents should reflect on social class, patriotism, class membership, and other "controversial issues."

HUTCHINS, ROBERT M. *The Conflict in Education in a Democratic Society.* New York: Harper, 1953.   The author, formerly the chancellor of the

University of Chicago, has long been associated with the point of view that schools exist to develop intellectual powers.

MORRIS, VAN CLEVE. *Philosophy and the American School.* Boston: Houghton Mifflin, 1961.   A widely used and excellent textbook in philosophy of education. See especially parts V and VI.

MORRIS, VAN CLEVE, *et al. Becoming an Educator.* Boston: Houghton Mifflin, 1963.   An introductory textbook that is both interesting and readable. Read Part One, "The Study of Education," and Part Two, "The Foundations of Education," especially "The Philosophy of Education" by Van Cleve Morris.

NEWMAN, JOHN HENRY CARDINAL. *The Idea of a University.* New York: American Press, 1941.   Although written betwen 1854 and 1858, this book sets forth principles that universities have attempted to implement during this century.

OLSEN, EDWARD G. *The School and Community Reader: Education in Perspective.* New York: Macmillan, 1963.   See Chapter One, "Our Times in Crisis," for an interesting collection of essays dealing with educational goals.

The Pursuit of Excellence: Education and the Future of America. Garden City: Doubleday, 1958. (The "Rockefeller Report" on Education.)   A summary of a project sponsored by the Rockefeller Brothers Fund, in which major problems of education are discussed.

ULICH, ROBERT. *Philosophy of Education.* New York: American Book, 1961.   A textbook presentation of the idealistic point of view by one of its outstanding proponents.

III

The Organization and Administration of American Education

A school or a school system, like any other complex organization, needs a structure if it is not to be merely a number of people working at cross purposes. Administrative decisions directly affect not only the teacher but the student as well. For anything like a complete picture of our schools one needs a basic understanding of the complexity, diversity, and magnitude of this aspect of American public education and some of the issues confronting those who administer and control public education.

Most laymen believe that the schools are under the absolute jurisdiction of a "local" unit of government. This belief is analyzed in Donald C. Orlich's "Administration of Public Education in the United States" and Thomas D. Bailey's "The Folklore of Local Control." The former article also discusses the administrative relationships between the local, state, and federal units of government. It is important to understand which unit is responsible for what and how that responsibility has been delegated—whether legally or traditionally.

"Do Small Districts Assure Better Local Control?" a résumé of research concerning California school districts, presents some interesting conclusions about size of school district and quality of education. The article should not be taken lightly, since in 1963 over half the operating school districts in the United States had fewer than 300 children attending school in their systems.

Many writers have tended to ignore the fact that there are political pressures on the school systems. Such an approach has been detrimental to American education, since it has eliminated politics from open discussion in the schools. Sim Wilde's "Pressure Groups and Public Schools" and Donald C. Orlich's "Schools and Politics" indicate how the schools, by virtue of their existence within a governmental structure, are influenced by pressure groups in their decision making. One needs to become aware of the subtle as well as the obvious pressures exerted on schools. Finally, if professional educators are to give direction and guidance to those directly involved in political decision making regarding the schools, they too must become involved in the political arena.

Administration of Public Education in the United States

by DONALD C. ORLICH

The beginning student of American education often assumes falsely that the federal government controls and administers the public schools. But if American public education has made a single unique contribution to school administration, it is the lack of a national or federal minister of education who hands down school policy from the national capital. This lack usually surprises foreign educators, especially those from Europe, where national ministers of education have ultimate authority over all schools.

"Local control" has often, and erroneously, been said to characterize educational administration in America. This concept will be examined, but a short discussion of how the basic administrative structure became established must precede such an examination, so that we may understand the implications of "local control."

SOME FACTORS INFLUENCING CONTROL
OF PUBLIC EDUCATION

The structure of American educational organization was well on its way to being formed by the time of the Revolutionary War. During the creation and ratification of the Constitution of the United States, education was much discussed, but it was omitted completely from the final draft of the Constitution submitted to the states for ratification.

This was surprising, since our close allies, the French, had a nationally centralized system of education, and Washington himself favored the establishing of a national university. Jefferson and many others were acutely aware of the power of education to control thought. Having experienced what they considered tyranny, they wanted to keep careful checks on the national government to avoid centralizing power. Thus local control—*absolute* local control—over schools was maintained. Typically, local schools were only elementary schools, for there was comparatively little "public" secondary education; and outside New England almost no publicly supported education existed. Another historical fact that contributed to the lack of national concern over education was that at the time we were a loosely connected group of states struggling to maintain economic, social, and military balance. In times of chaos, it is seldom possible to give much attention to the educational institution.

Yet it should not be assumed that the Founding Fathers were not interested in education. Thomas Jefferson was himself the founder of the University of Virginia, and many of the Founding Fathers were university graduates. These men knew that only through education could a citizenry become sufficiently enlightened to sustain our constitutional-representative democracy.

The framers of the Constitution compromised on the issue of federal control of education by omitting control of education from the Constitutional powers of the national government, thereby apparently delegating education to the states. This apparent delegation became a reality with the passage of the Tenth Amendment to the Constitution, which states, "The powers not delegated to the United States by the Constitution, nor prohibited by it to the States, are reserved to the States respectively, or to the People." The Tenth Amendment has been interpreted by the courts as giving the respective states jurisdiction over education.[1] The federal government does not directly control American education because it was never given the basic constitutional mandate to do so.

STATE CONTROL OF EDUCATION

Who, then, has basic administrative control over education? The various state constitutions are most explicit in their statements concerning educational control. For example, Article IX, Section 1

[1] Robert R. Hamilton and E. Edmund Reutter, Jr., *Legal Aspects of School Board Operation* (New York: Bureau of Publications, Teachers College, Columbia University 1958), p. 1.

of the constitution of the State of Hawaii states in part that: "The State shall provide for the establishment, support and control of a statewide system of public schools free from sectarian control, a state university, public libraries and such other educational institutions as may be deemed desirable, including physical facilities therefor."

Note that the state has been given the duty to establish and maintain the public schools in Hawaii. Of course, the body that acts for the state is the state legislature. All state constitutions have articles similar to that found in the Hawaiian constitution. The wording may be slightly different, but the meaning is clearly the same: *Education is a state responsibility.* At state constitutional conventions the people, through their elected representatives, have expressly given the control of public education to geographical areas known as "states."

How can state legislatures conduct the everyday business of schools when they are usually in session only a short time during any biennium?[2] This problem was resolved in Iowa, as in other states, by further delegation of authority. The Iowa constitution specifies that "The educational interest of the State, including Common Schools and other educational institutions, shall be under the management of a Board of Education." The Iowa state board of education has very broad powers: the constitution also states that "All rules and regulations made by the Board shall . . . have the force and effect of law." Of course, the Iowa state legislature (General Assembly) may amend or repeal acts of the state board.

The state constitution requires the establishment of a state board of education that ultimately receives its authority from the state legislature. The legal authority for the establishment of the state board of education came through the state constitution; however, the duties of the state board are prescribed by law. The laws are those that are established by the state legislature. As representatives of the people, state legislatures cannot ignore the responsibility inherent in their plenary, or complete, power over their respective public schools.

A state superintendent of public instruction is provided for in the California constitution; typically state constitutions provide for such an official. But the methods of selection vary greatly. As of 1963, in twenty-one states superintendents were elected by the eligible voters, while in twenty-nine states superintendents were appointed. Basically, the state superintendent receives his authority from two sources: the legislature and the state board of education. The duties of the office

---

[2] A few state legislatures meet annually, but the majority of state legislatures meets biennially, or once every two years.

are mainly executive—that is, the state superintendent executes the decisions of the state board or the legislature. Since the state board of education and the legislature are not in continuous session, some agency must fulfill the educational obligations. It is usually through the state department of education that specific responsibilities are delegated to experts in various aspects of school administration—for finance, curriculum, specialized services, and research, to name but a few. The state department is the agency that enables the state superintendent to carry out his responsibilities. The directives and orders issued by the office of the state superintendent must be complied with by local administrators.

Local School Districts   All state legislatures except that of Hawaii have seen fit to delegate further some of the responsibility for public education to local school districts through either an elected or an appointed board of school trustees.[3] Although many citizens think of school districts as something ordained or sacred, they are nothing more than arbitrary divisions, and they receive all their authority from the state legislature. To repeat: school districts are areas over which a specific local school board has limited jurisdiction. State legislatures can alter or abolish existing school districts through the passage of appropriate measures. School districts are not sovereign entities; they exist for specific purposes, just as do other special local units, such as water districts, sewer districts, and special improvement districts. The number of school districts varies from one in Hawaii to seventeen in Nevada to thousands in Nebraska, South Dakota, and Iowa. School districts are neither school buildings nor schools per se; they are geographical areas.

The local district comes under the jurisdiction of the local school board, whose members are either elected or appointed. The number of people on a local board varies greatly throughout the United States, but a board most frequently has five, seven, or nine members. The state statutes generally specify the board's duties. Rules and regulations issued by the state board of education and the state superintendent must also be obeyed by local boards of education.

Experts in school administration agree that local boards should establish *local school policy*, or the general objectives or directions of the schools. The local district superintendent of schools should implement policy. But we still find school boards investigating such earth-shaking problems as, "What kind of paper towel shall we purchase?" and "Where is that two-foot hole in the roof that the janitor reported?"

---

[3] "Board of school trustees," "board of education," "school board," "local board," and "board" are synonyms.

School boards, as governmental or state agencies, are creatures of the legislature and serve as arms of the legislature. School-board members act as local agents of the state, performing certain specified functions.[4] The courts consistently have held that school-board members are, in fact, state officials and not local officials. Their realm of responsibility extends beyond the narrow locale in which they reside. They owe it to the state to provide for the education of the district's youth, since it is the state that is demanding that the children be educated. This may be the legal interpretation, but it is difficult to find school-board members who worry about educational problems other than those in their own district.

The powers and duties of the school board usually vary from state to state and, within a state, from district to district. The appointment of a district superintendent of schools may well be one of the most important actions a school board can take. Typically the local superintendent acts as the executive officer of the board. This means that he carries out the board's policies and acts as its chief administrative officer. Most school-board members in the United States serve without pay. If they do receive any remuneration it is usually a salary for serving as clerk of the board or reimbursement for some expense incurred while conducting official board business. The district superintendent is, of course, a full-time, professionally educated individual who works with the board and the professional staff. Thus the phrase "educational leader" usually describes the superintendent.

As one of the district's educational leaders, the district superintendent bears a great responsibility. Aided by other staff members, he plans, organizes, coordinates, and directs the district's educational efforts. This is no small task, even in districts with only eight or ten teachers. A larger district usually has an administrative staff consisting of assistant superintendents whose duties concern finance or curriculum, and consultants or directors in special fields such as physical education, music, guidance and counseling, and health. These latter personnel help the teacher and the pupil.

Just as it is impossible for the legislature to direct all of a state's educational enterprises, it is often impossible for the superintendent to supervise personally all the schools within a district. This brings forth another class of administrator that all naughty boys and girls learn about the hard way: the school principal. The principal is held responsible for his own school.

[4] Lee O. Garber, *The Yearbook of School Law, 1961* (Danville: Interstate Printers and Publishers, 1961), pp. 20-21.

Last, but certainly not least, comes the teacher, who stands on the educational front line.

THE UNITED STATES OFFICE OF EDUCATION

Although our nation does not have a minister or secretary of education, we do have a Commissioner of Education heading the United States Office of Education (USOE), located in Washington, D.C. This agency is under the jurisdiction of the Secretary of Health, Education, and Welfare, a member of the Cabinet. The United States Commissioner of Education has neither the power, the prestige, nor the status of the European ministers of education. For example, the French Minister of Education can issue an "edict" that has the status of a law with which all French schools must comply. The United States Commissioner of Education has no such authority to issue directives to American schools.

Nevertheless, the USOE is an important educational institution. It is currently organized into three basic bureaus: (1) Educational Assistance Programs, (2) Educational Research and Development, and (3) International Education. Each bureau is further subdivided into divisions—for example, the Division of Elementary and Secondary Education. The latter are divided further into branches and the branches into sections, each with specialized functions.[5]

The basic functions of the USOE are (1) fact-finding—collecting and disseminating educational information and statistics; (2) research—studying problems that are of interest to the Congress, states, school boards, administrators, teachers, and scholars; (3) service—aiding either state or local educational agencies with specialists in various educational areas who act as consultants or help direct educational surveys; and (4) administration—administering federal funds in educational programs not specifically under the jurisdiction of any other federal agency.

Programs administered by the USOE include the cooperative research program, in which funds are allocated to colleges or universities to study specific problems related to education; distribution of special federal funds to school districts (for maintenance and operation of schools) which contain a large number of children whose parents are connected with the armed services or other federal enter-

[5] *Educational Directory, 1962-63* (Washington, D.C.: U.S. Office of Education, Department of Health, Education, and Welfare, Government Printing Office, 1963), Part 5, pp. 1-16.

prises, such as air bases, dams, and defense industries; vocational education grants, which help support instruction in home economics and vocational agriculture; grants-in-aid to land-grant colleges; and grants for library services in rural areas.

The National Defense Education Act (NDEA) of 1958 is administered through the USOE. However, the NDEA is not a federal educational program per se; rather, it involves federally supported state programs of the following sorts: (1) loans to college and university students; (2) grants to states and loans to nonprofit private schools for the purchase of equipment and improvement of supervision to strengthen elementary and secondary instruction in science, mathematics, and modern foreign languages; (3) graduate-study fellowships; (4) grants to states and contractual arrangements with institutions of higher learning to strengthen guidance, counseling, and testing in secondary schools and to establish institutes for the training of secondary-school guidance and counseling personnel; (5) modern foreign-language institutes for language teachers at all academic levels and language area-study centers for work in rarely taught modern languages and for the conduct of research; (6) research and experimentation to secure more effective use of modern communications media for educational purposes; (7) grants to states for development of vocational education programs in scientific or technical fields; and (8) grants to states to improve the statistical services of state educational agencies.

The above programs are in the "service" domain of the USOE. One of the criticisms of the USOE by a former Commissioner of Education, Sterling M. McMurrin, was that there was too much emphasis on service and fact-finding and too little on educational leadership.[6] Whether or not McMurrin's criticism is well founded, there are indications that the USOE may play a greater leadership role in the future. Two new USOE studies—"Project English" and "Project Social Studies"—will help redefine the goals of the English and social-studies curricula. The next decade may see a federal educational leadership that has been conspicuous by its absence since 1867.[7]

THE PUBLIC'S ROLE IN ADMINISTRATION

We cannot conclude our discussion of school administration without a brief mention of the "body politic"—the total citizenry. In the

---

[6] Sterling M. McMurrin, "The U.S. Office of Education: An Inside View," *The Saturday Review*, 46 (February 16, 1963): 78-81.

[7] The prototype of the USOE was established on March 2, 1867.

last analysis, school administration depends on our citizenry. The American brand of democracy is one in which the citizens elect others to represent them in the legislative, executive, and often the judicial branches of government. The public must be interested in its institutions. Approximately nine out of ten school-board members are elected by direct vote.[8] The elected members are aware of the wishes of their constituents, and the attitudes of the citizenry are expressed through its leaders. If the legislators, state-board members, or school-board members are apathetic about school problems, one can safely assume that the citizens are not excited either. The leader is like the follower, only more so.[9] Citizen interest and effective administration are directly correlated. And since approximately 90 percent of our citizens have attended a school of one kind or another and are literate, the American people frequently tend to consider themselves "experts" in education. This supposed expertise has strong repercussions on the local level, where provincialism and localism abound. Thus school administration is complicated by a tremendously complex social matrix.

Further complications arise from the local or state "power structure." In all probability there is a handful of people on every level who can affect significantly the decisions of others, either knowingly or unknowingly.[10] Those high on the power ladder usually exhibit considerable social, economic, and political strength in any community. These are the "community leaders," who play key roles in all important civic activities. If we are correct in assuming that power structures exist, then it follows that those who directly administer the schools must identify and solicit support from the power group to provide better educational programs.

Lack of a strong national organization, subtle checks and balances, and diffuse complexity characterize the administration of American schools. However, in a representative democracy, individual citizens shoulder the basic responsibility for the conduct of the school, as they do for *all* governmental functions.

[8] Alpheus L. White, *Local School Boards: Organization and Practices* (Washington, D.C.: Office of Education, Department of Health, Education, and Welfare, Bulletin No. 8, Government Printing Office, 1962), pp. 8-10.

[9] Paul Pigors, *Leadership or Domination* (New York: Houghton Mifflin, 1935), p. 10.

[10] The interested student can read further in some of the following: C. Wright Mills, *The Power Elite;* Floyd Hunter, *Community Power Structure;* George Orwell, *Animal Farm;* Keith Goldhammer, "Community Power Structure and School Board Membership," *American School Board Journal,* 130 (March, 1955): 23-25; and Peter Rossie, "Power and Community Structure," *Midwest Journal of Political Science,* 4 (1960): 390-401.

The Folklore of Local Control*

by THOMAS D. BAILEY

Thomas D. Bailey is the Florida State Superintendent of Public Instruction. He has held key offices in several educational organizations and is a frequent contributor to educational journals.

Local control of schools as we know it today has certain important values we must not lose in American education. It allows maximum flexibility to meet the local educational needs and desires that differ from those in other communities. Because it involves direct investment of money and effort, it also stimulates community interest in the schools and a desire to make the most effective use of school facilities. Local control exercised through nonpaid—or low-paid—school boards is less expensive and probably more efficient over-all than highly centralized control would be.

But what is local control today? Those who think that such control involves the absolute right of local persons to make decisions without reference to higher authority have accepted folklore as fact, for local control of this type is nonexistent today.

Folklore is appealing. Customs, beliefs, and tales traditionally preserved among people become a part of the common culture. And folklore has a charm of childhood fantasy about it; its convictions linger despite common sense and scientific reasoning.

For example, many Americans still believe that whiskey is good for snake bite. We knock on wood for good luck. We think it is unlucky for three people to get a light from one match. These are examples of inherited folklore—convictions that persist even though they have no basis in reality. As I suggested above, the conviction that absolute local control is still essential or even possible falls in the same category.

The concept of local control in education is a time-honored one, but state and federal influences on education began early in our nation's history. Two good examples are the Northwest Ordinance of 1787 and the Supreme Court decision in the Dartmouth College case

---

* Thomas D. Bailey, "The Folklore of Local Control," *The NEA Journal*, 50 (December, 1961): 42-43. By permission of the editor.

in 1819. Local school boards for the past several decades have looked to state governments for financial support to provide adequate educational opportunities for all the people in their districts. Furthermore, such control as local boards exercise over education is done within a framework of state and federal laws, regulations, and directives.

In addition, some influence on the school curriculum has been exercised through the National Defense Education Act with its emphasis on science, mathematics, languages, and guidance. Federal vocational-education programs for many years have generally been influenced by laws and administrative directives. Even subsidies by private agencies, such as Ford Foundation subsidies for educational television, have to a degree "controlled" local school districts that have accepted them.

Accreditation standards by regional agencies control to a considerable degree the practices in local school systems. For years, college entrance requirements have determined to an extent what is taught in secondary schools. State athletic activities associations often rigidly control local schools with respect to certain athletic activities. The fact that such controls are not official does not make them any less real. The point is that such controls limit or remove from the local community the power to make *absolute* decisions.

For some time, local control in education as our forefathers knew it has been obsolescent in certain respects. The first school in which I taught more than forty years ago in South Carolina was a two-teacher school in a rural flagstop community with one general store and about five hundred inhabitants. We were three miles from a town of about two thousand population with a good school by the standards of that day. No one gave a thought to school consolidation, because the three miles of sand ruts between the communities were almost impassable for the automobiles in the area.

Several years ago, I drove through this community on a beautiful paved highway. I found that the former little school building had long since become a residence. The children now boarded buses each morning to attend well-equipped consolidated schools. Good roads, transportation, and the demand of our times for improved education have made the concept of local control of education obsolescent.

Today, the need for many small independent school districts is being debated far and wide in our country. These small administrative units—relatively expensive and uneconomical—contribute to mediocrity in education by today's standards. When will we banish the folklore of absolute local control and forget the obsolescence of the past? How soon will we decide on local control of education supported by a more balanced financial effort that provides honest control of excellent education for all?

I like to to think of myself as a middle-of-the-roader in a discussion of education, but I have rather frequent experiences with extremists. There are those who are recommending a national curriculum and a national testing program. I have heard it said a few times that the state and federal government should take over the responsibilities of operating public education in order to assure quality education for all. I do not agree with these people. Nor do I agree with those people at the other extreme who declare that localized foolishness would be preferable to centralized wisdom.

It is interesting to note that even citizens most in favor of traditional local controls seldom resist decisions made by a central authority if they agree with those decisions. To my knowledge, few citizens have raised objections to the state requirements for a minimum school term of at least 180 days; minimum qualifications for all teachers; mandated financial accounting for the handling of public funds; earmarking funds for certain purposes such as teachers' salaries, buildings, and transportation; or for prescribed procedures in appointing teachers.

Furthermore, even though absolute local control is a thing of the past, people in communities today can exercise very effective control over the decisions of state and federal agencies and even those of private organizations. Today, more than ever before, modern communications media, well-organized citizen groups, and increased leisure time make it possible for citizens to participate in local, state, and national meetings and to assist in formulating policies that deal with education.

Groups of citizens at the local level can wield much influence through legislators and administrators, not only in state government but also in federal legislation relating to education.

In my opinion, this extension of the influence on education by the citizens in each community is the new and modern approach to local control. Even financial assistance from state or federal agencies may be refused if the terms are contrary to the desires of local school officials.

What then are trends as we move into the "searching sixties"?
The mobility of our population has increased. In one year—1958-59—

one million children moved from one geographic area of our country to another, one million moved from one state to another, and two million from one county to another. With this increased mobility, education is a matter of national concern.

The variations which exist with regard to the ability of states to finance good education may be illustrated by these facts: The personal income per child of school age (5-17) in 1959 reached a national average of $8780. The average for Mississippi was $4045; at the top was Connecticut with $12,762. To cite another comparison, during 1958 the number of school-age children (5-17) per 1000 adults (ages 21-64) averaged nationally 470. In Mississippi, there were 612; in Connecticut, 413.

Other comparisons would reveal similar variations. These facts compound the problem facing our nation today.

The demands caused by national defense and international rivalry are now accentuating the obsolescence of old patterns and practices in education. Ex-Senator William Benton of Connecticut, upon his return from Moscow six years ago, warned, "Russian education is a bigger threat than the hydrogen bomb." President Kennedy recently declared, "The human mind is our fundamental resource."

Under today's conditions, can this nation afford to allow any geographical area to continue to take a pauper's oath as the excuse for providing only mediocrity in education? Should there be any geographical area in America where it is an educational liability for a child to be born and thereby be sentenced to poor or mediocre educational opportunities? Can this nation afford to allow large segments of its potential citizens to grow up within a society that is indifferent to the values of excellent education and the very survival of America?

It seems to me that the trends point to a realistic cooperative partnership of local, state, and federal governments in making possible quality education for all who can profit from such opportunities. This effort must of necessity provide for some desirable controls by all three divisions of government in the form of fiscal accounting and reporting.

The initiative of local citizens to improve education at the grass roots level must not be thwarted by any effort to provide financial assistance to local schools from state and federal sources. To those of us who have administrative responsibilities in education, the concept of local control believed by segments of our senior citizens is folklore and for some years has been outmoded.

Do Small Districts Assure Better Local Control?*

Once they were "typically American" but today the're a headache. Lack of programs, costs, and fears of reorganization plague one and all. What has happened, and why? Here is a look at this perplexing problem.

How good are small school districts? There's a romantic notion that they provide greater local control; that they have better, more personalized instruction; that they are able to keep tax costs down because they don't need the greater administrative hierarchy found in the larger districts.

But is this all true?

A recent study published by the University of California indicates that just the opposite may be true.[1] Using state and federal figures, and their own research questionnaires, Authors Edgar L. Morphet and John G. Ross found that:

Small districts do *not* really have local autonomy, but, instead, depend on help from county and state offices. And they let the "higher ups" do most of their thinking and planning.

Morphet and Moss conducted a survey of all districts in California with the aid of Vincent E. Merritt, administrative assistant in Sacramento County, California. Questionnaires were sent to all county superintendents with small districts, and to a sample of school board members and administrators in those districts. For purposes of this study, a high school district was considered small if it had fewer than three hundred students. Elementary school districts were small if they had no more than nine hundred students and unified districts had to top fifteen hundred students to climb out of the "small" classification.

Here's a point-by-point breakdown of the arguments for small districts, and the answers as supplied by the authors.

THE CLAIM: *Small districts have a greater amount of local autonomy.*

THE ANSWER: *Small districts do not have more local control; actually,*

* "Do Small Districts Assure Better Local Control?" *School Management*, 3 (June, 1961): 16, 18, 22. Reprinted by permission from *School Management*. Copyright 1961, School Management Magazines, Inc.

[1] LOCAL RESPONSIBILITY FOR EDUCATION IN SMALL SCHOOL DISTRICTS, 1961 Legislative Problems No. 1, Bureau of Public Administration, University of California, Berkeley, January 1961.

*they have less. Local reponsibility in small school districts really could
be described as more fiction than fact. Here's why:*

1. Their boards of education are drawn from a smaller base—
giving less opportunity to get high class people to serve voluntarily,
or even willingly. School board spokesmen and administrators, answering a questionnaire, admitted that getting the best people on the board
in a small district is an almost insurmountable problem. And, they
added, citizens seldom attended any school meeting.

2. Small districts are less independent fiscally. Again, board members and local administrators admitted that budgetary control is in the
hands of the county superintendent.

Nearly half of them stated that their county superintendent not
only prepares their budgets but also does their financial accounting
for them.

The county superintendents themselves, answering a similar questionnaire, claimed this figure is too low. Only 4.3% of the districts do
their own budgeting and accounting, they said.

3. Small districts do not even plan their own educational programs.
All respondents admitted, moreover, that they need help in such matters as budgets, legal questions and transportation. Thus they turn to
"outsiders" for direction—to the county and the state.

Summing up, it is found that small schools have less local authority
because they are more dependent upon others to help in so much of
their day-to-day activities.

THE CLAIM: *Small districts give more personalized instruction.*

THE ANSWER: *It isn't who you know, but what you know that counts.
When it comes to teaching, no one questions the value of individual
help and instruction by an informed teacher but the study shows that
small districts can neither get nor hold outstanding instructors.*

1. Morphet and Ross found that teachers in small districts usually
are poorly trained and poorly paid. The better teachers tend to migrate
to larger districts which have a better salary range and improved
programs.

2. Few small districts, the county superintendents said, have systematic programs for teacher recruitment, selection, evaluation or in-
service improvement, or for developing or improving their curriculums.

3. Too-small classes, all those surveyed agreed, hamper good educational programs. Equipment and supplies are below par. The administrator usually is a teaching principal and sole district supervisor who
has little time, or even ability, for a "double operation." Hence administrative services and procedures are largely omitted.

Although more than two-thirds of the small districts surveyed consider interviewing teacher candidates one of their chief functions, more than half of the boards leave teacher evaluation in the hands of the county superintendent, not the district administrator.

Summing up, small districts have no means to recruit, train or retain superior teachers. Moreover, working on a smaller tax base, they generally cannot afford to pay as much as larger neighboring districts.

THE CLAIM: *In small districts, the price is right.*

THE ANSWER: *Oh no it's not! You pay for what you get. Costs for smaller schools and districts are found to be higher, not lower, than in the larger districts. Even per pupil costs are greater.* In the state of Washington, for instance, grade schools with less than 50 pupils cost 60% more to operate than those with 150-300 pupils. In California, the elementary districts which are smaller spend up to 30% more per pupil; the same is true for high schools with less than six hundred students. SCHOOL MANAGEMENT'S Cost of Education Index graphically depicts the plight of the smaller districts. They pay less per student for instruction, teacher salaries and teaching materials, but more for administration and transportation than the national average.

The ideal school size for cost, the authors find, averages around 600 pupils in grade school, 500 in junior high school, and 600-800 in senior high school. The smaller the school, they say, the greater the cost of providing a satisfactory program. The lowest possible cost, they say, is in district systems of more than 10,000 students.

BOON OR BANE?

Conclusions as to the present day value or disservice of small districts are now apparent, according to Morphet and Ross:

They seldom plan or carry through projects or policies. They cost more to run, but can't provide adequate educational programs or opportunities by themselves. They are uneconomical, inefficient and lack required day-to-day services.

"Less *bona fide* responsibility has been exercised" in the small districts, the authors claim, and "local responsibility and control are not as complete or as vigorous as has often been assumed."

"If the people want local initiative and responsibility for schools, they can have it. Potentially, it can be much more effective and meaningful in reorganized districts. It is (then) possible for local control to become fact rather than fiction."

Pressure Groups and Public Schools*

by SIM WILDE

Sim Wilde is head of the Bureau of Class Instruction and head of the Bureau of School Relations, Extension Division, the University of North Carolina, Chapel Hill.

In order to understand the role of the schools in relation to pressure groups, it is necessary to look at the general nature and method of these groups. Marshall Dimock identifies a pressure group as "any organized association that tries to influence elections and legislation by rejecting or endorsing candidates, *by conducting systematic educational or propaganda campaigns among the public to promote or propose matters of public policy,* and by lobbying to influence the content or defeat of proposed legislation or decisions pending before administrators."[1:21] Again, Dimock says that pressure groups are "one of the means by which people participate in a democratic government."[1:22] Franz Neumann calls pressure groups "organizations by which social power is translated into political power." Finally, David Truman calls them "shared attitude groups that make certain claims upon other groups in the society."[4:37]

These definitions only help to point out to a school system that pressure groups, whether large or small, whether simply or highly organized, whether rich or poor, operate against any given agency for the express purpose of accomplishing its will or its way of thinking. This is not a subversive idea nor is it undemocratic. In fact, the public will is probably better served through the work of pressure groups than in any other way. Pressure groups represent people and people represent the public. The tug of war that goes on between various groups usually evolves into policy reasonably close to what the public wants. Interest groups serve a valuable aid to the formulation of policy by giving technical advice, serving as consultants in specialized areas, and by conveying how certain people feel about a certain problem. Without them, educators and government agents alike would find it

* Sim Wilde, "Pressure Groups and Public Schools," *The High School Journal,* 45 (December, 1961): 119-124. By permission of the editor.

extremely difficult to feel the public pulse and determine what the people want.

The methods of pressure groups are essentially the same: to apply as much pressure as possible against that agent which must make the decision, using any available means of communication, education, or propaganda. These methods may be open and above board by the use of paid advertising, protest meetings, letters, phone calls, delegations, and the like. Or, they may be more subtle, even at times illegal, in the form of boycots, bribery threats, and undue pressure brought to bear by powerful citizens in the community. Whatever the method, all the energies are channeled toward influencing more and more people to bring pressure on the agent, or toward influencing the agent making the decision to decide in favor of the pressure group.

Pressure groups, then, are important and necessary to the operation of good democratic government. The educator must realize this and must be prepared to handle intelligently those groups that might bring their influence to bear on the policies of the school system.

Many of the forces acting or reacting against the public schools are either spontaneous or loosely organized. However, there are some groups that are highly organized and from time to time bring intense pressure on school administrators. Five categories or general classifications are listed as representative of the major pressure groups that attempt to influence the schools. They are listed below with brief comment about each.

RELIGIOUS ORGANIZATIONS

This is one area of controversy that will play an increasing role in public school policy in the future. In the past the courts have consistently held that there is a "wall of separation" between the church and the state and have maintained that public schools are not the place to teach religion. However, this has not prohibited churches from using their influence in bringing about favorable legislation or in attempting to influence the policies of the public schools. Pressure has been brought to bear in many individual systems over such things as the teaching of certain ideologies, the use of public classrooms for religious instruction, the observance of religious holidays, and the use of public facilities for parochial school purposes. Now that education has become an issue on a national basis, the pressure from religious organizations will be increased and the administrator in each school system will need to examine present practices and procedures in order to be prepared for any pressure that might arise.

COMMERCIAL INTERESTS

This area of pressure is one that we will always have with us in the public schools. With the American spirit of competition and free enterprise, educators can expect continual pressure from firms and organizations whose primary interests are to propagandize the student for purposes of private profit or gain. In fact, many organizations can see no wrong in using the rich potential of children's minds and the easy accessibility for the distribution of materials the schools offer. One danger here is that many commercial firms will try to slip in their propaganda under the guise of education. A good example of this is the giving of free books, films, and filmstrips that insidiously promote their own commercial interests while throwing in some educational value. The task of the educator is to inform these interests gently but firmly that the school is a place strictly for the educational development of the child and not for any other purpose.

PRIVATE INDIVIDUALS

Though the weight of private philanthropy is felt largely in higher education, the public schools also feel the pressure from private individuals in the community. Colleges and universities have long faced dilemmas where a wealthy individual not only wanted to contribute money but wanted strings attached which would allow them some control over the policies of the college. In the public schools wealthy and/or influential people have at times attempted to force certain practices on policy but usually they do this through political channels. Superintendents, principals, and teachers have lost their jobs because of incurring the wrath of a powerful individual in the community. There is no set formula for dealing with this type of pressure just as there is no set way to deal with any of the pressure groups. But the educator needs to be on guard in his public relations so that private individuals do not find the schools a fertile ground in which to peddle their wares.

POLITICAL ORGANIZATIONS

No other area of pressure is so sentitive to the educator as that of politics. In too many of our communities across the nation, political parties control the schools to such an extent that all professional ethics have long been crushed out. Strangely enough, political pressure is usually generated in the local communities with less and less pressure on up to the national level. Political parties have rarely done much on the national level except include some plank in their platforms about education. But on the local scene, petty party politics has attempted in many places to influence the policies of the schools. In this state several years ago, an agency of the local politicians in power in one county was actually using school children to pass out campaign literature. This sort of practice is unquestionably using the schools to promote a personal gain and the educator should carefully guard against such activities. This is probably one situation when it would be better to be right and forbid such activities than to be re-elected.

At any rate the educator must remember that the schools teach about the political party system in America, its evils, its advantages, its disadvantages, but never in favor of any one system, and it would belie its own teaching if it allowed a political party to pressure the schools into serving as its mouthpiece.

SOCIAL ORGANIZATIONS

Of all the pressure groups, the social organizations feel they have the most justifiable causes to promote in the schools. Because their objectives usually include something about civic improvement or community betterment, they feel their programs and their projects are worthwhile enough to demand some of the school's time. These groups will want to plant a tree with all the school assembled to watch, or they will want to call a special assembly in chapel to present a program, or they will want the school to sponsor a dance or a social hour. Many of these projects are worthwhile, but they usually detract from the purposes of the school and add one more item to interruptions that can take away from the school day. Somehow the administrator must so interpret his school program that these organizations will not attempt to unduly influence the policies of the schools.

Although these are the five classifications of pressure groups listed in this paper, there is perhaps one other group with no organization framework that should be mentioned. The influence of this group is "silent pressure"—the attitude of being non-committal. In politics these people are called the "independents," whose vote no one can predict. To the school officials, they are the people who never speak, who never let their feelings be known until it is too late for them to do anything about it. The organized groups will be heard constantly. The minority groups of parents who have a special complaint will be heard from time to time. But the group that is seldom heard and seldom raises its voice in protest is the group that really decides the policy of the schools. By their silence they are permissive. But once aroused, they are a group that can bring terrific and relentless pressure on the school system. The only possible protection officials have against this group is to run a first class and efficient school system.

The fact that these pressure groups exist and attempt to influence the purposes of the schools is not, however, the problem facing public education today. The real problem is in how to react to these groups, what attitude to take concerning these pressures, how to weigh the arguments pro and con, how to weed out the bad, and how somehow to keep a good balance after the pounding and pulling of local, state, and national pressures. Without question, the school system of any community must be willing to listen to any group of citizens who pay for their schools. School officials who do not have a ready ear cocked to the public mind are officials who will soon find themselves in trouble.

Perhaps a philosophy of what the school's role is in relationship to other agencies in society would help the school administrator or school board to decide how to handle pressure groups. Certainly, the American school of the twentieth century is responsible for the formal educational development of the child. Other agencies, other forces, other groups play their part and have responsibilities to the children of the community. But when it is a matter of formal education, taking into account that the child is in school only a part of the day for part of the year, the school must firmly defend its right to plan the development of a child's education. This, surely, cannot be done by the school alone. Other groups must help to develop well-rounded children. But the school is the leader in this role of development and must insist that other agencies or pressure groups accept this leadership. If the school system is unable to do this in a community, then apparently that system needs to set its own house in order. Its leadership techniques or the men who are its leaders are not convincing the people that the schools are capable of leading them to the best educational development of their children.

Something should be said in closing about the role of the public school profession itself as a pressure group. Public schools receive their appropriations from legislatures and legislatures are the center of attention for most pressure groups. As education receives more and more recognition at the state and national level, it appears that the public schools must turn to the tactics of interest groups if they are to accomplish their purposes. The National Education Association is doing a great work now but barely more than fifty percent of our nation's teachers belong to the NEA. Members of the public school profession—teachers, principals, supervisors, superintendents, all—must join together to make their numbers more effective for the cause of education in America. True, this effort must be ethical and conducted in the highest, professional manner. If the teaching profession lowers itself to mere propaganda methods and forgets that its contribution to society is one primarily of service, then the goals sought for will not be worth the price paid. The education profession in America must exert ethical and well-channeled pressure from the lowliest member to the greatest professional organization if it is to see our public schools obtain the proper goals for the people of American communities.

BIBLIOGRAPHY

1. DIMOCK, MARSHALL E., *Business and Government*. New York, Henry Holt and Company, 1957.
2. EHRMANN, HENRY, editor, *Interest Groups on Four Continents*. Pittsburgh, University of Pittsburgh Press, 1958.
3. LEE, GORDON, *Education in Modern America*. New York, Henry Holt and Company, 1957.
4. TRUMAN, DAVID B., *The Governmental Process*. New York, Alfred A. Knopf, 1955.

*Schools and Politics**

by DONALD C. ORLICH

With increasing interest in education, a sharp rise in public participation can be predicted. If this assumption is valid, then educators must anticipate the accompanying corollary: there will be a sharp increase in political involvement in education.

Traditionally, educators have feared the reality of politics. The misconceptions involved in such an attitude are indicated in the following excerpt:

Actually, the notion that politics and education *should* not have anything to do with each other is based on a misunderstanding both of

* Adapted from Donald C. Orlich, "The Schools, The Public and Politics," *The American School Board Journal*, 147 (August, 1964): 8-10. By permission of the editor.

politics and of the role of education in a democracy and how that role is determined. And the idea that they *do* not have anything to do with each other flies in the face of the facts.

Public education is paid for by public funds, and public funds are raised, and allocated, through the political process. Through this process, the community—as small as the township, as large as the nation—decides both the total amount it is prepared to spend for a host of public benefits, and how the total amount will be split up among them all. In short, the political forum is where the citizenry fights about the things it cares about; it is where the public assigns priorities and establishes its values in rank order.

Not everyone comprehends this trading out of interests in the political market place. This is one reason why many political decisions do not in fact reflect accurately the most widely held public values but do often reflect those of "interests" which understand the political process very well indeed. In these cases, where does the fault lie except with those who are either too lazy or too naïve to press the case effectively for their own "interests"?

For the basic importance of the inseparability of politics and education is not the fact that public money supports public education but what that fact represents: that the education of its youth is a primary interest of the nation. And the nation has many legitimate concerns—for defense, health, highways, and welfare, as well as education. The equitable allocation of resources in support of these interests is an extraordinarily intricate—and political—business.[1]

The word "politics" seems generally to have acquired a nasty connotation, perhaps because it has been connected so often with graft, corruption, fence-sitting, and boondoggling. In most parts of the country there have been documentary reports of apparent "political evils" in the schools, such as that reported in Harold L. Gear's account of nineteenth-century San Francisco school politics, when a person wishing to teach in the public schools could *buy* a teaching position from a broker for $300 cash![2] There is also the type of school politics where the school-board chairman's brother is hired as a teacher or his sister-in-law is hired as the superintendent's secretary—in a state with a law against nepotism.

But the above are examples, not of politics but of *bad* politics. Political scientists have given us the proper definition of the word: politics is concerned with institutions and the processes of governing

---

[1] "Education and Politics," *Carnegie Corporation of New York Quarterly*, 11 (January, 1963):1. Quoted with permission of the editor.

[2] "The Rise of City-School Superintendency as an Influence in Educational Policy" (Unpublished Doctor's dissertation, Harvard U., 1950), pp. 46-47.

them.[3] As a long-standing institution, education is one major aspect of government.

DIFFICULTIES SURROUNDING EDUCATION AND POLITICS

One problem in local politics is that school patrons are not kept informed about what is going on in the schools. This does not mean, of course, that all plans should be made public when they are in a nebulous state; but as firm educational commitments are developed, the school board and administration have the obligation to inform the public by publishing pertinent details and issuing policy statements. (This, of course, assumes that the professional staff will have been *included* in some phase of the initial decision-making process.)

John E. Corbally, Jr.'s study of a selected group of California board members and citizens revealed that if board members gave different answers to the same questions when posed by different citizens, the citizens blamed the ambiguity not on lack of policy but on hidden causes.[4] The implications of Corbally's findings indicate the need for policy formulation, since school-board members are in a position of public trust and hence are a "suspect" group. In this respect school-board members must be cognizant of the role they play at the "grass-roots" level in the great American game of politics. The politics involved in school affairs should approach the ideal as nearly as possible and should be consistent with American representative democracy.

IMPLICATIONS FOR EDUCATORS

Ours is not an egalitarian society. It never has been. At all times in our society there are many cooperating and competing groups. Each group has a different philosophy, set of attitudes and goals, and methods by which to reach its goals. Our "natural" pluralism is deepened by such group orientations. The American Legion and the American Civil Liberties Union both stand for "basic human rights," but there is a wide difference in their definitions of the term and their proposals for achieving such rights.

The implication of the above discussion would seem to be that educators must become more political-minded and—more important than that—must form a series of pressure groups. For some reason, the

[3] See V. O. Key, Jr., *Politics, Parties, and Pressure Groups* (2nd ed.; New York: Thomas Y. Crowell, 1950), p. 1.

[4] "A Study of Critical Elements of School Board-Community Relations" (Unpublished Doctor's dissertation, U. of California, Berkeley, 1955), p. 135.

words *pressure group* have an ominous ring in the ears of the public when used by those involved in public education.

But pressure groups are neither illegal nor un-American! The First Amendment to the United States Constitution states: "Congress shall make no law respecting an establishment of religion or prohibiting the free exercise thereof; or abridging the freedom of speech, or of the press; or the right of the people peaceably to assemble, and to petition the government for redress of grievances."

The words "to petition the government for redress of grievances" have been interpreted to mean that individuals or groups can approach Congressmen in an attempt to influence legislative policy and action. Thus lobbying is quite legal. Since most state constitutions contain statements similar to that found in the First Amendment, educators who do not lobby for legislation for the betterment of the schools and the profession are simply ignoring one of their Constitutional rights.

Other lobbyists are active in all state legislatures. Information concerning registration of lobbyists shows that in 1959 there were 4,534 lobbyists registered in Texas. In Massachusetts 301 lobbyists spent $317,232 in 1961. In 1959 the New York legislature was influenced by 188 lobbyists spending $369,497 on their various activities. Wisconsin in 1959 had 284 registered lobbyists representing 413 different interests and spending an estimated $400,000.[5] In 1963 the 150-member legislature in Montana was lobbied by 214 lobbyists representing 190 different employers.[6] These figures indicate the extensive use of lobbying at the state level.

It is doubtful that many legislators described themselves as "threatened" by lobbyists from the stockgrowers' association, bankers' association, or machinists' council. Yet in some states, when educators attempt to make use of their "inalienable rights," the cry of "threat" is always heard from some legislators. As indicated above, such a cry is unjustified in the light of state and federal constitutional principles, and members of the teaching profession, through professional education groups, must participate in the political arena.

On the national scene the picture resembles that found at the state level. According to the *Congressional Quarterly Weekly Report*, in 1962 there were 304 organizations registered to do business with the

[5] *The Book of States: 1962-1963.* (Chicago: Council of State Governments, 1962), XIV, 86.

[6] "Lobbyists Registered with the Office of Secretary of State: 38th Legislative Assembly," mimeographed list, distributed by Frank Murray, Montana Secretary of State (Helena: 1963), 10 pp.

Congress of the United States. These groups spent over $4,200,000 to make their viewpoints known to Congressmen.

A sample of the general categories of these groups shows that there were 170 business groups who spent a total of $1,836,125.93. Thirty-seven employee and labor groups spent $945,206.18, while nineteen professional groups spent $344,455.24.[7]

Let us select a few members of the above groups and compare their 1962 expenditures with the $41,599.27 spent by the National Education Association. In that year the United Federation of Postal Clerks spent $125,732.90; the American Legion, $102,931.25; the National Association of Letter Carriers, $83,435.28; and the American Medical Association, $83,075.87.[8]

ROLE OF THE TEACHER IN POLITICS

If our schools are to "encourage the teaching of the principles on which our country was founded," the right to organize for the promotion of one's interests must be recognized as one such traditional principle. Political compromises and agreements are ultimately reached through the interplay of pressure groups resulting from such organization. This is a vital element of representative democracy in a pluralistic society.

Teachers must be able to participate in the democratic processes guaranteed under our federal Constitution. *For many years, we have lived with the paradox of demanding that teachers inculcate the democratic principles of participation in politics and yet expecting teachers themselves not to participate!* This paradox seems to undermine the essential position of the teacher. Participation by the teaching profession in pressure politics is no more "unprofessional" than such participation by the American Medical Association!

Lieberman, in *The Future of Public Education*, has pointed out that teachers' organizations have concerned themselves not with the power structure that makes educational policy, but rather with innocuous public-relations programs. His statement that "A thousand PTA's convinced of the need for righer salaries for teachers are not as valuable as one congressman who knows that the organized teachers can mobilize enough votes to unseat him at the next election" is relevant.[9] Lieber-

---

[7] Data from the *Congressional Quarterly Weekly Report*, 21 (No. 36, for week ending September 6, 1963): 1544. By permission of the editor.

[8] *Ibid.*, 1542-1546.

[9] Myron Lieberman, *The Future of Public Education* (Chicago: U. of Chicago Press, 1960), pp. 4-5, 237-238.

man is pointing out that teachers and their associations have not really understood pressure politics or the workings of our nation's "power structure."

Since education is a state responsibility, educators and, especially, educational associations must recognize that it is at the state level that the greatest pressure must be applied. This is the level where informed education pressure groups must organize and operate. Teachers must support such lobbying activities financially, and the lobbyists must have at their disposal accurate and detailed information to be made available to legislators at a moment's notice.

A case study, *Schoolmen and Politics*, illustrates the impact of politics on public-school financing. The study vividly portrays the concerted efforts of Northeastern educators and points up the fact that it takes professional knowledge, leadership, organization, and hard work, plus political "know-how," to solicit support for public education.[10]

To fit various circumstances, there would be degrees of pressure-group participation, including: (1) recognizing educational needs and informing the legislature of these needs; (2) representing the interests of the state's teachers; (3) planning and drafting legislation beneficial to education and the people; and (4) advising legislative subcommittees. Legislators admit that, with the ever-increasing number of bills they must study, reliable testimony can help committees better understanding a bill.

Before any group action must come individual effort and action. Any group seeking redress of grievances is, in the last analysis, comprised of individuals who care about their own rights, privileges, and responsibilities. They must be interested in expending the energy involved in acting on their own behalf.

The late John F. Kennedy, while a United States Senator, summed up the situation:

> It is disheartening to me, and I think alarming to our Republic, to realize how poorly the political profession is regarded in America. . . . *Unfortunately this disdain for the political profession is not only shared but intensified by the educational profession.* . . . This disdain for the political profession in our schools and communities did not matter quite as much in the days when active participation in the political affairs of the nation was limited to a select few. *But today, the implications of national politics necessarily make politicians of all of us.*[11]

[10] Stephen K. Bailey, *et al.*, *Schoolmen and Politics* (Syracuse: Syracuse U. Press, 1962).

[11] John F. Kennedy, "The Education of an American Politician," in *Schools on the Threshold of a New Era* (Washington, D. C.: NEA, American Association of School Administrators, 1957), pp. 158-159. (Official Report.) Quoted with permission of the AASA. [Italics added]

SUGGESTED ACTIVITIES

1. Draw an organization chart illustrating the chain of delegation of legal authority from the federal Constitution down to the school principal. (a) Does such a chart mean that the state legislature is always superior to or "higher" than the local board? (b) Find out what the concept "line-and-staff" means. Is American education characterized by a "line-and-staff" hierarchy?

2. Given all the points made in the "Folklore of Local Control" and "Do Small Districts Assure Better Local Control?" what would you predict for the future of small local school districts? Is this future in any way connected with our rural-to-urban population shift?

3. If small school districts do not really provide personalized instruction, greater local responsibility, and lower per-pupil costs, why do so many Americans believe that they do?

4. What effects will the recently passed civil rights bill have on some aspects of local control of education?

5. Interview a number of public-school teachers, both elementary- and high-school, and ask them the following question: "In what ways do you perceive pressure groups as influencing the activities of your school?" Then interview a number of community and business leaders and ask the same question. How do their answers differ from those of the teachers? If their answers do not differ, is this significant? How?

6. Are district school-board members appointed or elected in your school district? If they are elected, compare the number of eligible and registered voters with those who actually voted in your district's most recent school election.

7. Obtain a copy of your state school laws and list the duties specifically delegated to the district superintendent of schools. Then list those duties specifically delegated to the local district school board. Compare the legally delegated duties of each. Does the result surprise you?

8. Poll 20 randomly selected residents of your home town. Ask them to name the school-district superintendent and all the members of the local school board. Compare your findings with those of several class members who come from other towns.

9. The school-district minutes are public property and can be examined by any citizen. Ask your local school-district clerk to let you see the minutes of your school district of the last ten years. (a) List the school-board members for this period and then ascertain their occupations, religions, and residences. (b) Decide for yourself whether or not the school board consists of a good "cross section" of the citizenry of your town.

SUGGESTED READINGS

BAILEY, STEPHEN K., FROST, RICHARD T., MARSH, PAUL E., AND WOOD, ROBERT C. *Schoolmen and Politics.* Syracuse: Syracuse U. Press, 1963.   An excellent study of the methods by which various school groups banded together to obtain more state support for education in the Northeast.

BARTKY, JOHN A. *Administration as Educational Leadership.* Stanford: Stanford U. Press, 1956.   Provides insights into the "human" problems of administering schools.

CAMPBELL, ROALD F. AND GREGG, RUSSELL T. *Administrative Behavior in Education.* New York: Harper, 1957.   A highly theoretical book that will offer the more advanced reader an excellent point of departure for discussion of administrative principles.

FOSHAY, ARTHUR (ed.). *The Rand-McNally Handbook of Education.* Chicago: Rand-McNally, 1963.   A standard reference work containing much information pertaining to all aspects of education in the United States.

GRAHAM, GRACE. *The Public School in the American Community.* New York: Harper and Row, 1963.   See especially Chapter 10, "Power and Participation in Community and School" (pp. 349-377), for an excellent discussion of decision making.

GRIFFITHS, DANIEL E. (ed.). *Behavioral Science and Educational Administration.* Chicago: U. of Chicago Press, 1964. (The Sixty-third Yearbook of the National Society for the Study of Education.)   An excellent collection of readings in the human aspects of administration.

HAMILTON, ROBERT R. AND REUTTER, E. EDMUND, JR. *Legal Aspects of School Board Operation.* New York: Bureau of Publications, Teachers College, Columbia University, 1958.   An excellent nontechnical presentation of the basic legal rights, duties, privileges, and responsibilities of those involved with public schools.

HUNTER, FLOYD. *Community Power Structure.* Chapel Hill: U. of North Carolina Press, 1953.   A classic in the field of sociology. Hunter's work describes the operation of the community power structure.

KIMBROUGH, RALPH B. *Political Power and Educational Decision-Making.* Chicago: Rand McNally, 1964.   A detailed analysis of policy decision-making processes as they exist at the local school district level, this book offers the more advanced student insights into policy-making problems.

MASTERS, NICHOLAS A., SALISBURY, ROBERT H., AND ELIOT, THOMAS H. *State Politics and the Public Schools.* New York: Knopf, 1964.   A well-documented examination of the political background of education and the positions taken by educators in state political systems.

Progress of Public Education in the United States of America 1963-64. Washington, D. C.: Office of Education, U. S. Department of Health, Education, and Welfare, 1964.   Served as the U. S. Office of Education report to a UNESCO conference in Geneva, Switzerland. Contains current information on enrollments, administration, and finance on our educational system.

RELLER, THEODORE L. AND MORPHET, EDGAR L. (eds.). *Comparative Educational Administration.* Englewood Cliffs: Prentice-Hall, 1963.   Compares school administrative practices of several nations with those of the United States.

IV

Financing the Schools

In the matter of financing schools, two major points stand out: (1) it is big business; and (2) there is *no one way* to accomplish the task. Since fiscal policies are seldom decided on totally agreed-upon criteria, the basic theme of this section touches on different financial problems and their points of conflict. It must be realized that this section is but an introduction to the problems and issues involved in raising the money to support our schools.

The article by Donald C. Orlich, "Financing the Public Schools," treats basic principles applicable to public-school fiscal policies. The data presented are by no means all-encompassing: various indexes of support have been omitted, as have cost per pupil expenditures, first because their derivations and interpretations tend to become quickly out-dated, and second because indexes used in school finance are influenced by local or state attitudes and conditions which play the key role in their application. Since it is a property tax base from which the local school district derives most of its revenue, property taxation receives major attention.

The concern about federal aid to education is discussed in Shermis' "The Semantics of Federal Aid and Federal Control." The emotional impact that federal aid to education has had on the public is analyzed in this article.

A great deal, both pro and con, has been written about the question of federal aid to education. Much of the argument has been emotional, but the articles by Albert H. Quie, "Federal Aid to Elementary and Secondary Schools: An Unnecessary Danger," and Edith Green, "The Present Need for Federal Aid to Education," do not have this emotional tinge.

Undoubtedly compromises concerning general federal aid to the public schools will be made to solve the problems of integration and aid to private or parochial schools. No matter what the final outcome, it will certainly have political as well as educational implications.

Financing the Public Schools

by DONALD C. ORLICH

The American public-school system is one of our biggest national businesses. In many communities the public-school system is the single largest employer and may have a budget comparable to that of the largest private corporation in the community.

While we will not here consider the financing of private or parochial schools, we should remember that those supporting nonpublic schools also share in the public financing of education.

Information pertaining to school finance comes from the approximately 31,000 local school districts in the United States. To collect data from this number of districts is, naturally, quite a problem. State superintendents compile statewide statistics and forward them to the United States Office of Education. This process is rather slow, and any researcher utilizing these data must be content to use statistics that are not current. Other reliable national statistics are compiled and disseminated by the United States Department of Commerce and the United States Bureau of the Census. In addition, the Research Division of the National Education Association, an association that represents over 900,000 teachers, gathers current data, usually in the form of estimates, but quite accurate and reliable. Indeed, more meaningful than the raw data are interpretation and the prediction of trends.

LOCAL AND STATE SCHOOL FINANCING

As of the school year 1962-63, there were only 17 states contributing at least 50 percent of the funds for educational expenditures in local school districts. The state contributing the smallest percentage was Nebraska, where state contributions accounted for 6 percent; North Carolina contributed the greatest percentage, with state appropriations accounting for 69.8 percent.[1] Since federal aid to education accounts for less than 4 percent, it is easy to see where the major burden of support falls—on the local school district. According to the *Digest of Educational Statistics 1963 Edition,* the sources of support for public education at the elementary and secondary levels for the 1962-63 school year were as follows:

Federal Aid to Education	3.6%
State Aid	39.4%
Local Support	57.0%
Total	100.0%

It may seem rather ironical that state legislatures have given local units the chief responsibility for financing the public educational enterprise, while keeping for themselves final authority and ultimate legal responsibility. Furthermore, as we shall see, the local district is the governmental unit that can command the least financial resources.

The usual sources for state financing of education are appropriations from the state general fund—which comes from personal and corporate income taxes and general and selective sales, excise, and various other taxes—and a state permanent endowment fund. (The permanent endowment fund is discussed later.) School districts rely on the property tax, and we shall examine this tax in some detail.

Property and Assessments We must first define a term common to all public finance—*tax base.* A tax base can be defined as those tangible or nontangible units which are taxed to support governmental services. The more units there are to tax, the broader the tax base; the fewer units there are to tax, the narrower the tax base. Typically, *tangible* units include real property, such as real estate; livestock; and personal property, such as clothing, jewelry, and furniture. *Nontangible* units include nonproperty items, such as, among many others, personal incomes, business receipts, inheritances, utilities, licenses, and admissions.

The primary source of revenue for local support of schools is the *property tax.* The term *local* refers to such geographical units as the county, the city, and the school district. The property tax consists of the *assessment* of a *tax rate* on a specified *tax base,* or specific types of property. The importance of the property tax cannot be overemphasized, since, in 1961, it accounted for approximately 88 percent of the total tax revenue of local governments.

[1] *Digest of Educational Statistics 1963 Edition* (Washington, D.C.: U.S. Office of Education, Department of Health, Education, and Welfare, 1963), Table 31, p. 42.

To the economist, assessed or taxable value usually means the true market value of the property—that is, the price that would be paid by a willing buyer and agreed to by a willing seller.[2] But the local officials who assess property are not economists! In 40 of the 50 states the assessors may be elected by direct vote of the people. In a total of 18 states, provisions have been made that the assessors may be appointed as either city, county, or township officials.[3] Most assessors are elected on the county level; those appointed are usually in larger cities. Property on which school taxes are levied is usually assessed at the local level or the county unit level. As a matter of fact, 91.8 percent of the nation's property falling into this category is assessed at the local level. And the tendency of local assessors is to assess property at a rate far below the true market value.

There was a noticeable increase in the value of locally assessed real property during the period from 1956 to 1961. One major factor in this increase apparently was the rising valuations.[4] In other words, there is a general trend in the United States to assess real property at a somewhat higher rate than in the past. But the reassessment of property is always a "hot political potato" in any state, especially where the assessors are *elected* at the local level.

There is no generally acceptable formula for assessing property in the United States: the practice varies among states and within any one state. For example, a study completed in 1954 for the state of Washington revealed that within King County (Seattle) alone the ratios of assessed value to estimated market value on residential property ranged from less than 2 percent to over 800 percent. The average assessment ratios among counties ranged from a low of 13.3 percent to a high of 38.5 percent. The statewide average assessment ratios for different property types varied from 18.9 percent to 37.7 percent.[5] These widespread variations indicate that it is difficult to establish equitable assessment standards.

The assessed values are usually higher for industrial, commercial, and residential properties than for farmlands: a tract of farmland does not

[2] William J. Schultz and C. Lowell Harriss, *American Public Finance* (7th ed.; Englewood Cliffs: Prentice-Hall, 1959), pp. 373-374.

[3] *Public School Finance Programs of the United States 1957-1958* (Washington, D.C.: U.S. Office of Education, Department of Health, Education, and Welfare, 1960), p. 51. (Misc. No. 33.)

[4] "Assessed Values for Property Taxation," *1962 Census of Governments* (Washington, D.C.: U.S. Department of Commerce, Bureau of Census, November, 1962), p. 2. (Preliminary Report No. 5.)

[5] *A Study of Real Property Assessments in the State of Washington* (Seattle: U. of Washington, December, 1954), pp. 17-2, 11, 12, 20. (A Report of the Subcommittee on Revenue and Taxation of the Washington State Legislative Council, 1953-1955 Biennium.)

have the market value of a lot in a business district. Land varies in worth with its location. For example, it has been estimated that a piece of land near Times Square is worth over $1,000 per square foot! Businessmen, homeowners, and realtors are most cognizant of the relationship between the location of a piece of property and its "value."

Not all lands or property are assessed for taxation. Federal lands and property are exempt, as are national forests, state-owned lands, county, city, and school properties, and church properties. It has been estimated, indeed, that approximately 25 percent of all property in the United States is exempt from taxation.

Real property is defined as immovable property, such as land and buildings. Real property is differentiated from *personal property* in that the latter can be rather easily moved. Personal property is divided into tangibles—clothing, jewelry, furniture, and other similar material things—and intangibles—insurance policies, stocks, and bonds. Tangible property is usually assessed for property taxation, while intangibles may or may not be assessed for taxation. Most profit from intangibles —other than that from tax-free, low-yield government bonds—is taxed through the income tax; or, as the writers of the *World Tax Series* state, the enforcement of taxes on intangible personal property "reaches the nadir of tax administration. . . ."[6]

The Process of Property Taxation   A mill is 1/1,000 of a dollar. A cent is 1/100 of a dollar; thus *a mill is 1/10 of a cent*. Since the cent is the coin of smallest denomination minted in the United States, the mill has only computational utility. Tax levies are computed on "so many mills per dollar" of assessed value.

In the property-taxing process, property assessment is the first and, needless to say, the most important, difficult, and subjective step. After the property is assessed, a *tax levy* is placed on the property. The following is a simplified example:

1. The county government makes its budget—the money it will need for all services—roads, sewers, parks, hospitals, schools, and so on.

2. It is then determined how much of the money needed to implement this budget will come from various sources. Let us assume that, after the money from all other sources is deducted, there remains a need of $1 million. This is the amount that must be raised from the property tax.

3. Suppose now that the actual market value of all taxable real property in the county is $40 million. A tax rate of 25 mills applied against this figure would raise the desired amount ($40 million ×

---

[6] *Taxation in the United States* (Chicago: Commerce Clearing House, 1963), p. 170. (*World Tax Series*, Harvard Law School International Program on Taxation.)

0.025). For various reasons—tradition, political considerations, and so on—it is not customary to use the full market value in computing tax rates. Thus the property is given an *assessed* value, to which the rate is applied. If it is decided to assess taxable property at half its market value, a rate of 50 mills will raise the needed sum ($20 million × 0.050); if the assessment is one-fourth the market value, the rate will have to be 100 mills to raise the needed sum. (The elements governing the decisions on assessment and tax rates are often complex; many county governments have a legal limit on the tax *rate*.)

4. Let us suppose that the assessment in your county is one-fourth of market value and the tax rate 100 mills. (We are simplifying—there may be different rates for different types of property.) You own a house that could be sold for $25,000. The *assessed* value will be $6,250 and your property tax $625 ($6,250 × 0.10). This money will be used to help pay for roads, sewers, parks, hospitals—and schools.

The above procedure seems simple enough. Yet when the local government employs property as *the* measure of wealth and therefore *the* basis of taxation, it is actually using a nineteenth-century concept, because land is no longer the great source of personal wealth that it was. Goldsmith points out that there has been a continuous decline in the percentage of national wealth accounted for by land since the nineteenth century.[7] However, local governments have found no substitute for the property tax, which accounts for nearly 90 percent of all local funds for schools.

How does the national trend toward intangible wealth fit into a specific state picture? Here no safe generalization can be made. If any state's chief resource and wealth is land, then the land should be the major tax base for school financing. But when this is not the situation, the following could provide a broad tax base on which to build a *state* tax structure: (1) personal income taxes; (2) corporation income taxes; (3) general sales or excise taxes on motor fuel, alcoholic beverages,[8] tobacco products, and amusements; (4) property taxes; (5) severance taxes—those placed on businesses engaged in utilizing natural resources for commercial purposes: mining, oil, cement, and lumber; (6) death and gift taxes; (7) bank, public utility, and insurance company taxes. To determine which and how many of the above seven

---

[7] Raymond W. Goldsmith, *The National Wealth of the United States in the Postwar Period* (Princeton: Princeton U. Press, 1962), pp. 47-50. (A Study by The National Bureau of Economic Research.)

[8] It may be of interest to the reader to know that alcoholic beverages are taxed in all states—even in those where their sale is illegal!

types of taxes would yield sufficient return, each state must study its own financial needs and fiscal structure.

The view advanced here is that *the state and not the school district* should have *basic* responsibility for financing the public schools. The variation in wealth among respective school districts within *any* state of the United States is fantastic. The amount of wealth, measured in assessed valuation per individual student, within Idaho's 117 school districts, for example, varies from approximately $200,000 to $2,500. The variation is perhaps even greater than the above figures indicate, because in Idaho, as in many other states, the school districts with the greatest number of children to educate have the least wealth behind each child. A strong state-aid program would tend to remove such inequities.

A unified state-support program would also tend to equalize the differences among counties—that is, a rich county receives less state support than a poorer county. In Idaho, Pocatello, with approximately $2,600 assessed value per child for 11,000 students, receives greater state aid than American Falls, with its $12,000 assessed valuation per child for 1,200 students.

Since property is one of the main sources of school revenue, the manner in which it is assessed is of utmost importance. If there are low assessment ratios, then the mill levies must be high; high assessment ratios require lower mill levies to raise an equal amount of revenue. Assume that a particular county has an assessment ratio of 10 percent. This means that the market value of a piece of property is 10 times its assessed value. Thus a house which would actually sell for $10,000 is assessed at $1,000. Now if on this property a 10-mill levy is applied, the amount of tax money yielded is $10. On the other hand, if this same property is assessed at half its market price, or $5,000, it will require only a 2-mill levy to raise the same $10 in tax revenue.

Almost all states have limitations on the number of mills that can be assessed on property for school expenditures. The implications are rather obvious. If the assessment ratios are low, then the district schools are not obtaining their *fair* share of the tax revenue for supplying the best possible education. This is really why we have school taxes—to educate the children.

THE ROLE OF THE FEDERAL GOVERNMENT
IN SUPPORTING EDUCATION

The federal government helped lay a basic foundation for all schools with the passage of the Northwest Ordinances in 1785 and 1787. The

Continental Congress expressed its faith in education in Article III of the 1787 Ordinance: "Religion, morality, and knowledge being necessary to good government and the happiness of mankind, schools and the means of education shall forever be encouraged." In selling public lands, the federal government encouraged education by giving section 16 of each township to the state for educational purposes.[9] These *land grants,* as they were called, were doubled in 1848, then redoubled in 1896, so that as the last states entered the union, four sections of the public domain—2, 16, 32, and 36—were reserved for school purposes. These lands were under state jurisdiction, *not* that of the local districts. With the proceeds from the sale, rent, development, or leasing of these lands, states established permanent school funds to aid in financing the public schools. The farsightedness of some constitutional conventions is typified by the Texas constitution, which states, in part, that "All Funds, land and other property heretofore set apart and appropriated for the support of public schools . . . shall constitute a perpetual public school fund. . . . And no law shall ever be enacted appropriating any part of the permanent or available school fund to any other purpose whatever. . . ."

The original thirteen states and nine other states do not have any state school lands. The school-land acreage ranges from Alaska's estimated 21,000,000 to Nevada's 5,441 acres.

Other special federal grants to education include the allocation of 25 percent of the revenue from federal forests and nonmetallic deposits, and 37.5 percent of the revenue received from federal leases and royalties.

In 1862 the Morrill Act provided for the establishment of "land-grant" colleges. This was followed by the Second Morrill Act, the Hatch Act, and the Smith-Lever Act, all of which were concerned with agriculture, agricultural experimental stations, and home economics. We have, therefore, a long history of federal financial assistance to public education.

The Smith-Hughes Act of 1917 provided federal subsidies for sec-

[9] The public domain is the land belonging to the public. Most of the land area west of the Appalachians once belonged to the federal government—was public domain. These lands typically were surveyed into six-square-mile areas called *townships.* Each township was made up of *36 sections,* each section containing one square mile. The sections were numbered consecutively, beginning with section one in the northeast corner.

N

6	5	4	3	2	1
7	8	9	10	11	12
18	17	16	15	14	13
19	20	21	22	23	24
30	29	28	27	26	25
31	32	33	34	35	36

W   E

S

ondary vocational education, which included instruction in agriculture, various trades, commerce, and home economics. Between 1929 and 1946, four additional federal laws supplemented the Smith-Hughes Act. The latter group of laws extended the programs to include vocational guidance and distributive education.

During the depression of the 1930's, several government-sponsored programs related to education were implemented. At this time the federal government created a host of agencies that attempted to combine some form of employment with some kind of basic vocational education. The CCC, the Civilian Conservation Corps, was designed to help conserve our natural resources, especially forests and watersheds. The Corps consisted of several hundred thousand teen-age boys, most of them unemployed city dwellers. The CCC also provided the rudiments of vocational education, combined with some formal education. The NYA, the National Youth Administration, aided needy students by providing work for them. Under the WPA, the Works Progress Administration, public-school buildings were repaired or constructed.

Early in 1940, under the auspices of the United States Office of Education, several intensive, short-term training courses were offered through the secondary schools to develop skilled workers needed for the defense effort. During the 1940's the Department of Agriculture instituted the federally subsidized school-lunch program, using food surpluses.

Under Public Law 16, commonly called the "G.I. Bill," which was enacted in 1944, Americans who had served in World War II attended the college of their choice, with the government paying for fees, books, and room and board. The program was repeated under P.L. 550 for the Korean War veterans, but instead of the government's paying for each specific item, assistance to these veterans was in the form of a single monthly check. More than 3 million veterans received a total of some $6 billion under these acts.[10]

During the Korean War two other federal laws were enacted—P.L. 815 and 874—to provide school construction and general financial aid in areas where federal activities resulted in adding to local school systems children who would not normally be there. Areas such as Cape Kennedy (Canaveral), military forts, dam sites, and defense installations are affected by these Acts.

In addition to specific school aid, there are other national expenditures that indirectly affect education. These are the "R and D" (re-

[10] John F. Kennedy, *The President's Message to The Congress of the U.S.*, January 29, 1963.

search and development) outlays that are now quite common. Expenditures for research and development have been steadily increasing. According to the 1962 Economic Report of the President, during 1961 the federal government appropriated $6.125 billion and private enterprise $4.372 billion, for a total of $10.497 billion, to aid in research and development. The National Science Foundation is one of many federal agencies that foster basic research in the sciences. Through the NSF, federal subsidies have supported university research programs as well as graduate study in all fields of science. Stipends are paid to students to work toward advanced degrees. The expenditures for the NSF's work increased from $4 million in 1953 to an estimated $128 million in 1962, and in all probability they will continue to rise.

The newest federal "crash" education program is the National Defense Education Act (NDEA), which has made federal funds available for the improvement of instruction in science and foreign languages, for guidance, and for the compilation and publication of educational statistics. The NDEA sponsorship of institutes for teachers in science, foreign languages, and guidance has been very popular. From 1959 to 1963 some 11,000 high-school counselors received specialized education at either short-term summer institutes or year-long sessions. In 1963 alone, over 132 institutes in guidance and foreign languages were sponsored by the NDEA.

Thus, though general federal aid to education has not yet been approved, it is obvious that the Congress has long since committed itself to the principle of federal aid. Apparently the major barriers to general federal aid are the problems involving integration and aid to private and parochial schools. These problems are certainly deep-seated and emotion-laden, but once they are solved, federal aid will come through the front door of the schools rather than the back, as is now the case.

WHY HAVE SCHOOL COSTS INCREASED?

Five components seem to be responsible for the increase in school costs. These are mounting enrollments, extensions of the school program, enrichment of the school program, better preparation of teachers, and inflation.

Enrollments in public, private, and parochial schools continue to shatter each preceding year's record. The student explosion is due in part to state compulsory attendance laws. All states have compulsory attendance laws, although Mississippi, South Carolina, and Virginia have allowed each local unit to establish minimum age limits for leaving school. During the 1962-63 school year over 96 percent of the total population aged 6 through 17 were enrolled in public, parochial, or private schools.[11]

In addition, schools now have extended their holding power. According to the November-December, 1962, issue of *School Life*, published by the United States Office of Education, the *retention* rate from the fifth grade through high-school graduation has more than doubled in the past 30 years. The increase in retention rate is even greater between the fifth grade and the first year in college: about 34 percent of our former fifth graders now go on to college, compared with only 12 percent 30 years ago. This means that there are greater percentages of all age groups attending school, since they are staying in school much longer than they did before. It seems likely that within the next two decades, completion of grade 14 will become the acceptable end of education. In other words, the completion of junior college in years to come will probably be as common as high-school graduation is today.

Another factor in increased enrollments is the change in general economic conditions. In the early years of this century, parents did not encourage their children to stay in school or even to complete elementary school, because the family needed the additional revenue. This is no longer true except in a few backward communities and states. Or perhaps there has been a compromise: the children go to school and the mother works.

During the school year 1962-63 there was a total of 51,300,000 students—28 percent of our population—enrolled in all types of institutions offering elementary, secondary, and higher education: 39,700,000 children were enrolled in full-time public schools; 6,700,000 in non-public schools; 300,000 in other types of schools, including federal Indian schools, federally operated elementary and secondary schools on posts, practice schools in teacher-training institutions, and residential schools for exceptional children; and 4,600,000 in institutions of higher education.[12] These figures will probably continue to rise.

The second factor in higher school costs is the lengthening of the school year from an average of 144 days in 1900 to 180 days in 1962. If school "keeps" for a longer period of the year, the costs must be expected to climb.

---

[11] *Progress of Public Education in the United States of America 1962-63* (Washington, D.C.: U.S. Office of Education, Department of Health, Education, and Welfare, 1963), p. 5.

[12] *Ibid.*, p. 5.

To illustrate the enrichment of the public-school program, a short list of offerings that are found in today's schools that were not found in the schools only a few years ago will suffice: vocational education, adult education, driver education, health services, gymnasiums and other facilities for physical exercise, classrooms for the mentally and physically handicapped, decent libraries, school-lunch programs, school-transportation programs, and guidance services. All these are in addition to expansion of the academic curriculum.

The fourth factor involved in increased school costs pertains to teacher preparation. Most teachers are now entering the classroom with at least a bachelor's degree. (This may not be true in every state or locale, especially at the elementary-school level.) As more teachers complete their B.A. degree, and as more teachers attain their master's or doctor's degrees, the salaries will tend to rise. (Teachers are paid more for both greater preparation and increased experience.) And more and more men are entering the teaching profession.

The final item contributing to increased school costs is inflation. The United States has experienced an almost uninterrupted inflationary rise since the turn of the twentieth century. For American education merely to maintain the *status quo*, expenditures must increase proportionately.

School costs will continue to rise. In a country that gains in population, believes strongly in education, and wants to raise the standard of living, there is no alternative to investing more money in the educational enterprise.

The Semantics of Federal Aid and Federal Control*

by S. SAMUEL SHERMIS

In any discussion of crucial social problems, one of the most persistent and noteworthy characteristics of human beings is their tendency to become hypnotized by symbols. Such symbols, possessing enormous emotional power, act to fix attention on a rigid category of meanings; at the same time, they exclude consideration of other cate-

* S. Samuel Shermis, "The Semantics of Federal Aid and Federal Control," *Phi Delta Kappan*, 43 (October, 1961):35-37. By permission of the editor.

gories of meaning. This is particularly true in discussions of federal aid to education.

The argument goes like this: Federal aid, say its supporters, is a necessity at this time. No, no, challenge opponents; federal aid inevitably leads to repressive federal control, and no one wants that. The supporters reply that such need not necessarily be the case, that federal aid has been given in other areas and has certainly not led to federal control. Opponents then cite instances where federal aid has indeed brought on controls. And so the argument goes. So long as it centers on the spectre of federal control, other more significant aspects of the situation are ignored.

THE BACKGROUND OF FEAR OF "CONTROL"

Let us examine the background of the long-standing fear of federal control on the part of the American people. It is apparent that Americans have entertained a powerful, and very likely irrational, fear of centralized control. An explanation of this fear would have to take into consideration the early history, and even the European background, of colonists during our country's settlement in the seventeenth and eighteenth centuries. European immigrants who had suffered under arbitrary and despotic governments tended to see centralized governments as being actually and potentially repressive. A brief citation of such despotism would include both the Tudor monarchy and the Commonwealth and Protectorate governments of England; it would include the absolutist kings of France and Spain; it would include the small but tyrannical princelings of the Germanies. In short, the background of our founding fathers was rich in experiences that would make them fear the unlimited power of centralized authority.

Transplanted to a new world, this fear was reflected in the expression, "The best government is that which governs least." This famous statement accurately expresses the idea that citizens must look upon centralized government with eternal suspicion and oppose every attempt of the government to arrogate powers to itself. Every new power claimed by the centralized government, it is feared, will lead to an inevitable curtailment of personal liberties. So strong was this belief that opponents of the Constitution of 1788 would not rest until a specific bill of rights was appended in order to guarantee that hard-fought freedoms would not be removed by arbitrary decision.

The nineteenth century and what has been called "Social Darwinism," the philosophy of Herbert Spencer, added a new dimension to the long-standing fear of authority. According to Spencer, whose theories were generally ignored in Europe but enthusiastically accepted in this country, society consists of many conflicting elements. Given a natural progression of events, the strongest and most capable group will win in the battle for the survival of the fittest. The true role of government was that of a passive mediator, an umpire, a neutral referee. Government was not to interfere, but merely to mediate the ongoing and absolutely necessary conflict.

But since those days conditions have changed mightily, and newer ways of looking at society and at the role of government have evolved. Still, alongside these newer ways remain strong remnants of earlier thinking. Despite the New Deal, despite the growth of cities, the expansion of population, the new interdependence of peoples, and rapidly accelerating technological development, Americans find themselves on both horns of a vicious dilemma: They desperately seek a solution to their problems, but they entertain grave fears about the very source of that solution.

Our divided attitude has resulted in a tragic time lapse between the onset of any social problem and attempts to deal with it—not only in education, but in almost all other fields. The Industrial Revolution made its appearance in the early nineteenth century; but federal regulations on wages, hours, safety, and sanitation, and federal health, sickness, and accident benefits had to wait until the 1930's.

Reading the literature of this period, one finds a good deal of mention of probable and possible federal control. Virtually every federal law concerning industrial welfare was passed in the teeth of fear of "federal control." It would appear, then, that the emotional impact of the word "control" has acted so as to preclude dispassionate analysis of actual conditions. Since "federal control" is *a priori* presumed to be something wicked—so presumed by both opponents and proponents of federal aid—frequently little effort is made to go beyond the terms to see just what it is that is being discussed.

THE SPECIFICS OF CONTROL

Let us address ourselves to the question: Is federal control inherently bad? Those who would answer "yes" to this question seem unconsciously to assume that the federal government is a crushing, impersonal, bureaucratic organization unable to restrain itself from eradicating personal liberties. The writer will freely grant that whenever the larger governing unit has become active in an area of human behavior, liberties are frequently obliterated. *But*, this is not the whole issue. The question that ought to be asked is not simply, "Are we going to lose a liberty?" but "What is the nature of the personal liberty at stake?" Or, to put it in another way, "Is that which the government proposes to do more or less valuable than the liberty that is being threatened?"

Let us cite some historical examples to illustrate the point. At one time it was assumed that justice was largely of purely personal concern. It was the duty of the family or clan of the injured one to punish the evildoer. Should your brother bloody me in a fight, my brothers or cousins would then seek rightful and just retribution. It was the right of the family, its sacred and inviolable right, to punish anyone who committed a crime involving property or personal injury. When punishment of criminals and lawbreakers became the concern of society, individuals were indeed deprived of their freedom to dispense justice personally. It would appear quite obvious that they lost a right. Is there anyone today who would wish to restore this right, or does it appear that the ongoing march of civilization demanded that individuals relinquish this right in favor of a centralized authority?

By the same token, the right to own or control human beings was assumed to be a sacred and God-given prerogative. For many centuries the strong and powerful had owned slaves and had used them to perform menial duties. The Bible, it was said, obviously sanctioned such a custom. It was altogether right and desirable that one human being should treat another as if he were a chattel. In some parts of America the Emancipation Proclamation of 1863 was greeted by the lament that a sacred property right was being removed by a repressive central authority. But today we generally agree that our way of life is such that this right ought to have been given up.

In the world of commerce sixty years ago the prevalent ethic was that of *caveat emptor*—let the buyer beware. It was the right of producers to sell any commodity, be it ever so poisonous, corrosive, or destructive. It was the right of advertisers to advance any and every claim with regard to their product. Useless or even dangerous patent medicines were invested with "miraculous healing properties" while buyers wasted money, postponed competent medical care, and sometimes damaged themselves irreparably. When the Pure Food and Drug Act of 1904 was passed and when Federal legislation was enacted to inspect and regulate meat-packing centers, the cry was heard that the federal government was depriving helpless individuals of sacred rights. But today the right to make a profit no longer takes precedence over consideration of public health.

History, therefore, does not reveal to me any instances of the kind of absolute right about which many talk today. Those who express fear that certain rights will be removed tacitly assume that these rights are inherent in the very nature of things, that they are immutable realities. Surely the social sciences have long since revealed that what has passed for natural law or rights are not anything of the sort, but are, rather, deeply ingrained values and customs. Were we to come to the conclusion that the rights which we feel are sacred and unchangeable are not absolutistic laws of nature but are values which must be seen in the context of other values, a good deal of the rigidity of the present discussion would disappear.

These three examples ought to suggest that it is quite in order for the public represented by the federal government to take away a right —even an old, cherished, and presumably sacred right—in the interests of a greater good. Thus the focus of attention needs to be placed not on the disappearance of a particular right but on whether the alternative is better or worse. Instead of considering the situation as if it were embedded in an absolute, we ought to take specific circumstances into account. Absolutes are not open to inspection or verification. Specific situations should be decided on their merits.

Should federal aid to education be enacted next year, it is quite possible that changes would be made in the state or local administrative structure. On the other hand, it is possible that there may not be such changes. History is replete with instances wherein federal subsidies have not resulted in federal control. Assistance to railroads did not result in federal control. Control came quite a few years after the practice began, and then only because of circumstances unassociated with the original aid. This, however, is not the issue. The issue ought to be, "Are federal aid and possible control preferable to the alternative?" If federal aid is indeed associated with some control, what will this mean *specifically?* When the GI Bill was instituted after World War II, federal accreditation of educational institutions was somehow seen as preferable to allowing war veterans to be fleeced by diploma mills and fraudulent or ineffective educational institutions. This was clearly federal control. Was it a good or bad practice? Did unwarranted restrictions on curriculum or on academic freedom result from this federal control?

I would like to suggest five questions which, if asked, might prove considerably more fruitful than the disputation concerning federal aid and federal control:

1. Do federal aid and/or control necessarily mean an *unjustifiable* reduction of significant personal liberties?

2. Is the traditional concept of local autonomy over education adequate for today's circumstances?

3. What agency or agencies can provide the necessary financing for public education? Are present financing procedures adequate to meet educational expenses?

4. Is it possible for equitable and effective machinery to be set up in such a way that federal aid will accomplish what needs to be done?

5. If education does not receive more adequate financing, if schools are not built, if teachers are not properly compensated, if students do not develop their abilities, what is going to happen?

SUMMARY

In this discussion I have tried to indicate a new approach to guide discussion of federal aid to education. I have contended that a long-standing fear of centralized authority—a fear which I maintain is both irrational and unjustifiable—has prevented clear analysis of the major issues. I have suggested that an exclusive preoccupation with an emotionally charged phrase, "federal control," has deflected examination of other important aspects of a crucial national issue. I have noted that while entrance of the larger governing unit has led to elimination of certain rights, it seems that the net gains—new rights, if you will—more than offset the losses. I have also tried to indicate that critical needs of specific situations ought to force discussion into channels which will be considerably more fruitful. When the hypnotic force of the words "federal control" loses its power, we shall then be able to examine the issue in a more meaningful and fruitful way.

Federal Aid to Elementary and Secondary Schools: An Unnecessary Danger*

by ALBERT H. QUIE

The Honorable Albert H. Quie is a member of the United States House of Representatives from Minnesota's first congressional district. A Republican, he has served in the House since 1958. He has served as a school-board member and is a member of the House Committee on Education and Labor. He was the ranking minority member of the House Select Subcommittee on Education.

* Albert H. Quie, "Federal Aid to Elementary and Secondary Schools: An Unnecessary Danger," *The High School Journal,* 45 (January, 1962): 143-151. By permission of the editor.

One of the most unfortunate aspects of the recent discussions concerning the question of Federal assistance to education, with specific reference to elementary and secondary schools, is that a great deal of emotionalism has become involved. This is perhaps most clearly demonstrated by the parochial school issue. In part, however, I feel that the height of feeling generated over the problem of Federal assistance to lower education is intentional: included in the general school assistance proposal submitted by the Administration are the so-called Impacted Area Laws enacted by the Eighty-First Congress. To be extended and associated with the present education proposal, are P.L. 815, which authorizes assistance for construction of facilities in federally impacted areas, and P.L. 874, which authorizes financial assistance to school districts in impacted areas for their current operating expenses. Both of these laws expired on June 30, 1961, and legislation is required in this Congressional session in order that they may be extended for the coming school year. It has been well established that these laws cover an area of Federal responsibility, and their existence has been highly justified. Their inclusion in the present general school bill amounts to little more than an attempt to gain support for the whole proposal on the strength of two laws of acknowledged need and effectiveness.

What I propose to do here is to try to clear the air around this whole question. I feel that because of misunderstanding and misrepresentation, only some of the more obvious factors pertaining to education in America have been examined. Investigation must be made beyond the mere presentation of figures—into proper evaluation of them and of the factors which were involved in their compilation. Most importantly, there must be no separation in the definition of WHAT constitutes a problem and WHY a given problem really exists. A great volume of statistical data has been presented by the Administration, but I feel that certain factors which account for the figures arrived at are generally overlooked, and the implication is made that certain shortages are "absolute" and must be met with Federal action.

Supporters of the Administration's bill to provide assistance throughout the nation for elementary and secondary education attempt to justify their program on the basis of a nationwide need. What has been the record of the support of education by the state and local governments? President Kennedy this year sent to Congress a message in which he said that over the next ten years, this country must construct about 600,000 classrooms in order to keep up with the needs of increased enrollments and the replacement of obsolete facilities. In the past five years, however, an average of better than 69,000 classrooms have been built annually. Some 81,000 classrooms have been built since 1956 over-and-above the needs of that period brought on by increased enrollments and obsolesence. Administration spokesmen indicate that, nevertheless, the "estimated shortage" has remained about the same since 1956—about 140,000 classrooms. I will refer back to this figure later on in this statement, however, a partial reason for this is that the standard for what constitutes a classroom shortage has been changing. In recent years, several states have re-evaluated their shortages upwards of several thousands of classrooms per year. There are no uniform standards applied to the collection of this data, which is left up to the local superintendent or to the state officials. There are absolutely no guarantees as to the reliability of their judgments, and the methods by which the data in question is gathered has not been without a great deal of criticism. The facts remain that in the past five years, the number of classrooms in use has increased by 28.3 per cent, while enrollments increased by only 19.6 per cent; and, more than one-half of the classrooms now in use have been built since World War II.

Facts bear out a similar situation with respect to the teacher supply. While the public school enrollment increased 19.6 per cent in the last five years, the number of teachers increased by 24.3 per cent. At the present time, the national average of students per certified teacher is 26.0, whereas seven years ago it was 28.4. Furthermore, the outlook for future teacher supply is very good. The Office of Education has projected an 82 per cent increase in earned college degrees for the 1958-1968 period, and the present level of college students preparing for teachers' certificates, 31 per cent, is expected to remain fairly constant. In the next ten years, the number of certified teachers is expected to double, while the school-age population is projected to increase by about 20 per cent.

A focal point in this controversy is the actual record and ability of the state and local governments to support elementary and secondary education. Expenditures for school support have increased from 4 per cent of the National Income in 1950, $241.8 billion, to 6 per cent of the National Income in 1960, $418.4 billion. This surely shows a willingness of the people of this country to make expenditures for education. The future prospects, moreover, indicate that the task of financing our public schools will probably be considerably easier in the 1960's than it has been in the past decade. The average annual increases in enrollment for the second half of the coming decade are projected to be only about one-half of that which we experienced in the second half of the past decade, or, average increases of 600,000 students per year as compared with the late average of 1,200,000 per year. And, the American economy is expected to maintain at least the rate it has for the past ten years; reputable economists have projected our GNP to rise from $500 billion to $700 billion by 1970.

School support has traditionally come from two sources: the state and the local governments, with the exception of limited Federal participation in programs of special national concern. Because I believe that the facts concerning the economic capacity of state and local units have been misrepresented, there are several points which I would like to bring out. The financial picture of the state and local governments indicates that in the 1927 to 1959 period, taxes multiplied by about five times; yet, the taxes as a percentage of the National Income remained about the same. Correspondingly, the Federal taxes multiplied by about twenty times, and Federal taxes as a percentage of the National Income increased by over four times. This revenue expansion, for all levels, has been uneven. Proponents of broad Federal action are quick to point out that since World War II, state and local revenues increased by about 256 per cent, whereas Federal revenues have increased by about 68 per cent. The reason for this disparity is that Federal revenues, in the past, have made their greatest expansion in wartime. In peacetime, the path is open for the lower levels to meet their obligations and increase, if necessary, their revenues. Illustration of the rate of increase in local and state taxes is evidently intended to prove that those taxes have been extended too greatly, and that recourse should be made to Federal taxing power. The facts, however, just do not bear this out. Besides the fact that Federal, state, and local taxes all come from the same people, the state and local taxes are still relatively low. It has been pointed out, for example, that typical state income taxes range from one to seven percent of personal income, while the Federal counterparts range from twenty to ninety-one percent of personal income.

The allegation that the Federal government has superior taxing powers is without foundation, for the only tax source which is available to the Federal government and which is not available to the states are the import duties. The only source of income for school support on the local level is the property tax. While it is true that there are limits to the amount of financing which can come from this tax base alone, the limits are frequently artificially set. Many states have set up legal restrictions on the size of property taxes and the size of the public debt, the same way that many states have set up prohibitions to public universities from contracting long-term loans.

What actually is being done? Last year a new record for school bonds approved at elections was set, both in the amount of funds and the percentage of approval. The volume of approved school bonds exceeded that for all other types of bonds. Last year, the sale of state and local bonds for school financing reached a new record of 7.2 billion dollars.

The facts I have presented represent the total picture of our educational system across the nation. It is evident that there is not a problem of finding support for our elementary and secondary schools. What many proponents of present legislation do not seem to realize is that the traditional sources of school support have by no means reached the limits of their capacities. This is not to say that I reject all allegations that there are problems which are confronting our schools. Nevertheless, since the Administration has proposed a general program of education, nation-wide figures must be taken into account. The point is, there just is not a serious crisis across the nation which warrants nation-wide Federal assistance to the elementary and secondary schools.

I feel that the issue is easier to comprehend when it is discussed on a concrete basis. For this reason, I would like to approach the problem in the light of provisions in the bill submitted by the Administration. As our educational system operates at the present, the state legislatures and the local boards of education make the decisions concerning the division of school funds and the distribution of support among the various units. The proposed program of Federal assistance would give to state educational agencies the decisions of distribution of Federal funds among the local units and division of funds between teachers' salaries and school construction. It would authorize the payment of allotments to the states on the basis of estimates made by the U.S. Commissioner of Education. State agencies would submit to the Commissioner an application which would provide for the specific distribution of the allotments. Final approval of these applications would be up to the Commissioner. This would greatly strengthen the position of the State educational agencies at the expense of the voters, the local boards of education, and the state legislatures. The provisions of this bill will take the power to decide the size of school funds from the states and communities and substitute a Federal formula in their place. In this program, which is designed to offer general and nation-wide assistance, there is no truly adequate means of accounting for discrepancies in the ability to raise standards and the actual effort expended towards that goal. State agencies of Education will allocate funds on the basis of need—and this is important—determined by the State agencies of Education. Federal funds are to be granted outright; there is no provision requiring local and state funds to match the Federal allotments. If a project is considered to meet the qualifications of need, then it may receive Federal monies. It is certain that many communities would postpone their school construction plans for several years, if necessary, in order to enhance their chances of qualifying their projects for Federal grants. Furthermore, many bond issues would be likely to fail in those districts which the state education agencies determined not to include among those to receive Federal aid since they may receive Federal monies if they wait. This could actually slow up school construction.

When this Nation's finances are involved in foreign aid, we have a right to expect, and even demand (as is the case at the present with respect to our foreign aid to Latin and South America) that funds are being supplied to "help others help themselves." The Administration's general education bill does have a "maintenance of effort" provision which is intended to see that efforts by the state and local levels are maintained and increased. This does not really amount to much, however. In the first place, Federal funds would be made available without any mandatory matching from the state. The psychological effect of Federal assistance being considered to be just a "gift" is well known—without a mandatory matching to unlock Federal funds, the threat of a reduction of one-third in the size of the "gift from the government" will not have the stimulating effect some would lead us to believe. Secondly, the whole "maintenance of effort" provision is inoperative for the first year; only the second and third years of the program would be affected. The over-all intention of this bill has much merit, for it seeks to strengthen our system of education. But I am confident that, if enacted, the failure of this measure to achieve the desired aims will lead to demands for tighter control over the Federal funds. This action, to me, would be inevitable, and it would spell the end to what has traditionally been the strength of our educational system.

With state education agencies allocating Federal funds to areas of substantiated need, it would be well to look deeper into the question of "need" as it would be facing the state agencies in the future (and as it has been facing state agencies in the determination of classroom and teacher shortages). The most recent figures available indicate that throughout the nation there are 42,428 different school districts, 35,297 of which are currently operating schools. A recent study of school district organization indicates that in twenty-one states, the average geographical areas of the school districts are less than 49 square miles, or seven miles square. A great deal could be said of the change which has taken place just in transportation since these districts were drawn up. Twenty-three states across the nation have thus far met the problem with legislation making possible mandatory redistricting. In these twenty-three states, there are fewer districts of less than 1,200 students than in any other ten states combined which have not adopted compulsory legislation.

Of the 35,297 operating school districts in America, there are 14,862 which have less than 50 students. This means that over 42 per cent of all school districts in the nation have less than 50 pupils enrolled. Adequate size is essential to the operation of a school program. A grade school needs at least one teacher for each grade level. Many experts feel that a school system embracing all 12 grades must have as many as 1200 students before it can offer adequate opportunities in education and meet the demands of this modern era. Regardless of the accuracy of that allegation, the fragmentation which exists is undoubtedly the major factor contributing to the figures which are being cited to show that there is a "grave shortage of classrooms and teachers." Of course the figures have some validity, but only partially, for they are a result of what has become a weakness in our system of education. The important thing to remember here is that, because of the nature of these "shortages," specific and not general measures should be taken to solve the problem. The Administration refutes the claim that money will be a panacea to the current problems, but I cannot understand what else is involved in their proposed legislation. No amount of money will ever make it practical for a very small school district with very small enrollment to employ qualified teachers in the sciences, mathematics, Latin and modern foreign languages. The school district is the heart of our educational system—and it is also at the heart of the educational problem. Here, in the very small school district, is where state education agencies gather figures for obsolete classrooms; here is where a teacher's skills are inefficiently used; here is where teachers of insufficient qualifications are to be found.

Let the state of Nebraska serve as an example of the manner by which the proposed legislation will affect elementary and secondary education. I believe that it is very fair to single out one state in this matter, since the Administration has designed its proposal on the premise that there is need in all areas of the nation, and Federal assistance would be granted to each and every state. Bear in mind that the "intention" of the bill in question is not only to provide "needed assistance" but also to give stimulus to efforts on lower levels. To justify a general assistance bill, there must be adequate justification from every area in which its effect will be felt—otherwise, assistance ought not to be designed on a broad and general basis.

The latest statistics available in Washington indicate that the state of Nebraska has 3,255 school districts actually operating schools—more than any other state in the Union. Of this number, 2,760 operate schools with less than 50 pupils enrolled—82 per cent of the total. The average geographical area per operating public school system in Nebraska is only 23.7 square miles, or less than 5 miles square. The most recent figures available to government planners indicate that the state government, which has a variety of tax sources to choose from, contributes only 6.5 per cent of the total revenues which go into school support. The various local units, which for the most part are dependent solely upon the property tax and bond issues for education revenues, contributed 88.9 per cent of the total. From this great dependence upon local support, it might be expected that revenue expansion would be somewhat inflexible and limited. The state of Nebraska depends on local support of education to a greater extent than any other of the fifty states, and the state government contributes a smaller percentage of school support than any other state. Nevertheless, the grant of Federal funds which would be made to Nebraska would amount to 90 per cent of what the state government itself contributed. Furthermore, the size of the grant to Nebraska would exceed the revenues taken out of the state to pay for the program.

I fail completely to understand just how the proponents of this general Federal assistance bill can justify their program when such obvious areas of local and state ability exists. The addition of $6 million in Nebraska for educational support will most certainly tend to perpetuate the situation as it exists. To be sure, Nebraska could find a use for $6 million, but will these funds encourage the state government to significantly alter the antedated organization of school systems and increase the state contributions toward education support, commensurate with its responsibilities? I think not.

There are, of course, problems which exist which are not directly related to school redistricting. One such problem is the existence of "curtailed sessions." Examination of this problem reveals that it is most often present in the urban and suburban areas, and specifically in those areas which are experiencing rapid growth of population and and business activity. Actually, more than one-half of the schools which report split-sessions are located in the four most populous and wealthy states. Now, the Administration program is designed to allocate $720 million in 1962 to be distributed among the various states, and from the state agencies to designated areas of need. It is easy to forget that $720 million must be raised in taxes to finance this program, with the higher-income states taking a proportionately larger share of the taxes, and receiving a proportionately smaller share of the Federal funds in return. Although the program has since been expanded, estimates made on the original bill indicate that New York, for example, would be paying $88.4 million in taxes for the general education bill, and would be receiving in return from the government $37.7 million; California would be paying $67.1 million and would be receiving in return $57.7 million. I just cannot believe that this represents a net gain for two states which have a problem of overcrowding and curtailed school sessions.

This bill aims at no emergency, provides no specific remedies; indeed, it makes no attempt even to define particular needs. It is analogous to a pain-killer being used in an illness—it may perhaps relieve some effects, but it will not cure anything. The shortcomings will continue to exist, and so therefore will the program of Federal participation. Administration spokesmen have frankly admitted that they expect this program, if enacted, to encrease in scope and to be on a continuing basis. I would like to emphasize the word "relieve." This legislation could do no more, and the role of the Federal government in education would, by necessity, become ever-larger.

A general program of Federal aid to the nation's schools, with specific reference to the legislation being proposed by the Administration, is actually dangerous. The history of American education is one of local and state initiative and support. If present proposals go into effect, there will be a loss of local and voter power; there will be a serious stifling of incentive and effort, and there will be increased necessities for Federal participation. An ill-defined and nation-wide assistance program is essentially dangerous because it is not needed. It is dangerous because it would not be truly effective—it would have a tendency to perpetuate the shortcomings which presently exist in our system of education, and shortages and poor quality education would be a continuing problem.

As a member of the Education and Labor Committee of the House, and two of its subcommittees, I have a sincere interest in the welfare of American education. My approach to Federal participation in matters dealing with education is not "obstructionist" nor is it "dogmatic." I have and shall continue to support measures for which there is a proven need, measures which will be both sound and effective. It is precisely for these reasons that I am in opposition to a general Federal aid program for elementary and secondary schools.

The Present Need for Federal Aid to Education*

by EDITH GREEN

The Honorable Edith Green is a member of the United States House of Representatives from Oregon's third congressional district. A Democrat, she has served in the House since 1954. Representative Green is a former school teacher and the former director of public relations for the Oregon Education Association. She is a member of the House Committee on Education and Labor and was the chairman of the House Select Subcommittee on Education.

In affirming the case for Federal aid to our education system, it is necessary, but not sufficient, to discuss the statistical evidence of need for help. This I intend to do before the end of this article. But all the statistical evidence, all the figures showing the shortage of facilities and the inadequacy of our national effort in education will fall far short of convincing those who feel that education is not a matter of national concern. It is to this question of principle that we must first address ourselves.

In my capacity as a member of the House Committee on Education and Labor, a large percentage of my daily mail deals with educational matters. Some of these letters, both from my own State and from elsewhere, oppose Federal aid to the schools in terms which can be summed up as follows:

> We in_____oppose Federal aid to education because we don't need it. Our community is meeting its school needs, and we object to being taxed in order to make up for the failures of the people of_____.
> Let them work to meet their own needs, as we have worked to meet ours.

In all fairness, this is a compelling argument—leaving aside for the moment the accuracy or inaccuracy of the assertions involved. The fundamental question which must be answered in considering Federal

---

* Edith Green, "The Present Need for Federal Aid to Education," *The High School Journal*, 45 (January, 1962): 136-142. By permission of the editor.

aid to the schools is not whether or not the schools are in need, but whether or not there is a reason for Federal concern.

I believe there is.

To begin with, there is little historical justification for the argument that the Federal Government has no constitutional basis upon which to take an active interest in promoting education. It is quite true that public education was not mentioned in the Constitution among the powers specifically delegated to the Congress. Neither was the development of atomic energy, nor the maintenance of an air force. And these omissions all stem from the same historical fact. Public education was not specified by the Founding Fathers because, with a few rare exceptions, the basic idea of public education is newer than the Constitution. At the same time that our Constitution was written, most schools in this country were under private auspices. Provision was not specifically made for an interest in a system which had not yet begun to achieve anything resembling the significance it has today.

But this does not mean that the Founding Fathers were indifferent to the possibility of a Federal role in education. George Washington, who had presided over the Constitutional Convention, said, in his first Presidential message to the Congress.

> There is nothing which can better deserve your patronage than the promotion of science and literature. . . . Whether this desirable object will be best promoted by affording aids to seminaries of learning already established, by the institution of a general university, *or by any other expedients* will be well worthy of a place in the deliberations of the Legislature. (emphasis added)

The subsequent history of Congressional interest in education offers ample evidence of the continuing Federal concern in this field. The Republican Policy Committee of the House of Representatives recently prepared a list of precedents for Federal aid to education. The precedents thus listed are as follows:

1. Land-grant colleges.
2. Surplus revenues for education. (In 1837, the Congress distributed the surplus revenues then in the Treasury to the States for educational purposes.)
3. Vocational Education.
4. RFC loans for Public Schools and Teachers' Salaries.
5. Veterans Education and Training (G.I. Bill, Korean G.I. Bill).
6. International Educational Exchange (Fulbright and Smith-Mundt Act).
7. Rural Library Services.
8. National School Lunch Act.

9. Federally Impacted Areas Legislation.
10. College Housing Loans.
11. Cooperative Research.
12. White House Conference on Education.
13. President's Committee on Education Beyond the High School.
14. Teachers of Mentally Retarded Children.
15. War Orphans' Educational Assistance.
16. National Defense Education Act.

(That particular Committee report makes the incredible leap from those facts to the conclusion that the Federal Government has never had an "intention to provide Federal support for education on a secondary or primary level." I hope I shall not be accused of partisanship if I confess my inability to see how these premises support that conclusion.)

In summation, the historical evidence is strongly on the side of the right of the Federal Government to take an interest in education, when there is a need.

The advent of Sputnik in October of 1957 did not *create* the intimate connection between our nation's educational adequacy and its basic strength. But it did call this connection to the attention of a great many people who had hitherto overlooked the importance of education. With the passage of the National Defense Education Act, the Congress officially recognized the fact that our defense is deeply rooted in our schools. The increasing technological complexity of our defense establishment gives further emphasis to this connection. To those who boast of the adequacy of their own local school system, and who assert that the quality of the schools in the next county or next state, or across the nation, is no concern of theirs we can point out that a defense system which depends upon adequate schools, depends upon adequate schools *throughout the nation*. If a talented and well-motivated teen-ager in Indiana does not receive the kind of high school training he ought to have in order to develop a latent interest in physics, the people of Georgia and California may suffer ten years later because the nation has lost a potential nuclear physicist. "No school district," we can say, "is an island. It is a piece of the continent: a part of the main."

But even this argument, compelling as it may be, would lose its validity should the unlikeliest of miracles come to pass, and the cold war crisis [be] settled. The case for Federal aid to our schools, on a long-range, across-the-board basis, cannot be firmly established even on such a seemingly permanent aspect of the national scene as the struggle for democracy's survival. If the case is to be made, it ought to be made in terms of the inherently permanent needs of a free society, and not on the shifting exigencies of external problems.

But this case can be made. The impact of our educational system—and of its inadequacies—is obviously not limited to the field of military or scientific endeavor.

If schools in Montana are unable to equip Montana youth to compete for skilled occupations, then Montana will be a poorer market for Florida products. And even this argument, based on the assumption that Americans tend to remain in the place where they were born, falls short of recognizing the vitally important fact that ours is one of the most mobile of populations. In an article in the May, 1960, *Phi Delta Kappan*, Mr. W. W. Carpenter of the University of Missouri discussed the problems of pupil migration and its impact upon educational standards. In that article, Mr. Carpenter points out that:

> Children are no longer citizens of just one State. They are citizens of the nation. Their education or lack of it is of concern to the entire Nation because they not only may but do live in several States, not just one.
>
> Many of the future citizens of State A, for example are being born in the 49 other States and educated or not educated in the public schools of these States. Many are born into misery and poverty; many are denied good schools and quality teaching; and some have been denied many of the rights for which America was established. On the other hand, many are superior in mind, body, and spirit and have attended superior schools and have been taught by master teachers. The citizens of State A appreciate receiving the latter into the State. But the children born into poverty, disease, crime, delinquency, immorality; children who are hungry, ill clothed, neglected, and denied human rights and good schools bring with them ignorance, disease and disrespect for the law.

As Mr. Carpenter points out, our national mobility has resulted in making the quality of education in a given area a matter of direct and pressing concern for the people of other areas. Economic and social standards, anywhere in the nation, can be damaged by inadequate education—anywhere in the nation. We are not separated from one another by state boundaries. Americans have never ceased the restless wandering that subdued a continent. The automobile, the airplane, the telephone, radio, television, and all the other means we have developed to reduce distance to a myth have had the effect of allowing not only the benefits of our economy, but also the weaknesses of our society to spread throughout the nation. A poor school is a weak link in the nation's strength, not just in the strength of the State in which it is located.

The fact, then, that the adequacy of our schools has a national impact is the basis for the judgment that the Federal government has a legitimate and continuing interest in the ability of our schools to meet, not just the challenge of Sputnik, but all the challenges of the 20th century.

The next question, obviously, is whether or not there is any need for school assistance at any level. If the schools have no problems, then the case for Federal assistance is, at best, only a hypothetical one.

Let's look, then, at the need itself. In my capacity as Chairman of the Special Subcommittee on Education of the House Education and Labor Committee, I had the privilege of presiding over a number of hearings on the President's proposal for assistance to the nation's colleges and universities. The original bill, as first recommended by the President, called for a two-fold program of assistance to the colleges and to college students—loans to the institutions for the construction of classrooms and libraries, and scholarships for deserving and needy young people to enable them to begin and to pursue undergraduate studies. At the time this article is being written, the scholarship provisions have been temporarily set aside, and there is no way of being certain what will happen with the academic facilities proposal. But the facts involving need have not changed, and it is to those facts that I wish to address myself here.

College enrollments now total 3,600,000, and they are expected to increase by over a million in the next five years. By 1970, according to conservative estimates, over 6,000,000 students will be enrolled in— or seeking admission to—our nation's colleges and universities. Estimates are tricky things, but it does seem safe to state that within a decade, the college population will be at least 2/3 again as large as it is today. And if these conservative estimates are correct, the colleges will fall short of meeting their financial needs for academic facilities by $1.5 billion in 1965, and $2.5 billion in 1970.

These needs, of course, must be met from a variety of sources. Increased tuitions are inevitable. Increased tax support for the State and municipal universities are inevitable. Alumni groups and educational foundations will, unquestionably, be meeting increased demand with increased generosity. But all of these possible sources can only help to fill the gap. If the Federal Government has an interest in educational adequacy—and I believe we have demonstrated it does—then the Federal Government, too, will have to help meet these needs.

Inadequacies in the academic physical plant are not, of course, the only problem facing our country in considering its system of higher education. Of even greater significance is the fact that large numbers of students—talented and with superior ability—are unable to enter our colleges and universities because of their own insufficient financial resources.

According to testimony before the House Committee by Dean Charles C. Cole, Jr., of Lafayette College, Easton Pa., speaking for the Association for Higher Education—

> . . . the Educational Testing Service conducted a questionnaire and tests among a 5-percent sample of the Nation's public secondary school seniors. The results of that survey revealed that insufficient financial resources prevented between 60,000 and 100,000 persons of superior ability from enrolling in college *each year*. Another group *of similar size and ability* apparently lack the interest or motivation for college. (Emphasis added)

In short, according to this respected authority, between 120,000 and 200,000 young people, who could profit from a college education—and whose abilities and talents the nation desperately needs—are absent from our college freshman classes each year. Half of these people are, according to Dr. Cole, not motivated toward college. How large a portion of these people lack the motivation because they see no hope of being able to finance a college education, I cannot tell. Presumably, the figure is substantial. But, even if we restrict ourselves to the 100,000 young people who want to enter the colleges and cannot, the loss of talent, the waste of brainpower is appalling!

President Kennedy, in his message urging passage of this legislation said,

> We must assure ourselves that every talented young person who has the ability to pursue a program of higher education will be able to do so if he chooses, regardless of his financial means.

President Eisenhower in 1958 told the Congress,

> Many able high school graduates do not go on to college. This represents a waste of needed talent.

The late Senator Robert Taft, speaking to the question of Federal aid to education said,

> It does not have the glamor that other things have, but it seems to me that we must go forward in the field of education for our people, and I know of no way of going forward in that field to any substantial degree without providing some Federal financial assistance. (Congressional Record, March 24, 1948)

The hard facts about the needs of our schools are not in evidence only at the level of higher education. Inadequate funds for facilities

—and for the other costs of education, including the salaries of teachers —must be supplemented from other sources.

According to testimony before another Subcommittee of the Education and Labor Committee, enrollment in the elementary and secondary schools of the nation increased by 11 million in the 1950's. In the 1960's, conservative estimates are that enrollment will continue to expand at a rate of 1.1 million students per year until 1965, after which —perhaps—enrollment *increases* will taper off to a rate of approximately 600,000 per year. These increases will call for adding 400,000 more teachers to the staffs of the nation's elementary and secondary schools by the end of the 60's. If we are to keep even the teachers we have, not to speak of recruiting 400,000 teachers, salary levels are going to have to be raised.

The public-school teacher in 1958 had an average annual income of $4,827. If he was just beginning to teach that year, his salary averaged $3,900, while the engineer who embarked on his profession in the same year averaged $6,120; the accountant $5,352, and the salesman $5,280.

I need not pursue this point further to indicate that there is a need for more money to pay the salaries of the teachers we will need in the next decade, and to continue to attract the kind of teacher our children deserve to the educational profession.

In hearings before this same Subcommittee, Dr. Ralph Flynt, Assistant U.S. Commissioner of Education, advised the Committee that 607,000 new classrooms would have to be built in the next ten years. Half of these would be needed to cope with increased enrollments, and the other half to meet the current backlog of 131,600 classrooms and to replace the 168,000 inadequate or substandard rooms now in use.

These statistics present a compelling picture for Federal action, and for Federal assistance.

In conclusion, I must say that this article was being written at a time when the House was on the verge of coming to grips with the school assistance issue, after many weary months of partisan and pressure group politics. As I put this article in the mail, I cannot tell what the Congress will finally send to the President in the form of education legislation. But it is apparently safe to say that it will be less than he requested—and less than is needed to meet the needs of our schools throughout the nation.

The Federal Government has the authority to act. The impact of action—or of inaction—will be nation-wide. Our economic well-being, the health of our social structure, and the very survival of freedom itself may well rest with the willingness of the Congress to respond, appropriately and in time, to the educational challenge of the Sixties.

SUGGESTED ACTIVITIES

1. Is there any relationship between the size of a school district and the financial support given to schools in that district? How would you gather data relevant to this question?

2. Request the following information from the Secretary of State in the state from which you come: The amount of money spent by your state education association in lobbying activities at the past five legislative sessions and the amount of money spent by the state taxpayers' league for the same purpose during the same period. Compare the amounts of money spent by these two organizations. Can you draw any inferences or conclusions?

3. Consult a labor-union leader and ask him the following question: "Would you be in favor of more financial assistance from the federal government to expand and improve vocational and industrial education in the public secondary schools?" After he has answered, then ask: "Are you in favor of more or less local control over education?" Do you perceive any contradiction in his answers?

4. Find out how many local school districts in your state are obtaining federal funds either directly or indirectly. Now obtain the stand that your state school-board association has taken on federal aid to education. (Hint: your state department has detailed financial reports on file in the college library.)

5. Find the percent of funds that the federal, state, and local governments contribute to support education in your state. How do local districts raise revenue for school support?

6. Public education is often referred to as "free." Make a list of all the fees, excluding bus fare and lunch fees, that were either mandatory or almost mandatory each year in your local high school? Any conclusions?

7. Find out if your state has any limit on the number of mills that the local school board can levy on the district's property for operation of schools. (a) Ask the local county assessor what the ratio is between assessed value and estimated market value for residential property. (b) In the light of the assessor's answer, how do the assessing practices affect local support of education?

SUGGESTED READINGS

BENSON, CHARLES S. *Perspectives on the Economics of Education.* Boston: Houghton Mifflin, 1963.   A collection of readings on school finance and management. The beginning student can benefit from the articles pertaining to the principles of taxation and public finance.

BURKE, ARVID J. *Financing Public Schools in the United States.* rev. ed.; New York: Harper, 1957.   An excellent reference work in the problems and issues of school financing.

Digest of Educational Statistics: 1964 Edition. Washington, D.C.: Office of Education, U.S. Department of Health, Education, and Welfare, 1964. An excellent source of statistical data on all phases of public and private education in the United States.

GALBRAITH, JOHN KENNETH. *The Affluent Society.* Boston: Houghton Mifflin, 1958.   This book caused a national sensation because the author presents a convincing argument that the American people have spent far more on the private sector than on the public sector of their economy. This thesis has important implications for public education.

JOHNS, R. L. AND MORPHET, E. L. (eds.). *Problems and Issues in Public School Finance.* New York: National Conference of Professors of Educational Administration, Teachers College, Columbia U., 1952.   Although the statistics in this work are outdated, the discussion about trends and financial problems is excellent.

MUNSE, ALBERT R. AND MCLOONE, EUGENE P. *Public School Finance Programs of the United States, 1957-1958.* Washington, D.C.: Office of Education, U.S. Department of Health, Education, and Welfare, 1960.   Although some of its data are now dated, this volume is one of the best sources for information about state public school finance programs.

SCHULTZ, THEODORE W. "Investment in Human Capital," *American Economic Review,* 51 (March, 1961):1-16.   Schultz's analysis of education as an investment in people is highly relevant to public finance.

SCHULTZ, THEODORE W. *The Economic Value of Education.* New York: Columbia U. Press, 1963.   An excellent, thought-provoking book.

SHULTZ, WILLIAM J. AND HARRIS, C. LOWELL. *American Public Finance.* 7th ed.; Englewood Cliffs: Prentice-Hall, 1959.   This volume, long a standard reference in public finance, is written for the advanced student.

V

Forces Shaping The Curriculum

The term "curriculum" does not refer simply to what is taught in the classroom. Other elements include extracurricular activities, the overall goals, assumptions about the mind, the relationship between the content of a discipline to immature children, the determination of what goes into a textbook, the legality of required subjects, and how the total school program has been created. Principles discussed in this section are all facets of the curriculum.

The first essay in the section, "The Curriculum: Attitudes, Problems, and Practices," is an overview of the meaning of curriculum. After a consideration of the part individual differences play in curricular practices, unrecognized but important forces in curriculum planning are discussed. The educational objectives of a school system have a direct bearing on or relationship to what is taught, how it is taught, and to whom it is taught.

"Influences on the Curriculum: Theories of Mind," by S. Samuel Shermis, presents a theoretical construct of how and why we learn. The three theories of mind, with their accompanying corollaries, can be identified in various forms throughout the United States.

In "What Content and When?" Dorothy M. Fraser further analyzes the content of the curriculum, with emphasis on the importance of basic learning theory.

One often hears that the "golden age" of American education lies in the past. This assumption about our schools may not stand up under careful examination, especially when one studies textbooks used in the "good old days" as John A. Nietz does in "Some Findings from Analyses of Old Textbooks."

What amounted to a revolution in thinking about the public-school curriculum occurred in the early decades of this century. This complex and often misunderstood movement is discussed in William Van Til's article "Is Progressive Education Obsolete?"

There are numerous direct and indirect influences from pressure groups that bear on the curriculum of the public schools. Jack Nelson's "What Is the Problem?" points up this phenomenon.

The Curriculum: Attitudes, Problems, and Practices

by S. SAMUEL SHERMIS and DONALD C. ORLICH

WHAT DOES "CURRICULUM" MEAN?

Most persons think of curriculum as simply "that which is taught in the schools." The difficulty in defining curriculum more precisely is that its meaning will be entirely dependent on one's philosophy, psychology, and notions of teaching method, because all of these factors determine the actual curriculum. There is no such thing as *the* curriculum, since there is no universal agreement as to what should constitute it. In brief, the meaning of *curriculum* depends entirely on time, place, circumstance, and personal preference.

TWO APPROACHES TO CURRICULUM DESIGN

We shall examine two approaches to curriculum design. The first views the curriculum as subject matter; the second means by "curriculum" a set of experiences. There are many curriculum theories, but most approaches can be categorized under one or the other of the headings of subject matter or experiences. (This is an oversimplification, but it is one that may help at this point.)

Curriculum as Subject Matter Those who view curriculum as subject matter usually assume that the goal of education is simply to transmit the cultural heritage. This means that the school's major function is to pass on to children information that is considered desirable for them to know. That which has occurred in the past is usually accepted as having inherent value. The literature, language, beliefs, values, art, music, and methods of computation that have existed in the past are assumed to be sufficiently important to warrant being passed on to *all* students. The rationale is that no culture can survive unless these aspects of the culture are directly, consciously, carefully, and thoroughly transmitted to the children who are to inherit the culture.[1]

The basic educational philosophy of those who would transmit the cultural heritage and omit all other types of learning is known as "authoritarianism." Authoritarianism is the position that adults ought to have the authority and responsibility for determining what children should know. It implies, of course, that adults *know* what is good and what is valuable.

The goal of this authoritarian, subject-centered approach is knowledge of subject matter *in and for itself*. It is simply good and desirable for children to learn arithmetic, spelling, reading, and history. These subjects possess value in and of themselves. They may or may not be a means to something else; if they are, it is incidental. They may or may not induce a child to appreciate or understand his cultural heritage.

The anthropological fact is that for a culture to survive, to renew itself, there must be a conscious attempt to transmit the cultural heritage. Therefore, those people who believe in a subject-centered, authoritarian approach to curriculum are, in part at least, quite correct in the stress they place on "subject matter." However, they are typically conservative,[2] tending to ignore the future and to confine themselves to the past and the present.

Curriculum as Experiences Because the above position tends to give short shrift to the future, another approach to curriculum has developed. This theory sees curriculum as a set of "desirable experiences." The emphasis is not on knowledge of any particular piece of information but on a "process" or skill to be mastered. Subject matter is used to develop facility in this process or set of processes. For example, students must acquire the ability to handle number concepts; to promote this ability, arithmetic, algebra, geometry, and other mathematics courses are taught. The subject matter is simply a tool

---

[1] See John Dewey's *Democracy and Education* (New York: Macmillan, 1916), Chs. I and II for a discussion of the importance of transmitting the cultural heritage.

[2] A "conservative" is usually defined as one who accepts the present as being most desirable. He can usually be expected to resist any attempt to change or modify what *is*. A "liberal" tends to look on change as desirable. The liberal is not entirely satisfied with the present; he sees many unfair and undesirable practices and wishes to change them. This distinction is useful provided one understands that there are no such things as "pure" liberals or conservatives.

or a means: it is not an end in itself. For another example, to be able to make political decisions, students study history, civics, social problems, and geography. By studying these subjects in the "right way" and by having a set of experiences, the individual is presumed to become a more "effective" person. These experiences include not only studying books but such things as observing a real trial, interviewing the commissioner of water works, or surveying community recreational needs.

The former approach—curriculum as subject matter—is extremely ancient. (This is *not* to be construed as meaning that it is necessarily "bad.") The ancient Hebrews used their religious writings, the Torah and Talmud, as "subject matter to be learned." The Europeans of the Middle Ages and Renaissance employed a subject-matter curriculum called the "Seven Liberal Arts." For centuries, university students studied seven subjects: astronomy, arithmetic, geometry, music, logic, rhetoric, and grammar. The present-day American conception of liberal arts, or the liberal college education, is rooted in this approach.

The experience curriculum assumes that experiences which children attempt under the school's direction will help produce a certain kind of person. This person is supposed to be, above all, "intelligent."[3] He is supposed to be able to "adjust" to the life around him. He is supposed to be able to "plan intelligently." He is supposed to be the kind of person who knows what ought to be changed and along what lines it ought to be changed. He "appreciates" his cultural heritage but, of course, is not enslaved by it. He is well-rounded. He can participate in group activities but is also an "individual." He chooses his leisure-time activities and recreation well, and his vocation wisely. He keeps up with current events, rears his family properly, reads good books, enjoys good music, and participates in civic activities. He epitomizes the "good" American. In fact, he does not exist!

Analysis of the Two Basic Approaches to Curriculum   Both curricular theories can be criticized. The subject-matter curriculum may produce a "well-trained" individual, one who knows persons, places, dates, formulas, and so forth. But it does not actively further much discernment or awareness. It does not necessarily produce a person who is critically aware of what he knows, does, and thinks. He probably is not even aware that he is operating under an authoritarian approach!

---

[3] "Intelligent" and "intelligence" are weasel-words; there is no clear understanding of what "intelligence" is or does. However, those who advocate the experience curriculum want, above all, students to be "intelligent." See John Dewey's works—for example, *Experience and Education* (New York: Macmillan, 1953).

On the other hand, those who deny the intrinsic importance of subject matter are also open to criticism. What they have done, in effect, is to separate the *content* of knowing from the *process* of knowing. They have somehow assumed that while *knowing* is important, what is *known* is not!

The weakness of the experience approach may be seen in some of the recent curricular modifications brought about by the "experience-centered" advocates. A course commonly taught in high school is "Social Problems" or "Contemporary Problems." The typical tendency is to study dating etiquette, teen-age problems, how to get along with your family, and the correct method of handling personal finances. When John Dewey introduced the concept of experience and suggested that the curriculum ought to begin with the concerns of students, he did not advocate that the curriculum *begin and end here*. He believed that the curriculum ought to begin with students' immediate concerns and then proceed to a higher, more abstract level. Thus, when the high-school curriculum concentrates on only the temporary problems of teen-agers, it errs in two respects: (1) it is not preparing the way for more advanced studies, and (2) it is not providing students with the deep insights and knowledge they actually need to solve problems, present or future. That is, students remain ignorant of the underlying meaning of what they supposedly know.

AMERICAN VALUES AND THE CURRICULUM

The extensive borrowing, adopting, synthesizing, and innovating have made our pluralistic society a collection of conflicting cultural traits. These conflicts have influenced what is taught in the schools. Schools are a part of society; they do not exist independently of the values, techniques, beliefs, and aspirations of that society. Therefore, conflicts generated by our culture have worked their way into the program of studies. Let us now look at some of the conflicts within the American curriculum.

We believe, as a society, that everyone should understand that which is "basic and fundamental." We call the "Three R's" the "fundamentals" of the American elementary school. However, the curriculum of the elementary school is not confined to the "Three R's." It includes health, science, art, physical education, music, woodworking, home economics, safety, fire prevention, manners, morals, social activities, dramatics, and so on and on. These "nonfundamental" subjects were placed in the curriculum because many people thought they were important. They illustrate the tendency of the American curriculum to snowball. We add courses as they are deemed necessary, but we rarely discard any. All of these subjects, of course, are important. But what is their order of relative importance? American schools have not provided an answer to this question. After all, if a seven-year-old child gets killed on his bicycle, it would obviously have been of "fundamental" importance to teach bicycle safety. So from 8:45 to 9:00 A.M. all bicycle owners may be required to take a legislature-enacted course, "The Fundamentals of Safety."[4]

Much of our public-school and university curriculum has come to us, practically unchanged, from the traditional, classical curriculum of the past. This curriculum, stemming from the ancient Greeks and Romans and the Europeans of the Middle Ages, was designed for an elite—an aristocracy. It included philosophy, literature, mathematics, and rhetoric (a term for formal speaking). It was designed to train the leaders of a society based on the assumption that some were born to rule and others were born to be ruled. Although it is often difficult to see how some parts of the curriculum fit into a modern democracy, it is indeed a cherished and beloved part of our life. However, the older aristocratic curriculum is only a part of the American curriculum.

Existing side by side with the classical curriculum are the more recent innovations stemming from American beliefs in democracy and equality. An examination of the "typical" American high school will reveal not one but three kinds of curricula under one roof. There is one curriculum for college-bound youths, another for those who intend to end their formal education with high school, and still another one for those who are expected to learn a trade in high school. This arrangement is scorned by many Europeans who until very recently have believed that there is but *one* goal and *one* curriculum —the classical—for secondary schools. But in the American public schools we wish to have all students considered social equals, regardless of what they study. We, in turn, look askance at the class-oriented curricula—one kind for those who work with their hands and another for those who work with their minds. This is our democratic theory.

The practice, however, is somewhat different. While we talk as if all men are created equal, and say that the high-school home-economics student is "just as good" a student as the college-bound math student, our feelings are by no means this democratic. There is in actuality a "pecking order" of subjects, students, and teachers. "Every-

---

[4] Schools in all the fifty states include courses—in some cases, safety—legislated into the curriculum.

one" knows that the teacher of mathematics and science is a brighter, better-trained, and more widely read person than the physical-education teacher. We suspect that even the physical-education teacher is aware of this belief. Of course, he doesn't like this and will deny that there is any "difference." After all, we are all created equal—although it is obvious that some are "more equal than others."

One can detect many other contradictions in American schools. A rather recent goal of American education is to provide vocational training. By and large, this is a twentieth-century development. The high school can and should teach students "a trade." Thus, agriculture, wood shop, metal shop, and auto mechanics are common offerings. The problem is that the typical procedure is to assume that only the student who is not intelligent enough to succeed in an academic curriculum is to be "counseled" into a vocational curriculum. The result of this is that vocational courses commonly are taken by students who are academic underachievers; they are failures in one curriculum and are generally recognized as failures. And they frequently do very poorly in their vocational courses.

At the turn of the twentieth century a group of theorists asserted that the curriculum should be based on student "interests." These theorists maintained that when students are interested in something, they do it well and enthusiastically. Thus the theorists set about making the curriculum flexible and responsive to the interests, wishes, and wants of students. The result of this was a curriculum that jumped, skipped, and hopped from "Fly-Casting" to "How the Ancient Egyptians Lived." Arithmetic was taught by having students operate a mock grocery store or post office. Students were probably interested but, as the critics of this position have pointed out, they did not learn much. As of this writing, this is a discredited approach to curriculum; yet one may pick up many educational journals and note that on one page there are advocates of a curriculum that appeals to student interests and on another page others asserting that the student does not know what he is really interested in.

During the 1930's and 1940's another set of theorists decided that interests were not a good basis on which to build curriculum. Curriculum, it was asserted, ought to be based on "needs." In an analysis of the term "need," one of the authors found it had seven different meanings. That is to say, the advocates of "needs" as the basis of curriculum had no clear idea of who needed what, when, and for what purpose. However, it was assumed that "needs" were superior to "interests." The teacher "knows" what students "need"—so goes the theory. What the theory ignores, among other things, is how the teacher is to decide which "need" ought to be met. After all, what does a sixteen-year-old adolescent boy "need"? A biologist might argue that he "needs" a sixteen-year-old adolescent girl (having, presumably, similar needs). It is a simple matter to see that it would be difficult to plan a curriculum on this particular "need."

Needs did become a curriculum basis—along with interests, vocation, leadership training, mental discipline, and a few other things. One of the other things was "personality development." Schools, it was asserted, have the reponsibility of creating students with desirable personalities. The term "personality" usually was not distinguished from the term "character" by theorists and teachers. The theory of personality development led to such "reforms" as more emphasis on extracurricular activities, teen-age problems courses, student council, pep club, social activities, and counseling. And it became somewhat difficult to distinguish the "curriculum" from the "extracurriculum." The solution to this difficulty was a semantic triumph: "cocurricular activities."

After all, who is to say that a dance is less educational than a trigonometry course? In fact, it could be argued that one learns many more "useful" things in planning and attending a well-conducted dance than in a mathematics course. There is no point in denying the importance of a "well-rounded personality" in this country. And there is no point in saying that dances and clubs are useless, since they do provide important extracurricular values. The question is, "How important?" Is learning to be poised and gracious more or less important than learning to handle logarithms? The schools have no answer because, essentially, the American people have no answer. Trigonometry and the Halloween Hop both seem important.

Although citizenship training was an early nineteenth-century addition to the public-school curriculum, it was reemphasized with new determination during the depression of the 1930's. Social critics knew that if America was to survive, we would need students who were more intelligent about citizenship than those of the previous generations. Therefore, students were given a curriculum designed to make them "better citizens." They were to study economic, social, and political practices in this country, with a view toward improving such practices. But there were at least three difficulties: (1) Few teachers, administrators, and board members could distinguish between scholarly study and patriotism. (2) Since it was realized that none of the social studies could be studied in isolation, the tendency was to "fuse" or "integrate" the social studies; economics, history, political science, sociology, and geography were all parts of a whole. As it actually worked out, this did not change the previous practice of studying unrelated, irrelevant, isolated facts. (3) Instead of being presented from a genuine problems approach, instead of being a presentation of social phenomena and methods of improving them, the social studies continued as a detailed study of the structure of American government and history—in short, as facts without analyses of meanings.

A curricular reform that could have had real impact was that advocated by John Dewey. Dewey advocated a curriculum based on problems. He defined a problem as anything that gives rise to doubt and uncertainty. This theory is not to be confused with the needs or interest theories. Dewey did actually have a rather careful and definite idea of the type of problem suitable for inclusion in the curriculum. He thought that the problems to be studied would meet two criteria: (1) they would be significant and important to the culture, and (2) they would be important and relevant to the student.

Although Dewey had an important contribution to make to this field, it would appear that his disciples did not understand his theories. Instead of choosing problems that were important to the total culture and studying them, as Dewey advocated, the problems approach soon degenerated into "What should I do on a date?" "How can I learn to make change?" and "Why do adolescents have bad skin?" Genuine comprehension and successful application of Dewey's problem-solving theory hinge on extensive knowledge of Dewey's philosophy. In general, this extensive knowledge did not and does not exist. Teachers and professors of education know of Dewey, are familiar with the term "problem," but have little understanding of the extensive theorizing in which Dewey engaged.[5]

It is quite apparent that recent reforms in the science and mathematics curricula are based on the problem-solving approach. These curricula involve problems that must be solved by students utilizing the scientific method. These curricula stress "discovery" of relationships and "inquiry" into the "structure" of the world of things and ideas. The same terms were used by Dewey in the early 1900's. Interestingly enough, the proponents of the newer curricula in science and mathematics are not educators and know little about Dewey's theories. They are by and large scientists and mathematicians who, without realizing it, have come to the same conclusions reached by Dewey. A discussion of the new curriculum theory is found in a slender volume by Jerome Bruner.[6]

[5] Dewey wrote from 1884 to 1948, a period of 64 years. It is calculated that his books total 18,000 pages, and his journal articles 5,000!

[6] *The Process of Education* (Cambridge: Harvard U. Press, 1960).

CURRICULUM AND INDIVIDUAL DIFFERENCES

Although psychologists and educators have known for some time that there are differences among human beings, this knowledge has been applied only recently. For many years all students, regardless of intelligence, interest, or ability, studied approximately the same things. American curriculum makers have attempted recently to devise curricula to "meet the needs" of different levels of ability. There is one kind of curriculum for the average, one kind for the bright and gifted, and another kind for the child who is either a slow learner or retarded. Again, this is *theory*. What has actually happened is that the same curriculum is offered to those with different levels of ability but is covered at different rates of speed. This is, however, a start, and we may be on the trail of devising a curriculum that is adaptable to different levels of ability.

Another factor that has affected curriculum is awareness of the students' home environments. It has been realized that children who live in a slum have a markedly different outlook, set of experiences, and interests than the suburban dweller. James B. Conant's book *Slums and Suburbs*[7] brought this fact to the attention of the American public. In response to his book, investigations and projects have been carried out to devise different teaching methods and more appropriate curricula. This curricular practice is of very recent origin and is found chiefly in larger metropolitan areas.

Another curriculum problem, really inseparable from the problem of slums, is that raised by minorities. Negro, Mexican, and Puerto Rican children typically live in run-down districts and usually belong to the lower socioeconomic class. These children and/or their families usually have the following traits: they do not plan; they are not interested in the long-range future; they have little concern for formal education; their sexual mores are much less restrictive than those of the middle class; they usually experience considerable learning difficulties; they are apt to be in trouble with the law; they do not typically hold down well-paid or rewarding jobs; and they do not seem to profit from the customary curriculum. A consideration of the kinds of educational experiences these children should have raises many issues. The education they have been exposed to is almost completely irrelevant and is generally a total failure.[8]

Psychologists recently have become very much interested in "cre-

---

[7] New York: McGraw-Hill, 1961.

[8] See the Vol. 45, November, 1963, issue of the educational journal *Phi Delta Kappan* for an extensive discussion of the "culturally deprived child."

ativity." It was recognized by many people that creative thinkers, artists, and scientists are necessary to our civilization. Therefore, numerous psychologists and educators have attempted to measure creativity and to devise curricula that would enhance it. The problem, once again, is that there is little agreement as to what "creativity" means and even less as to the kind of curriculum that will enhance it.

The entire concept of "creativity" raises problems. Since it is an anthropological fact that the cultural heritage has to be passed on to the young, it does not seem likely that schools are equipped to deal with creativity. The hallmark of creativity is an original response to or novel manner of looking at the world. It is doubtful that most teachers know how to handle an original or creative response. Usually the creative child threatens the teacher's authority. In view of the fact that creativity requires some knowledge of the cultural heritage, how much traditional knowledge is to be mixed with how much creativity in the classroom? Finally, so little is known about the identification, the care, and the treatment of creative children that most recent talk about creativity is just that—talk.

SOME ODD INFLUENCES ON THE CURRICULUM

Other factors than those evolving from formal curriculum theory influence the curriculum.

The geographic location of a school has much influence on what it offers. For example, the important biological theory of evolution is usually barred from fair consideration in many states. These states, preferring a literal Biblical interpretation of the origin of life, either do not make mention of Charles Darwin's theory, misinterpret it, or water it down. By the same token, one does not often see racial issues dealt with in the South as they are in other areas. The racial issue is, to use the words of one professor, a "closed area."[9]

Another interesting, if not generally acknowledged, influence on curriculum is that of geography on vocational offerings. One of the authors taught in a California high school in which the agricultural curriculum was almost entirely devoted to viticulture—the raising and processing of grapes. In another high school in which he taught a few years later, the agricultural curriculum was almost entirely given over to animal husbandry.

In some school districts the custom is to hire only local teachers who were brought up in the area. The practice effectively prevents new

[9] See Maurice Hunt and Lawrence Metcalf, *Teaching High School Social Studies* (New York: Harper and Brothers, 1955), for a discussion of the "closed areas."

ideas from "contaminating" the curriculum. Thus, the curriculum in these areas is almost totally conservative—resistant to change.

Another fact is that most curricula are designed by the middle class for children of the middle class. The texts, their illustrations, the contents, the teaching methods, and the grading practices are designed to further middle-class values and beliefs. Since our country is geared toward the middle class, this sounds like a reasonable approach. However, as we pointed out earlier in the brief discussion on slums and minorities, the very large numbers of children living in lower-class areas—both city slums and rural slums—can relate poorly if at all to the middle-class-oriented curriculum. For instance, the first-grade reader usually depicts a father who works in an office and returns to a suburban home where two well-dressed, white, presumably Protestant children are playing happily on a well-manicured lawn. This picture is totally alien and irrelevant to the lower-class city dweller, who may never have been exposed to the comfortable homes, offices, green lawns, and happy excursions to the farm emphasized so strongly by typical first-grade readers. The significance is that the curriculum is oriented toward the middle class, and lower-class students are simply excluded from any vital relationship to what is studied.[10]

Although the school is supposed to be "nonpolitical" and neutral in controversial matters, schools tend to reflect the conservative point of view. This inherent conservatism of an education that must transmit the cultural heritage is not surprising. There is an additional factor that makes schools conservative. The median age of women teachers (and six out of seven elementary-school teachers are women) is approximately forty-six years.[11] Since individuals tend to become more conservative as they grow older, students do much of their basic learning under teachers who are inherently conservative. Thus the schools are not politically neutral. They perpetuate a conservative point of view that is not recognized as such.

Another factor leads not only to conservatism, but to reactionism.[12]

[10] Otto Klineberg, "Life Is Fun in a Smiling, Fair-Skinned World," *Saturday Review*, 47 (February 16, 1963): 75. For a thorough discussion of the schools' responsibility for moral education see the October, 1964 issue of *Phi Delta Kappan* (Vol. 46).

[11] *NEA Research Bulletin*, 41 (February, 1963): 3.

[12] The term "reactionary" refers to an extreme position. Whereas the conservative wishes to keep things about the way they are now, the reactionary wishes to return to a previous historical age that he perceives as "golden." The reactionary not only is typically opposed to the present state and to future change, but wishes to pass legislation that would negate all the social legislation of this century. Typically he is against organized labor, the United Nations, liberal church groups, federal aid to education, state support of education, and civil rights.

In many states reactionaries have placed tremendous pressure on local boards, state legislatures, and publishers to delete from the curriculum what reactionaries consider objectionable and unpatriotic material. Thus there are numerous instances of the "extreme right" (another name for reactionary groups) forcing publishers to delete references to the United Nations from social-studies textbooks. Any mention of the entire controversy involving the Supreme Court and civil rights has been completely eliminated from some social-science textbooks. There is even a case in which an entire state has required adoption of a textbook, to be studied by all high-school seniors, which attempts to indoctrinate them in beliefs of racial inferiority. This same type of person not only forces publishers to alter textbooks, but also is active in banning books from public and school libraries. A book frequently objected to is *1984* by George Orwell. Other authors whom the reactionary element sees as "injurious" include John Steinbeck, J. D. Salinger, and Plato. What this all means is that a particular segment of the population does indeed determine *local* curriculum. These groups typically are not discussed in textbooks in curriculum theory, but their influence is no less real for that.[13]

Probably one of the most important influences on the curriculum is the publisher. In effect, much of the curriculum, as interpreted by the classroom teacher, is based on textbooks. Although publishers are generally desirous of providing the most intelligent and effective textbooks possible, some publishers surrender to pressures that cause controversial material to be omitted from textbooks. In one instance, a state textbook committee called in the director of research of a popular encyclopedia that is often used in classrooms. The state board demanded that certain passages, offensive to the local biases of that state, be omitted.

The picture is therefore mixed. On the one hand, publishers influence curriculum in a desirable way by turning out textbooks that are carefully edited, well printed, beautifully illustrated, graded for age levels, rich in teaching aids, and designed for maximum effective use by teachers and students. On the other hand, by deleting material that may be offensive to some persons or in various sections of the country, publishers must accept some blame for perpetuating the bland, noncontroversial texts that do not enhance awareness of social problems. Of course, the principal blame here lies with the schools,

13 Joseph A. King, "Books and Banners: A Case History," *Saturday Review,* 47 (November 9, 1963): 28-29, 66, presents an interesting case study of a California incident.

which, yielding to various pressures, simply will not buy any other type of book in quantities sufficient to keep a publisher in business.

The present emphasis on mathematics and science, an emphasis that almost dominates the high-school curriculum and is rapidly becoming effective on the elementary level, is not an accident. When, in October, 1957, the Russians orbited a satellite, Americans were shocked beyond measure. "How," they asked themselves, "can a nation of illiterate peasants be so scientifically sophisticated?" The immediate response was to blame American education. Immediately, money was appropriated by the federal and state legislatures to train and retrain teachers in mathematics and science. In addition, more stress was put on modern foreign languages and counseling, apparently so that trained guidance personnel would "counsel" bright children into science, engineering, and mathematics careers.

This illustrates rather perfectly the tendency of American schools to be extremely responsive to most major current developments or "needs" in our society. There was little thought about whether or not science and mathematics were entirely appropriate for everyone. There was little consideration as to which aspects of science would be emphasized. There was almost no concern for other elements in the curriculum, such as the humanities—literature and the fine arts. There was so little reflection about the broader impact on curriculum that an individual was heard to make the following comment: "If the Russians suddenly decided to concentrate on metaphysical poetry, America would immediately fall into line and start emphasizing metaphysical poetry in universities, high schools, and elementary schools." This joke does not appear to be far from the truth; let any segment of our population feel a "need," and very soon the need is translated into curriculum.

Although the obvious sources of curriculum are books, state departments of education, colleges of education, and theorists, ultimately it is the individual classroom teacher who translates all the theories and materials into subject matter or experiences for his students. The training, interests, personality, beliefs, and values of the individual classroom teacher have considerable influence on what is really taught. Not infrequently a college instructor will spend a great deal of class time discussing a relatively trivial matter about which he happens to be writing a thesis. Thus a rather narrow area of the subject becomes —for all practical purposes—curriculum.

The same thing happens in public schools. In theory the biology curriculum may be quite well balanced. But if the teacher is weak in zoology, it can be predicted that students will not spend much time on zoology. On the other hand, if the teacher is most enthusiastic about the mating habits of the light-bellied brant (a northern goose), it is likely that students will spend a significant portion of the semester studying this subject. This type of influence on curriculum is not necessarily bad; it is simply unrecognized. And because it is not seen for what it is, the influence is actually irresponsible and weakening.

Analysis and Implications   Why is American curriculum this way? The answer is complex, but we shall attempt to give some reasons:

First, because of pluralism it is unlikely that one viewpoint, one curricular emphasis, or one set of values will long predominate. The combined push, pull, and tug of different groups working toward different goals will find its way into American schools. Thus the vocational emphasis in schools is a response both to the lower class and to the farming population. The recent emphasis on mathematics and science is essentially a product of the Cold War. The very recent emphasis on general "physical fitness" is partly a reaction to the previous overemphasis on producing winning football and basketball teams. The emphasis on modern foreign languages, many years overdue, is a reaction to the sudden realization that we live in a world in which not everyone speaks English.[14] It is likely that the emphasis on band and orchestra in some areas is a response to the middle-class yen for "culture."

The curriculum will bend—almost unlimitedly—to accommodate itself to the time, location, tensions, "felt needs," economic events, and wishes of a particular population. It is difficult to say that this is completely bad. After all, Americans have believed for a long time that the curriculum should be responsive to the wishes of the American people. But how does a school determine what *ought* to be taught? If it is true that the squeakiest wheel gets the grease, and if dozens of wheels are squeaking, groaning, and shrieking, how are the school commissions to decide which wheel is "right"?

Second, today's curriculum is the result of philosophical conflict, not only among and between professional curriculum makers and laymen but often within a single person's views. A current book by John Gardner, *Excellence: Can We Be Equal and Excellent Too?*[15] discusses the contradiction inherent in the long-standing American beliefs that all are equal and that it is important to stress excellence in

---

[14] Not everybody is happy about including foreign languages in the curriculum. A national weekly magazine quoted a Southern state superintendent of public instruction as saying that if English was good enough for Jesus Christ, it is good enough for us!

[15] New York: Harper and Row, 1961.

our schools. If all are equal, it is difficult to say that some people are excellent—that is, better than others. (Gardner's conclusion is that people can be excellent in a variety of ways: we can produce excellent bricklayers, poets, and engineers, and each person is excellent in his own way. This is easier said than done.) As a culture, America has not yet settled on what should be general, widely distributed education and what is properly education for those who are able, talented, and intelligent. Until this issue is clarified and resolved, we are likely to slide back and forth between stressing academic excellence for the bright and emphasizing education for all American young people, regardless of their intellectual capacities.

The third aspect of this analysis of curriculum involves the notion of social lag. In brief, the theory of social lag is that the beliefs, values, and much of the thinking of a society are very apt to "lag behind" technical and other "hard" developments. For example, Americans still talk about individualism and the glories of being independent. In fact, the "rugged individualist" disappeared with the closing of the frontier at the end of the nineteenth century. However, the belief and the faith in this image are still widely held.

Social lag affects curriculum. Though nuclear physics has been vital since World War I, it has been slighted in high-school physics classes and textbooks. Agriculture offers another case in point. Although fewer and fewer people earn their living on farms, nearly one third of all students other than those in home economics who are receiving federally aided vocational training are in the field of agriculture.[16] In other words, the vast majority are being trained for unemployment. It would appear that vocational training ought to emphasize automation and electronic operations, but very few schools are actually implementing such a program. American language teaching has traditionally emphasized Western languages, both ancient and modern, such as French, German, Spanish, and Latin. Though Soviet Russia, China, and the African countries have been realities for a long time, we rarely find students even at the university level studying Swahili (an African dialect), Chinese, or Russian. We are not advocating throwing modern Western foreign languages out and replacing them with Swahili. We are merely observing that in the area of foreign languages the schools lag far behind the political, social, and economic realities. In another area, even though 20 percent of the nation's work force belong to a union of some kind, there is almost no place in the

[16] *Progress of Public Education in the United States of America: 1963-64*, U. S. Department of Health, Education, and Welfare, Office of Education, Washington, D.C.: 1964, p. 11, Table 4.

curriculum for the study of the history and practices of the labor movement. Too, this kind of avoidance of social issues is extremely conservative, and by denying the realities of the situation, it has led to widespread ignorance of economics. Thus quite typically Americans have little or no understanding or appreciation of the role of unions in our economy; all most of us usually have is a vague feeling that unions are a kind of necessary evil.

The American curriculum constantly lags far behind realities, and much of the content of our curriculum, as well as our teaching methodology, is obsolete. American children emerging from a formal education carry a picture in their heads of a world that existed ten, twenty, or fifty years ago and does not exist today. The question is, "How can an individual deal with the present by employing an inappropriate set of concepts, beliefs, and values?"

SUMMARY

We realize that we have raised more questions than we have answered, posed more problems than can be solved at present, and perhaps left the reader in a state of bewilderment and confusion.

A pluralistic society predictably yields the kind of curriculum we have described—a patchwork. It will produce conflicts and confusion in educational psychology, methods, philosophy, administration, and finance. Simple solutions and absolutistic thinking are not called for— they will not work. What is required first of all is an understanding of the nature of our society and the manner in which curriculum is created. Once students of education—that is, teachers—have this understanding, they are in a position to do something about the curriculum.

What can be done about it? Teachers, if they are to be true professionals—that is, independent and autonomous—must take a more decisive and vigorous part in making curricular decisions. A physician will not allow the patient to tell him what medicine to prescribe or how to remove the patient's appendix. It is largely the fault of teachers that they have had to cope with such a vast and powerful array of pressures that distort and weaken the curriculum. Better-educated teachers, who understood the basic techniques of reading instruction, would not need a detailed guide to tell them how to teach reading. Social-science teachers would not have to yield to the pressures of ultra-right-wing groups if they were sure of what constitutes social science and social studies. Biology teachers with backbone and a greater knowledge of the biological sciences would be forced to yield neither to nineteenth-century thought nor to legislators whose knowledge of experimental science is negligible. In addition to being aware of the nature of our culture, teachers need to know more about what they are teaching, and they need to organize themselves into the kind of association that is able to resist unfair and reactionary community pressures.

The hoary argument between advocates of "method" and supporters of "subject matter" is outdated and absurd. To teach, one must teach something: one cannot separate legitimately the content of knowledge from the process of knowing. All teachers need to be reasonably sophisticated and informed about the subject matter appropriate to the age, interests, and intelligence of the students they teach. In addition, they need to be informed about the methods, techniques, philosophies, psychologies, and learning theories of education.

To the introductory student of education, all of this may appear somewhat complex. As a matter of fact, we have merely scratched the surface of curriculum problems; this is but a brief and incomplete treatment of an area that will require years of your time and study.

Influences on the Curriculum: Theories of Mind

by S. SAMUEL SHERMIS

Of the various influences that have shaped the American curriculum, one of the most important is different theories of mind.

Several theories of mind have been developed. Most people are unaware of the meaning and influence of these theories on curriculum; even those in the field of education are not conscious of the impact these theories of mind have had on curricular offerings. Let us look at three theories of mind to see how they are related to the curriculum.

THE VAT THEORY

One of the oldest theories is what we might call the "Vat Theory." According to this theory, the mind is like a vat; it is a receptacle. Into this receptacle are poured facts, ideas, concepts, values, and whatever else is in the curriculum. Of course, this pouring process is executed carefully. Just the right amount of material must be poured in just the right way.

Those who hold this view—and they may not know that they hold it—usually state that the material being poured into the vat is designed to be used at a later time. Whether or not the student sees the material as useful or interesting now is not important. The material is to be learned, stored, and remembered, so that when it has to be used, it is available.

This theory of mind has had the following curricular effects:

1. The subject matter is determined by adult authorities who are felt to know best what should be learned.

2. The subject matter is often difficult and frequently inappropriate for children. This, however, is regarded as desirable, since the subject matter is not for children, anyhow; it is for the adults they will later become.

3. The subject matter lends itself to memorization.

4. Since children may not like the subject matter, it is necessary to force them to learn. This has led to stern discipline, and often to corporal punishment.

THE THEORY OF MENTAL DISCIPLINE

An extremely old theory of mind might be called "Mental Discipline." In the nineteenth century the theory of mental discipline became known as "Faculty Psychology," the view that the mind consists of separate faculties. Many different faculties, or powers, reside in the mind, and each faculty is different from every other faculty. The following were usually listed as faculties: memory, willpower, appreciation, logic, imagination. Often other powers were named, depending on who was doing the naming.

The various faculties of the mind were conceived as being somewhat like muscles. The more you exercise a muscle, the better developed it becomes. Thus, the theory went, the more you exercise the various faculties, the better developed they become. It was believed that for each faculty there was subject matter that would develop it. For the faculty of memory, one studied history: memorization of names and dates was just what was needed to train this faculty. For the faculty of appreciation, one studied music and art: these subjects would develop the powers of imagination. For the faculty of logic, mathematics—especially geometry—was highly recommended: a continuing study of the deductive logic of mathematics "made one logical." For the faculty of will, almost any topic would do—provided one didn't like it. The theory was that by being forced to do that which was dull or unpleasant, one's willpower would be developed. This may explain why for so many years it was considered desirable for students to be a little miserable.

This theory of mind has not died out entirely. Ask a teacher, preferably one who has been teaching quite a long time, to defend the teaching of, say, mathematics. The reply probably will be something like this: "The study of mathematics helps develop your mind so that you will be more logical."

DEWEY'S THEORY OF MIND: MIND AS A FUNCTION

A more recent theory, and one that is not generally understood or accepted, is John Dewey's theory of mind. As Dewey and some of his disciples saw it, mind is not a *thing*. It is not a muscle: one cannot "strengthen" faculties, as faculty psychologists believed. Nor should the mind be looked on as a receptacle, a vat. "Mind" is rather a verb. One can speak of "minding." That is, "mind" is a term for all the ways in which any individual copes with his environment.

An individual—from an individual amoeba to an individual person—lives in an environment. He must learn to operate in this environment. The amoeba must avoid harmful conditions and must seek food. A cat must catch mice. A mouse must avoid being caught. To describe these activities, some thinkers have used the word "adjust" to an environment.[1] Unless an individual adjusts to his environment, he will perish. It is thinking, the process of mind, that enables people to live, to survive. Thus the mind is that which enables individuals to "get by" in an environment.

---

[1] In the past few years, the word "adjust" has come in for some severe—and probably deserved—criticism. Critics have attacked Dewey and his disciples for their emphasis on adjustment. However, many of the critics did not read Dewey very carefully. By "adjustment" Dewey did not mean mere conformity; he did not wish to see people happily and dully conform to their social or physical environments. Dewey saw the word "adjust" as having various meanings. One meaning was, indeed, concerned with conformity. After all, if you do not conform to your physical environment, you may die. For instance, one cannot eat razor blades; they are neither digestible nor nutritious. Thus, one has to conform to a razor blade on its terms. On the other hand, adjusting, as Dewey saw it, also meant intelligently changing the environment. Dewey was extremely critical of society and its ways; he never advocated blind conformity to our culture. Rather, he frequently stated that students should learn enough about our society to be able to help change it.

As Dewey saw it, the purpose of an education was, in part, to enable children to learn to think—that is, to learn to use their minds most intelligently. Therefore, the curriculum ought to consist of those experiences that serve to promote the thinking process. Although Dewey unfortunately was rather vague as to what kind of curriculum would promote this thinking process, he was most emphatic in his belief that the traditional, classical curriculum was not adequate as it was usually employed.

Dewey's disciples attempted to implement his views on the relationship of the mind to curriculum. Whether they were successful or not is highly debatable. Some of their curricular innovations were adopted by many schools in this country. Here are some of the implications, as Dewey's disciples saw them, of Dewey's theories:

1. The curriculum ought to be appropriate to the age, ability, and maturity level of the student.

2. The curriculum ought to be such that, as interest is developed, students exert effort. "Interest" and "effort" are not contradictory terms.

3. The curriculum ought to consist of problems. Only problems lead to thinking.

4. The curriculum, instead of being an abstract study of what adults have thought important, ought to help students develop an independent capacity to deal with the world.

5. Adults and teachers ought not to force children to study. The impetus should come from the curriculum itself. If the curriculum is important and relevant to them, students will not have to be forced. If it is not, it should be changed—but only after one is sure the fault lies in the curriculum and not elsewhere.

IMPLICATIONS

What is the significance of these three thories of mind?[2]

1. Theory guides and directs practice.

2. Different theories lead to different practices.

3. A combination of different theories often leads to practice that is confused and ineffective.

If we examine these three theories of mind, we see that they are indeed quite different from one another. Each theory goes in a dif-

[2] There are, of course, other theories of mind. These are merely three of the best-known and most important.

ferent direction. Each theory leads to different assumptions about curriculum and to different teaching methods.

What Americans have done is to combine theories that are, in reality, quite different.[3] We tend to be proud of the fact that we do not respect theory, that we can and do combine theories whenever we feel like doing so. However, this creates very large problems. When we combine three rather different theories of mind, we also combine three rather different practices. A "vat" theory of mind leads to promotion of memorization of subject matter for future use. A "functional" theory of mind leads to teaching which insists that subject matter is for the present as well as for the future. What happens when, as we have done, we combine both the "vat" and the "functional" theories? The answer is that some parts of our curriculum are designed to be memorized and filed away for future use, and other aspects of our curriculum are designed to be useful immediately. Students taking, say, agriculture are expected to be able to make immediate use of the skills and facts they learn. Students taking Latin are not expected to use Latin conversationally; Latin has another, quite different, function.

This leads to confusion and ineffectiveness. What does it do to a student to be told that "this class" is designed to have immediate, practical value, but that he is not expected to realize the immediate value of "that class"? What does it do to teaching methods when one class is operated on the assumption that a student is "exercising his faculties" and another class is based on the belief that he is simply storing up knowledge for future use by memorizing unrelated facts? What happens when teachers operate, unconsciously, with one theory of mind and students with another? For example, the teacher may assume that this subject matter has use only in the students' future life, but the students themselves feel that they should derive immediate benefit from the subject matter.

What happens to our entire culture when students feel that they are in high school and college for vocational reasons and at the same time many other people feel that "true" education has nothing to do

---

[3] This mixing is known as "eclecticism." Technically, eclecticism refers to mixing the *best* of different theories. However, eclecticism in practice does not always mean combining the best of different theories; second, eclecticism says nothing about whether the combination of various aspects of different theories is logically contradictory or logically consistent. Americans, who have been called "pragmatic," are often blithely indifferent to theoretical inconsistency. Our whole culture is a prototype of eclecticism. We have often operated on the assumption "If it works, let's go ahead and use it. Never mind theory." But what does it mean for something "to work"?

with job training? Does this not invite controversy, confusion, and divisiveness? Does it not also tend to weaken the public's support for education?

Americans, in their educational undertakings, have tended to borrow quite indiscriminately. They mix points of view that lead in different directions. "Eclecticism" has been regarded as one of our major assets. But is it necessarily an asset when we don't know much about what we are mixing?

What Content and When?*

by DOROTHY McCLURE FRASER

Dorothy McClure Fraser is professor of education at Hunter College. She is one of the writers for the NEA Project on Instruction, and she has written CURRENT CURRICULUM STUDIES IN ACADEMIC SUBJECTS *and* DECIDING WHAT TO TEACH.

In the quest for excellence that is so much discussed today, a great deal of attention is being given to the content of instruction—to what is taught or is not taught in the schools. The debate has raised a multitude of questions and criticisms. Is the curriculum dominated by "soft" subjects? Do the schools fail to teach children as much as they could and should learn? Should more time be devoted to the sciences and mathematics? Should foreign language instruction begin in the elementary school?

Such questions cannot be discussed intelligently without first understanding what it is that we are seeking, what it is that we mean by excellence. Nor can they be discussed without recognizing the place of content in learning, the need for a continually fresh look at content selection, and the importance of considering what *should* be taught as well as what *can* be taught.

Let us, then, take a look at these four considerations which provide a setting within which to discuss some of the issues about content in the elementary school program.

* Dorothy McClure Fraser, "What Content and When?" *The National Elementary Principal*, 42 (September, 1962): 13-19. Copyright 1962, Department of Elementary School Principals, National Education Association. By permission of the editor and the author.

WHAT KIND OF EXCELLENCE?

We are all for excellence, just as we are all for home and mother. But excellence in education is being interpreted in many different and contradictory ways.

To some, excellence in education seems to mean a "return" to the three R's and a slightly modernized version of the nineteenth-century curriculum. To some, it apparently means longer and harder assignments on the assumption that the child who works harder, who does twice as much homework, will be twice as smart or excellent. To some, excellence in education seems to mean formal instruction in reading in the kindergarten and teaching set theory in the first grade. To some, it means rigid standards of grading, of academic achievement, and of promotion, with failure and repetition for children who do not meet these arbitrary standards. To some, excellence is for the gifted few, or at best for the superior minority, with the implication that the school's duty is to develop excellence for this group even at the expense of the rest of the school population.

To others, excellence is a goal for every individual and is to be achieved by developing each person's full potentialities, whether they be great or limited. This is the interpretation with which I want to associate myself. John Gardner expressed this point of view well when he wrote:

> Our society cannot achieve greatness unless individuals at many levels of ability accept the need for high standards of performance and strive to achieve those standards within the limits possible for them. We want the highest conceivable excellence, of course, in the activities crucial to our effectiveness and creativity as a society; but that isn't enough. If the man in the street says, "Those fellows at the top have to be good, but I'm just a slob and can act like one"—then our days of greatness are behind us. We must foster a conception of excellence which may be applied to every degree of ability and to every socially acceptable activity. A missile may blow up on its launching pad because the designer was incompetent or because the mechanic who adjusted the last valve was incompetent. The same is true of everything else in our society.[1]

Education for excellence, in this view, can be achieved only by school programs that are planned to develop in each child the desire and the tools to make the best possible use of whatever abilities he has. This cannot be done through uniform prescriptions about content,

[1] Gardner, John W. *Excellence, Can We Be Equal and Excellent Too?* New York: Harper & Brothers, 1961. p. 131.

learning experiences, and promotion standards. It can only be done by taking into account what is known about ways of dealing with individual differences.

PLACE OF CONTENT IN LEARNING

Many suggestions for achieving excellence in education have stressed the amount and kinds of facts to be taught. To evaluate these suggestions, we must identify the place of facts in learning.

Facts are building blocks to be used by children in developing concepts. These concepts, in turn, are to be used in developing the understandings, ideas, and generalizations that furnish the structure or structures of knowledge. Facts, therefore, are basic in learning. But they are not the starting point in planning for organized or structured learning. Instead, the planner begins by identifying the understandings, ideas, and generalizations to be developed, then analyzes these to determine the concepts that are involved, and as a last step selects the specific facts to be taught. The planner also considers the usefulness of specific content for the child's development of values and skills, because he knows that mastery of content alone does not produce the kind of excellence we need.

Usually, there are several or even many sets of facts that children could use to develop given concepts and generalizations. The question, then, is not, "What are the facts that all children should learn?" but rather, "What facts will be most useful to these children in developing the desired concepts and generalizations, and at the same time facilitate their growth in values and skills?" The facts to be used must be selected in terms of learning goals and in terms of their usefulness to the particular children who are doing the learning.

TRADITION NOT A GUIDE

Tradition is not a guide for content selection. Content that was pertinent and useful for the learning of an earlier generation may no longer be the most useful for the learning of children whose lives will extend into the twenty-first century. No content should be retained in the curriculum merely because it has "always" been there. Nor, on the other hand, should new content be rejected simply because it is new. Instead, we need a continuing review and evaluation of the content of the elementary school program in order to select that which will most effectively facilitate the attainment of educational goals.

WHAT CAN VS. WHAT SHOULD BE TAUGHT

Evidence that particular content can be learned by children of a given age and level of ability does not prove that it should be taught. Certainly, one criterion for the selection of content is whether or not the pupils can learn it. But having proved that elementary school children can learn a foreign language or gain some understanding of atomic and molecular theory, for example, does not automatically indicate that learning it would be a desirable use of their time and energy. Other questions must be considered. For example: How will the child's total school program be affected? Will other content, potentially more significant at the child's present stage of learning and growth, have to be minimized or dropped to make time for this study? Are there other content areas not receiving adequate attention that deserve a higher priority? Is the topic or subject one that the child can learn more easily at a later stage of maturity? In short, how does this study fit into the total picture—into the broad range of the educational goals of the school and into the developmental pattern of the child?

To make this point is not to deny the importance—indeed, the urgency—of continuing research to identify the topics and subjects children of a given stage of maturity can and cannot comprehend. We need such research. The point is that having discovered that children can study certain content effectively, we must apply appropriate criteria to determine the priority that it should be given in the child's total program.

With these points in mind, we can turn to a consideration of some of the specific issues related to the content of the elementary school curriculum. There are a number of such issues that might be discussed. But among them, two seem to be particularly significant. They have to do with, first, the relation of the disciplines or organized bodies of knowledge to the elementary school curriculum and, second, the desirability of moving down some content formerly treated in the secondary school.

THE DISCIPLINES AND THE CURRICULUM

Three factors have always influenced the selection of content for the school curriculum: first, the learner's capacities and how he learns; second, society's needs and goals and its demands on the schools; and third, the knowledge available to be taught. Throughout most of the history of formal education, the emphasis has been on the third factor, the systematically organized bodies of knowledge or the "disciplines." It was assumed that the schools would best serve society's needs by transmitting to each new generation as much as possible of the organized knowledge that was available and that could be comprehended by the learners.

With the rise of systematic study of human development, psychology of learning, and educational sociology in the twentieth century, the emphasis shifted in curriculum planning for the elementary school. The nature of the pupil and his learning processes and the more explicitly stated social goals for the school became the major bases for the selection of content to be taught. Specialists in human development placed great emphasis on the concept of readiness as a factor in selection of content for children at a given state of maturity. Many of these specialists viewed readiness as an integral part of maturation, a process that they concluded could *not* be hurried but must develop according to the child's natural growth pattern. Systematically organized bodies of knowledge came to be viewed as storehouses of factual data from which to choose appropriate information. This material was then arranged in a curriculum that was designed to meet not only the changing needs of a dynamic society, but also the new conception of the needs of the learner.

The trend away from an elementary school curriculum structured on the disciplines was not a "retreat from content," as some have charged, for our twentieth-century schools present a broader range of content than children were previously offered. Nor was it a trend away from structured, organized learning. It represented, however, a drastic change in the basis on which the content was selected and in the structures around which the content was organized. Systematic study of selected branches of human knowledge—the disciplines—was not a primary consideration in the selection and placement of content in the elementary school curriculum, although in some fields, such as mathematics, it was assumed that certain steps must come before others.

EMPHASIS ON STRUCTURE

In the past decade, the pendulum has apparently begun to swing back. A new interest among academic scholars in the school curriculum and in analyzing the structures of their own disciplines has contributed to this swing of the pendulum. The view is advanced that the most important basis for the selection and placement of content is the structure of the discipline from which the content is drawn. One adherent of this view, a professor who is engaged in one of the elementary school science projects, has written:

> The initial guideline for curriculum construction, in our view, is the discipline itself. It is *not* the apparent interests of children. It is *not* the social utility of science. Children's interests are important. So are the uses of science in daily life. The Project staff does not minimize these goals. But we feel that a deep interest in science can stem from a curriculum built on the discipline itself. And a significant understanding of the usefulness of science can result from a basic understanding of the subject.[2]

Many who propose that the structure of the disciplines should be the determining factor in the selection and sequence of content also insist that each discipline must be studied separately if its integrity and meaningfulness are to be maintained.

Those who would emphasize the structure of the disciplines as the basis for selection of content in the elementary school urge that by teaching the overarching concepts and generalizations of the field of knowledge at an early age, we will enable the pupil to learn specific facts more meaningfully and retain them longer.

Teachers and educational psychologists have long recognized that more is learned when the learner is able to relate specifics to a meaningful conceptual framework. For example, we know that nonsense syllables are learned more slowly and forgotten more quickly than meaningful words and phrases. A memorized fact—or a memorized generalization—is almost a nonsense syllable. The memorized fact will not carry the same meaning as it would if it were learned in relation to and as part of a broader context, nor will it be retained as long. A generalization has meaning only as it is developed from supporting facts and ideas. Modern school programs take these principles into account by teaching in units of a size and level that the learner can comprehend *at his stage of maturity*. Disagreements between the educator and the academician about teaching the structure of the disciplines to young children arise *not over the importance of structured learning*, but over what *kind* of structure is appropriate for the elementary school pupil.

It is important to recognize that there are, within each field of knowledge, generalizations or principles (structures) of varying degrees of concreteness or abstractness and varying degrees of simplicity or complexity. Structures that will be readily absorbed at an early age

[2] Atkin, J. Myron. "The University of Illinois Elementary School Science Project." *Elementary School Science Bulletin* 66:3, December 1961.

may have little resemblance to those in the minds of the scholars who are advocating the early teaching of general principles. Even a structure or frame of reference that is easily comprehended by the high school student may be confusing to a primary grade child and may actually interfere with his learning.

HOW MANY STRUCTURES IN THE CURRICULUM?

Generally accepted principles of learning suggest that the structures—that is, the principles, theories, or generalizations—over which a child will gain and retain control will be those that he frequently uses and applies. This raises the question of how many separate structures the younger learner can handle successfully at one time. Attempting to teach many separate structures may result in none being fully developed or applied frequently enough for pupils to retain them. Another question is whether the learner who is presented with many separate subject structures is likely to have difficulty in relating specifics to the correct structure. The effort to teach too many structures may cause one to interfere with another, so that none are useful to the pupil for organizing his learning.

These comments do not deny the urgency of introducing generalizations, theories, and principles as early in the pupil's career as is feasible. As the child develops concepts and generalizations, he gains powerful tools for learning and thinking. He can use this conceptual structure for a topic or a field of knowledge to select, relate, and organize pertinent materials and to revise his conceptual structure at a more mature level.

Indeed, as John Dewey pointed out over two decades ago, the essence of the educative process is the "progressive organization of knowledge." Recognizing that experience is basic to learning, he reminded his readers, "No experience is truly educative that does not tend both to knowledge of more facts and entertaining of more ideas and to a better, a more orderly, arrangement of them."[3] In short, the organized subject matter and structures of the disciplines constitute the *goal* toward which the learner must move. They are not the starting point. The level of the structure that is taught at any stage must be related to the learner's experience, background and maturity. The assumption that the problems of curriculum planning can be solved

---

[3] Ratner, Joseph, editor. *Intelligence in the Modern World: John Dewey's Philosophy.* New York: Modern Library Inc., 1939. p. 677. For Dewey's full discussion of this point, see: Dewey, John. *Experience and Education.* New York: The Macmillan Company, 1938. p. 86-112.

by inviting the scholar to lay out the structure of his discipline and then transferring it bodily into the school curriculum will lead only to confusion of the learner.

The limit of the number of separate structures that can be taught concurrently and effectively must also be considered in relation to the total curriculum. There are more disciplines that could be taught than can be handled separately in the time available. Two alternatives present themselves. One is to study the various groups of disciplines to determine what simple unifying structures within each of the broad groupings the young child can develop and how we can lead him to the more advanced structures that are involved in the separate disciplines. In many schools, we have tried to do this by formulating our curriculum with broad fields in the elementary grades and then leading into separate subjects in the senior high school. If, as some academic specialists maintain, it is impossible to find simple structures that are suitable for introducing the young child to broad fields, then the second alternative is to select a very limited number of separate disciplines to be introduced in the elementary school.

Whichever alternative is selected, if the pupil's school experience is to result in meaningful learning, it cannot be atomized into so many separate subjects that he has no opportunity to comprehend any of them or, if he comprehends them, to retain the learning. Those who urge early teaching of the structures of separate disciplines must face this practical fact: Even if the structure of each discipline could be presented so that elementary school children could grasp it, there would remain the impossibility of teaching all or even a large proportion of the diciplines as separate subjects. As the "battle of the disciplines" develops, with each discipline seeking separate treatment in the elementary school program, we should point out that the subjects to be studied by a pupil as discrete subjects must be limited to the number he can pursue to a useful level of competence within the available school time.

CONTENT PLACEMENT—THE DOWNWARD MOVE

A second issue concerning the selection and placement of content that is being debated has to do with the desirability of introducing younger children to content that has been reserved for the later school years. An outstanding physicist, Jerrold Zacharias, has urged that most, if not all, curriculum areas should be "rolled back" three or four years to teach more advanced content earlier in the school program. Several of the foundation supported curriculum projects in elementary school mathematics and science are devoted to introducing younger children to topics that conventionally appear in the junior or senior high school. The movement to teach foreign languages in the elementary school would add another subject to the elementary school curriculum.

Many leaders in elementary education, on the other hand, have objected to adding new and difficult topics and subjects to the curriculum. They point out that the school program is already crowded with factual information. It is their view that efforts to teach advanced topics to young children not only may fail to accomplish the desired results at the time but also may actually handicap the child's future progress in the subject. Some specialists in human development have warned of the injury "forced learning" may do to children's emotional development, which in turn may handicap intellectual achievement.

Pressures to "move content down" seem to have developed for several reasons. One is the longer period of preparation needed today for scientists, doctors, or specialists in any field. This has resulted in demands from the colleges that the secondary school carry students further into the various fields of knowledge than they formerly did. The secondary schools, in turn, have called on the elementary schools to step up the academic content of their programs.

Another factor in recommendations for "moving content down" has been the emergence of new views on the subject of readiness. Some psychologists today, while recognizing the dangers of "forced learning," suggest that there has been an undue and rather sentimental emphasis on *waiting* for children to develop readiness for various school experiences, and that much waste of children's time and talent has occurred as a result. Instead, it is suggested, teachers can "get behind the child and push him into readiness" for learning many things at an earlier age than he is expected to learn them in most schools today.

Other educators have pointed out that the experience background of most children today is considerably broader and deeper than was true of children a generation ago. This richer background has been developed through travel, television viewing, and other such activities. Therefore, the children are probably ready to attack more mature ideas and experiences. Indeed, there are fragments of evidence to suggest that children may come to school with more knowledge about some curriculum topics than the school attempts to teach them. To the extent this is true, the school program will fail to stimulate the interests and intellectual growth of pupils.

NEED TO STUDY PLACEMENT PROPOSALS

We should consider seriously whether our present programs are challenging to the youngsters of the 1960's and make the adjustments that are needed to begin where modern children actually are. Most of the current proposals to "move content down" deserve thoughtful consideration and evaluation before they are accepted, rejected, or perhaps adapted in some way for use in the school program. We need to look beneath the labels to see what is really being proposed.

Science   In considering proposals about the teaching of science, we must recognize that this area has been neglected in many elementary school programs. Some of the current proposals for introducing science may be unrealistic in the depth of study they assume most children can achieve. But they may help to redress an imbalance that has long existed in both the elementary and secondary school. We should study these proposals with an open mind and be ready to adopt them, or adapt parts of them, if they will help orient youngsters to the modern world in which science and technology are such important forces.

Foreign Languages   In considering foreign language study in the elementary schools, we should keep in mind the warning of the foreign language specialists that it is better to have no teaching of foreign language in the early school years unless certain minimum conditions can be met. According to the policy statement of the Modern Language Association, foreign language instruction in the elementary school should not be undertaken unless:

- It is an integral part of the school day.
- It is an integral part of the total foreign language program in the school system.
- There is close articulation with later foreign language learning that children will experience.
- There are available enough elementary school teachers with an adequate command of the foreign language.
- There are available adequate learning materials.
- The program has the support of the administration of the school system and of the secondary school teachers of foreign language.[4]

[4] Modern Language Association, Foreign Language Program Research Center. *Foreign Languages in the Elementary School: A Second Statement of Policy.* New York: the Center, 1961.

These conditions require that the elementary school principal and members of the staff weigh the advantages to their particular pupils of devoting the children's time and the school's resources to foreign language study, as opposed to spending the time and resources in other pursuits. Unless foreign language teaching in the elementary school is to be done well and with continuity, even the foreign language specialists—or *especially* the foreign language specialists—would urge that it be left to the secondary school.

Mathematics In certain other subjects, terminology may have been a block to communication between the subject specialists and elementary school personnel. For example, when the mathematician suggests that algebra or geometry be introduced in the elementary grades, the elementary specialist may assume (and many have done so) that the intention is to teach these subjects as they have traditionally been presented in the ninth and tenth grades. The mathematician, however, may be proposing to give primary grade children experiences with algebra and geometry at a level comparable to the level at which young children should be taught to "read maps." This is usually described as a "readiness level," although basic concepts of map interpretation are being introduced.

Economics Again, when the economist suggests that young children study basic economic concepts, he is likely to be urging that topics already in the curriculum be treated in order to lay a basis for children's understanding these concepts. For example, economists say that one of the fundamental generalizations of their discipline is that there is a continuing conflict between people's unlimited wants and the limited resources that are available to satisfy these wants, and that a rational solution to this conflict must be found. In the primary grades, children can take first steps toward understanding this generalization by considering the need to reconcile all the desires of family members with the money the family has to spend.

All of this suggests that in dealing with proposals to introduce into the elementary grades content that has traditionally been reserved for later school years, leaders in elementary education need to consider exactly what the proposals mean and what is likely to be the effect on children's total learning and growth. Proposals that would emphasize memoriter learning or cripple efforts to develop a balanced, well-rounded school program for youngsters can only be rejected. Proposals that seem likely to result in an enriched and more challenging school program deserve careful study, followed by suitable applications.

GUIDELINES FOR IMPROVEMENT

As we work to improve the selection and placement of content in the elementary school program, there are at least five guidelines we should follow.

Content is the means to selected goals and does not represent a goal in itself. Factual information is the material that is used by children to develop concepts, understandings, values, and skills. There is no fixed body of content that all children must "master." Content should be selected in terms of its significance to an understanding of the modern world and its learnability for the children to whom it is to be presented. Individual differences among pupils, as well as their common characteristics, must be taken into account in selecting the content and learning experiences for a particular class.

Content should be placed so that children can gain a sequential development, from one school year to the next, of the generalizations, values, and skills that are the goals of education. This requires identification and detailed analysis of educational goals in terms of generalizations, values, and skills. The level at which these concepts and generalizations can be treated at each grade level can then be considered and content appropriate for developing the concepts and generalizations can be selected. Continuity from one school year to the next can be consciously planned.

The existing program should be examined to determine whether it is failing to challenge pupils and, if so, what can be done through better selection and placement of content to raise children's standards of performance and broaden their learning horizons. Perhaps a program of readiness experiences, planned to enable children to begin the conscious development of generalizations, values, and skills in the various subjects at a somewhat earlier age than has been assumed possible, will pay great learning dividends. Perhaps we have been underestimating the background that many children today bring to the classroom. Perhaps we have pitched our program—or parts of it—to a level that was appropriate a generation ago but is not sufficiently demanding of today's youngsters. On the other hand, we have a half century of research in child development and psychology of learning that we must not dismiss because of slogans that call for "rigor" and "hard content." Without being stampeded by current proposals for "rolling the content back" into earlier school years, we need to take a fresh look at this whole situation.

The selection and placement of content must help youngsters learn in a structured manner so that they establish relationships and grow toward an increasingly mature organization of their knowledge. Every bit of content that a youngster studies should be related to a conceptual framework he can understand. These conceptual frameworks will consist of important ideas and generalizations that are the structures of the disciplines as scholars see them. The child's conceptual framework will be much simpler, much less elaborated, than that of the scholar, but it can be consistent with the frame of reference he should develop as he grows up. We must apply what we know of child development and the learning process to organize and use content to lead the pupil toward comprehension of the structures of the disciplines. We must organize the content into large blocks of study comprehensible to the child.

We must not permit pressure for teaching the structures of separate subjects to fragment the curriculum, so that we turn back to a daily schedule that allots fifteen minutes to spelling, thirty minutes to reading, twenty minutes to history, and so on.

Curriculum research must be adequately financed, broad in scope, and draw on the cooperative efforts of public school personnel, academic scholars, scholars in the appropriate fields of professional education, and informed lay persons. This guideline looks to the future. We need answers to many questions about the selection and placement of content, answers based on evidence gained through experimentation. Each of the groups named above has a contribution to make to such experimentation. Teachers and administrators bring to the job a firsthand knowledge of their pupils, the schools in which they work, and the educational goals they are trying to achieve. Specialists in the academic disciplines bring a knowledge of the structure, method, and content of their fields. Scholars in the educational disciplines can bring to bear the latest research in learning, human development, and school-society relationships, and informed analyses of philosophical problems that are involved in the decision-making process. Informed lay persons can raise pertinent questions and contribute to balanced judgments. Each group can make its contribution, however, only if it understands its appropriate role and is willing to stay within it and respect the competency and the contributions of the other groups that are involved.

These five guidelines call for continued and even increased effort on our part and for fresh creative thinking about the instructional program of our schools. The effort that is demanded will be great, but it will be a small price to pay if it can bring better learning opportunities for the boys and girls of our nation.

Some Findings from Analyses of Old Textbooks*

by JOHN A. NIETZ

John A. Nietz is professor emeritus at the University of Pittsburgh. He is an expert in educational history, specializing in the history of textbooks. Dr. Nietz has written extensively in education journals and has written OLD TEXTBOOKS and THE CONSTITUTIONAL AND LEGAL BASES OF THE PUBLIC SCHOOL SYSTEM OF PENNSYLVANIA.

Much of the treatment in the textbooks in the history of education deals more fully with the development of educational thought than of actual practice. It is the thesis of the writer that an analysis of the actual textbook used in the past will reveal a truer history of what was actually taught in the schools than a study of the educational theories. This does not mean that the theories should not be studied, but failing to deal with what was actually taught results in an incomplete understanding of the history of education.

It has been the privilege of the writer to have directed a number of studies involving the analyses of old American textbooks. This article deals with the significance of some of the findings of some of these studies. Space limitation of such an article permits only meager reference to some of the more obvious contributions of these studies to a fuller understanding of the history of education in the United States.

Nearly every one of the studies referred to in this article has found that what has been commonly written about the evolution of these subject fields in American educational history has been partly, and sometimes largely, false. One of the outstanding examples of this was in the field of what is now called civics. Mason[1] found that much of what has been written about evolution of civil government (civics) in the schools of the United States was largely wrong. Among the persons whose statements were partly or largely wrong were Burke Hinsdale in his *How to Study and Teach History* (1894), Henry

---

* John A. Nietz, "Some Findings from Analyses of Old Textbooks," *History of Education Journal*, 10 (Nos. 1-4, 1959): 20-28. By permission of the editor.

[1] All studies referred to in the body of this article are listed in the bibliography.

Bourne in *The Teaching of History and Civics in the Elementary and Secondary School* (1903), Monroe in the *Encyclopedia of Education*, and a number of more recent writers. Several said that civil government was not introduced into the schools until after the middle of 19th century. Another said that no civil government text was published between 1848 and 1873, and so on. As a fact, Mason discovered and analyzed seventy of these textbooks published in the United States before 1890, all of which bore separate titles. He did not count the numerous editions in which many of these appeared. Chronologically, two appeared before 1800, two during the period 1800-24, twenty-two during 1825-49, eighteen during 1850-74, and twenty-six during 1875-90.

The titles of many subject fields have changed since their introduction into the curriculum of American schools. Only two of the forty-five textbooks analyzed by Shank bore the title of physics, most of others were entitled natural philosophy. One was called Philosophical Conversations, and several Natural and Experimental Philosophy.

Herk, in his study of sixty-six American Psychology textbooks prior to 1890, found many and varied titles for this field. Only twenty used the title of psychology, and most of these appeared after 1870. Some of the other most common titles were: Intellectual Philosophy, Mental Philosophy, Mental Science, Science of the Mind, The Human Mind, The Laws of Being, The Human Intellect, and Improvement of the Mind.

Many of the old grammar textbooks did not bear the title of grammar. For example, the most commonly used Latin grammar text to be used in England for several centuries and also in the colonial Latin grammar schools of America was Lily's *Rules Construed*. Too, the first popular American Latin grammar was Ezekiel Cheever's *A Short Introduction to the Latin Tongue: Being the Accidence*. A similar title was used by Caleb Bingham for a textbook written in English for girls. Its full title was: *The Young Lady's Accidence: or, a Short and Easy Introduction to English Grammar* (1787).

Another subject field in which many of the early titles were different was arithmetic. Many early arithmetic authors, all of whose books went through numerous editions, entitled their textbooks *Schoolmaster's Assistant*. This was first true of an arithmetic written in England about 1750 by Thomas Dilworth and then went through many printings in America. The full title was: *The Schoolmaster's Assistant, Being a Compendium of Arithmetic*. Similar titles were used by Joseph Crukshank, Nathan Daboll, Donald Fraser, Zachariah Jess, Jeremiah Paul, Stephen Pike, and John Todd. It may also be interesting to note how many of the given names of these authors were Biblical. The following authors used the title *Calculator* for their books: John Armstrong, Howard Frusher, William Slocomb, Thomas Smiley, Joseph Stockton, and Almon Ticknor.

The textbooks in the field now known as civics possibly had the most variations in titles of all the textbook fields. No particular title had become common until after 1900. Among the titles used before 1900 were the following: *Citizen's Manual, American Government, American Manual, Principles of Government, Young American, Patriot's Manual, Political Manual, Voter's Textbook, United States Government, Civil Government, Our Government, Politics for Young Americans, Constitutional Instructor, Constitutional Textbook, Governmental Instructor, Political Classbook,* and *Our Republic.*

The first outstanding example of preparing a series of textbooks in a graded manner was when Comenius wrote the *Janua Linguarum Reserata* in 1631, and later the *Vestibulum, Atrium,* and *Palatium.* Even after Comenius set a good example, it was not until more than a century later before it was common to write textbooks in series. View the slow development of graded American textbooks.

The *New England Primer* was virtually the entire elementary school curriculum in the colonial period. The first significant American attempt to produce a sort of graded textbook series was done by Noah Webster, called the *Grammatical Institute of the English Language* in three parts. Part I was the Speller (1784); Part II, Grammar; and Part III, Reader. Even though there were three books, yet the fact that each book was in a different subject field destroyed its graded value.

Lindley Murray published his *English Reader* in 1779, which was later followed by the *Sequel to the English Reader* and still later by *Introduction to the English Reader;* yet these scarcely constituted a graded series, since none of them was sufficiently easy to be used as a beginning reading book.

It was not until the 1830's that graded textbooks appeared in several subject fields, the most famous of which was the McGuffey *Readers.* A series of readers written by Samuel Worcester antedated the McGuffey books, but these never gained wide usage. S. G. Goodrich, writing under the pen name of Peter Parley, wrote graded books in several fields in the 1830's, namely, in reading, geography, American history, and world history. Joseph Ray and also Charles Davies began writing graded arithmetics in the 1830's. Following the 1830's it was common for most elementary textbooks to appear in graded series.

The next question to be asked is, how well were these series graded? Space does not permit an extensive analysis, yet some light can be thrown on some findings regarding the best known of all these series, namely, the McGuffey *Readers*. The writer recently had one of his graduate students analyze the vocabulary of the first edition of McGuffey's *Second Reader* by means of the Yoakum Readability Formula. He found the vocabulary to be of eighth grade reading level. The *Third Reader* contained a selection entitled "Metaphysics."

Hughes found that all of the editions of the McGuffey *Fourth*, *Fifth*, and *Sixth Readers* contained a total of 1067 separate titles. Of these, 247 appeared in readers of more than one level, 607 appeared more than once in readers of the same level, and 607 appeared only once. The fact that more than 23% appeared in readers of more than one level is proof that experience with the use of the early readers revealed poor grading. Five of the fifteen most frequently repeated titles appeared in readers of all three grades. Thus by trial and error the gradation improved in the later editions.

Jacobs found that the United States History textbooks published before 1885 on an average devoted 44.65% of the content to matters of war and 19.28% to government and politics, and only 1.52% to to social, recreational, religious, and educational matters. Certainly, an analysis of recent history textbooks would reveal a very different pattern.

Several studies show that the early textbooks in several fields devoted much space to religion, with such emphasis declining after 1850 and nearly disappearing in some fields after 1900. For example, Robinson found that the readers used in the colonies prior to 1775 devoted 85% of the space to religion and 8% to morals; those between 1775 and 1825, 22% to religion, and 28% to morals; those between 1825 and 1875, 7.5% to the religion and 23% to morals; and those between 1875 and 1915, only 1.5% to religion and 7% to morals.

Hughes, who analyzed the contents of all of the editions of the fourth, fifth, and sixth famous McGuffey Readers, found that the lessons devoted to religion and morals even exceeded the percentages reported in the Robinson study and that the decline was not so marked in them. The first edition of the third reader in 1837 devoted 32.6% to religion and 11.2% to morals. The popular 1879 edition of the three readers devoted 8.7% to religion and 25.2% to morals. The last edition in 1901 still devoted 5.9% of the lesson to religion and 26.3% to morals.

Wilson, in his analysis of 134 geographies published in the United States before 1895, found that the 68 books before 1850 devoted an average of 5.8% of the content to religion, while the books between 1875 and 1895 only 1.23%.

The two main emphases in early readers were religion, as already shown, and elocution. Even before readers appeared in graded series Caleb Bingham wrote two rather popular readers, *American Preceptor* (1794), emphasizing religion and morals, and the *Columbian Orator* 1806, containing reading selections for developing powers of elocution. Too, the first edition of the fifth in the famous McGuffey series was entitled *Rhetorical Guide: or Fifth Reader*. The first 60 pages of this reader dealt with "Principles of Elocution." The first reading selection on page 61 was prefaced with the statement that all the lessons were selected according to their suitability for elocutionary reading. These two aims or emphases were foremost in nearly all readers before 1900.

Barton analyzed sitxy-two 19th century and 20th century textbooks in physiology and hygiene. She compared the emphases according to the percentage of pages devoted to the different aspects of the field. Marked differences were found regarding the space devoted to certain aspects in the two centuries. For example, 22.5% of the space dealt with the nervous system in the 19th century and 12.4% in the 20th; only 1.6% on disease in the former and 13.4% in the present century; 0.87% on the circulatory system in the earlier and 5.5% in the 20th century. In other words, the authors of the present century paid less attention to systems but more to factors involving the functioning of these systems, as disease, nutrition, and cleanliness.

Shank's analysis of 45 American natural philosophy (physics) textbooks before 1880 reveals that the content dealt with the following topics: Structure of matter, mechanics, sound, heat, magnetism and electricity, optics, astronomy, mathematics, and miscellaneous matters. He determined the average percentage of space devoted to each topic for each of four eighteen-year periods and for the entire period. It was found that 40.3% of all space dealt with mechanics, 18% to optics, 16.7% to magnetism and electricity, 7.9% to heat, and less than 7% to each of the other topics. Too, it was found that the percentage of space devoted to each of the topics for each of the four sub-periods was rather constant except for two topics, namely, heat and astronomy. The books of the first period devoted only 1.4% to heat, and the last period devoted 12.3%. During the first period 20.5% was on astronomy and only 1.4% during the last.

Hess analyzed 86 rhetoric and composition textbooks published in the United States before 1870. He found that in the earlier books the emphasis was definitely on rhetoric and literary criticism, but that after 1840 the emphasis gradually shifted toward composition. To illustrate the nature of the treatment in an early book, Andrews, in *Elements of Rhetorick and Belles Lettres*, 1813, designated the following:

> as important figures—Allegory, Prosopopeia, Apostrophe, and Parabole or Similtude to which may be added Antithesis or Opposition, Interrogation, Exclamation, Vision, Amplification, Climax, Correction, and Suppression.

and listed,

> metaphor, metonymy, synecdoche, and irony as primary tropes, and antonomasia, communication, extenuation, euphemism, catachresis, and hyperbole as secondary tropes.

Every one of the studies involving the analysis of old textbooks has shown the *evolution* of something regarding nature of these books. Space permits reference to only a few illustrations. One very interesting and exhaustive study was made by Steiner in tracing the origin and developmental use of the concept of percentage in arithmetic. After examining hundreds of arithmetics published in the United States before 1860, he discovered that at least 140 included one or more topics that would now be classified as applications of percentage. He found twenty different percentage topics used by one or more authors, but that no arithmetic used all twenty. It was found that Lee's book (1797) was the first to present special symbols for U.S. money, Daboll gave us the dollar sign ($), Gough (1788) first suggested the over-all subject of percentage, Barnard (1830) first treated percentage as an abstract concept, Putnam first presented the percent symbol (%), and Robinson (1860) was the first to complete the development of the concept of percentage.

Alan C. Lloyd analyzed 248 American typewriting textbooks. He found that the development of the content and nature of these books may be divided into three periods, as follows: 1880-1900, The Period of Exploration and Indefiniteness; 1900-1930, The Period of Experimentation and Development; and 1930-1950, The Period of Crystallization of Refinement.

During the first period there was considerable confusion, since there were variations in typewriters and in their operating procedures. During the second period the typewriter was standardized, but much diversification in the matter of teaching typewriting. Then during the third period there was a trend toward adapting books to the curriculum, toward using group procedures rather than individual instruction, toward the crystallization of objectives, and toward the use of constructive practice activities for developing typewriting skill. Lloyd says:

> The pattern of development in American typewriting textbooks has consistently moved from the vague to the definite, from the general to the specific, from the haphazard to the focused, from the brief and cursory to the extensive and systematic, and from the individual to classroom work. (p. 334)

Korona, in his analysis of 103 old bookkeeping textbooks, found that even though both single-entry and double-entry systems were recognized rather early, yet many of those who included both failed to present any procedure for changing a set of books from single to double entry. No writer before 1865 mentioned this procedure. In most of the early books, if both were mentioned, they were treated separately.

Korona also found that Jones, in 1841, was the first author to reject the method of beginning the study of bookkeeping through journalizing transactions. He favored an approach through the ledger and statements rather than the journal. Thus Jones laid the foundation for two approaches which later became common in bookkeeping —the account or ledger approach and the balance sheet approach.

An analysis of 45 American natural philosophy (physics) textbooks before 1880 by Shank reveals some interesting findings. All the books contained suggested demonstrations, but many of the earlier books included no demonstration dealing with heat and three none with sound. For all the books an average of 42.9% of the demonstrations related to mechanics. Too, the books of the first sub-period contained no problems whatever, and those of the second sub-period contained only problems relating to machines. The books during the third and fourth sub-periods contained problems relating to mechanics, heat, sound, and optics. Eighty-seven per cent of all the problems dealt with mechanics.

There was a considerable lag in time between the appearance or discovery of new knowledge and its use in textbooks. In regard to some matters or ideas this appears to have been inertia and in other cases fear of public reaction. For example, in Workman's *American Accountant*, 1793, which really was an arithmetic, there appears in full resolution of 1786 of the Congress of the United States creating the United States monetary system of mills, cents, dimes, and dollars. Too, advertisements in the back of the book use the U.S. system. Yet the problems in the text were still based on the old English monetary system. In fact, some arithmetics continued using English monetary problems considerably after 1800. Inertia and lack of up-to-dateness on the part of textbook authors apparently account for such a lag.

In some fields this lag could well have been caused by fear of public opinion regarding the introduction of the new ideas in textbooks. This likely was true in the field of Biology. Mendel's laws of heredity were discovered about 1860, yet Cretzinger found that they were not commonly presented in secondary school textbooks until about 1900. The theory in evolution was formulated by Charles Darwin in 1858, but found little acceptance in textbooks until after 1900. Since these theories conflicted with the religious views held by many, textbook authors, or their publishers, hesitated in presenting these theories in texts.

Early textbooks often contained biased content. Seemingly the authors not only failed to observe care to avoid such content, but purposely introduced such content by misrepresenting or adversely criticising certain attitudes, beliefs, or customs which they did not favor and over-valuing those which they did favor. This seemed to be true in early readers, such as the *New England Primer;* in early history books; and particularly in early geography books. These biases were involved in such matters as religion and customs, and were applied to national groups and to other races.

Sahli found much of this type of content in his analysis of early American geographies. Since some of the earliest geography textbooks were written by New England ministers, they were very critical of other religions. For example, the Morse text (1790) said, "The religion of the Spanish monarchy; and it is, in these countries, of the most bigotted, superstitious and tyrannical character." Adams' text (1818), in writing of Russia's religion, said, "The established religion is the Greek church, but little differing from Popery." Davies (1805) claimed that the Irish priests ruled with "blind superstition and ignorance." On the other hand, Parish (1810) wrote, "The Scotch clergy are men of learning and piety." Similar compliments were given Protestants by other authors.

Similarly numerous uncomplimentary comments were made of other nationalities and races. Morse (1790) said of the Mexicans, "From idleness and constitution, their whole business is amour and intrigue; their ladies, of consequence, are not distinguished for their chastity or domestic virtues." Smith (1816) wrote, "The people of Brazil are said to be sunk in effeminate luxury, to be lazy and proud." Davies (1805) wrote, "The Saxons are a lively and contented people; the

Prussians appear dull and gloomy"; while Dwight (1806) said they were "fond of show and parade in their dress." The authors generally held that the Hungarians were a strong, robust people, but rude, revengeful, and warlike. Morse wrote that the Italians "are amourous and addicted to original indulgences, revengeful, and masters of the art of dissimulation." Dwight (1806) referred to the Turks as "morose, treacherous, furiously passionate, unsocial, and unfriendly to people of all other nations." On the other hand, the Swiss received more consistent approval than any other people in Europe. For example, Woodbridge (1835) wrote, "The Swiss are generally well educated, and are remarkable for their bravery, industry and virtue."

Culler, who analyzed 97 later geographies (1840-90) found that the treatment of religion decreased and became more tolerant. Likewise, less bias on national and racial matters was exhibited.

BIBLIOGRAPHY[1]

1. BARTON, HELEN N. "A Study of the Development of Textbooks in Physiology and Hygiene in the U.S." 1942.

2. CRETZINGER, JOHN I. "An Analysis of Principles or Generalizations Appearing in Biological Textbooks Used in the Secondary Schools of the United States from 1800 to 1933." 1939.

3. CULLER, NED. "The Development of American Geography Textbooks Prior to 1890." 1945.

4. HERK, MICHAEL. "An Analysis of Early American Psychology Textbooks Prior to 1890." 1950.

5. HESS, GLENN. "An Analysis of Early American Rhetoric and Composition Textbooks from 1784 to 1870." 1949.

6. HUGHES, RAYMOND G. "An Analysis of the 4th, 5th, and 6th McGuffey Readers," 1943.

7. JACOBS, CHAUNCEY D. "A Study of the Development of School Textbooks in United States History from 1795 to 1885." 1939.

8. KORONA, LOUIS W. "The Development of Bookkeeping Textbooks Used in American Schools Prior to 1893." 1943.

9. LLOYD, ALAN C. "The Development of American Typewriting Textbooks." 1951.

10. MASON, WAYNE E. "Analysis of Early American Civil Government Textbooks." 1944.

11. ROBINSON, R. R. *Two Centuries of Change in the Content of School Readers*. Nashville: George Peabody College for Teachers, 1930.

[1] With the exception of item number eleven, all the works cited in this list are unpublished doctoral dissertations at the University of Pittsburgh.

12. SAHLI, JOHN R. "An Analysis of Early American Geography Text-books from 1784 to 1840." 1941.

13. SHANK, PAUL. "The Evolution of Natural Philosophy (Physics) Text-books Prior to 1890." 1951.

14. STEINER, ROBERT L. "Percentage and Its Applications as Developed in American Arithmetics Through 1860." 1946.

15. WILSON, KARL K. "Historical Survey of the Religious Content of American Geography Textbooks from 1784 to 1895." 1951.

Is Progressive Education Obsolete?*

by WILLIAM VAN TIL

William Van Til is chairman of the department of second-ary education at New York University. He is a former president of the Association for Supervision and Curriculum Develop-ment of the NEA. His varied writings in the field of education include THE MAKING OF A MODERN EDUCATOR *and* ECONOMIC ROADS FOR AMERICAN DEMOCRACY.

Is progressive education outmoded? One's first impulse is to say "yes." Who today, among the voices being heard on education, is talking about the concerns which characterized many leaders of edu-cation during the first half of the twentieth century? Specifically, who today is talking about the ideas which occupied John Dewey, George Counts, Boyd H. Bode, and William Heard Kilpatrick, those symbols of the intellectual leadership of the "new education," symbols of the varied versions of the progressive movement in education? Practically nobody, at least nobody who is being heard widely.

Instead, American education in the early 1960s is engrossed with the application of technology to education, with competing new proposals for organization of the school program, and with stress on reconstruction of academic disciplines. The mass media foster the interest in technology, organization, and disciplines. If an educator tries to be heard on more fundamental aspects, he often encounters the silent treatment.

---

* William Van Til, "Is Progressive Education Obsolete?" *Saturday Review,* 45 (February 17, 1962): 56-57, 82-84. By permission of the editor and the author.

The Industrial Revolution has finally reached education. As a result, matters of technology have virtually become table talk in education today. In professional discussions and in the mass media reporting we hear constantly about educational television, language laboratories, courses on film, and programmed learning through teaching machines.

A second stress in today's education emphasizes organization of the school program. Proposals are varied and often conflicting. They include such organizational proposals as team teaching, the dual progress plan, the nongraded school, and increasing the course requirements within the existing Carnegie unit structure.

Currently, a third stress is the new interest in the academic disciplines. In part, the emphasis is upon updating knowledge through efforts by specialists in the disciplines. The work of such groups as the Physical Science Study Committee and the varied mathematics programs at Yale, Maryland, and Illinois are watched intently. Science, mathematics, and foreign languages ride high as the favored fields of the national government, which has become a significant curriculum maker on the elementary and high school levels. The fields of English and physical education make frantic and failing attempts to latch onto the benefits of the National Defense Education Act; leadership in reconstruction of the curriculum in these fields has been assumed by the College Entrance Examination Board and by a football coach, respectively. There are indications that Commissioner McMurrin intends to attempt to do for the arts as well as for English what post-Sputnik apprehension did for the sciences. Rumors, alarms, and confusions surround the status of the social studies. The phrase "structures of the disciplines" is being bandied about, with none too clear a definition emerging as yet.

Technology, organization, and the disciplines seem a far cry from the philosophical, social, and psychological ideas that engaged the leaders of the progressive movement in education in the first half of the twentieth century. There appears to have been a change in "fashions in ideas," to use the chilling and accurate phrase Irwin Edman coined for a phenomenon of our times. Consequently, progressive education seems outmoded. Lawrence A. Cremin even consigned it to history in his "The Transformation of the School: Progressivism in American Education, 1876-1957." He began his preface as follows: "The death of the Progressive Education Association in 1955 and the passing of its journal, *Progressive Education*, two years later marked the end of an era in American pedagogy. Yet one would scarcely have known it from the pitifully small group of mourners at both funerals." Martin Mayer recapitulated the Cremin position in his widely read book, "The Schools."

One might readily conclude that progressive education is outmoded save for a stubborn fact. The fact is that the questions raised by the progressive movement in education are not obsolete. They will not die. They cannot be killed. They cannot be exorcised by any voodooism yet known to technology, organization, or the reconstruction of disciplines which remains aloof from these questions.

The basic questions which men like John Dewey, William Heard Kilpatrick, George Counts, and Boyd H. Bode raised are inescapable questions: What are the aims of education? Upon what foundations should the school program be built? Given such aims and foundations, what should the schools teach? To these probing and fundamental questions, matters of organization and technique, while important, are necessarily subordinate.

The progressive education movement of the first half of the twentieth century, symbolized by Dewey, Kilpatrick, Counts, and Bode, was essentially a quest for workable answers for our times to questions such as these. No one claims that the Holy Grail was found; no one claims that the questioners came up with final, definitive, eternal answers. The "new educators" did not completely agree among themselves on workable answers for our times. But at least the "new educators" asked the right questions.

One wing of the progressive movement sought the answers primarily in the potential of the individual learner. A pioneer in this respect was the man whose ninetieth birthday was celebrated on November 20, 1961—William Heard Kilpatrick. Many of today's schoolmen will remember Kilpatrick's classes in the Horace Mann Auditorium of Teachers College, Columbia University. Hundreds attended each session, yet the quiet man with the mane of white hair used committees and reports so skillfully that each student found opportunities to speak out and battle over ideas.

The heart of Kilpatrick's first major contribution to education, "The Project Method," was founded on his faith in the potential of the individual learner. In back of the recurrent Kilpatrickian phrases which valued "purposeful activity," "intrinsic motivation," "planning," in back of his opposition to "extrinsic subject matter" which disregarded individuals, in back of his opposition to meaningless rote learning, lay Kilpatrick's belief that clues to significant content can be found within the learner and can be developed fully in collaboration with a mature adult who fosters self-direction and independent thought. The later Kilpatrick increased his stress on the importance of social orientation and the urgency of meeting social problems. But the mark Kilpatrick lastingly left on the progressive movement still derives largely from his faith in the potentiality of the learner when that potentiality is cultivated by skillful and sensitive teachers. To many educators, probably to most, insight into the relationship between the individual and his education was the major contribution of the progressive education which Kilpatrick espoused, though he was concerned for philosophical and social, as well as psychological, foundations. And—mistake it not—the insight derived from Kilpatrick made a massive contribution to education in an era that had lost sight of the importance of the learner and his purposes and potential.

A second wing of the progressive movement set forth answers to the perennial questions of aims, foundations, and content largely in terms of the society which surrounded the schools. George Counts, a battler for socially oriented schools in a democracy, serves as a symbol of this emphasis. To George Counts, for instance, the times cried out for an education realistically geared to the new social order which was emerging. He threw his eloquent challenge to the Progressive Education Association assembled in convention in 1932. He amplified his ideas in the pamphlet "Dare the Schools Build A New Social Order?" and for years educators found themselves forced to face the issues Counts raised. Whether one condemned aspects of his viewpoint as indoctrination and a potential abuse of the method of intelligence, thus classifying it as a new liberal's version of authoritarianism, or whether one hailed it as a realistic recognition of the overpowering importance of social problems, as an indication that the social sciences had come of age, an educator who heard Counts had to take into account stress on society. The role of education with respect to social change and to reform was an imperative and recurrent theme with Counts and his fellow social reconstructionists. The pivotal place of social realities in education could not be forgotten after Counts was heard, even though indoctrination might be repudiated.

George Counts lived his faith. He helped turn back Communist infiltration of teachers' unions. He was a tower of strength in the Liberal Party; he was a candidate for public office and in the vanguard of social movements of his time. He is still active in his retirement.

To others equally immersed in the progressive movement, democratic values were central to all considerations. For instance, to Boyd H. Bode, the Lincoln-like man from Illinois who made his major contribution through Ohio State University, the crucial need was for the clarification of differences between the democratic way of life and the way of its authoritarian competitors. As he saw it, the road out of value confusion led through a remorseless and unremitting use of the method of intelligence in human affairs. To Bode, progressive education was at the crossroads and a child-centered view would never suffice. Nor was indoctrination the road to a better world. He conducted his classes in philosophy of education through the Socratic method and he fostered thought with every heckling, humorous, or trenchant exchange of ideas into day-by-day learning experiences.

I venture for your consideration the bold hypothesis that each of these men touched on part of the whole, that each perceived and particularly stressed an aspect of education which we neglect at our peril, that each succeeded nobly, and, where he failed, failed gallantly in building the "new education." Each asked the right questions; each responded with relevant contributions toward workable answers for our times.

The thinker who came closest to the reconciliation of the individual, society, and philosophical foundations—was the extraordinary John Dewey, whose centennial was celebrated by the John Dewey Society three years ago through meetings in scores of universities across the nation. The word "extraordinary" is used advisedly. During his long lifetime, this incredible man lived a full life as a person, participated in social and civic action, conducted the most famous laboratory school in history, became the father figure of the progressive education movement (and, to shift the analogy, sometimes served as mother hen by reconciling conflicts and even smoothing ruffled feathers in the flock), became a towering figure in philosophy, and, in the process, managed to leave for posterity a legacy of 5,000 pages of articles and 18,000 pages in book form.

Yet even Dewey, prodigious though his endeavors were, never achieved extensive translation of his ideas into a new curriculum. Underbrush in philosophy needed to be cleared. After his Laboratory School experimentation, and after setting forth his pedagogical creed in such books as "The School and Society" and "Democracy and Education," Dewey gave himself to this Herculean labor as he built his philosophy of experimentalism. He constantly reacted to trends and tendencies in progressive education, as he did in his critique "Experience and Education." He made only occasional critical forays into program building. He would be the first to admit, were he alive, that much remained to be done to implement his ideas on what he preferred to term simply "education," rather than "progressive education."

So we turn back to the thinking of representative intellectual leaders of the progressive movement in education, not in any spirit of ancestor worship, but for the inescapable questions they raised and for the insights they contributed toward workable solutions for our times. Cremin says it well in his final paragraphs: "There remained a timelessness about many of the problems the progressives raised and the solutions they proposed. . . . And for all the talk about pedagogical breakthroughs and crash programs, the authentic progressive vision remained strangely pertinent to the problems of mid-century America. Perhaps it only awaited the reformulation and resuscitation that would ultimately derive from a larger research and reform in American life and thought." With these words Cremin partially redeems the strange inconsistency of pointing out brilliantly in early chapters that social currents created progressive education well before the official establishment of a Progressive Education Association, yet conveying the impression in his final chapter that the demise of an organization and a magazine meant the death of progressive education. The fact that ideas live beyond organizations apparently escaped the overanxious gravediggers who gleefully greeted Cremin's book as the definitive obituary for progressive education as a force in American ideas.

The questions raised and many of the tentative answers ventured by the early leaders of progressive education are not dead nor will they die. In time, the sponsors of new educational technology, the advocates of varied forms of educational organization, the proponents of study of the structure of separate disciplines, must face the inescapable questions and consider the possible solutions proposed.

The problem for sponsors and users of programmed learning through teaching machines does not lie in the capacity of the machine to produce positive reinforcement, whether it takes the form of a kind word, a pat on the head, or, indeed, a bottle of Coca-Cola. Given technical ingenuity, a reinforcing reward will be forthcoming. The harder problem for sponsors and users of the teaching machine is whether positive reinforcement will be used to bring nearer George Orwell's "1984" and Aldous Huxley's "Brave New World," or whether programmed learning, using positive reinforcement selectively and with discrimination, will reduce the skill-drudgery of education and free teachers and students for more humane aspects of learning and human development, such as creativity, the use of reflective thought, and experiences in freedom. Consider, for instance, this quotation from "Walden Two," a Utopia envisioned by the pioneer of teaching machines, B. F. Skinner of Harvard, a Utopia which appears to some of us an authoritarian nightmare world of behavioristic conditioning.

T. E. Frazier, spokesman for "Walden Two," says approvingly, "Now that we *know* how positive reinforcement works and why negative doesn't . . . we can be more deliberate, and hence more successful, in our cultural design. We can achieve a sort of control under which the controlled, even though they are following a code much more scrupulously than was ever the case under the old system, nevertheless *feel free.* They are doing what they want to do, not what they are forced to do. That's the source of the tremendous power of positive reinforcement—there's no restraint and no revolt. By a careful cultural design, we control not the final behavior, but the *inclination* to behave—the motives, the desires, the wishes.

"The curious thing is that in that case *the question of freedom never arises.*"

In the light of this quotation we can understand why Aldous Huxley recently reminded us in "Brave New World Revisited" that it may be later than we think. He wrote of his conclusion, "The older dictators fell because they never could supply their subjects with enough bread, enough circuses, enough miracles and mysteries. Nor did they possess a really effective system of mind-manipulation. . . . Under a scientific dictator, education will really work—with the result that most men and women will grow up to love their servitude and will never dream of revolution. There seems to be no good reason why a thoroughly scientific dictatorship should ever be overthrown."

The problem before the sponsors of educational television is not how wide a circle over six states, or indeed a nation, can be reached by a plane flying for Midwest Airborne Television. Nor is it bouncing beams off satellites for global television. Technology will solve those problems. The real problem is whether the device will realize the gloomy prophecy of an old Vanderbilt University professor who once said at a meeting of the American Association of University Professors, "Gentlemen, the time is coming when one Harvard University professor will determine through his history course on television what history is taught in the United States—and even if it's Arthur Schlesinger, Jr., I say the hell with it!"—or whether imaginative educational TV will provide learners with a magic carpet to a wider world of experience made at once more expansive and more closely detailed.

The problem before the sponsors and users of team teaching is not precisely how many students to instruct at any given time in any given space. It is not whether a new magical number combination, proposed for better staff utilization, or some flexible magic of numbers out of Lexington, Massachusetts, will take the place of the former magic number—25 or 30 in each classroom. Experience and, we hope, genuine controlled experimentation, will supply the answer here. The real problem is whether team teaching actually will improve learning, whether it will evolve toward emphasis on the *interrelationships* of subject matter, whether it can provide sufficient personalized contacts with teachers and sufficient firsthand experiences by students to enable young people to deal with significant problems.

The problem before the sponsors and users of the dual progress plan is not the technical difficulty of introducing specialized science, mathematics, and arts teachers into elementary school organization through the demonstrations at Ossining and Long Beach in New York. The real problem for the sponsors and users of the dual progress plan is recognized by the originator of the plan as whether the dual progress plan will or will not better answer some of Dewey's persistent queries; George Stoddard poses the issue in his new book, "The Dual Progress Plan," which should be read along with the Association for Supervision and Curriculum Development pamphlet, "The Self-Contained Classroom," for differing organizational approaches to possibly compatible goals.

The problem before the liberal arts professors currently reconstructing and updating knowledge in such disciplines as physics, biology, and mathematics is not whether they can cram all of man's new knowledge into separate water-tight compartments, which will then be siphoned off during the elementary and high school years. They can't. Even if they could, they would endlessly face true obsolescence, for knowledge swiftly dates and, like fish, won't keep. The real problem, of which some of the reconstructors of disciplines are aware and of which others appear quite unaware, is whether the scholars can identify concepts in their new knowledge which can be made meaningful to children and youth, appropriate to both the general and specialized education needed for living in today's society, crucial in the process of critical thinking and problem solving—or whether their reconstructed and amplified knowledge, however new, will prove to be inert subject matter in Alfred North Whitehead's sense.

The problem for those who are studying the structures of the disciplines may be first to make clear what they mean. Granted that they can and do, the question will face them as to whether their studies of structures of disciplines are to be achieved as culminations built upon the experience of learners, as Dewey recommended. Or will their studies of structures of disciplines be evasions of problems central to general education, formal orientations to content which bear little relationship to how young people live and learn?

One can derive little encouragement for the future of study of the structure of the disciplines from the views of Charles R. Keller, director of the John Hay Fellows Program, who believes "too many social studies teachers have emphasized the creation of good citizens rather than the content and discipline of their subjects." He says, "Attitudes cannot be taught in formal classroom situations. We weaken education—and schools—when we try to do so. What students should do in school is to study subjects and become acquainted with facts and ideas. Subjects as such have disciplines that will help to develop students' minds." Is this the conception of educational aims and psychology of learning which is to characterize the new advocacy of studying the structure of disciplines? Surely this was not the conception of Arthur W. Foshay when, in his presidential address to the Association for Supervision and Curriculum Development in 1961, he advised "that we educators take directly into account the nature of the organized bodies of knowledge, in addition to the nature of the growing child and the nature of our society, as we try to make curriculum decisions."

If their work is to have meaning, rather than to be innovation for unclear purposes, the sponsors and users of the new technology, organization, and approaches to disciplines must come to terms with the questions that engaged the intellectual leadership of the progressive movement in education. Questions of "why" and "what" have necessary precedence over questions of "how" and "when." The inescapable questions relate to the aims of education, the foundations of the program, and what the schools should teach as appropriate content based on such aims and foundations.

Is, then, the progressive movement in education obsolete? I think not. The questions raised by the "new education" are remorseless, inevitable, demanding. The answers provided by the intellectual leaders of the progressive movement were promising beginnings, useful leads, valid foreshadowings.

When considerations of "why" are dodged, we get prescriptions which simply cannot be appraised. One cannot truly evaluate the proposals made in widely read books which are characterized by indifference to aims and purposes in the early chapters and which then constantly smuggle in unanalyzed value assumptions through the remainder of the pages. Two knights entered in the educational jousting show this tendency: both the great and good James B. Conant and the provocative and prancing Martin Mayer.

Conant, for instance, does not set forth aims for education in "The American High School Today." Yet he steadily makes assumptions as to what knowledge is of most worth.

In "Slums and Suburbs," Conant says, "It is after visits to schools like these that I grow impatient with both critics and defenders of public education who ignore the realities of school situations to engage in fruitless debate about educational philosophy, purposes, and the like. These situations call for action, not hair-splitting arguments." Yet, "Slums and Suburbs" is permeated with proposals for action which must be based on philosophic assumptions.

In "The Schools," Martin Mayer colorfully rejects all possible formulations of aims. He says, "It is well to rid oneself immediately of this business of 'the aims of education.' Discussions on this subject are among the dullest and most fruitless of human pursuits. Whatever the ideal general 'aims of educaton' may be, they certainly cannot be accomplished in schools." He then proceeds to lace through his book individualistic approbations and denunciations based on his acceptance of undefined aims.

One of the myths of our times is that the several tendencies which characterized what is broadly termed progressive education prevailed, were fully achieved, and are now being repudiated. This sedulously cultivated myth is incomprehensible. The reality is that progressive education has never been tried on any significant scale.

As the inescapable queries reassert themselves and the tentative proposals of the varied interpretations of progressive education are reconsidered, educators will find it necessary to utilize the insights of Dewey, Bode, Counts, and Kilpatrick. An education which takes into account the individual, his society, and his values—an education which builds upon the soundest possible scholarship derivative from psychological, social, and philosophical foundations—is imperative in developing a curriculum appropriate for twentieth-century man.

The central questions posed and the relevant contributions toward workable answers for our times made by such interpreters of the progressive movement in education are not obsolete. They must and will persist. In time, they will be embodied in the form of new proposals for modern education, new syntheses which build upon our predecessors, as is common in the world of ideas. The overanxious gravediggers, and those who currently give them comfort, will discover as this twentieth century moves along that what they have mistaken for a corpse is indeed very much alive.

What Is the Problem? *

by JACK NELSON

Jack Nelson is on the staff of the ATLANTA CONSTITUTION *and is a coauthor of* THE CENSORS AND THE SCHOOLS. *He has won two journalism honors, the Pulitzer Prize and a Nieman Fellowship to Harvard.*

In nearly a third of our state legislatures, textbooks came under fire from the early part of 1958 until the end of 1962.

Censorship groups stepped up their activities in 1961 and 1962. Their successes, coupled with the proliferation of right-wing groups to distribute their propaganda and to join in their attacks on books, portended even more activities for 1963 and after.

In one state, home of several groups which produce propaganda for attacks on texts, numerous book battles erupted. In one case, a publishing house deleted an entire chapter on the United Nations from an eighth-grade civics book.

In another state, the textbook selection committee, after screening books for material protested by several groups, made a number of recommendations to the publishers for deletions of some phrases that might have been considered objectionable. The publishers are making the changes.

In still another state, the legislature authorized a special textbook investigating committee two years ago. Hearings were held in several sections of the state, but according to a state association official, no matter where the committee met, it heard many of the same witnesses and substantially the same testimony from extremists bent on changing textbooks to agree with their viewpoint.

As a result, the state education association, the parent-teacher association, and the school board association developed a brochure which presented affirmatively the facts concerning selection and distribution of textbooks for public schools. The pamphlet was given wide distribution throughout the state.

In addition, the state education association journal carried a series of articles informing teachers concerning the textbook attacks and point-

* Jack Nelson, "What Is the Problem?" *The NEA Journal,* 52 (May. 1963): 19-21. By permission of the editor.

ing out other aspects of textbook selection and use at the local level. Some of these stories were picked up by various newspapers in the state.

For the time being at least, the drive to censor textbooks in that state seemingly has died out. The current state legislature, with more than half its regular session completed, has given no consideration to textbook censorship.

However, no state escapes the effects of attacks on schoolbooks. When censors in one state force a publisher to alter a textbook, that book may be sold, as altered, in other states. More important, perhaps, is the impact widespread attacks have on textbook publishers, who are highly competitive. Publishers generally acknowledge that in order to sell books they must avoid controversy and offending special interest groups.

Where the censors scored best, they operated in a vacuum. They escaped comprehensive coverage by the press and they met little organized opposition. In some instances, conservative newspapers editorially acquiesced in, or even supported, censorship efforts. At the same time, the groups attacking textbooks were well organized and well financed, and they put up a solid front for their views.

The mushrooming attacks on textbooks also took their toll in school libraries. Hundreds of books were withdrawn from library shelves in states from coast to coast. The American Book Publishers Council, Inc., reported that in 1961 alone, censorship groups attacked texts and school library books in at least eighteen states.

By far the greatest pressure for censorship emanates from right-wing sources and is based on ideological grounds. While some pressure comes from other groups, it is sporadic, unorganized, and, as a rule, not too successful. The National Association for the Advancement of Colored People, the Anti-Defamation League of B'nai B'rith, and, on occasion, other crusading or religious organizations have screened textbooks for matter they consider objectionable. But for the most part, these forces work independently of each other.

By contrast, the ultraconservatives—America's Future, the Daughters of the American Revolution, the Sons of the American Revolution, the John Birch Society, and other organizations—distribute each other's propaganda and carry out concerted campaigns. This practice frequently escapes public attention.

In 1961, in Meriden, Connecticut, a vigilant press, education officials who were willing to take a strong stand, and at least two local patriotic organizations which were not beguiled by the "canned reports" from other states quickly extinguished a censorship fire before it came near the book-burning stage.

In that city, local critics of school textbooks used an unsolicited publication from the DAR entitled *Textbook Study*. It was an alarming report. A DAR committee has examined 220 public-school books and blacklisted 170 of them for being "subversive." Only 50 of the books met "minimum DAR standards." The names of the authors of the condemned texts read like rosters of the American Historical Association and other social-science organizations.

What was wrong with the books? "Unfortunately there is a perceivable pattern of 'economic determinism' running through the unsatisfactory texts on all subjects," according to the *Textbook Study*. "History books and economic texts contain uncomplimentary pictures of slum areas or of long lines of the unemployed during 'The Great Depression,' one book even labeling such a photograph 'A Long Line of Unemployed Waiting for Christmas Dinners.'"

The local critics had also received a copy of a thirteen-year-old report called *A Bill of Grievances* from the Sons of the American Revolution. From America's Future, in New Rochelle, New York, they obtained a series of textbook reviews and a copy of *What's Happened to Our Schools?* by Rosalie M. Gordon, who once attacked the U.S. Supreme Court in another booklet entitled *Nine Men Against America*. They had also purchased a pamphlet titled *The Left Swing in Education* and a book titled *Brainwashing in the High Schools* by E. Merrill Root, a small-college English professor turned critic of "subversive" textbooks.

Some of the conservative national groups and critics exchange mailing lists, and many of their most avid members belong to two or more groups. The Texans for America, for example, drew heavily on the DAR and the John Birch Society for their members.

While some of the groups have different axes to grind, they find common cause in Communism as a domestic threat and manage to associate it with everything else they fear or hate.

Organized attempts to influence the contents and selection of schoolbooks are nothing new, of course. After the Civil War, forces in the North and the South each tried to dictate their own version of history, and just two years after the conflict, a New York publisher advertised: "Books prepared for Southern schools by Southern authors, and therefore free from matter offensive to Southern people."

Prominent national forces in today's textbook battles are Root and his book, the DAR, and America's Future. Root is presently on the

Committee of Endorsers of the John Birch Society, and on the mast-head of its magazine as an associate editor. He has written many articles on "subversive" texts for ultraconservative publications and has given speeches on the same topic in many parts of the country. His words have been cited by censors in every major textbook battle of recent years. At least one state has hired him as an "expert" to inves-tigate texts, and an Illinois legislative committee called him to testify on a textbook censorship bill.

The thesis of Root's book, which quickly became a favorite hand-book of the censors after its publication in 1958, was that the U.S. is losing the Cold War, largely because distorted history texts have indoctrinated students with un-American ideas. The book was billed as an objective analysis of eleven American history texts which, Root said, "parallel the Communist line."

Academic sources generally ridiculed Root and his methods of evaluation, which included measuring the amount of space devoted to conservative presidents as compared to liberal ones. Ray Allen Billing-ton, professor of American history at Northwestern University, rebuked Root for insinuating that textbook authors "have connived together or are under the direction of some Moscow-inspired force bent on undermining popular faith in the nation."

But many newspapers, including some reputable and influential ones, printed favorable reviews, apparently accepting Root's charges without analyzing his methods and without checking the texts of which he wrote. As an NEA memorandum noted at the time, his book "stim-ulated other groups and persons to call for censorship action in all branches of school work. Proposals cover fields from American his-tory to zoology and suggest action from book-burning to labeling of 'dangerous' books."

In March 1959, soon after publication of Root's book, the National Defense Committee of the DAR began distributing its *Textbook Study*, mentioned previously. In the study, books were evaluated, the DAR reported, "in the light of the excellent prior study made by the Sons of the American Revolution in 1949 . . . to determine if our young students are emphatically taught love of God and Country or are being corrupted to accept socialism and materialism."

Despite repeated inquiries from the NEA and others, the Daughters have never identified their "experts" who criticized the books. In *Textbook Study*, which is still being distributed, they listed all of the condemned books with "an analysis of general reasons" for branding them un-American or "unsatisfactory." The reasons included that the textbooks were "guardedly patriotic," that they showed a "perceivable pattern of economic determinism," and that they left the impression that "some central source within the educational apparatus directs and dictates what textbooks must emphasize."

Citing a rash of textbook battles in 1959, the American Library Committee warned of the strong trend of censorship and declared: "Of all the programs by organized groups, the DAR textbook investigation, at both the national and state level, was the most specific and . . . most threatening."

America's Future is one of the nation's principal propagandists against textbooks. It operates on an annual budget it reports to be in excess of a quarter of a million dollars and is controlled by a group of business and industrial executives. Three of its textbook reviewers are editors of *American Opinion*, the monthly publication of Birch Society President Robert Welch. Two other reviewers of America's Future also have written for the Birch publication.

In 1958, America's Future launched *Operation Textbook*, saying it would provide "authoritative, objective reviews," but stating, at the same time, that the reviews would show that ". . . through the textbooks used in the schools, particularly in the field of the so-called 'social sciences,' the progressive revolutionaries have done their most damaging work in the past quarter of a century. But so slyly and slickly has the collectivist-internationalist philosophy been inserted . . . that it is difficult, if not impossible, for the average parent or school board member any longer to tell what is a good textbook and what is not."

Literature from America's Future has been used by book censorship groups throughout the country. Its publications are used by the John Birch Society, the DAR, and some local Legion posts in censorship campaigns.

America's Future has expressed constant concern that the public school system—not just the textbooks—is purposely subverting the nation's youth. In *What's Happened to Our Schools?*, mentioned previously, Rosalie M. Gordon, secretary of the organization and editor of its regular publication, wrote:

> No one who has watched closely what has been going on in our public school system in America these past two decades can escape the feeling that something drastic—and rather terrible—has happened to it. What is more, it is rather difficult to believe that it has happened by accident, that there has not been a planned, slyly executed, and almost successful attempt to deliberately undereducate our children in order

to make them into an unquestioning mass who would follow meekly those who wish to turn the American Republic into a socialistic society.

America's Future and other groups are entitled to harbor such fears about this country's schools, and even to use such fears as the basis for attacks on textbooks. But the public, in evaluating these attacks, also should be aware of their basis. They should have sufficient information about the groups and their criticisms to determine whether the groups are judging a book on its merits or on the basis of their own fears and prejudices.

SUGGESTED ACTIVITIES

1. Ask the following persons for a definition of "curriculum": a member of your community not associated with the schools; a public-school teacher; and a professor of education. Are there any *real* distinctions among the various definitions? If so, what general conclusions can you draw?

2. Make several visits to a first-grade and a sixth-grade classroom. Note the emphasis on desirable experiences in the former and on subject matter in the latter. What are the differences in teaching techniques and curricula in the classes?

3. Since high-school civics is required for almost all students, one would reasonably expect that those students would recognize their civic obligations by voting later in elections. Find out what percentage of Americans voted during local, state, and national elections. What conclusions seem warranted?

4. One group of curriculum theorists constantly refers to the "basics." *Precisely* what is meant by "basic subjects"? How does a subject become basic? Have those subjects that we consider basic today always been so considered? Poll several persons, including laymen, college professors of various disciplines, elementary-school teachers, and high-school teachers and ask them to name those subjects they consider basic. How much agreement do you find?

5. Home economics is considered a "practical" subject, while English literature is usually not so considered. Attempt to reverse the usual distinction, and argue that literature is extremely practical for some and that home economics can be highly theoretical.

6. In European countries the responsibility for vocational training of adolescents is not customarily that of academic institutions. Find out how Denmark, England, France, and Germany handle vocational training. Could we profit by their approaches? Why or why not?

7. The status of physical education in high schools and colleges is not as secure as it might be. This subject is frequently attacked by proponents of "basic" subjects as being nonintellectual and therefore having no place in an academic setting. Could one conceivably argue that physical education ought to be one of the liberal arts? (Hint: Find the original definition of "liberal arts.")

8. Professor Bestor has blamed "educational theorists" for the weaknesses in the American curriculum. In the light of the essay by Shermis and Orlich and the article by Birnbaum, how correct is he? Give evidence for your reply.

9. Should you ask almost anyone the question, "What should schools teach?" you are apt to get a rather firm, definite answer. Furthermore, people are likely to defend their positions with a good deal of warmth. Why?

10. List the requirements in your state for high-school graduation. In the light of your findings, what are the arguments for and against greater local autonomy in establishing requirements?

11. Ask several elementary-school teachers to defend the teaching of reading to *all* young children. In your analysis of their reasons, attempt to deduce the theories of mind to which they are subscribing.

12. Dr. James B. Conant has argued that European and American schools differ in one major respect: schools in the United States assume the responsibility for developing a much wider range of talents than European schools. Consult some of Conant's educational writings to discover which talents American schools attempt to develop. Is this concern for developing a wide range of talents completely desirable? Why or why not?

13. If team teaching becomes an accepted curriculum practice in the future, what changes can be anticipated in the teaching of elementary, junior high, and senior high schools? What will happen to the "traditional" role of the elementary-school teacher?

14. Boyer argues that public schools could benefit by academic freedom. By this he means that students should have the right to discuss a wider range of topics, many of them heretofore barred from discussion and study. Find which books or subjects the following organizations would favor not allowing students to read or discuss. Verify each position.

a. The Anti-Defamation League of the B'nai B'rith
b. The National Association for the Advancement of Colored People
c. The White Citizens Council
d. The Women's Christian Temperance Union
e. The National Association of Manufacturers
f. The American Medical Association
g. The Catholic Church
h. The John Birch Society
i. The American Legion

SUGGESTED READINGS

ALCORN, MARVIN D. AND LINLEY, JAMES M. *Issues in Curriculum Development: A Book of Readings.* New York: World Book, 1959.   Essays and readings that cover a broad range of issues in curriculum construction.

BAYLES, ERNEST E. *The Theory and Practice of Teaching.* New York: Harper, 1950.   An attempt to discuss curriculum and teaching methods from a unified position. The author, one of the leading philosophical experimentalists in this country, attempts to indicate the nature of the implementation of the philosophy of John Dewey.

BENJAMIN, HAROLD. *The Saber-Tooth Curriculum.* New York: McGraw-Hill, 1939. (Now published in paper.)   A devastatingly witty satire which provides insights into the problem of lag in the curriculum.

BIGGE, MORRIS L. *Learning Theories for Teachers.* New York: Harper and Row, 1964.   An excellent introduction to learning theory. The author is especially interested in developing the contributions of Kurt Lewin, a major innovator in learning theory.

BRACKENBURY, ROBERT L. *Getting Down to Cases.* New York: Putnam's, 1959.   A lucid and interesting discussion, designed especially for beginners, of the relationship between philosophy and education. A particularly interesting chapter is "Democracy and the Teaching of Controversial Issues."

BRUNER, JEROME S. *The Process of Education.* Cambridge: Harvard U. Press, 1960.   There appears to be a return to some of the curricular concepts of John Dewey in the author's suggestion that the curriculum ought to be revised to de-emphasize isolated facts and emphasize relationships, concepts, and structure.

CASWELL, HOLLIS (ed.). *The American High School.* New York: Harper, 1946.   Although this is an older work, the essays by curriculum experts deal with topics still vital.

CONANT, JAMES B. *The American High School Today.* New York: McGraw-Hill, 1959.   An influential appraisal of the curriculum of our nation's high schools. Contains a series of recommendations that have been taken seriously by many persons in education.

———. *Education in the Junior High School Years.* Princeton: Educational Testing Service, 1960.   In this follow-up to *The American High School Today,* Conant provides a lucid and keen analysis of the strengths and weaknesses of the junior high school, with a series of recommendations.

DEWEY, JOHN. *Democracy and Education.* New York: Macmillan, 1916. A classic still relevant to education today. Dewey discusses the relationship between curriculum and democratic philosophy.

FRASER, DOROTHY M. *Current Curriculum Studies in Academic Subjects.* Washington, D.C.: National Education Association, 1962.   A most interesting and up-to-date account of the "new" curricula.

GARDNER, JOHN W. *Excellence: Can We Be Equal and Excellent Too?* New York: Harper, 1961.   Discusses the cultural conflict which results when schools must provide education for persons with a wide variety of talents.

GOWAN, JOHN C. *An Annotated Bibliography on the Academically Talented.* Washington, D.C.: National Education Association Project on the Academically Talented Student, 1961.   A useful bibliography of books and articles written about the academically gifted student.

GWYNN, J. MINOR. *Curriculum Principles and Social Trends.* 3rd ed.; New York: Macmillan, 1960.   A standard reference in curriculum. See especially Part V, "Other Influences on Curriculum Change," and Part VI, "Looking to the Future in Curriculum Revision."

HILGARD, ERNEST R. (ed.). *Theories of Learning and Instruction.* Chicago: U. of Chicago Press, 1964. (The Sixty-third Yearbook of the National Society for the Study of Education.)   A collection of essays constituting a sophisticated discussion of the relationship between educational activities and theories of learning. Of particular interest is the first essay, "The Influence of Learning Theories on Education (1900-1950)," which is a summary of the history of learning theory.

Innovation and Experiment in Education. Washington, D.C., U.S. Government Printing Office, 1964. (The President's Science Advisory Committee.) Summarizes the contributions that research and development can make to educational instruction, materials, teacher education, and school management.

JAMESON, MARSHALL C. AND HICKS, WILLIAM VERNON. *Elementary School Curriculum: From Theory to Practice.* New York: American Book, 1960. A practical introductory text.

KRUG, EDWARD A. *The Secondary School Curriculum.* New York: Harper, 1960. A standard textbook dealing with the high-school curriculum.

LEE, J. MURRAY AND LEE, DORRIS MAY. *The Child and His Curriculum.* New York: Appleton-Century-Crofts, 1960. A popular textbook for those studying elementary curriculum.

PHENIX, PHILIP. *Realms of Meaning.* New York: McGraw-Hill, 1964. A highly sophisticated book exploring the relationship between curriculum and philosophical assumptions.

RAGAN, WILLIAM BURK. *Modern Elementary Curriculum.* rev. ed.; New York: Holt, 1960. A popular textbook in elementary-school curriculum.

SHANE, HAROLD G. AND MC SWAIN, EDWARD T. *Evaluation and the Elementary Curriculum.* New York: Holt, 1958. An excellent sourcebook for those interested in the elementary school.

SMITH, B. OTHANEL, STANLEY, WILLIAM O., AND SHORES, J. HARLAN. *Fundamentals of Curriculum Development.* New York: Harcourt, Brace and World, 1957. An excellent reference work in curriculum development.

SMITH, G. KERRY (ed.). *Higher Education in an Age of Revolutions.* Washington, D.C.: National Education Association, 1962. (Association for Higher Education.) Short articles on a variety of problems in higher education.

TRUMP, J. LLOYD AND BAYNHAM, DORSEY. *Guide to Better Schools.* Chicago: Rand-McNally, 1962. A series of rather conservative recommendations designed to show how to utilize schools more efficiently. The authors support team teaching.

TYLER, RALPH W. *Social Forces Influencing American Education.* Chicago: U. of Chicago Press, 1961. (The Sixtieth Yearbook of the National Society for the Study of Education.) A useful reference book.

VI

The Profession of Education

This section is concerned with teaching as a profession. Implications for the educational practitioner as well as his professional organizations will be discussed. This topic is in some respects the most important of all, since professional services are only as good as those who render them.

The lead essay, "Teaching as a Profession," attempts to perform an anatomical analysis of teachers, their status, their problems, and their organizations. What is the relationship of group status to group success? By what criteria is an occupation judged to determine whether it is a "profession"? What organizations are available so that teachers may group together to strive for common professional interests? These questions are explored in a summary of problems associated with "being" a profession.

"The Code of Ethics for the Education Profession" is included to give the reader an understanding of the types of behavior which are approved by those associated with teaching. It is important to remember that the Code is not the exclusive property of the National Education Association. It has been adopted by several other organizations associated with education, including Phi Delta Kappa, a men's education honorary society devoted to the improvement of teaching, research, and educational services in general.

John H. Marvin's "The Role of the Code in the Education Profession" is a detailed accounting of how the Code of Ethics actually functions. Marvin points out that ethical behavior is *not* something that is absolute or immutable. Like any other code, it requires interpretation on the part of those who observe it in their activities. He discusses the problems in applying the code to individual cases, as well as the actual implementation of the code at local, state, or national levels.

"Professional Ethics and the NEA," by Myron Lieberman, presents a more critical view of professional ethics. Lieberman attempts to show that the code as currently written "won't work because those in teaching don't want it to." It is all well and good to write a code of ethics, says Lieberman, but if it isn't applied or is easily circumvented, what real value does it have?

Arthur Kratzmann's "The Alberta Teachers Association: A Vision Vindicated," by giving a brief history of the Alberta, Canada, teachers association, provides a contrast with American professional practices.

Teaching as a Profession

by S. SAMUEL SHERMIS
and DONALD C. ORLICH

THE HISTORICAL BACKGROUND

The Colonial Teacher To understand where the teaching profession is heading, one must first understand something about the history of teachers—where the teaching profession came from.

In seventeenth-century colonial education, teachers had status not much above that of an indentured servant and indeed, some teachers *were* indentured servants.[1] A few teachers were well trained, highly educated, and almost aristocratic in their background, but teachers in general were little more than semiliterate. They had only the rudi-

[1] The following advertisement appeared in the *Maryland Gazette or Baltimore Advertiser,* May 30 and June 6 and 13, 1786.

Men and Women Servants
JUST ARRIVED

In the Ship *Paca,* Robert Caulfield, Master, in five Weeks from Belfast and Cork, a number of healthy Men and Women SERVANTS.

Among them several valuable tradesmen, viz.

Carpenters, Shoemakers, Coopers, Blacksmiths, Staymakers, Bookbinders, Clothiers, Dyers, Butchers, Schoolmasters, Millwrights, and Labourers.

Their indentures are to be disposed of by the Subscribers,

Brown, and Maris
William Wilson

Baltimore, May 29, 1786

ments of reading, writing, and "ciphering" (a term meaning to figure arithmetically). They were minor members of the community at best, and lived at the periphery of the social structure.

A typical primary-school teacher was known as the "dame" who held class in what was known as a "dame school." The dame school was the forerunner of the kindergarten-primary school of today. It combined the following two social functions: giving young children the rudiments of reading by teaching them their "letters"; and providing suitable employment for the aged widow, who without any source of income would have been a liability—a community charge. The "dame" kept school in her kitchen and taught from a dozen to twenty children the alphabet, basic prayers, hymns, and some Scripture. For these services the children's parents paid her a pittance or provided her with food, shelter, or firewood. Typically she had no formal academic preparation. She quite literally often taught the children all she knew academically.

The Latin-grammar schoolmaster, usually a man, often had some formal training and academic preparation, though there was no guarantee. When he was also the minister, the town could be certain that he had received some formal training, possibly a college degree. (Harvard College was founded in 1636, before enactment of the Massachusetts "public" school legislation of 1642 and 1647.) All too often, though, the schoolmaster was an itinerant, traveling through the colonies and resembling a wandering European minstrel—except that he didn't sing well. Quite often he was a ne'er-do-well and had the status of one.

The typical arrangement was to pay the schoolmaster chiefly "in kind." He boarded with a member of the community or received room and board plus a few shillings. The understanding was that he was a community servant, at the beck and call of the townspeople. Among his "community" duties he was to instruct in catechism, clean the church, lead in church hymns, prepare funeral invitations, dig graves, and toll the bell. Social, political, and religious restraints rendered him an ineffectual, second-class citizen. For a picturesque, unsympathetic, but not unrealistic view of the colonial schoolmaster, read Washington Irving's "The Legend of Sleepy Hollow." The tall, gangling, ugly, not very bright Ichabod Crane, neither effective nor industrious, is a stereotype of the schoolmaster. When Irving had Brom Bones throw a pumpkin at Ichabod's head and frighten him out of town, he was symbolizing the attitude of the time.

In short, the colonial schoolmaster was a poorly prepared, poorly treated, and poorly integrated member of the community. He seemed to many to provide proof that those who can't do, teach!

The Nineteenth-Century Teacher   There are rich and numerous descriptions of nineteenth-century American education, from which we can derive the following generalizations:

1. In the unsettled frontier communities of the time, teaching and most other intellectual activities were considered either irrelevant or necessary evils.[2]

2. The teacher continued to be a community servant, subject to the whims and desires of the local townspeople and the board of trustees.

3. Women were beginning to enter teaching in greater numbers. This had at least two consequences: (a) the teacher was a young, docile, unmarried woman, with some normal-school education, who aspired to a clean, respectable existence; and (b) she was cheap labor.

4. The educated, genteel, white-collar worker was a comparative rarity, and the occupation of teaching provided a first step toward middle-class respectability. This point is made in the classical cliché that teaching was "not a *profession*, but a *progression*."

Considering the sociological facts of life, one could not expect much more. The United States was still largely rural. Rural communities, usually conservative in outlook and often Fundamentalist in religion,[3] tended to limit rather stringently what could be taught. This meant that teaching was merely the transmission of the most simple aspects of our cultural heritage—middle-class morality and the "Three R's." The amount of intellectual training required for this kind of teaching was minimal. Nineteenth-century teacher education was characterized by only a bare minimum of university or college study, usually one year or less.

In the cities, to be sure, there were always a few high-quality, intellectually oriented schools. But these schools were usually private. One of the major problems facing the nineteenth-century city public school was how and what to teach several million immigrants from all parts of Europe. Few immigrant children could speak or read English. Many of them were still wedded to the customs and values of the "Old Country." The function of the American public school was to equip these children for American life.

[2] See Richard Hofstadter, *Anti-intellectualism in American Life* (New York: Knopf, 1963), Ch. 2.

[3] Fundamentalism is that branch of Protestantism that holds to a precise, literal interpretation of the Bible. The Bible is the source of both ethical and scientific truths. Fundamentalists are often hostile to intellectual endeavors. (See Hofstadter, Chs. 3 and 4, on Fundamentalism and anti-intellectualism.)

Unfortunately, the job of training fifty or sixty immigrant children carried little prestige, glamour, or reward. The nineteenth-century city public-school teacher, like her rural counterpart, transmitted the "Three R's" and passed on middle-class morality, gave a smattering of United States history and civics, and earnestly attempted to enculturate the immigrant's child into the mainstream of American life. By and large the teacher was successful, but he could scarcely be considered a hero of American life, as were the entrepreneur, the capitalist, and the industrialist. The teacher was a necessary, but not especially valued, member of the community.

In the nineteenth century teachers began to talk of their "profession," and "career" teachers began to be mentioned. There arose concern for the creation of a trained, expert class of professional administrators—superintendents and principals. But teaching still usually did not attract or retain first-rate minds. If we examine the biographies of nineteenth- and twentieth-century historical figures, we see that many spent a year or two teaching, but only as a prelude to becoming lawyers, politicians, or some other kind of middle-class professional. Teaching, unlike most other professions, long was merely a stopover point for people of ability (President Lyndon B. Johnson, for instance, spent two years at it), and until rather recently it has typically been only a way station for all but relatively few of the first-class minds. In the nineteenth century, men and women gravitated toward teaching either because they could not do anything more demanding or because it was a respectable life. Then—as now—many women teachers taught a few years before marriage, and very few women viewed teaching as a lifelong, professional career.

TEACHING AND THE ADMINISTRATIVE STRUCTURE

We shall now consider the relationship between education as a profession and the structure of educational administration. Until the twentieth century the organization and administration of public schools was almost exclusively "local." Decisions as to hiring teachers, selecting curricula, building schools, and most other matters concerning education were made by the local board of trustees, which was either elected or appointed by the local townspeople. Educational policies, in other words, were not made by the practicing "professionals." Traditionally policies have been made by laymen—those outside the field of education. This is most significant because: (1) those who know least about educational matters have had the most to say in determining such matters, and (2) this has tended to retard the growth of education as a "profession." A profession, as we note later, is characterized by internal controls—decisions are made by those educated, trained, and practicing in that particular field. This type of control is precisely what has been lacking in education:

> Those serving on the board of directors of a business corporation usually get there after long years of business experience. Military men, physicians, lawyers—all gain positions of responsibility only after long years of training. But the new school board member usually leaps directly from no experience in school administration to a position of top authority over the entire school system in his community.[4]

The consequences are that the duly constituted legal administrative structure generally operates independently of the wishes, desires, orientation, and values of practicing teachers. Typically, decisions that bear on teaching and on teachers are not made by teachers themselves. For instance, a teacher frequently must use a textbook not of his own choosing. He may teach a class for which he is unprepared because the superintendent just happens to need an algebra teacher for the fifth period. Within the curriculum of a particular class, he may be required to teach a unit he considers irrelevant.[5] The teacher is bound and his activities circumscribed by rules and regulations that are not remotely of his own choosing. A typical school-board policy specifies when the teacher must arrive and leave. These administration-made requirements leave the teacher feeling as if the bulk of the teaching process is determined elsewhere.

When an individual must perform duties and functions he has not had a choice in determining, he often tends to do so in a superficial, routine, and mechanical manner. He seldom assumes responsibility for seeing that they are done properly. He often is not committed to the overall task. Not having had a choice in making what ought to be professional decisions, the teacher does not feel a part of the entire educational and professional organization. Thus the teacher is often apathetic and unconcerned about what ought to be his primary concerns. He is, then, typically "nonprofessional" in his attitudes and orientation.

---

[4] Henry J. Toy, Jr., "Lay Participation in Public Education," in *Improving Public Education Through School Board Action* (Pittsburgh: U. of Pittsburgh Press, 1950), p. 19.

[5] One of the authors once was required to teach two units in a high-school social-studies class. One concerned driver education, and the other, first aid. He was prepared to teach neither. Nor did he consider them to be especially relevant to social studies. However, he taught them!

Jean D. Grambs made a most interesting comparison between the teaching profession and such American ethnic and racial minorities as Negroes, Jews, and ". . . ethnic groups in which the process of Americanization has not as yet been completed." These groups and teachers were all characterized by the following behavioral traits: defensiveness and cynicism, apathy, poor self-concepts, limited aspirations and success, high frustration level and low level of status, and poor group solidarity.[6] Although Grambs' analysis has flaws, it suggests the social orientation of teachers.

With this cursory historical background, we can turn to the definition and criteria of a profession and to a consideration of the two major teaching organizations.

WHAT IS A PROFESSION?

The teaching profession can be organized in one of two ways: along the lines of a craft union or along the lines of a "professional" organization. The former would resemble the AFL-CIO, the latter, the American Bar Association or the American Medical Association. Of course, there is another option: to have no organization at all. But an occupational group cannot realize its own interests without an organization through which to accomplish its desired goals.

The organization associated with the position that envisions teaching as a profession is the National Education Association (NEA). The NEA, established in 1857, has maintained for over a century that: (1) teaching is or ought to be a profession and (2) the only long-range, fruitful approach to realizing the goals of teachers is a nationwide organization composed of semiautonomous state units and further developed to include local education associations. The goal of this organization is now and has always been to secure recognition for teachers as "professionals." Although the NEA is not always clear as to what it means by a "profession," it constantly reiterates the goal of professionalism.

We must now attempt to answer the following questions: "What is a profession?" and "Is teaching a profession?"

Although commentators on professionalism do not agree entirely on the criteria for a profession, we can make the following generalizations:

1. *Learning a profession involves learning by intellectual endeavor many concepts and principles.* Medicine, law, and engineering, to

6 "Teachers as a Minority Group," *The Journal of Educational Sociology,* 22 (February, 1949): 400-405.

mention professions widely recognized as such, contain many complex ideas and principles. These principles require long years of advanced study to be comprehended. Medicine is typically a seven- to nine-year program, and law usually requires a minimum of seven years of college or university preparation.

2. *A profession has a body of techniques that are applied in specific situations and that can be transmitted.* Medicine requires an individual physician to understand the principles of surgery and to be able to apply these same principles as techniques when called on—for instance, to perform an appendectomy. A lawyer learns principles of contracts and applies these same principles when arguing a case involving a disputed contractual point.

3. *A profession is internally organized and contains the apparatus for self-discipline.* Medicine is organized from within, not controlled by a lay body. Only physicians belong to the American Medical Association, and only physicians decide who is to be allowed to become a physician. This group has constructed its own code of ethics, and this code is widely understood by physicians. When in doubt about an ethical problem, a physician can—and, indeed, does—turn to the national office of the American Medical Association for a decision as to what is ethical.

4. *A profession is altruistically motivated.* The emphasis is on a service to be rendered, not on a fee to be collected. The physician, although he surely collects a fee, is theoretically concerned first of all with providing a service that is of real importance. No one questions that it is important to be healthy and that physicians provide a significant service to humanity when they cure or prevent illness.

5. *A profession must allow independence.* An individual physician can work either for himself or for an employer. An individual attorney can hang out a shingle and go into business on his own, or he can hire out to a firm, which in turn is retained by a client.

6. *A profession is recognized as such and commands high prestige.* Few would dispute the right of attorneys, physicians, engineers, and architects to be called professionals. On the other hand, we are not in the habit of categorizing shoemakers, electricians, and bricklayers as "professionals."

A profession is not a static arrangement. It is possible for a job classified as an "occupation" to evolve into a "profession." A profession is often in process of "becoming." An example of an occupation that apparently evolved into a profession only within the last three decades is that of the certified public accountants. This is because they have adopted a professional code of ethics which is part of the legal structure of many states and because they have required extensive educational preparation. They are no longer "mere bookkeepers," but are, in fact, analysts. They require high standards for entry, and possess a professional organizational structure.

The point regarding prestige[7] needs elaboration. *Prestige* usually refers to a kind of "glow" that surrounds a given person *because* he belongs to a particular, highly respected organization or occupation. It is widely recognized that a United States Supreme Court Justice commands high prestige. People "look up" to him. He—and the group to which he belongs—has status. Ordinarily status is derived from desirable conditions of work, high salary, recognition as having contributed something important, and other similar attributes.

The above six criteria define a profession. Unless a given occupational grouping meets these criteria, one usually does not speak of it as a profession.[8]

IS TEACHING A PROFESSION?

The field of education does indeed contain many intellectual principles and concepts. But it is also true that much in education, as it is taught, is lowered to the level of "Now, do it like this," or "Now we do this"—much as a mechanic is taught to adjust a carburetor. That is, there are still too many "rule of thumb" procedures in education and too few principles, theories, and concepts. There are concepts in psychology, theories of learning, growth, and development, educational history and philosophy or sociology, curriculum, and so on that are very legitimate, but not all practitioners in education understand or have been exposed to these concepts. About 85 percent of all teachers have at least one degree, with approximately 24 percent of the entire teaching corps having master's degrees.[9] Since 15 percent of all practicing teachers do not possess any degree—and this proportion is even higher in several states or communities—they can hardly be considered to be practicing an intellectual endeavor! The point is that since one-sixth of the nation's teaching force do not hold a bachelor's degree, they have not been adequately exposed to the concepts in their field. Thus their claim to professional status is, to this extent, weakened!

[7] *Prestige* is usually accorded a given person; *status* is usually accorded a group. The two terms are related in that they refer to a situation in which individuals and groups command high regard and respect.

[8] Of course we talk about "professional" football players and golfers. In this sense the term designates one who is not an amateur and who therefore receives pay. The "professional" tennis player, for instance, differs from the amateur in that he is paid for his services.

[9] *NEA Research Bulletin*, 41 (February, 1963): 4.

The concepts and theories in education can indeed be transmitted, and techniques can be applied in given circumstances. One can learn theories of discipline and then apply these theories, much as a physician learns to understand symptomatology and applies his knowledge in diagnosing Suzy's case of measles.

Teachers do have an organization; in fact, they have two. Yet one may teach without belonging to either, and many teachers do. Estimates show that approximately half of all elementary- and secondary-school teachers do not belong to any teachers' organization. It is difficult to find a physician who does not belong to a medical association of some type, and you will search even longer before finding an attorney who feels that he can ignore the local, state, and national bar associations. But it is not at all difficult to find a teacher who neither knows or lives by "The Code of Ethics for the Education Profession." Indeed, very few teachers are disciplined by their own profession. They may be fired by the school board, but they are rarely given a hearing by their peers for breaking a well-known and well-defined ethical principle. It is extremely debatable whether or not teachers have a true professional organization—that is, whether or not they truly have internal organization.

That teachers have altruistic motives is much less questionable. By and large, they are highly motivated to work for what they consider humanitarian goals. Teachers are extremely concerned about the welfare of students—about whether or not the students understand what they should, whether they are well-adjusted, and the like. But it may be that the altruistic motivation has actually been a barrier to professionalism. Teachers have been so concerned to do "good" that they have usually neglected the hard realities of bargaining, salaries, and working conditions. Teaching has often been looked on as a "calling," and teachers themselves often consider such matters as academic freedom, extra pay for extra work, and hard bargaining beneath them.

Teaching is not, nor is it likely to be, characterized by a high degree of autonomy or independence. A teacher cannot make "ends meet" by being a tutor—that is, working as an independent agent. The vast majority of teachers must work for someone else (the public educational system).

The status of teaching is not very clear. While sociological studies have shown that teachers *can* command great respect,[10] in some communities teachers are looked on as the servants of the community and are called on to do a wide variety of miscellaneous jobs, from teach-

[10] Frederic W. Terrien, "Who Thinks What About Educators?" *American Journal of Sociology*, 59 (September, 1953): 150-158.

ing Sunday school to taking tickets at football games. Neither this type of work nor patrolling boys' lavatories to check on smokers enhances teachers' prestige.

The Three Status Levels   In teaching, there are at least three levels of professional awareness, corresponding to the elementary-school teacher, the secondary-school teacher, and the college teacher. Each position is characterized by different aspirations and techniques, a different level of training and intellectual ability, and a different value structure.

1. *Elementary-school teaching.* The elementary-school teacher in America occupies the lowest rung on the ladder of professionalism. Although much lip service has been paid to the importance of having the "best-prepared" teacher at the elementary level, quite typically superintendents hire the youngest, the least educated, and the least experienced persons to teach in the elementary-school grades. In many states it is common to find nineteen- and twenty-year-old girls with two or fewer years of college or junior-college training holding class in elementary schools. Sometimes these novices, attending extension courses, night-school classes, and summer sessions, accumulate enough credits to earn the bachelor's degree. But too often they teach for two or three years and then, on finding a likely candidate, abandon their academic aspirations for marriage and a family. Teaching at the elementary-school level has a long tradition of being the least promising, least stable, and least attractive career.

The women who do remain as elementary teachers frequently have families and a husband who is a full-time worker and usually the chief breadwinner. This means that to many—if not most—married female elementary teachers, teaching is only a sideline. They make enough money to augment their husbands' incomes, to buy little extras, or to finance the vacations. Or they teach because teaching is more interesting than being a housewife. For the woman with growing children away most of the day, teaching affords a relief from cooking, cleaning, TV-watching, or gossiping. Such teachers can scarcely be classified as dedicated, career-minded professionals; for them teaching is really incidental.

The unmarried, career-oriented woman teacher poses another problem almost as serious. Even though a woman teacher is career-oriented, she often is not *professionally* inclined. That is, she may not be very much concerned about wages, conditions of work, fringe benefits, and the like. For her, teaching is a means of rising socially, just as it was in the nineteenth century. The social prestige of being a teacher—of having a more or less consistent income and of doing "clean" work—

is of more significance than the economic aspects of the profession. That is, for a young woman whose father was, say, a railroad worker, a miner, or a bricklayer, the social benefits deriving from teaching tend to outweigh the professional requirements of securing higher wages, more favorable work conditions, and fringe benefits. The social status of teaching is far more important to this type of woman than mere monetary considerations.

The male elementary-school teacher tends to be younger than his female counterpart and to be better prepared. But he has had less teaching experience.[11] Nevertheless, the male elementary teacher comes closer to meeting the criteria for a professional than does the female, and we can only hope that an increasing number of men will be attracted to teaching in the elementary grades.

2. *Secondary-school teaching.* The secondary-school teacher is often much better prepared, more academically oriented, and more professionally directed than the elementary teacher. There are more males in high-school than in elementary teaching, and because of this we find more principal breadwinners. Merely the fact of being a breadwinner does not mean that one is necessarily more professional, of course, but it does stimulate professional concern. Typically the high-school teacher—because of the emphasis on subject matter—is academically better prepared. He probably has a bachelor's degree, and quite frequently is working toward a master's degree.

There is also more opportunity for both advancement and diversification in high-school work. The high-school teacher may look forward to becoming an administrator, a counselor, a superintendent, a coordinator for a city or county system, or some other specialized person, and these positions tend to be better paid and command more prestige.

When the United States Congress decided, in this century, to assist education, emphasis was placed on the secondary schools. The Smith-Hughes and Smith-Lever Acts at the time of World War I were designed to assist vocational and homemaking education, both secondary-school specialties. The recent National Defense Education Act was designed to improve the teaching of science, mathematics, and languages on the secondary-school level and to train counselors.

Because of the above, professional "values" will be found more frequently at the high-school level than at the elementary-school level.

---

[11] *U.S. Census of Population: 1960. Subject Reports. Characteristics of Teachers.* (Washington, D.C.: U.S. Bureau of the Census, U.S. Government Printing Office, 1964), Tables 3, 4, 7, pp. 8, 13, 35. See also the *NEA Research Bulletin,* 41 (February, 1963):4.

The higher academic requirements and the greater tenure of employment tend to generate concern about long-term, serious, professional goals. The career-conscious teacher finds it important to work for better teaching conditions, medical insurance, a free period, seniority, tenure, the abolition of unfair and discriminatory practices, and a long-range study of school issues. These goals can be implemented only by a strong, organized, and rather militant profession.

3. *College teaching.* The college teacher is on another professional level. Typically he (and most college professors are males) is a highly educated person, who has had an average of seven years of higher education. Often he has a terminal degree, usually a doctorate. His concerns are highly intellectual. He does not regard college teaching as a way station or a sideline. He is typically a researcher, a teacher, or a combination of both. He may do consulting work on the side, but the consulting is a sideline. The typical full-time woman college teacher also is a productive academician, not a housewife who is teaching as a sideline. One would think, therefore, that there would be a uniformly high level of professionalism in university and college teaching. But there is not.

The low level of professionalism on the university campus is *probably* the result of the college teacher's preoccupation with intellectual matters; he does not have the energy or interest to organize for securing higher wages or better conditions. Too, teaching conditions in a typical university are much superior to those found in a typical elementary or high school. Instead of teaching five, six, or seven hours a day and being confronted with frequent requests for "extracurricular" supervision, the college professor may teach a total of ten, twelve, or fourteen hours a week. The remainder of his time is spent in research, reading, writing, advising, and related activities. Nor is he restricted physically; he may wander from library to lecture hall to seminar room to student union to informal luncheon meetings. Comparatively, the college teacher has an almost leisurely existence, with problems of grading, disciplining, chaperoning, listening to irate parents, wiping runny noses, and the like absent or kept to a bare minimum.[12]

The college professor, then, is apt to be an intelligent, highly educated, and very independent individual. He may belong to one or several professional and scholarly organizations. But the idea of band-

---

12 Woe unto the high-school teacher who flunks the son of a prominent citizen or the daughter of a school-board member. The college teacher, however, ordinarily can grade his students without concern for community pressure, though he may feel pressure at times from the administration.

ing together to fight the dean, chancellor, or board of trustees usually does not even occur to him.[13] The college professor, concerned about his academic specialty, his promotion, his publications, and his prestige, does not have the time, the energy, or the interest to seek collective, professional action to secure professional goals. That is, while the professor is professionally oriented with regard to academic values, he is almost unconcerned about other professional values.

The status of the professor with a Ph.D. degree is much higher than that of the public-school teacher. The college teacher enjoys respect not usually accorded to the woman in elementary-school teaching or even to the high-school instructor. Having "arrived"—that is, having the prestige that other teachers can only wish for—he is often content to bask in admiration and allow others to worry about collective bargaining and wringing concessions from the board of trustees.[14]

Therefore, if we use the criteria generally accepted as defining a profession, *we can characterize teaching either as a nonprofession, as a profession only to a limited degree, or as an occupation striving to become a profession.*

Why Should Teaching Be a Profession,   The NEA has strenuously advocated professionalism for teachers. Its journals and speakers stress the theme that teaching either is or should be—by the very nature of things—a profession, and that any other arrangement is wrong. The NEA feels that only by being professionals can teachers obtain what they want, deserve, and need. This raises the compound question: What should teachers want and what do they need? The NEA would probably answer this question by saying that teachers need:

1. A salary commensurate with the importance of teaching.

2. Prestige sufficient to allow them to teach effectively. This prestige is essential for working relationships with students.

3. A working relationship with the community. The teacher is not a servant of the community but a person empowered by the community to do an important and special job. He needs to relate well to the parents of students and to the community in general.

4. A close relationship with administrators and a working relationship with the local boards of education. The teachers are copart-

---

[13] Professors occasionally *do* become angry enough to fight the administration. And when they do, the results can be spectacular. See the reports on the California Loyalty Oath of the 1950's and the response of the faculty of the University of California.

[14] There are exceptions; there are unions or other organizations for college professors on college campuses. But it is the exception rather than the rule to see collective action by the faculty to wrest economic gains from the regents.

tiers in the educative process with administrators and boards of education. Collectively, they should be "one big happy family."

5. A high level of education. Teachers should be truly educated persons, with the process of education continuing.

6. An understanding of the basic principles of learning. This would be accompanied by the acceptance of education for all children in a democracy.

7. A thorough grasp of the skills, techniques, and methods of imparting our cultural heritage to the students so that they may learn better. This implies a continuing interest in and knowledge of testing, audio-visual techniques, counseling, financing of education, subject matter, teaching methods, and the democratic philosophy.

8. Membership in a professional organization to gain the goals of the "profession."

How can all of these be acquired? There is no sure method, of course, but the NEA would hold that progress can be made if teachers will join the NEA at the national level and its affiliated state and local organizations, work patiently with the community and the state and federal legislatures, and help do an effective job of educating the public. Teachers need to contribute their time, money, and energy for an organizational program that, in time, will result in a uniformly high set of conditions, high salary, and high prestige.

TEACHING AS A UNION ACTIVITY

The position of the American Federation of Teachers (AFT), an affiliate of the national AFL-CIO, is quite different in emphasis, method, and philosophy from that of the NEA. The AFT maintains that the NEA has lost sight of reality in its insistence on "professionalism."[15] The AFT holds that, by refusing to deal with political and economic realities and by ignoring the meaning of power, pressure, and the strength that comes from bargaining and striking, the NEA renders itself ineffective. The AFT has affiliated with the organized labor movement and has made use of some of the traditional weapons of labor, including the strike. The strike is regarded by the NEA as "unprofessional" and unacceptable. To this the AFT retorts that by refusing to consider striking or hard bargaining, the NEA has rendered itself a weak and essentially useless organization. AFT writ-

[15] For an interesting discussion of union membership and "professionalism" see Robert W. Clopton, "An Answer to the 'Unprofessional' Dodge About Unions," *The American Teacher Magazine*, 46 (April, 1962): 28. *The American Teacher* (newspaper) of November, 1963, also discusses this point.

ings imply that because the NEA is the dominant teachers' organization, the salary of teachers has suffered.

The AFT has attempted basically to realize the following objectives:

1. To secure a strong, close-knit, powerful classroom teachers' organization.

2. To avail itself of the power that is supposed to come from close relations with organized labor as a whole.

3. To fight for higher teachers' salaries and other economic gains.

4. To form an effective counterorganization to the alliance of administrators and board members, whom it considers "management" and therefore inevitably antagonistic to the aims of the teachers, whom it considers "workers."

5. To bring teachers such benefits of unionized labor as job security, seniority rights, collective bargaining, grievance procedures, and written agreements with local boards of education.

The AFT has generally, but not always, excluded principals and superintendents from its membership, in line with the logical division of "labor" and "management." The AFT maintains that the NEA's inclusion of administrators in the organization is a mistake. (The American Association of School Administrators is an affiliate of the NEA.) The AFT asks how administrators, who hire and fire teachers, can share the goals of teachers. At the AFL-CIO Second Constitutional Convention in 1957, the AFT was instrumental in having a resolution adopted by that convention which stated in part that the NEA, *"dominated as it is by the school administrators, does not and cannot fulfill that need* [classroom teachers' organization] because it is in effect a company union."[16] The NEA has strongly maintained that the administrators and classroom teachers have the same aims, values, goals, and interests—they are all working for the public good in a common endeavor. The AFT apparently considers this position unrealistic.

The approach of the AFT involves organizing teachers into local units. This organization typically has taken place in large cities rather than in smaller towns or rural areas. By appealing to the Wagner Act and other national and state laws that guarantee unions the right to act as bargaining agents, the AFT seeks to represent teachers. What this "representation" has come to mean—both in teachers' unions and in other union organizations—is face-to-face confrontation with "management"—in this case the board of trustees and the superintendent.

---

[16] "AFL-CIO Calls NEA Company Union," *The American Teacher Magazine,* 42 (February, 1958): 11. (The AFT submitted the original resolution, which stated that the NEA *was* a company union. However, the AFL-CIO Resolutions Committee "watered it down" to state, "in effect a company union.")

It is during this meeting that collective bargaining takes place. The bargaining is for a series of demands including improved working conditions, a method of handling grievances, higher wages, and fringe benefits. The board may or may not act favorably on all demands and will often counter with some compromise offer. If needs be, the local can back up its demands by threatening to withhold services, which is tantamount to striking.[17]

By such means, which obviously have succeeded in industry, the AFT hopes to improve the lot of teachers.

A BRIEF HISTORY OF
THE TWO TEACHERS' ORGANIZATIONS

The National Education Association The NEA was founded in August, 1857 and was first known as the National Teachers Association. In 1870 its name was changed to the National Educational Association. The NEA at that time was actually the result of a merger of three teachers' groups. In 1906 the United States Congress offered the organization a national charter; a year later the charter was accepted. In 1907 the name was changed to National Education Association.

In 1857 the NEA had 43 members. As of 1964 the membership approached 900,000. Although this phenomenal increase in membership had a variety of causes, there is the possibility that in many districts administrators "pressure" some teachers to join.[18] What the membership would be without this apparent coercion is not known.

Once any person who taught in the schools could join the NEA. Since August 31, 1964, however, the NEA has required a bachelor's degree and a standard teaching certificate from any person desiring to become an active member. Those not able to fulfill these qualifications for active membership may become associate members, without the privilege of voting for delegates for the Delegate Assembly or holding office in the organization.

The NEA is the national parent organization; there are 64 state and over 8,000 local affiliated associations. Teachers in a particular school may send delegates to the school-district organization or they all may meet jointly as a district, depending on the size of the school system.

---

[17] See the *American Teacher Magazine*, February, 1961, for a rather comprehensive picture of AFT views on legislation, bargaining, salaries, fringe benefits, working conditions, merit pay, and grievance procedures.

[18] A news item in *The American Teacher* newspaper of September, 1963, stated that some districts in Iowa and New Jersey were making membership in the NEA mandatory as a condition of employment.

The American Federation of Teachers   The AFT, lacking the "pure" professional teaching background of the NEA, grew out of the nineteenth-century labor movement, and first formally affiliated with the American Federation of Labor in 1902. It has grown only recently. In 1920 the AFT could claim about 9,800 members, while the NEA had approximately 53,000. In 1964, the AFT membership was approximately 90,000, as compared with the NEA's almost 900,000.

The AFT is essentially urban. Locals typically are found in larger cities or in towns in which the organized labor movement is a part of the local power structure. For example, powerful AFT teachers' locals are to be found in New York City, St. Paul, Chicago, Butte, Seattle, and Los Angeles. At present, the status of the AFT is dependent on the success of its tactics in several geographically unrelated school districts. The more successful the AFT is in wresting gains from school boards, as it did in New York City during 1962 and 1963, the more likely it is that it will challenge the NEA as the spokesman for teachers. However, the AFT can be expected to have a difficult time. Not only is the NEA a formidable opponent, but associations of school boards and administrators have gone on record as opposing virtually all of the operations and tactics that are the heart and soul of the AFT.[19]

The NEA and the AFT—A Comparison   It is rather difficult to compare the NEA and AFT because their aims, organizations, and procedures differ greatly. As we have indicated, the AFT is organized much like a trade union. The NEA is a huge, sprawling organization, with numerous kinds of interests and activities.

The NEA is analogous to a circus in that it has many main rings and several dozen sideshows. Actually, the NEA is a collection of several organizations. There is the parent body consisting largely of teachers and administrators from all fifty states. There are organizations within the jurisdiction of the NEA designed to further specialized teaching interests. For example, there is the National Council for the Social Studies, consisting of social-studies teachers throughout the country. Similarly, there are organizations for teachers of foreign languages, science, physical education, and so on.

An important department or subordinate organization of the NEA is the American Association of School Administrators, whose members

[19] The NEA takes the position that negotiations are transacted *through* the district superintendent to the board. The AFT holds that negotiations can proceed directly from the teachers negotiating committee to the board. Whereas the NEA holds that the superintendent is the professional partner of the teacher, the AFT asserts that the superintendent is, in fact, aligned with management—the board of education.

are principals and superintendents. The AASA has an extremely strong role in formulating NEA policies. This is the object of criticism by some within the NEA, as well as by the AFT. In addition to 33 departments there are 14 headquarters divisions and 26 commissions and committees. The scope of this giant organization extends from kindergarten to the university graduate school. (There is also the student NEA, a college-student organization affiliated with the NEA.)

In addition to embracing a multiplicity of organizations, the NEA is active in a wide variety of areas. The National Council for Accreditation of Teacher Education, currently under some heavy fire,[20] helps determine standards of teacher education in education departments and colleges throughout the country. Another very important function of the NEA is that of gathering data. In this field it is of acknowledged preeminence, actually augmenting the United States Office of Education. Data are gathered on every conceivable topic of interest to educators—salaries of teachers, average teaching time of elementary and secondary teachers, teacher preparation, age and sex of teachers, amount of money spent by states on education, subjects taught, how they are taught and by whom, and so on. These data are often used in formulating legislative proposals and making policy at various levels.

The NEA publishes a wide variety of journals, pamphlets, brochures, books, and monographs (special studies on one topic). The *NEA Journal* is one of the most—if not the most—widely read journals in the field of education. Some of the NEA publications report research findings; others are designed to influence high-school students to enter teaching. Some publications inform teachers about important trends and movements within education, such as merit pay. Some deal at considerable length with research about the learning process—for example, teaching machines and programmed learning—and the learning theory involved in these innovations. Material is designed for classroom teachers, as well as for college professors of education. Other materials are aimed at the lay public to inform it of the needs of education. The NEA, in reality one of the world's largest publishing concerns, publishes books, journals, tips, summaries of research, lists of pending legislation, analyses of trends, reports of promising techniques, pep talks, and literature on almost every other conceivable topic relating to education.

[20] For some insight into this controversey see "Will Wisconsin Accredit NCATE?" *Phi Delta Kappan*, 44 (January, 1963): 154-159. Other interesting points are made by James B. Conant, *The Education of American Teachers* (New York: McGraw-Hill, 1963).

All of the functions and organizations referred to above can be classified broadly as supplying "in-service education" for teachers through the pooling of information by education specialists. The NEA has an important "informative" function; as a disseminator of information the NEA is very, very good. This enterprise is ably supported, since the NEA has the greatest income of all educational organizations in the country.

It is in the area of improving teaching conditions and raising salaries that the NEA is apparently unsuccessful, if success means: (1) higher classroom teachers salaries, (2) improved fringe benefits, and (3) steadily improving on-the-job conditions. Let us examine each criterion in greater detail.

According to the United States Office of Education, *Digest of Educational Statistics, 1963*, the average salary of all classroom teachers was $5,735. And according to the statistic derived by the NEA the "average teacher" has about eleven years of experience.[21] This salary is not impressive when compared with the earnings in other professions, such as law, medicine, and engineering. Nor is it impressive when compared with wages earned by skilled and semiskilled workers who are unionized. A source of desperation and cynicism for many teachers is the fact that teachers in a given town often earn less than unionized pipe fitters and electricians—individuals who usually have not gone to college. The NEA is quite aware of this and continues to work for improvement of salaries. Naturally, the NEA alone cannot be blamed for inadequate salaries; there are too many other variables.

Teaching conditions—perhaps even more than salaries—are a source of grievance to teachers. According to a *Life* article on this topic, resentment of working conditions was a prime factor in driving many from the teaching profession.[22] Teachers often work as many as fifty hours a week—teaching, grading papers, supervising recess, and chaperoning dances and other student social activities. Much of this work is unremunerated, the thanks of the parents apparently being considered sufficient compensation.[23] In most cases, there is no effective machinery for dealing with teachers' complaints. Teachers either must swallow them or, as many do, move on to another school district where "the grass is greener."

[21] *NEA Research Bulletin*, 41 (February, 1963): 3.

[22] Richard Meryman, "How We Drive Teachers To Quit," *Life*, 53 (November 16, 1962): 104-106, 109-114.

[23] The teachers in Yonkers, New York in January of 1964 announced that they would not spend their time on extracurricular activities. This announcement came after the local board, having promised a 10 percent salary increase, was able to deliver only a 2.5 percent increase. The teachers then threatened to withhold some of their services.

Most teachers' complaints are directed against administrators. A principal or superintendent may have very limited power, or he may rule like a ship's captain of the nineteenth century—akin to an absolute monarch. Although the latter type is dying out, enough tyrants remain to plague far too many teachers. These administrators, often themselves not especially distinguished as scholars or teachers, frequently make the lives of their teachers miserable by techniques ranging from constant harassment to requiring the filling out of a multiplicity of forms, a task that in some school districts takes a disproportionate amount of the teacher's time. The most frequently voiced complaint of teachers—one that would require several dozen volumes to illustrate fully—is that their administrators do not back them up with regard to discipline. Some administrators act as though disciplinary problems always are the fault of the teacher. But it is difficult to blame poor discipline on the teacher in a school district in which a high proportion of the students are in school through the courtesy of the local parole and probation department!

"Fringe benefits" refers to such items as medical insurance, paid vacations, paid holidays, retirement plans, sick leave, and other non-salary conditions of employment. It is in the area of fringe benefits that virtually all teachers' organizations are well behind *all* unions in accomplishment. Although fringe benefits are considered sufficiently important by union leaders to be goals of hard collective bargaining, the NEA has not seen fit to deal realistically with these facets of modern economic life.

It is precisely these areas—salary, working conditions, and fringe benefits—that the AFT is attempting to use as selling points in its drive to recruit teachers or to lure them away from the NEA. The AFT boasts of its ability to win higher salaries, better conditions, and more fringe benefits for its member teachers. In this endeavor it has had only limited success, but even limited success is not insignificant where so little success is known.

A basic assumption of all unions is that, if they do not obtain what they seek, they can walk out on the job. The phrase "walk out on the job" is synonymous with "withholding service" and "striking." The strike has been a potent weapon in the generally successful program of labor during the last two decades of the nineteenth century and thus far in the twentieth century. A strike can be positively crippling to a business with its profits dependent on the constant flow of goods to the buying public. When a group of workers halts its work, thereby preventing goods from being marketed, the employer is hurt in a most sensitive part of his anatomy—his pocketbook.

But it is not clear whether or not a teacher has recourse to the same economic sanctions as other workers. In teaching, it is by no means clear just who the "employer" is. Is the employer the administrator, the school board, the local district, or the state? In addition, many states prohibit public officials and public servants from going out on strike. A strike is not considered a legitimate way for post-office workers, police officers, sanitation engineers, or anyone else who ministers directly or indirectly to the public health or safety to achieve his desires. Where teachers have been classified as public officials— for example, in New York—it is simply not legal for teachers to strike. There the Conlon-Wadlin Law permits jail sentences and fines for those who violate this restriction. Thus the teachers' strike has an extremely doubtful legal status at this time. Yet recourse to a strike— the ultimate weapon—is essential to hard bargaining.

Although the legal status of teachers' strikes has not been clearly decided by the courts, the AFT does not appear to be concerned about it. The AFT position seems to be that a strike of one or two days is neither a serious imposition on the public nor a serious threat to the public's health and welfare. If, by striking, the teacher wins necessary salary gains or improved working conditions, the strike is clearly worth it. The AFT is a proponent of "hard bargaining," and feels—perhaps with some justification—that only through hard bargaining can teachers obtain what is rightly theirs.

An example of the AFT procedures and tactics is provided by the famous "threatened" New York City strike of September, 1963. Led by Charles Cogen, president of the United Federation of Teachers of New York, an AFT local, the New York City teachers considered striking to win their demands. In April, 1962, they had gone out on strike—for one day—and as if by some miracle $13 million was found by Mayor Wagner of New York City and Governor Rockefeller to meet this crisis. In 1963 the New York City teachers wanted a total increase of $29 million. It was again declared that this amount of money was impossible to raise: it had not been budgeted and no one could predict whether or not it would be budgeted. Through a "marathon" bargaining session and the threat of a strike, $24 million was found, this amount to be distributed over a two-year period, with the average gain about $580 per teacher.[24] The AFT has advertised

---

[24] For more about the issues involved read John Scanlon, "Strikes, Sanctions and the Schools," *Saturday Reveiw,* 47 (October 19, 1963): 51-55, 70-74. Another treatment of the New York City strike is in *Time Magazine,* 82 (November 15, 1963): 86-92.

this as a successful fight and since 1963 has stepped up its membership drive. The solution may not be this simple in all school districts. The New York City schools are in reality an arm of the city government. The city council adopts the school budget, even though the schools receive a good deal of state aid. (New York City had an educational budget of approximately $600 million for the 1963-64 school year!)

The NEA has made limited use of what it calls "sanctions." "Sanctions" refers to the practice of requesting teachers and administrators not to apply for employment in designated school districts. Since sanctions have been employed in only a few instances, it may be premature to judge their success. In the famous Little Lake, California case, the sanction was totally ineffective, desipte NEA claims to the contrary. In 1963 in Utah the threat of a statewide sanction may have played an important role in winning Utah teachers some financial gains. But the effectiveness of sanctions, although legal (as opposed to strikes, which often are not legal), is still doubtful.[25]

Apparently some state education associations are becoming more militant, as evidenced by the 1964 "two-day recess" of the Utah Education Association. This recess, called without the official support of the NEA, lead to the Utah Education Association's receiving a mild rebuke at the 1964 NEA convention in Seattle. However, as of late summer 1964, there was still a national sanction leveled against the entire state of Utah. Apparently there is some inconsistency between these two actions. It would appear that the NEA and the state educational associations are not decided as to the degree of militancy required to gain their professional and economic goals.

The scope of the AFT is severely limited. Its reseach functions are limited typically to salaries and working conditions. While in one respect this may be considered a weakness, it may also be a potential strength. Its limited scope allows the AFT to pursue its restricted goals with enthusiasm and vigor, without dissipating its energy on hundreds of different projects.

Emotional Considerations The fact—sad from the AFT's viewpoint —is that teachers have descended from the "genteel" tradition. This means that teachers consider themselves to be thoroughly middle-class, "nice" people, and "nice" people do not affiliate with organized

[25] The reader is referred to the following articles in the *Phi Delta Kappan,* an educational journal of great renown: "Collective Bargaining and Strikes? Or Professional Negotiations and Sanctions?" 44 (October, 1962): 1-11; and Lavor K. Chaffin, "Utah Teachers Prod Legislature with Threat of Boycott," 44 (May, 1963): 358-359.

labor. Teachers wear white shirts or neat dresses, have regular hours, do not lift, tug, or pull, and in general comport themselves like professionals.[26] When the subject of respectability and tactics was being discussed in a college class, one graduate student said, "I don't care if the AFT could get us higher wages, I still don't consider myself a union member."

Since teachers see themselves as white-collar, middle-class, and respectable, they logically cannot resort to "union tactics." They will receive their just desserts when the public recognizes that they deserve what they are asking. "Pounding the bricks," a union phrase meaning "to go on strike," is regarded by the average teacher as something foreign and hoodlum-like. It is simply not for him.

As a result, teachers are foregoing real improvements in wages and conditions of work. Only through concerted group action can people succeed in having their demands met. That is, only by organizing, employing bargaining agents and political lobbyists and, if need be, striking, can a group realize its goals. However true this may be, the entire situation is perceived by most educators as not being worth the bother; the means required to obtain an obviously desirable goal simply are not for them.

The AFT has alienated most teachers by insisting on its affiliation with organized labor, by scoffing at the NEA's reliance on professionalism and professional means, and by emphasizing the teacher-administrator incompatibility. This alienation may be a deterrent to the AFT's growth. If nothing else, the AFT most certainly will continue to evoke the wrath of local boards.

Social, Economic, and Political Considerations Neither the AFT nor the NEA has come to grips with a hard fact of our social life: as teachers become more powerful and autonomous, they can bring to bear more pressure, and the traditional American concept of "local control" will weaken. Historically, schools and teachers have been under the exclusive and fairly absolute control of local residents, especially in small rural towns. The board—elected by local residents—has come to represent "the people." The board has traditionally set wages and conditions of labor, hired and fired teachers, and, in ways which seem to many to be quite unfair, controlled the private lives of

---

[26] This point about "snobbishness" is made in *The American Teacher* newspaper, June, 1963, in an article by John Dewey entitled "Why I Am a Member of the Teachers Union." The article was written by Dewey in 1928. John Dewey was a strong advocate of and member of the AFT.

teachers.[27] When and if teachers' organizations, either union or professional, become more powerful, this kind of local control is apt to disappear. Though the local area recently has had much of its real control eroded, most Americans still perceive the school as naturally and desirably being under local control. "After all," it is said, "only the local people know local problems." (Of course, this does not mean that they will remedy them.) But the establishment of a strong, independent, autonomous organization will mean that an increasing number of decisions will be taken out of the hands of the local boards and placed in the hands of the state and/or national teachers' organizations. To repeat: neither the AFT nor the NEA seems to have appreciated this fact.

There is an important political fact that is also frequently overlooked. States have the constitutional responsibility of administering the public schools in all fifty states. This responsibility is taken very seriously. Legislatures, state boards of education, state departments of education, and state superintendents all share in conducting the state's educational affairs. Collectively they are powerful and really "run" things. Neither a professional nor a union type of teacher organization can afford to overlook this legal fact. Greater "professional" autonomy implies the establishment of powerful state organizations that would lobby in state legislatures for laws beneficial to teachers. The AFT

---

[27] The following is a contract that teachers were required to sign in a North Carolina town during the 1930's and is not unlike others used at the time:

I promise to take a vital interest in all phases of Sunday-school work, donating of my time, service, and money without stint for the uplift of the community. I promise to abstain from all dancing, immodest dressing, and other conduct unbecoming a teacher and a lady. I promise not to go out with any young men except insofar as it may be necessary to stimulate Sunday-school work. I promise not to fall in love, to become engaged, or secretly married. I promise to remain in the dormitory or on the school grounds when not actively engaged in school or church work elsewhere. I promise not to encourage or tolerate the least familiarity on the part of my boy pupils. I promise to sleep at least eight hours a night, to eat carefully, and to take every precaution to keep in the best of health and spirits in order that I may better be able to render efficient service to my pupils. I promise to remember that I owe a duty to the townspeople who are paying my wages, that I owe respect to the school board and the superintendent that hired me, and that I shall consider myself at all times the willing servant of the school board and the townspeople and that I shall cooperate with them to the limit of my ability in any movement aimed at the betterment of the town, the pupils, or the schools.

Of course, at the time of this contract the nation was in the midst of the Great Depression and such coercion was not uncommon. Yet this quotation still vividly illustrates the point.

does not have a series of powerful state organizations, and it does not possess the financial resources to operate effectively at both the local and the state levels. The NEA, through its state associations, has not provided for powerful lobbies in all states; only a few state associations have a firm grasp of political realities and understand the use of political power. Presently neither the NEA nor the AFT is operating effectively at the state level.

However, there are already-existing statewide NEA organizations with headquarters typically in the state's capital city. It is theoretically possible for these organizations to create a powerful lobby in each state. That they have not done so is due in part to their reluctance to grasp political power, their lack of willingness to contribute financially to such a venture, and their inability to organize effectively at local, state, and national levels. As Myron Lieberman has said, educators do not recognize the existence of political power; they have almost ignored the existence, meaning, and function of pressure groups in a democracy.[28]

As we have noted, our political life is characterized by a series of nudges, pushes, and pulls. Legislators are approached by individuals or organizations and are influenced by various bits of information. Or these same representatives are approached and strongly reminded that unless they vote for this or that piece of absolutely necessary legislation, the forces of an organization will do their utmost to see that the legislators are retired to private life come the next election. This type of practice has come to be called such unsavory terms as "back-scratching," "political coercion," and "threats." It does not sound "nice." This is, however, the way things are—at least in a representative democracy; labor long has understood the uses of political power. Note the title of an AFL-CIO subcommittee: "Committee on Political Education."

The NEA, with its approximately 900,000 members, has not understood this simple and probably inescapable fact of our political life. NEA groups continue to operate on the genteel level by reminding PTA's and another that teachers are a fine group of people who deserve better. As compared with the approaches of the organized and powerful Taxpayers Associations, Farmers Alliances, National Association of Manufacturers, Chambers of Commerce, American Medical Association, and others, this approach has been singularly unproductive. Teachers are not supported by the same kinds of legis-

[28] Myron Lieberman, *The Future of Public Education* (Chicago: U. of Chicago Press, 1960), pp. 236-244.

lation that have benefited farmers, post-office employees, physicians, typesetters, and dockhands. As of this writing, there is no convincing evidence that the picture will change. The AFT is an urban phenomenon, thriving in large cities and oriented toward a liberal political position. The NEA, on the other hand, has just recently begun to understand how the complexity of city life is related to "professional associations." It was only during 1962-63 that the NEA established a unit within its complex structure to deal specifically with urban educational problems. The NEA's "Urban Project" is a belated attempt to strengthen the role of their organization in urban communities, to advance the welfare of city teachers, and to improve city schools. If the NEA policy-making forces will also take a long and hard look at the problems accompanying education—social and civil rights—the NEA may hope to gain in stature. It should also be noted that the NEA still maintains totally segregated state and local educational associations in the South; but the AFT will not tolerate such racial discrimination in its organizational framework. The NEA policy-making forces, at both the national and the state levels, are conservative in the areas of political and civil rights. This type of conservatism may well be the result of vested interests and the rural character of these organizations. Perhaps the NEA, like many other organizations, finds it difficult to stand criticism and benefit from it.[29] However, at the Seattle convention of the NEA in 1964, those states which still possessed a segregated organization were warned to integrate.

We have attempted to dissect two very much alive organizations. This attempt is further complicated by the fact that both the AFT and the NEA are continuing to make some slight changes in their organizational complexions. Only recently "bargaining elections" have been held in Denver, Little Lake, New Rochelle, Milwaukee, and other cities, and the NEA has successfully defeated the AFT in its efforts to act as the teachers' bargaining agent with the school boards. But the whole concept of "bargaining agent" is an AFT notion! The NEA

[29] See the March, 1964, Vol. 45, issue of the *Phi Delta Kappan* for five excellent articles on teacher organizations. Especially important is the article by Charles Tyner, "Neglected Landmark: California's Jack Owens Case." This article presents only one side of the case, but it does help substantiate the authors' claim that the NEA is somewhat conservative when it comes to civil rights. The other side of the case is discussed in Jack Williamson's "Only One 'Landmark' but Much Confusion in California's Jack Owens Case," *Phi Delta Kappan*, 45 (April, 1964): 339-341.

recently coined the phrase "professional negotiations"—a semantic triumph for that old friend of organized labor, collective bargaining.

IN CONCLUSION

It is obvious that neither the NEA nor the AFT meets the criteria for a genuinely effective organization. Either the NEA is blissfully unaware of political power and its uses in a democracy, or it does not wish to move rapidly into this area. The AFT apparently is equally unaware of the legitimate striving of teachers to belong to a respectable profession. The NEA is weak in the area of bringing about real economic gains. The AFT, by insisting on what is probably an inappropriate philosophy, has managed to antagonize most teachers. Furthermore, the AFT's myopic position often borders on anti-intellectualism; too many educational problems are ignored because they are not economic.

What is the answer? The existence of two organizations seems pointless, confusing, weakening, and absurd. It has led to a division within the ranks of teachers and has created confusion outside educational circles in the minds of the lay public. It has prevented teachers from taking a unified stance, from utilizing the total resource of personalities, strategies, and finances. What is clearly needed is *one unified national teachers' organization*.[30]

There must be a common meeting ground for the two organizations to be able to effect a merger. At present, officials in both associations throw up their hands in shock and horror when merger is mentioned. This attitude is as destructive and self-defeating as were the divisions in organized labor during the 1930's and 1940's. The differences in philosophy—which exist and which are important—should not serve to defeat the *aims* of all teachers.

In view of the strengths and weaknesses of both organizations—the functions, resources, structure, and membership of the NEA and the tactics of the AFT—they could well be merged into a revitalized and unified organization. Such an organization could effect improvements in salaries and conditions of teaching—the two areas most in need of improvement. What is required is a change of attitude. However, this is not easy to bring about.

The question remains: Why a powerful organization, professional or otherwise? The answer is simple: Ultimately, a better professional organization means better classroom teaching. *This is one major reason for professional organization.*

[30]This is a major point in Lieberman's *Future of Public Education*.

The Code of Ethics for the Education Profession

This document constitutes the report of the NEA Committee on Professional Ethics in response to the mandate from the 1961 Representative Assembly that the Committee should provide leadership in drawing up a uniform Code of Ethics for the education profession. The Code was accepted by the 1963 Representative Assembly as the Code of Ethics governing the NEA. The Representative Assembly further instructed the NEA Committee on Professional Ethics to conduct a nationwide survey every five years and to recommend revisions that will reflect changing professional standards.

Although developed chiefly under the auspices of the NEA, the Code is considered to belong to the profession, and not to be the exclusive property of any organization.

PREAMBLE

We, professional educators of the United States of America, affirm our belief in the worth and dignity of man. We recognize the supreme importance of the pursuit of truth, the encouragement of scholarship, and the promotion of democratic citizenship. We regard as essential to these goals the protection of freedom to learn and to teach and the guarantee of equal educational opportunity for all. We affirm and accept our responsibility to practice our profession according to the highest ethical standards.

We acknowledge the magnitude of the profession we have chosen, and engage ourselves, individually and collectively, to judge our colleagues and to be judged by them in accordance with the applicable provisions of this Code.

PRINCIPLE I
Commitment to the Student

We measure success by the progress of each student toward achievement of his maximum potential. We therefore work to stimulate the spirit of inquiry, the acquisition of knowledge and understanding, and the thoughtful formulation of worthy goals. We recognize the importance of cooperative relationships with other community institutions, especially the home.

In fulfilling our obligations to the student, we—

1. Deal justly and considerately with each student.
2. Encourage the student to study varying points of view and respect his right to form his own judgment.
3. Withhold confidential information about a student or his home unless we deem that its release serves professional purposes, benefits the student, or is required by law.
4. Make discreet use of available information about the student.
5. Conduct conferences with or concerning students in an appropriate place and manner.
6. Refrain from commenting unprofessionally about a student or his home.
7. Avoid exploiting our professional relationship with any student.
8. Tutor only in accordance with officially approved policies.
9. Inform appropriate individuals and agencies of the student's educational needs and assist in providing an understanding of his educational experiences.
10. Seek constantly to improve learning facilities and opportunities.

PRINCIPLE II
Commitment to the Community

We believe that patriotism in its highest form requires dedication to the principles of our democratic heritage. We share with all other citizens the responsibility for the development of sound public policy. As educators, we are particularly accountable for participating in the development of educational programs and policies and for interpreting them to the public.

In fulfilling our obligations to the community, we—

1. Share the responsibility for improving the educational opportunities for all.
2. Recognize that each educational institution may have a person authorized to interpret its official policies.
3. Acknowledge the right and responsibility of the public to participate in the formulation of educational policy.
4. Evaluate through appropriate professional procedures conditions within a district or institution of learning, make known serious deficiencies, and take any action deemed necessary and proper.
5. Use educational facilities for intended purposes consistent with applicable policy, law, and regulation.

6. Assume full political and citizenship responsibilities, but refrain from exploiting the institutional privileges of our professional positions to promote political candidates or partisan activities.
7. Protect the educational program against undesirable infringement.

PRINCIPLE III
Commitment to the Profession

We believe that the quality of the services of the education profession directly influences the future of the nation and its citizens. We therefore exert every effort to raise educational standards, to improve our service, to promote a climate in which the exercise of professional judgment is encouraged, and to achieve conditions which attract persons worthy of the trust to careers in education. Aware of the value of united effort, we contribute actively to the support, planning, and programs of our professional organizations.

In fulfilling our obligations to the profession, we—

1. Recognize that a profession must accept responsibility for the conduct of its members and understand that our own conduct may be regarded as representative.
2. Participate and conduct ourselves in a responsible manner in the development and implementation of policies affecting education.
3. Cooperate in the selective recruitment of prospective teachers and in the orientation of student teachers, interns, and those colleagues new to their positions.
4. Accord just and equitable treatment to all members of the profession in the exercise of their professional rights and responsibilities, and support them when unjustly accused or mistreated.
5. Refrain from assigning professional duties to non-professional personnel when such assignment is not in the best interest of the student.
6. Provide, upon request, a statement of specific reason for administrative recommendations that lead to the denial of increments, significant changes in employment, or termination of employment.
7. Refrain from exerting undue influence based on the authority of our positions in the determination of professional decisions by colleagues.
8. Keep the trust under which confidential information is exchanged.
9. Make appropriate use of time granted for professional purposes.
10. Interpret and use the writings of others and the findings of educational research with intellectual honesty.

11. Maintain our integrity when dissenting by basing our public criticism of education on valid assumptions as established by careful evaluation of facts or hypotheses.
12. Represent honestly our professional qualifications and identify ourselves only with reputable educational institutions.
13. Respond accurately to requests for evaluations of colleagues seeking professional positions.
14. Provide applicants seeking information about a position with an honest description of the assignment, the conditions of work, and related matters.

PRINCIPLE IV
Commitment to Professional Employment Practices

We regard the employment agreement as a solemn pledge to be executed both in spirit and in fact in a manner consistent with the highest ideals of professional service. Sound professional personnel relationships with governing boards are built upon personal integrity, dignity, and mutual respect.

In fulfilling our obligations to professional employment practices, we—

1. Apply for or offer a position on the basis of professional and legal qualifications.
2. Apply for a specific position only when it is known to be vacant and refrain from such practices as underbidding or commenting adversely about other candidates.
3. Fill no vacancy except where the terms, conditions, policies, and practices permit the exercise of our professional judgment and skill, and where a climate conducive to professional service exists.
4. Adhere to the conditions of a contract or to the terms of an appointment until either has been terminated legally or by mutual consent.
5. Give prompt notice of any change in availability of service, in status of applications, or in change in position.
6. Conduct professional business through the recognized educational and professional channels.
7. Accept no gratuities or gifts of significance that might influence our judgment in the exercise of our professional duties.
8. Engage in no outside employment that will impair the effectiveness of our professional service and permit no commercial exploitation of our professional position.

The Role of the Code
in the Education Profession*

by JOHN H. MARVIN

John H. Marvin is an Associate Professor of Education, Pennsylvania State University, and was formally the Associate Secretary for Ethics of the National Education Association. It was through the standing committee on Professional Ethics that the current Code of Ethics was written.

After the events of the past few months occurring in the neighboring state of Utah,[1] you may well wonder whether professional ethics is anything but remotely related to some of the burning questions confronting professional associations at this time. Thus, even before mentioning the Code of Ethics of the Education Profession, it is more appropriate to establish the close relationship of ethics to professional development and welfare. As a classroom teacher, I was quite conscious of the interrelationship of many parts of the profession, but ethics always seemed to be in limbo.

DEFINING QUALITY IN EDUCATION

One of our problems in education has been to establish and identify just what "quality education" really means. It will be impossible to ever do this until we find the answer to the question "Education for What?" The profession as a whole has left much to be desired by not defining both questions in words that the public understands.

* From John H. Marvin, "The Role of the Code in the Education Profession," a speech delivered in Pocatello, Idaho, July 16, 1963. By permission of John H. Marvin.

[1] In the spring of 1963, a sanction was threatened by the Utah teachers against the school system of Utah. The Utah Education Association broke off all negotiations with the boards of education over the problem of inadequate public-school financing.

During the summer the governor of Utah appointed a committee to study increased financial aid. This action led to further contract negotiations and the Utah schools opened on schedule. See the following for more detailed accounts: Lavor K. Chaffin, "Utah Teachers Prod Legislature with Threat of Boycott," *Phi Delta Kappan*, 44 (May, 1963): 358-359; "Of Strikes, Boycotts, Overkill, and Billions," *Phi Delta Kappan*, 44 (June, 1963): 397-398; and *The NEA Journal*, 52 (September, 1963): 4.

The result of this omission is the failure of many boards of education and state legislatures to act with intelligence when we submit requests for ever-increasing sums of money for a quality educational system. Frequently there is a tendency on the part of influential lay persons to look at the proverbial tree instead of the forest. Instead of regarding salary increases as a means of maintaining or upgrading certificated personnel in the district or state, there is a strong tendency to think of *one* poor teacher, like Mrs. Mary Doe down the road, who patently is not worth a nickel more in salary.

We would be less than honest to maintain that all teachers deserve higher salaries. The sad fact is that we as a profession have not undertaken anywhere near our share of responsibility for the quality of our practitioners. Initially the problem arose because many in our own ranks confused the sacred right of the public to formulate educational goals and policies with control over who enters and remains in the profession. We in the profession ought to be able to identify qualified practitioners better than those who have had no experience or background. This is one of our professional responsibilities.

The truth of the matter is that in most instances we fail in defining the relationship between quality and expenditure. We would also have difficulty applying a set of standards against individuals who may be cited by a board member or legislator to determine whether they, in fact, deserve the rights that go with a profession or whether, in fact, the legislator does not have a leg on which to stand. Since I have taken the liberty of assigning partial responsibility for the current situation to the profession, we should move hurriedly to make clear the nature of this intangible term.

WHAT CHARACTERIZES A PROFESSION?

Let us examine the characteristics of a profession and then measure teaching against these characteristics. All professions are composed of practitioners who render a public service by applying specialized skills developed by training acquired normally through association with an institution of higher education. On this score teaching certainly qualifies. Unfortunately, some observers attempt to oversimplify the concept of a profession by using this as the sole characteristic. Such simplification is dangerous and misleading. It would not, for example, distinguish between a profession and many other occupations in the service industries.

Professions are marked by voluntary associations of practitioners who are interested in improving the quality of their service. Educators certainly do well on this score when we consider the number of professional organizations composed by and for educators. An extensive survey conducted in 1962 devoted to establishing NEA professional priorities revealed major concern by members to establish curriculum development and improvement as the first priority. Surely, we are demonstrably devoted to improving the quality of our service.

However, these next two characteristics of a profession reveal our failings. The first of these constitutes a challenge to all professions—that is, a profession protects its competent practitioners who are unjustly attacked *and* protects the public from its incompetent members. No profession has, to its own satisfaction, comprehensively defined competence in terms of specific standards relating to the knowledge, skills, and attitudes that a so-called competent practitioner applies. Other professions have, however, made greater strides. Accreditation of professional schools of preparation is far more broadly accepted for other professions than is true of education. The National Commission for the Accreditation of Teacher Education is only a decade old and even now is under attack that threatens its very existence. Law and medicine both use licensing examinations as a partial determinant of competence. However, we as educators are perhaps most acutely aware of the gap that may exist between ability to reflect knowledge on paper and the ability to employ it properly under performance conditions. That interest is high in this realm is reflected in the widespread and rapid growth of TEPS—the NEA Commission on Teacher Education and Professional Standards. Secondly, so far as the professional association movement is concerned, the vital and critical task of agreeing on standards of competency is perhaps the main goal of the TEPS movement.

The definition and application of competency standards is one of the really great problems confronting education. If we do not come to grips with the problems involved, I can assure you that the public will not tolerate the vacuum. From this void will develop increasing pressures for merit salary programs. This, however, is a simple answer that will not suffice in the face of the increasing complexities of modern education.

Thus, we have far to go in the identification and implementation of programs related to competency. As such, it is the largest single problem confronting not only teaching, but all major professions. The acceptance of this challenge is a firm indication of whether teachers really mean business about being a profession, or whether this is a goal that we would prefer merely to talk about. The final characteristic of a profession is more easily identified. The profession has a great deal more direction in finding a solution. The question is whether the profession is prepared to take the necessary measures. A profession protects its ethical practitioners who are unjustly accused and it defends the public from its unethical members.

PROFESSIONAL ETHICS—THEIR IMPLICATIONS

Professional ethics has been plagued with misconception. These must be put to rest before further headway can be made.

Let us start with the title of the document itself. It is called a "code for the Education Profession." There is a distinct and major difference between a profession and a professional association. The latter is only a segment, albeit an important one, of a profession. Heretofore codes have been identified with professional associations in education. Thus, they governed only those who belonged to the association. The Principle of Medical Ethics governs all physicians. It is sponsored by the American Medical Association which is comprised of just over seventy percent of the potential membership. All lawyers must adhere to the Canons of the Bar. This is sponsored by the American Bar Association, which has by generous estimate only forty percent of the nation's lawyers. In the same sense it is appropriate for the largest professional organization with over fifty percent of the nation's public-school licensed personnel as members to undertake the leadership in developing a code identified with the entire profession—not only one professional association. The one major difference is that law and medicine have not only provided for professional implementation, but legal as well, so that all practitioners are expected to adhere to their Codes. In education a few associations are beginning to consider ways and means of having an educator's code of ethics apply to all in the profession—not just those who voluntarily join a professional association.

Another myth is that the term "ethics," as used in professional ethics, has the same meaning as the word "ethics" when used by the philosopher. The latter uses the word to describe the system of values in a society, or to describe a school of thought. We in the profession use the word to describe the acceptable standards of behavior. Usually a system of philosophical ethics remains relatively constant. But, standards of acceptable behavior are as changing as society itself. In the past, professional codes of ethics were regarded in somewhat the same light as the Ten Commandments—fixed and unchanging, with no provision for orderly review and revision. However, there have been gradual reinterpretations of the absolute character of professional codes. The result has been that the NEA has torn up its previous codes and started all over about once every ten years. This time the Representative Assembly has authorized a complete review of the Code by the total profession once every five years with a provision for orderly change as may be deemed necessary.

Another weakness has been to delay education about professional ethics until the teacher is in the classroom. In part, this stems from the proliferations of codes that we have inadvertently fostered. Teacher-preparation institutions excuse their failure to do much, if anything, about ethics in part on the grounds that teachers are so mobile, and that there are so many codes, that it is pointless to spend much time on any single code. The 1952 NEA Code, for example, after ten years had only been adopted by 30 of the 64 state education associations. Virtually all other state associations had their own codes, and there are countless codes of ethics for local associations. Obviously, if this Code of Ethics of the Education Profession is to live up to its title, it must be adopted by the overwhelming bulk of associations for professional educators.[2]

AN EXAMINATION OF THE CODE

At this time I want to turn to the document itself and examine some of the key provisions which represent substantial changes.

Principle 1–Commitment to the Student Section 2, "Encourage the student to study varying points of view and respect his right to form his own judgment," is designed as a positive instrument for use by the profession. For example, a medical practitioner would be hard pressed indeed to refuse the request of close friends for prescriptions of illegal drugs. As the situation now stands, he can in good conscience couch the refusal in the medical code of ethics. By the same token, we would expect members of the profession to stand up against unreasonable infringements upon the freedom of students to study controversial materials. Not only can the member of the profession object to such restrictions as a violation of his own conscience, but he can also find support for them in his code of ethics.

Principle I, Section 3, "Withhold confidential information about a student or his home unless we deem that its release serves professional purposes, benefits the student, or is required by law," does recognize

---

[2] As of May, 1964, the Code has been adopted by 55 state associations, 11 NEA-affiliated departments, and Phi Delta Kappa (a professional fraternity for men in education). Thus, by virtue of its adoption by so many related organizations, the Code now applies to over 1,400,000 members of the profession!

that a member of the profession must have the freedom to discuss professional problems in an unfettered atmosphere. However, it does not condone the kind of casual gossip about students that sometimes occurs in teachers' lounges.

Principle I, Section 7, "Avoid exploiting our professional relationship with any student," deals with many types of undesirable exploitation of the teacher-student relationship. Although basically an extension of the provision regarding tutoring, it is much broader. It covers practices ranging from sales of commercial items to the parents of students to the publication by a professor of a book which consists of research papers prepared by graduate students, but where no recognition is made of their contributions.

Principle II—Commitment to the Community   Section 4, "Evaluate through appropriate professional procedures conditions within a district or institution of learning, make known serious deficiencies, and take any action deemed necessary and proper," states that the profession has an obligation to the public to evaluate school conditions and to make deficiencies, where such exist, known to the public. This is the basis of our professional sanctions program which rests largely upon persuading the public of the justice of our cause.

Principle II, Section 6, "Assume full political and citizenship responsibilities, but refrain from exploiting the institutional privileges of our professional positions to promote political candidates or partisan activities," is designed to encourage members of the profession to play an active role in political and civic affairs, but it makes clear that we draw the line at the use of public funds to support political candidates for partisan activities. As you in Idaho are well aware, what happens in the Legislature has an immediate consequence on your own future. However, flagrant violation of this privilege by using public money for partisan purposes is an open invitation to the passage of "little Hatch Acts"[3] which would serve to restrict severely any political activity on the part of those covered.

Principle III—Commitment to the Profession   Section 2, "Participate and conduct ourselves in a responsible manner in the development and implementation of policies affecting education," is written specifically with professional negotiations in mind. This is a privilege which many professional associations are seeking. This provision recognizes that associations share a responsibility to deal in a mature fashion with school boards. Before we consider applying sanctions to those outside of the education profession, we must give serious consideration

---

[3] The "Hatch Act" refers to legislation passed by the United States Congress which restricts political activity of Civil Service employees.

to the behavior of those within the profession. Sections 4, 6, and 7 all have definite implications for administrators. (Section 4: "Accord just and equitable treatment to all members of the profession in the exercise of their professional rights and responsibilities, and support them when unjustly accused or mistreated." Section 6: "Provide, upon request, a statement of specific reason for administrative recommendations that lead to the denial of increments, significant changes in employment, or termination of employment." Section 7: "Refrain from exerting undue influence based on the authority of our positions in the determination of professional decisions by colleagues.") One of the chief objections against any of the previous codes has been the use of the word "teacher" with an all-inclusive meaning. Although the intent was good, many casual readers have misinterpreted the word. This code gets away from the narrowly generic term "teacher" and has specific provisions which would apply essentially to persons involved directly in administration.

Principle III, Section 10, "Interpret and use the writings of others and the findings of educational research with intellectual honesty," grew out of the wishes of those engaged in educational research. By implication, it would also include adherence to the provisions of the copyright law. This section may also be used to inform a board that certain practices of reproduction of materials constitute a violation of the ethics of the profession. Some boards need to be told that if they continue to desire a quality program in education, they must make available the supplies and materials which are necessary to achieve the objective instead of expecting professional educators to take the time and trouble to reproduce comparatively inexpensive materials in a manner that is, in fact, illegal.

Principle IV—Commitment to Professional Employment Practices Section 7, "Accept no gratuities or gifts of significance that might influence our judgment in the exercise of our professional duties," sets forth a position statement on the matter of gifts. Some school boards completely forbid the acceptance of any gifts. This is not only impractical, but it also fails to recognize the psychological necessity of some youngsters in primary grades to give small presents to their teachers. Obviously, it would be impossible for a national committee to attempt to set a national monetary limit. Instead, it is up to local associations to give this section meaning in context of local conditions.

Principle IV, Section 8, "Engage in no outside employment that will impair the effectiveness of our professional service and permit no commercial exploitation of our professional position," again sets forth a principle which can only be given meaning on the basis of local situations and facts. Obviously, if a man goes to sleep in class as a result of overworking, this would constitute a dereliction of responsibility to education. Since teaching conditions vary so widely, even within the same school district, the committee did not attempt to do other than enunciate a principle which must be given meaning based on the facts of a case.

IMPLEMENTING THE CODE

I would assume that each principle of the code would be discussed at some length. I have covered some of the highlights and now would like to move on to the question of implementation. In 1962, at the Representative Assembly meeting in Denver, a motion was made to instruct the Commission on Professional Rights and Responsibilities and the NEA Committee on Professional Ethics to draw up a program of implementation of the code. We were given until the Representative Assembly of 1964 to complete the task. In my opinion, this is a far greater challenge than simply writing a code, since the profession has had so little background in dealing with codes of ethics other than writing them. The previous year had seen a motion to draw up a program of enforcement almost unanimously defeated by the NEA Convention. It becomes imperative for us to look at the differences between implementation and enforcement.

The primary purpose of implementation is to raise professional standards. Only after all else, by way of implementation, has failed is consideration given to formal enforcement measures. Since many problems in ethics have overtones relating to the misapplication of accepted personnel policy, it is extremely important that mechanism be developed to deal with both grievance and ethics cases. The local association Professional Rights and Responsibilities Committee should be capable of dealing with the professional problems of individual educators. Most local associations have not recognized any responsibility other than to deal with general policy as it affects all members of the association. This was true not only of ethics, but most other aspects of education. This is not altogether surprising. People do not like to become involved in the personal problems of others in a responsible fashion and it frequently requires some courage to have to face a colleague and tell him that his professional behavior leaves something to be desired. But if we in the profession reject this responsibility, we invite others to assume it. I submit that the end result will be far more satisfactory if we recognize our obligation.

When I speak of a national program, perforce, I am required to talk in broad generalities. A very few of the 64 state associations and few more than a handful of local associations have faced this challenge in ethics. For almost every allegation I make about the professional ethics program, some exception can be found. But real progress cannot come about until such time as we recognize the general inadequacy of the program that now exists in this field. My apologies to any of you who may be familiar with a good working program. My primary purpose today is to lay out the facts and the challenges so that you as professional leaders will seize the initiative that is required of educators if a meaningful program of ethics is to evolve. Neither the NEA nor the state associations can provide the fundamental program; this must emerge from determined local associations. The most important function of the state and national associations is to provide leadership so that the membership may respond.

There are three separate and distinct but highly related roles for the various levels of professional associations in developing an effective program in ethics. Since a code has no more meaning than the local association is willing to give to it, we would expect that local associations must take the responsibility for looking into alleged violations. If such a violation has occurred, the local association has a minimum responsibility and must be prepared to counsel with the individual offender and, when necessary, to point out the error of his ways. There are many minor infractions which are not of sufficient importance to call to the attention of a state agency. If the profession is serious about implementation, then it must be prepared to deal with those ethics problems before they are either forgotten or have grown into far more serious proportions than may be warranted. In summary the three basic roles for implementing the code of ethics are:

1. The state association must provide the leadership for the formation of effective local association committees. Beyond this, the state association must be available to step in when the local association needs assistance. Since the state association has limited resources, it can only handle the most serious cases. If the local associations are doing their share of the program, there will be plenty to keep state associations busy. In addition, the state association must also assume responsibility for the application of professional discipline. We have learned from recent cases before the Executive Committee of the NEA that the national level is simply too busy to give prolonged attention to cases of professional discipline. By spreading the responsibility across the fifty states, there should be few enough cases in any single year so that no association would become burdened with hearings.

2. The NEA must serve as the final interpretive body for the code and as an appeal body from decisions of state associations.

3. In a rural-oriented state it may not be practical to set up local association professional rights and responsibilities committees. Instead, the answer may be county professional rights and responsibilities committees which are prepared to meet on relatively short notice. Personnel problems always require a high degree of diplomacy. The local or county association professional rights and responsibilities committee is not a place for amateur "do-gooders" or simply to train leadership, but rather this committee needs to be composed of respected and experienced educators who are prepared to take appropriate action to maintain the integrity of the profession.

Several times during the course of this discussion I have made the point that implementation of the code is far more difficult than simply development of the document. Obviously, the first step in an implementation is adoption. The second is to make provision in the constitution or bylaws of the state association for adherence to the code of ethics as a condition of membership. Beyond this, careful planning and the courage to move ahead are required. Progress is seldom made painlessly.

Implementation cannot come about hastily, but it does require persistence. Perhaps Robert Frost's famous quotation is most appropriate: "The woods are lovely, dark and deep. But I have promises to keep, And miles to go before I sleep."

Professional Ethics and the NEA*

by MYRON LIEBERMAN

Myron Lieberman is chairman of the Professional Studies Division, Rhode Island College, Providence and a well-known critic of education—especially of the teaching profession. He has written widely in the field and has authored two highly provocative books, EDUCATION AS A PROFESSION *and* THE FUTURE OF PUBLIC EDUCATION.

Many educational leaders recognize that a code of ethics is an important element in professional status. Nevertheless, professional ethics

* Myron Lieberman, "Professional Ethics and the NEA," *Phi Delta Kappan,* 44 (April, 1963): 310-312. By permission of the editor.

has never been taken seriously by teachers. I do not mean by this that teachers are unconcerned about the ethical problems of education. I mean only that teachers as a group have never taken seriously the idea that they should formulate and enforce a code of ethics which would regulate teacher behavior in a meaningful way.

Teacher concern about professional status has led to the formulation of codes of educational ethics. These codes are not enforced—indeed, their content is unknown to most of the teachers supposedly regulated by them. More often than not, nothing is lost by this, because the content of these codes renders enforcement impossible. Teachers cannot conform to a code which is not clear or which imposes unrealistic standards and obligations upon them.

In recent years, some educators have been seeking a more effective approach to ethics in education. Some, like myself, were hoping that the NEA's Committee on Professional Ethics might provide the leadership and the ideas needed to achieve this goal. These hopes were based partly on the fact that the committee had been drafting a revision of the present NEA Code of Ethics, an atrocious collection of clichés, platitudes, evasions, and ambiguities. Unfortunately, now that the committee has submitted its proposed new code to the NEA's Board of Directors, it is clear that the NEA will continue to be preoccupied with the symbolism instead of the substance of professional ethics for several years to come. The proposed code falls so short of what is needed and what is possible that its adoption by the NEA's Representative Assembly this summer, in anything like its present form, will serve only to delay the development and enforcement of an adequate code of ethics for teachers.

Let me illustrate these points by a brief analysis of some of the sections in the code recently drafted by the NEA's Committee on Professional Ethics and submitted to the NEA's Board of Directors in February, 1963. [And approved by the board without change.] Sections 3 and 4 of Principle I of the code call upon teachers to:

"3. Withhold confidential information about a student or his home unless we deem that its release serves professional purposes, benefits the students, or is required by law.

"4. Make discreet use of available information about the student."

Now, the crux of the problem of disclosure is this: Under what circumstances may information acquired in the course of employment be disclosed? The proposed sections beg this issue. Section 3 assumes that teachers know what "confidential information" is, though the need is for a test to determine confidentiality.

The section on disclosure might read: "A teacher shall not disclose information acquired in the course of employment unless its release serves professional purposes, benefits the student, or is required by law." While this statement itself can easily be improved, it avoids the original's restriction to "confidential information" without any test of confidentiality.

Section 4 places an obligation upon teachers to "make discreet use of available information about the student." What does this add to the obligation imposed by Section 3? Instead of providing a criterion for disclosure, Section 4 merely asserts a platitude which would command universal agreement but provides no guide to practice.

Many teachers are involved in commercial relationships with their students. These relationships include, but are not limited to, tutoring their students for pay, selling encyclopedias to their families, operating summer camps which enroll students, and assigning instructional materials on which the teachers receive a royalty. Instead of coming to grips with these problems, the proposed code leaves them completely up in the air. For example, Section 7 of Principle I calls upon teachers to "avoid exploiting our professional relationship with any student." Section 8 calls upon teachers to "tutor only in accordance with officially approved policies."

The need here is not for a statement that exploitation is bad and should be avoided. It is for a clear-cut statement of what teacher action constitutes exploitation, at least of the kind that will evoke professional sanctions. Similarly, there is an abdication of professional responsibility in the section on tutoring. Teachers are to tutor only in accordance with "officially approved" policies—but "officially approved" by whom? The local school board? The local association? The state association? If the committee meant "officially approved" by the local school board, why did it not say so specifically?

In any case, if it appears desirable, teachers should allow for some local autonomy on tutoring. However, they should still lay down guidelines which would prevent situations wherein "officially approved policies" permit exploitation. Furthermore, there are many communities which have no "officially approved" policies. Are we to infer that there should be no ethical restrictions on teacher tutoring in such communities?

Some of the sections of the proposed code are nothing but pompous nonsense. For instance, Section 11 of Principle III calls upon teachers to *"Maintain our integrity when dissenting by* basing our public criticism of education on valid assumptions as established by careful evaluation of facts or hypotheses." (Italics added.) For the sake of argument, let us agree that it is desirable to have some professional regulation of public statements about education by educators. However, why should such regulation apply only to critics and dissenters? Ignore the fact that the proposed section does not specify or indicate: "dissenting" from whom? Surely, teachers do not want to be in the position of saying that only dissenters must base their comments upon "valid assumptions."

In any case, the first six words italicized in Section 11 should be omitted. They add nothing but confusion. What is left (after changing "basing" to "base") is still indefensible. I may make a public statement on education which is not based upon valid assumptions. In fact, I have made several such statements and I will undoubtedly make several more in the future. Nevertheless, although I have been and will often be *mistaken*, I hardly think that my past and future mistakes should be treated as unethical conduct. There is a world of difference between being mistaken and being unethical, even though the proposed section ignores the difference. The section as proposed makes every public criticism of education that involves dissent unethical unless based upon "valid assumptions as established by careful evaluation of facts or hypotheses." I pass over without further comment the fact that valid assumptions are not always based upon careful evaluation of facts or hypotheses.

Let me cite one other section to illustrate the low intellectual level characteristic of the entire code proposed by the NEA's Committee on Professional Ethics. Section 3 of Principle IV calls upon teachers to "fill no vacancy except where the terms, conditions, policies, and practices permit the exercise of our professional judgment and skill, and where a climate conducive to professional service exists." Do we really want to make it unethical to offer or accept ("fill" is typically ambiguous) a position where there is not *a climate conducive to professional service?* Undoubtedly, boycotts are desirable in some such situations. To enable teachers to boycott a system because of censorship of instructional materials, for example, their code of ethics should make such action possible from an ethical point of view. However, there are also situations wherein teachers might offer or accept positions in full knowledge that they do not exist within a professional climate, and we might have only praise for their determination to *develop* a climate conducive to professional service.

Some educators believe that it is desirable to have a code of ethics for teachers as long as such a code is not enforced. In their view, codes of ethics represent ideals and should be presented to teachers only as such.

This view is partly responsible for the poor quality of codes of professional ethics for teachers. If a code is going to be enforced, teachers may suffer severe penalties for some violations of it. This possibility creates strong pressure to draft a good code. On the other hand, the very knowledge that a code is not going to be enforced eliminates or reduces this pressure. Our laws would be less clear and less reasonable if their non-enforcement were taken for granted, as is the case with professional ethics in education.

No matter how good a code may be, it will eventually require interpretation and clarification. My own criticism of the proposed code takes this into account. However, there is a vast difference between applying a clear code to unclear situations and applying an unclear code to clear situations. The code proposed by the NEA, like its predecessors, cannot and will not be taken seriously as an effective step toward building a teaching profession. In its present form, it is simply another concession to the symbolism of professionalism while its substance goes unheeded in the area of educational ethics.

I should like to make a few other points which seem to me to be crucial to the future of professional ethics in the field of education. Educational codes of ethics are poorly drafted because there is a tacit understanding that they will not be enforced. At the same time, they are not enforced partly because their content does not deserve enforcement. In other words, the quality of our codes bears a reciprocal relationship to enforcement.

It is a fallacy to think that it *necessarily* takes a long time to promulgate a first-rate code of ethics. Teachers need only to examine the code of the American Psychological Association to see that an organization seriously interested in professional ethics can develop a defensible code and can get it accepted by the organization and operative in professional practice in less than five years. The NEA has been playing games on the subject for almost forty years. The defects in all of its codes, past, present, and proposed, stem from the association's basic failure to recognize the potential importance of the subject. This failure overshadows any particular defect in the codes and should be a concern of those who seek improvement in this area.

The Alberta Teachers' Association: A Vision Vindicated*

by ARTHUR KRATZMANN

Arthur Kratzmann is executive director of the Alberta School Trustees' Association, Edmonton, Canada.

Teachers' organizations in the United States, claims Myron Lieberman, are irrelevant in the national scene, are tragically futile in protecting the public interest and the legitimate vocational aspirations of American teachers, and are generally quite unimaginative and unproductive.[1] We may not, perhaps, accept this forthright critic's evaluation as accurate, particularly if we have vested interests in one of the national organizations. Yet if we are intellectually honest we are compelled to admit that teacher organizations in the United States fall far short of their potential, both in terms of membership welfare and with respect to service to the teaching clientele, not to mention general impact on educational progress.

How can this gap between the actual and potential be bridged? Again, it is Lieberman who has set forth the most comprehensive list of concrete recommendations and objectives. Many Americans consider them revolutionary and impractical; certainly, the proposals represent sharp departures from the present activities of the National Education Association and the American Federation of Teachers and their affiliates.

Yet if we look north of the forty-ninth parallel we find teacher organizations, particularly in Western Canada, which have incorporated into their *modus operandi* the great majority of Lieberman's recommendations. One of these, and perhaps the most progressive—the Alberta Teachers' Association—is the subject of this article. Some attempt will be made to determine a number of implications for the American scene. Of course, any cross-cultural comparisons are difficult to make; yet an analysis of the Canadian scene does suggest pos-

---

* Arthur Kratzmann, "The Alberta Teachers' Association: A Vision Vindicated," *Phi Delta Kappan*, 45 (March, 1964): 288-292. By permission of the editor.

[1] See Chapter IX of Myron Lieberman, *The Future of Public Education*. Chicago: The University of Chicago Press, 1960.

sibilities for the United States. If nothing else is achieved, it will become abundantly clear that Lieberman's proposals, while regarded by many in his own country as those of a radical visionary, have long since developed beyond the level of romanticism in Western Canada.

Included both as proposals in Lieberman's *The Future of Public Education* and as achievements of the Alberta Teachers' Association are the following: competitive salaries for staff officers of the association; relatively high dues for a state organization (ATA fees begin at $48); a membership-paid staff officer ratio of 1:2,000 (ATA—1:1943); abandonment of labor affiliation (ATA early considered, but decided against, affiliation); safeguards against administrator domination (school superintendents can be associate, but not active, members); mandatory membership (a legal requirement in Alberta since 1936); a check-off system of dues collection; an enforceable code of ethics (effective since 1936); a shift of emphasis from local to state levels (ATA has strong control over local activities); increased organizational pressure on school boards (the author is well aware of ATA's pressures!); collective bargaining (again, in Alberta since the Thirties); master contracts covering a wide range of working and living conditions (developed in Alberta with the advent of collective bargaining); formal grievance channels (ATA has both internal and external channels of appeal); professional control over entry to teaching (ATA has representation on teacher education and teacher certification committees); and impact upon curricula (ATA is represented on all state curriculum committees). Many more partial achievements of Lieberman's proposals could be added. But the list is sufficiently long to characterize the Alberta Teachers' Association as an *avant-garde* state organization in North America.

Emergence and Early Development of the ATA   The ATA, like many Canadian teachers' associations, emerged and developed rapidly at the close of the World War I period.[2] It was formed in 1918 from without the Alberta Education Association, which was a loosely-knit, diffuse organization including government officials, school administrators, teachers, and professional and lay people interested in education. The ATA, early named the Alberta Teachers' Alliance, represented a rebellion of Alberta teachers against substandard working and living conditions imposed by local school boards, and embodied a collective demand for improvement. As it emerged, in an atmosphere of

[2] See J. M. Paton, *The Role of Teacher's Organizations in Canadian Education.* Toronto: W. J. Gage Ltd., 1962.

sharp controversy, the organization took on rather distinctive characteristics for a Canadian association. It was for teachers only—senior administrators, labor, and the lay citizenry were excluded from its ranks; all teachers had equal membership rights and responsibilities. There were no divisions according to sex, teaching levels, subject specialties, and the like. And it established a comprehensive and revolutionary platform of welfare objectives and a militant air promising their early attainment. The major influences upon the ATA, apart from the catalytic conditions in Alberta, came from abroad. The AFT in the U.S. was creating appealing headlines at the time, and the accomplishments of the British National Union of Teachers were being propagandized by immigrant British teachers. John Barnett, an Englishman, was named as first secretary of the ATA and he left an indelible imprint upon the organization after thirty years of forthright and dedicated service.

The emergence of the ATA, with its demands for adequate contracts, salaries, pensions, administrative units, and working conditions, and with its challenges to the authority of officials of the Alberta Department of Education and school boards, evoked anticipated opposition—violent opposition—from the Minister of Education and the School Trustees' Association in Alberta. It was a case of a precocious youth upsetting the homeostasis of the traditional educational decision-making family. And precocious it was—for its constitution, its legislative and policy-formation patterns, its membership expectations, its general educational goals, and its welfare objectives were so well developed as to stand the test of time for decades, with only minor amendments. Despite the violent opposition from the time-honored power structure for education, the ATA fought, without compromise, for the realization of its platform. Twenty years later, as we shall see, most of the welfare objectives had been achieved, or at least the structures had been established for their eventual attainment.

Before these achievements are analyzed, the reader should realize that the Alberta Teachers' Association developed at the provincial (state) level within a system of government for education which placed very extensive powers in the hands of provincial legislators; the ATA area of influence was and is clearly bounded by the borders of Alberta; and furthermore, the association was and is the only state agency for Alberta teachers and has not had to compete for membership with any other teachers' organization. In these respects, the Canadian and United States contexts for state associations vary markedly.

ACHIEVEMENTS OF THE ATA

One is impressed, upon studying ATA documents, with the sheer volume of time and effort devoted to teacher-welfare issues and particularly to security of tenure, salaries, and pensions. As well, the stability of stated organizational objectives is strongly in evidence; year after year, the association approached the Alberta government with identical requests for provisions for continuous contracts for teachers, stated reasons for dismissals, government-endorsed salary schedules which would recognize training and experience, pensions provided by teacher and government contributions, and improved working and living conditions. And year after year, the Alberta School Trustees' Association brought pressures upon the legislature to offset ATA demands. In all matters of salary and tenure involving lack of agreement on the part of boards and individual teachers or groups of teachers, the association sought referral of the cases to a neutral board of reference; in fact, in all of their "welfare" dealings with school boards they have shown, until recently (when the welfare tide, based upon public opinion, has tended to ebb), a willingness to abide by the rulings of a third and neutral party.

For a number of reasons, the "golden years" for the association, in terms of improved social and economic status, came in the 1935-41 period. During these years the ATA included among its welfare accomplishments legislative sanction of the following: (1) Continuous contracts, with severance only upon the mutual agreement of both parties, and the right of the teachers to appeal against dismissal to a neutral board of reference. (2) Abolition of the individual form of contract, and teacher acceptance by letter assuring the positioning of the teacher on a group salary schedule. (3) The right to bargain collectively with school boards for salaries and for living and working conditions, as well as the right, in extreme conditions, to strike. (4) The legal definition of a salary schedule, making provisions for a minimum salary and annual increments for teaching experience. (5) Increases in the statutory minimum teacher's salary for Alberta. (6) A joint teacher-school board contributory retirement plan.

Since 1941, the legal bases and internal and external machinery already established have been used to make annual gains in membership welfare. The major progress during the Forties and Fifties related to salaries and to fringe benefits included in teachers' contracts, as well as to the inauguration of an improved pension plan.

Collective bargaining procedures are singled out for brief but special attention. While the ATA resisted the efforts of labor leaders to have the association affiliate with the organized labor movement, its officials nevertheless secured an official legal interpretation of the Labour Act of Alberta that extended to teachers the full range of bargaining privileges previously granted to labor in the private sector of the Alberta economy. Such benefits, sanctioned by a clause in the province's school act or code, included collective bargaining, closed-shop procedures, a dues check-off system, the use of neutral Labor Department conciliators in time of dispute, and the use of strike action as a final bargaining weapon. In every instance the ATA itself is the bargaining unit for local teachers, advising them at each stage, assisting them closely in times of dispute, and maintaining special funds to assist them during strikes. Teachers' locals tend to be coterminous with major administrative jurisdictions for education in the province.

Organizational Status and Recognition Since its inception, the ATA, considering itself to be the only body competent to form and transact the opinion of those engaged in teaching in Alberta, has striven for both improved internal controls and external impact. The 1918 Executive Council of the association envisioned the day when the organization would embody all Alberta teachers and when it would obtain recognition on all committees, boards, and authorities where curricula, instructional materials, examinations, and teacher training and certification were under discussion. These goals were realized many years ago. Undoubtedly, the passage of the Teaching Profession Act of 1935, together with its 1936 amendments, ranks as the outstanding turning point in the struggle for recognition and representation by the ATA.

This legislation, which was paralleled by similar statutes in Saskatchewan in 1935, and which was to be imitated by every Canadian province in later years, has been described by Paton as "a case of plucking success from the jaws of failure, or of dire necessity proving to be the mother of invention."[3] In an effort to offset the vicious circle of low membership, inadequate funds, and ineffectual organization, and to strengthen the ATA in its teacher welfare platform during the depression years, officials of the alliance sought and secured a mandate from Alberta teachers to seek legislation affording the ATA full professional status with mandatory membership and internal controls over member action. The first of these requests was met in 1935; the membership and discipline clauses were added in 1936. These were indeed revolutionary pieces of legislation.

The Teaching Profession Act was to have a great impact upon the internal control activities of the association. In the first place, it made

[3] *Ibid.*, p. 44.

membership of Alberta teachers in the ATA compulsory; no teacher could any longer remain as a non-joiner. This could perhaps have resulted in severe problems of fusion of opinion, attitude, and action on the part of dissident teachers had a supplementary clause of the act not given the ATA power to devise its own discipline by-laws and to secure machinery to enforce them. Consequently, teachers were not only compelled to join the association, they were forced to abide by ATA-formulated policies, including those which guaranteed a controlled and unified voice for the organization and those which spelled out member-member, member-association, and member-employer reciprocal rights and privileges. A third feature of the act was of vital significance for the ATA's material resources: The 1936 amendments not only brought all teachers into the association, it brought adequate financing. Association fees were high and have remained high when compared with the dues of other state associations.

The Teaching Profession Act also brought two very significant changes in the ATA's relationships with external persons and agencies. In the first place, the association for the first time became the state-sanctioned voice for Alberta teachers, a feature which the ATA fully clarified in its internal by-laws. Secondly, the association, in one legislative swoop, became potentially much more powerful in terms of membership, finances, and consequent impact upon the Alberta educational front. That the school trustees fought the legislation and that the government acquiesced reluctantly suggests that many realized what statutory membership would mean in the way of the mobilization of teacher opinion and action. Here was a body of teachers, dependent upon municipal and provincial funds for their salaries and conditions of work, being given the wherewithal, with legislative blessing, to grow strong enough to exert a great deal of control over their employers and conditions of employment.

A Change of Emphasis During the first thirty years of its development, the ATA was first and foremost a member-welfare association; only in recent years has it redirected its emphases so that it may be described as a service or a "commonweal" organization as well, promoting the interests both of the teaching clientele and the public-at-large in its internal and external activities.[4] The shift in emphasis, most marked during the past five years, appears to have resulted from: (1) a process of goal replacement necessary to maintain the

---

[4] These typologies of formal organizations are advanced by Peter M. Blau and W. Richard Scott in *Formal Organizations*. San Francisco: Chandler Publishing Co., 1962.

identity and cohesion of a group which had achieved most of its long-range objectives. (2) The constant appeals of the public and external Alberta agencies to shift ATA's focus from "union" to "professional" activities. (3) A readiness on the part of the membership to assume a larger responsibility, via their parent association, for on-the-job professional improvement.

Regardless of the motivation, the association now devotes large blocks of time and money to the sponsorship of small and large group meetings, conventions, seminars, and workshops, to the publication of service-oriented materials, and to the use of field consultative services related to the improvement of teaching. Having attained an adult status with respect to membership welfare, the organization is in the adolescent stages of maturity in terms of its extrinsic, public-service, or "professional" activities.

The ATA and the American Scene   The American Federation of Teachers and the National Education Association and their respective affiliates are offering teachers of the United States two different routes to economic paⱢity and professional stature. The former speaks of collective bargaining and coercive action to achieve welfare benefits, and has accomplished little by way of the direct promotion of general educational and instructional programs. The latter is concerned with professional negotiations, sanctions, a persuasive partnership with teaching communities, and the dissemination of materials designed to improve the teaching competence of members. There seems little chance of a reconciliation of differences, of a meeting of the ways.

What does this description of the activities of the Alberta Teachers' Association contribute to the discussion of these means of achieving an almost identical end? What it says is obviously limited by differences in societal contexts noted earlier. The ATA developed at the provincial level within a system of educational government which placed very broad powers in the hands of provincial legislators; it emerged and grew in a country which, educationally, has been more concerned with regional developments than with national trends; and it came to fruition without competition from any other professional organization. Nevertheless, the following observations, based upon ATA developments, appear to be pertinent to the American situation:

1. "Unionism" is unionism and "professionalism" is professionalism, and never the twain shall meet? Recent ATA activities would tend to discredit this American myth. Both types of activities are possible under one roof, to the advantage of both the teacher-group and the public. Any organization which ignores either welfare or service responsibilities, or which attempts to avoid similarities to the approach

of other competing agencies by purely semantic emphases, is destined to fall short of its true potential.

2. The ATA proved that teachers can fight for their place in the sun, independent of the largesse of other groups. Alberta teachers achieved their welfare and service stature without reliance upon labor affiliation or the direct contributions of senior school executives, this in contrast with American counterparts.

3. Myron Lieberman has called upon teachers to shift their emphasis from local to state and national levels. If the Alberta situation has any transfer value, it would appear that, as American teachers enter the state or federal power arena, boards of education will probably be forced to develop policies and procedures which will permit them to operate in the same sphere. One might, therefore, expect a vitalization of the state and national school board agencies.

4. In unity—in the teaching profession as elsewhere—there is strength. Following the 1935-36 legislation, the ATA became an increasingly powerful and recognized force in the Alberta power structure because, above all, it represented the entire teaching force of the province. The true potential of American teachers to influence school board and governmental decisions is probably offset by their division into two competing camps. If reconciliation or compromise is permanently offset by long-established vested interests, perhaps Lieberman's plea for a third agency may, in future years, represent the only possibility for capitalizing on the best of both existing organizations.

5. As American teacher groups become successful in formalizing collective bargaining procedures, the role of the school superintendent seems destined for close scrutiny and modification. In resolving the obvious conflict which occurs when "his" board of education—of which he is a line officer—is in open dispute with "his" teachers— of whom he is a professional colleague—he will likely become less of a decision-maker and more of an information-giver with respect to teacher welfare. At least this has been the lot of his Canadian counterpart.

6. Finally, it is suggested that the ATA, which has taken on many of the characteristics Lieberman has proposed, has, because of such actions, assumed a position of educational leadership in the province of Alberta, both for its own membership and for its clientele. It has developed successful channels of influence in the educational power structure of Alberta. While there have been instances where opposing agencies and individuals have deplored their militancy, their paternalism, and the sheer power which at times exudes from their head-

quarters, it cannot be denied that the ATA has achieved sound salaries, pensions, and other welfare benefits for its members and has, of late, evidenced its desire and ability for improving education through improved member service. These achievements, in my opinion, offer some vindication of the Lieberman vision.

SUGGESTED ACTIVITIES

1. Make a content analysis of the articles and editorials in one volume of *The American Teacher* (the AFT organ) and the *NEA Journal.* Compare the styles of writing and the major themes of the articles. Categorize the number and types of articles in each journal over a six-month period.

2. There is a legal precedent for requiring teachers to perform a "reasonable" number of extracurricular activities, such as supervising dances, sponsoring clubs, chaperoning tours, supervising the lunchroom, and loading the school bus. How does this situation compare with the professional activities of attorneys, physicians, and architects?

3. Do you know of any customs and *unwritten* rules in your home town which tend to restrict the personal lives of public-school teachers? How would you go about discovering whether such restrictions exist?

4. In the eyes of many people, teachers occupy a rather high position. If this is accepted as being true, why is it that teachers' salaries are not commensurate with their status? Could the same be said for Supreme Court justices, who are highly esteemed but who make a salary much less than would be made by any business official with comparable responsibilities? Discuss.

5. The NEA considers administrators part of the teaching "team"— that is, teachers and administrators are partners in the profession. The AFT considers administrators part of "management." Interview a number of administrators to discover whether they perceive themselves as "management" or as "partners" in the teaching profession.

6. Many teachers seem to fear that adoption of "union tactics," such as collective bargaining and the strike, would somehow result in diminished respect on the part of the public. (a) Do professions such

as medicine and law make use of such tactics? (b) Are such fears grounded in fact?

7. In what sense, if any, are the attitudes of college professors a barrier to the growth of professionalism of public-school teachers?

8. A checklist of criteria by which to measure a profession has been provided. That is, a definite meaning for the term "profession" has been given. Ask several public-school teachers what they mean by a "profession." Compare the answers with the criteria.

9. In what sense have state education laws been both a barrier and a boon to teacher professionalism?

10. A large segment of the teaching corps consists of temporary job holders. In what specific ways do those non-career-oriented men and women provide a barrier to the "professional" status of teaching?

11. One educational theorist, a physician teaching biology in a liberal-arts college, argues that a true academic discipline is one which is self-sufficient—that is, the subject matter of the discipline can "stand by itself" and the concepts are independent of concepts in other fields. Is this description true of medicine?

SUGGESTED READINGS

BARTKY, JOHN A. *Social Issues in Public Education.* Boston: Houghton Mifflin, 1963.   Chapter Eight, "The School and Culture," is most relevant to the teaching profession.

BRUBACHER, JOHN S. *Eclectic Philosophy of Education.* 2nd ed.; Englewood Cliffs: Prentice-Hall, 1962.   Readings pertaining to the philosophical bases for education. Prospective teachers should read articles in Sections 14 through 21.

CONANT, JAMES B. *The Education of American Teachers.* New York: McGraw-Hill, 1963.   This book has aroused professional educators because of its controversial analysis of such problems as teacher education and certification. Conant has many interesting suggestions for improving teacher education.

HODENFIELD, G. K. AND STINNETT, T. M. *The Education of Teachers.* Englewood Cliffs: Prentice-Hall, 1961.   A summary of the work of three national conferences that brought liberal-arts and education professors and public-school teachers together to discuss teacher education. It advances understanding of the basic problems of teacher education.

HUGGETT, ALBERT J. AND STINNETT, T. M. *Professional Problems of Teachers.* 2nd ed.; New York: Macmillan, 1963. A discussion of people, problems, and professional organizations associated with teaching.

KERSHAW, JOSEPH A. AND MC KEAN, ROLAND N. *Teacher Shortages and Salary Schedules.* New York: McGraw-Hill, 1962. This study presents a novel program for salary schedules which could aid in the recruitment and retention of better-qualified teachers.

LIEBERMAN, MYRON. *Education as a Profession.* Englewood Cliffs: Prentice-Hall, 1956. One of the revolutionary works in the field of education during this century. A must for anyone interested in teaching as a career.

———. *The Future of Public Education.* Chicago: U. of Chicago Press, 1960. A most provocative work that attempts to show the relationships among educational control, finance, and professionalism.

MORRIS, VAN CLEVE, et al. *Becoming an Educator.* Boston: Houghton Mifflin, 1963. An introductory education text. Chapter Eleven, "Teaching as a Career," provides some insights into the profession.

Opinions of the Committee on Professional Ethics. Washington, D.C.: National Education Association, 1964. This booklet is essential reading. It discusses views concerning the application of "The Code of Ethics for the Education Profession."

SMILEY, MARJORIE B. AND DIEKHOFF, JOHN. *Prologue to Teaching.* New York: Oxford U. Press, 1959. A book of readings and source materials. Part I has excellent materials pertaining to teaching and teachers.

SPINDLER, GEORGE D. *Education and Culture—Anthropological Approaches.* New York: Holt, Rinehart and Winston, 1963. This book of readings attempts to relate anthropology to education. See especially Part II, "Education in American Culture."

STANLEY, WILLIAM O., et al. *Social Foundations of Education.* New York: Holt, 1956. This collection of readings treats the "Social Aspects of the Teaching Profession" excellently in Part V.

U.S. BUREAU OF THE CENSUS. *U.S. Census of Population: 1960. Subject Reports. Characteristics of Teachers.* Washington, D.C.: U.S. Government Printing Office, 1964. (Final Report PC [2]-7D.) This report is a valuable source of national and regional data concerning age, earnings, education, etc. of teachers.

Index